GUILDFORD VIA COBHAM

THE ORIGINS AND IMPACT OF A COUNTRY RAILWAY

Howard Mallinson

Howard Mallinson

Subscribers' Edition
published 2006
by

Howard Mallinson
22 Gordon Road
Claygate
Surrey
KT10 0PQ

ISBN 0-9543934-2-2

Printed by BAS Printers, 1 Premier Way, Abbey Park, Romsey, Hants, SO51 9DQ

Not in an hour, but year by year,
As we grow poor and the lands grow dear,
Will come an alien people here,
      Will come where the Railway came.

(from Barbara Sayles Garner)

MY SEASON TICKET

Ever against my breast,
Safe in my pocket pressed,
Ready at my behest,
  Daintily pretty
Gilt-printed piece of leather,
Though fair or foul the weather,
Daily we go together
  Up to the City.
Yet, as I ride at ease,
Papers strewn on my knees,
And I hear "Seasons, please!"
  Shouted in warning:
Pockets I search in vain
All through and through again;
"Pray do not stop the train –
  Lost it this morning.
No, I have not a card,
Nor can I pay you, guard –
Truly my lot is hard;
  This is the reason,
Now I recall to mind
changing my clothes, I find
I left them all behind, –
  Money, cards, 'season.'"

———————————

Anon

GUILDFORD VIA COBHAM
THE ORIGINS AND IMPACT OF A COUNTRY RAILWAY

CONTENTS

Acknowledgements

Her Majesty, Queen Elizabeth II has given her consent to the publication of Chapter 6, and the author is grateful for this and the assistance given by the staff of the Royal Archives, Windsor Castle.

The author also acknowledges the assistance given by the staff of the House of Lords Record Office; the Surrey History Centre; the Local History Room of Kingston Museum and Heritage Service; Surrey Archaeological Society; Elmbridge Museum and Esher Library. Many private individuals have been generous with their efforts on my behalf. Philip Hutchinson helped with access to many Guildford artefacts and willingly made photographs and other material available. Tony Allen commented on part of the text as did Cllr Terence Patrick who was also very helpful in sourcing photographs for illustrations. Alan Roome also gave assistance with photographs of the New Line. On the same score must be thanked David Taylor and Stephen Spark, who both also gave useful information; Paul Langton, Peter Tatlow, Avril Gilbert supplied photographs and John Field also gave access to his goods yard records. Michael Baldwin gave me access both to his photographs and his recollections of working on the New Line. Michael Day of South West Circle made available many helpful parts of the Circle's archive. Gareth Clutton supplied useful material on John Clutton and the Institution of Civil Engineers and the Royal Institution of Chartered Surveyors helped in various ways. Alan Williams considered parts of the text and provided useful suggestions for enhancement. South West Trains assisted with traffic data and Gareth Leslie from *Guildford* assisted in various ways. In thanking all who have helped him, the author notes their willingness to give their time and enthusiasm.

The author is grateful to Tyra Till for her design work on the jacket and the Oxshott map and to John Gillham for his work on the coloured map showing the proposed and as built railways between Kingston and Guildford. Except where credited all the photographs are either by the author or from his collection of commercial postcards. The author is grateful to all those who have assisted with illustrations, including Alan Jackson, and the successors to the JN Faulkner, Lens of Sutton and H C Casserley collections. Special thanks must go to Surrey History Centre for their permission to use their collection of photographs of the New Line under construction; these are not individually credited within the text. Although every effort has been made to contact those who may have a copyright interest, it has not always been possible.

The author is especially grateful to the subscribers to this book; the willingness of so many to commit to buying the book, unseen, has had a beneficial impact on its quality. Without the numbers of subscribers it would have been difficult to contemplate the extra cost of the use of colour for some of the illustrations and the commissioning of maps, and generally it has been possible to produce the book to a higher quality than might have been possible with a commercial publication.

Those thanks made, it is impossible for the author to overstate his thanks to Alan Jackson. A notable author himself on railways and 20th century development in suburban London, he read the entire draft text and commented on it to great effect. The result, for which the author retains the sole responsibility, is a better balanced book. If readers are agreeably disposed to the contents they, as well as the author, will have cause for thanks for his painstaking trouble.

Abbreviations

In text

BR – British Railways
District Railway – Metropolitan District Railway
GWR – Great Western Railway
LB&SCR – London, Brighton & South Coast Railway
LC&DR – London, Chatham & Dover Railway
LSWR – London & South Western Railway
SE&CR – South Eastern & Chatham Railway
SER – South Eastern Railway
SR – Southern Railway

In notes

NA – National Archives, Kew

Preface

From the time my family moved to Surrey as a child the Guildford via Cobham railway, or the New Line as it is called in this book, has in one way or another touched my life. I have lived near three of it stations – London Road, Hinchley Wood and Claygate – and for 40 years bar a gap of five years travelled on it to London, like many others to earn a living. During that time the position of London in its global context has grown and its influence on demand for travel-to-work remains high: this is not new, as the reader will discover, for the influence of London and its global ascendancy was strong when the New Line was being considered. Whenever I travelled in the opposite direction the journey to Guildford was remarkable for the countryside through which the line runs. When the line was built an agricultural district stretched from Surbiton to Guildford providing, with domestic service, the major source of employment. Gradually the question posed itself: why was the New Line built? It was a question that this book explains. Was the obvious answer 'for the commuters' quite as obvious as it seemed? Or was the line built for the goods traffic? Or did the London & South Western Railway decide to build it as a relief for the main line via Woking? If the greater part of the population was engaged on the farms or in the mansions, there did not seem to be any certainty that the obvious answer 'for the commuters' was right: research has shown that the reason why the Guildford via Cobham line was built was because:

Lord Onslow, being short of funds due to a severe agricultural depression, so terrified the London & South Western Railway by promoting a line which would link the District Railway at Fulham with Guildford via Kingston that for fear of its monopoly being broken, its directors decided to build their own new line to keep the District Railway out. Onslow's legacy to the district was the so-called New Line to Guildford: his reward was the sale of land on which part of it was built and added value to his extensive land holdings in Guildford.

Property development is taking place today, still, in practically every settlement served by the New Line; the landowners who promoted it could see this demand coming: the builders begat the commuters.

An interest in the New Line explained and the reason given for why it was built, this book is about how it all happened; the characters behind it; the pre-history; the objectors and the how the stars in their courses caught the moment when the New Line could have been considered as a half-sensible idea. Recognising that there must be hundreds of thousands of people whose lives have been touched by the New Line, whether as schoolchildren, lovers, commuters, shoppers or as neighbours of it, the book is not just about explaining the origins of the railway, which is the role of Part 1, but discoursing on its impact on the various settlements which it serves. Part 2 covers the period from the opening of the New Line in 1885 and compares and contrasts its variable impact on each of the station settlements served by it.

That the New Line is a commuter railway now, and has been for the greater part of its life, is self-evident even if there was little traffic in the early days, but equally it is a country railway of huge charm. After the excesses of the 1930s the Metropolitan Green Belt has ensured that the building lines have been restrained, so that it remains a country railway today, albeit with considerable traffic since electrification. Travelling on the line today it is not easy, even if one should attempt it, to keep one's eyes from the passing country scenes. These are the reasons the book is titled Guildford via Cobham: the Origins and Impact of a Country Railway: it always was a country railway and it remains so, one of the very nearest to London.

The approach to referencing should be explained. Those readers who have an academic interest in the subject, may find the absence of some references in the text unhelpful, but in a book that is aimed at a general audience, and readers who will often have local knowledge, to have excessive interruptions to the text can be an irritation. This has been overcome by including references only on two bases: first to those sources that appeared to be new contributions to the literature; and secondly, to observe proper courtesy, where direct quotations from other texts have been taken. For readers who wish to go further into the background of a subject themselves an annotated bibliography is given in which the sources used are discussed. I express my thanks to the authors concerned for material that has informed this account.

Howard Mallinson
Claygate, April, 2006

Guildford via Cobham

Part 1: Origins

Chapter 1: The Main Line, 1838

1.1 Clandon Park, 2005: the seat of the Earls of Onslow. The 3rd Earl was an objector to the London & Southampton Railway, in respect of land he owned in Woking, but later he sold land for the station at Guildford. The 3rd Earl allowed Clandon Park to decay, but the 4th Earl, William Hillier, restored it to its past glory and became the driving force for the New Line to Guildford.

The story starts at Woking

On 12 May 1838, the directors of a new railway company and their guests sat down to a banquet at a London hotel. A celebration was taking place with mutual and hearty congratulations being exchanged and toasts to the future success of the 'high road to Europe': the hopes and expectations of the directors for the future were not misplaced; they had seen the genesis of a great railway company – a company which would ultimately build the New Line to Guildford, but not before having tried to prevent its conception and, failing in that, then to attempt to strangle a version of it in the womb.

Earlier in the day the party had had lunch on a common 25 miles from London, in a tent, for there was nothing there but the shantytown of the railway navvies. The party had been taken there and back by the first train to run on a new railway which, for the time being,

terminated on the isolated heath a mile or two from a tiny village called Woking (subsequently renamed Old Woking). The very act of going so far out of town for lunch, and being back for dinner in the same day, was as extraordinary as it would come to be commonplace. The journey to what we now call Woking had started at Nine Elms,[1] a low and marshy site near a wharf on the south bank of the Thames in London, and had immediately run from there through grazing land; it had taken 45 minutes, an astonishing average of 30 miles per hour. Nine Elms was chosen as a site for the terminus because the land required was undeveloped and was available cheaply. Most of London, and all the

---

[1] Nine Elms had been an economical site when first built and it would be the London terminus of the railway company until the 1½-mile extension to a site near Waterloo Bridge, built on a viaduct after considerable residential property demolition, was opened 10 years later in 1848.

better parts, were north of the river, but the Nine Elms site avoided the cost of crossing the Thames and buying and demolishing buildings to make way for the railway. It also avoided a common cause of delay: the Private Acts of Parliament gave railway promoters the statutory right to purchase the freehold of the required land but often companies tried to avoid passing through land they knew would be difficult to acquire at a reasonable price or even any price; deviations to the proposed route were then made and this is relevant to the subsequent events in the area under consideration in this book. Landowners had the right to petition Parliament with their objections. This gave a wealthy landowner considerable nuisance value, and we shall see later that this was a difficulty from which the promoters of the New Line suffered.

Plainly, the ultimate destination of the railway was not Woking Common: if an uninformed observer, glancing at the present-day railway map of the south of England, were to guess the destination of this unfinished railway he might suggest Salisbury and Exeter, and points west from there. The route from London to those cities certainly looks like an obvious target for the early pioneers: but it was not. In Britain neither the initiative for building a railway nor the routes that railways took were ever, it must be understood, the subject of rationalisation by some all-seeing wise body: least of all, were they the concern of governments: no one took a long-run strategic view.[2] The proof of government's *laissez-faire* attitude is that Parliament allowed two connecting railway companies to build their railways to different gauges. No: governments thought the whole matter a private affair, subject to the control but not the direction of Parliament. However, the battle of the gauges is not our concern here: we must observe, simply, that the new railway companies were operating in a free-market economy: if a railway idea made business sense, capital would move towards it; if the idea turned out to be foolish, that was not a matter to concern the government, for it was the market which would decide the fate of a project. Ultimately, it has to be said, the government became obliged to have a more hands-on approach to regulation, but that does not concern us here either: we are concerned generally with how railway routes evolved and in particular where this railway, which was temporarily terminating on a heath, was going to terminate.

The routes which railways took were a compromise between economics (an overarching factor in the early

days) and the topographical obstacles which had to be overcome, together with the additional factor, sometimes, of land ownerships being in difficult hands. The directors' guests at the Woking celebration included dukes and earls, several MPs and other notables such as Thomas Brassey, a man who was to become a famous railway construction contractor, and a man whose skill had rescued from an inauspicious start, the very works from Wandsworth to the Wey Navigation near Brooklands over which the first train had run. As the directors and their guests drank their champagne, they no more had in mind Exeter as the destination for their new railway than they did even Portsmouth; the directors had considered Guildford as a route to London, but the town had been dismissed from their thoughts. It was only brought back to mind later because another company – a competitor – sought powers to connect Woking to it. This irritation happened just as Woking was breaking into its key position on the emerging railway map. No: it was not Guildford but Southampton which was the objective, for this was a celebration by the London & Southampton Railway, incorporated under an 1834 Act of Parliament, a railway born of the strategic attributes of that harbour – attributes which were only developed in any substance after the railway came, to the mutual benefit of both.

Another proving run to Woking Common was operated just over a week later when 'nearly 400 ladies and gentlemen' were on an expedition, which required two trains to accommodate it. Sir Sam Fay, a notable railway manager of the late 19th and early 20th centuries, in writing a history of the company[3] just before the New Line opened, observed that: 'On every eminence along the line' (probably including Claygate

---

[2] An early exception to this was in 1863 when Parliament became concerned that the needs of urban London were inadequately met, so a Select Committee was charged with seeking a comprehensive Metropolitan plan. From this was born the idea of an Inner Circle line to link the termini north of the Thames. The execution of the plan was left to the private sector, which riven as it was by injurious competition, fumbled it. In 1874, when City of London interests, despairing at the inability of the Metropolitan and Metropolitan District companies to complete the Inner Circle, obtained their own powers to do so. This, of course, was enlightened self-interest by the private sector, not direct government action.

[3] *A Royal Road*, Sam Fay (1882).

MAP OF THE SOUTH WESTERN RAILWAY FROM NINE ELMS TO WEYBRIDGE

1.2 This map by Blackwood, dated 1842, shows the route of the London & South Western Railway from its terminus at Nine Elms as far as Weybridge, with intermediate stations at Wimbledon, Kingston (actually Surbiton), Ditton Marsh (Esher) and Walton on Thames: Weybridge and Woking, which was the country-end terminus at the time, are off the map to the west. The absence of any habitation near the stations is evident.

Lane and the Portsmouth Road in what was then Thames Ditton, where new bridges had been built to carry the line on its embankment) 'admiring rustics gathered in thousands to cheer the train, and on Woking Common, where tents had been pitched … a great crowd had assembled'. Crowds came to Surbiton too from all parts of the district for their first experience of a life-changing phenomenon. The first London & Southampton Railway train to run the whole distance from Nine Elms to Southampton was in 1840.

Choice of two routes

Most railway histories give no space to speculation about how Guildford was left out in the cold by the London & Southampton Railway but in a book about the New Line to Guildford it has a much greater relevance. In 1830 the civil engineer Francis Giles surveyed two routes between London and Southampton: in his letter to the promoters of the intended railway he wrote on 29 December 1830:

GENTLEMEN

I have made a preliminary survey of the line … between London and Southampton, for the purpose of … making a railway … and I find that two practicable lines might be formed … The first of these lines … will pass by Wandsworth, Kingston, Ditton, Weybridge, Guildford, Farnham, Alton, Alresford, and Winchester to Southampton, and will be in length about 73 miles … The second line will pursue the same course as the first … to Weybridge, from whence it will diverge to Basingstoke … [then on to] Winchester and Southampton … The distance will be about 78 miles, or about five miles longer.[4]

No historian has found the original plan referred to by Giles of the route to Guildford from Nine Elms: the point is highly relevant also to Kingston's railway, which we shall come to. There is some anecdotal evidence supplied by the reminiscences of Edward Ryde (1822-92), a renowned surveyor and a president of his professional body, whose astonishing workload included considerable railway work, including surveys and valuations for the LSWR in connection with the New Line. Ryde maintained a scrupulously methodical diary, which has survived and is now in the public domain.[5] When he was convalescing from an accident, he started some uncompleted notes for a history of Woking: writing in 1883 he states:

It has often been remarked of the railway from London to Southampton that it passes through very poor land; and that had it been laid out a short distance to the south [of Woking] and parallel to the present line it would have passed through very good agricultural land.[6]

This much is inarguable and is suggested by Giles. The nearest thing to a straight-line from London to Southampton would take in Guildford, Farnham, Alresford and Alton, and Weybridge is the ideal place to leave the Thames valley to hold the level ground of the Wey valley in which both Guildford and Farnham lie. Ryde, writing over 50 years after the event, offers his rationalisation of why the longer of the two routes

---

[4] *Surbiton: thirty-two years of local self-government 1855-1887*, Rowley W C Richardson, 1888, p 98.
[5] Surrey History Centre, Woking: 1262.
[6] Surrey History Centre, Woking: 1262/50/14.

surveyed by Giles was adopted: 'the landowner's opposition at all those places was so great that the application to Parliament was unsuccessful and the present line was resorted to in sheer desperation'. According to one of his peers, Ryde, 'excelled in the presentation of evidence having a special gift of marshalling figures and presenting a complex problem in a concise and lucid form'; it may appear churlish to cast doubt on the evidence of such a great witness but his reference to an 'unsuccessful application to Parliament' is wrong – if it ever existed it did not reach Parliament. The story that Ryde adopts – it could not have been direct knowledge for he was only a boy at the time – must have relied on the railway folklore which is more likely to be a cover promulgated by the promoters of the railway after the real reason for the strange route had been made invalid. Ryde probably relied on statements made after the application to Parliament that the line was laid down on the principle of avoiding estates, the owners of which might offer opposition: 'the line was therefore carried through a barren and desolate country, where the soil was so valueless, that the landowners were glad to get rid of it at any price'. Certainly, the route that was taken allows Ryde's remark its validity – the land on Woking Common is just one location that would fit the point – but to have wilfully forsaken the traffic of Guildford, Farnham, Alton and Alresford in exchange for a longer route to Southampton suggests that some of the story is incomplete.

Was there some better reason to forsake the additional traffic, which a new railway would capture, from the towns on what we might call the straight-line route? The evidence given to the Select Committee that considered the Bill in 1834 is littered with plausible and persuasive economic arguments for the railway, which are the more robust if the railway were to serve rather than by-pass the population on its route. Giles estimated the construction costs of the two routes as about equal (£1.2 million in 1830s £s), the shorter route being more expensive per mile than the longer because it would need a three-mile tunnel between Alton and Alresford.[7] Guildford, as we will see, is a natural railway town because it allows a reasonably easy penetration of the North Downs, but at the time it is plain that the point carried no weight. There is unfortunately no contemporary record of the deliberations over the route to prove it one way or the other, but there seems to be something like a magnetic attraction rather than the repulsion asserted by Ryde,

The Philip Hutchinson collection
1.3 Guildford High Street, looking east c1880.

that was keeping the railway running west, from Weybridge and avoiding Guildford.

If Southampton was the economic prize – and it was – what other reason could there be, in addition to the cheap land point, for the railway to run west as far as Basingstoke, before a great bend turned it south for the sea? Why did the railway take a route that included only one town of any significance – Winchester? Building the Southampton line through Guildford was considered but rejected because the directors could see beyond the great prize of Southampton: they had the much greater port of Bristol in their sights. If Southampton was to be made into a great entrepôt, how much more lucrative for a railway would be that

---

7 Those readers who are familiar with the Watercress Line between these two towns (opened in 1865 and now a heritage railway) will know that the route includes a famous five-mile bank graded at its steepest at 1 in 60 and known to local railwaymen as 'going over the Alps'. The steep gradient, which was unacceptable for a main line at that time, was the cheaper alternative to a tunnel.

western port which was already established? And a railway as far as Basingstoke already would give it a springboard from which to leap and carry the trade of two great ports, or so the directors thought when they proposed to Parliament that a branch should be run from their line at Basingstoke. In fact, the GWR with its broad gauge had ambitions of its own, and the London & Southampton Railway failed in its ambition of capturing Bristol's trade because they were obliged to withdraw the branch from their proposals in order to get their Bill through Parliament, and it was too late to go back on the route which was more or less parallel with the GWR's. This was an early manifestation of the competition, from which the two companies suffered, with their routes to the west. We cannot go into that here, but the keen competition between railway companies is a point to note, because it becomes highly relevant to this story. We have laid the ground, however, for an understanding of why Guildford, a bustling prosperous town at the time, with a heavy canal trade for the taking, did not get its railway.

Southampton

Agitation for a railway from Southampton had started as early as 1826, and by 1830 a preliminary prospectus for the Southampton, London & Branch Railway – the 'Branch' being the one to Bristol which had to be dropped – appeared in the local paper, whose editorial proclaimed: 'A new era is dawning on Southampton, and the march of events is rapidly lifting us over the usual progress of centuries'. This was even more prophetic than it appeared: the reader needs to put aside any conception of Southampton as a thriving port at this time, for in spite of its natural advantages, it had a poor reputation, with one of its promoters commenting on '… the present deplorable accommodation which is afforded to shipping in our port …'. The promoters of the railway were quick to make the connection between a new railway and a modernisation of the docks: they would feed each other. A few years later, it was asked: 'Who had heard of Southampton as a port until it got the railway …?' By holding meetings in Winchester, Basingstoke and Kingston, support for the idea of a new railway was to be canvassed: there was one town, however, which did not oblige; as we shall see, the railway history of Kingston will become key to the genesis of the New Line.

The line to Southampton was the first main line out of London south of the Thames.[8] We must take a little time

for a brief understanding of the economic case for building a railway to that port as one of the earliest priorities of the railway initiatives. The economic grounds for building a railway from Southampton were as robust, as was the paucity of economic rationalisation for building the New Line to Guildford 45 years later. We must remind ourselves of some realities of the 1830s – that London was the great port: that Napoleon had been dispatched to St Helena so recently that an older teenager would remember the explosion of joy which greeted the news of Waterloo; that strategic issues were still of considerable importance; no one could be certain that France was contained, and the hatred she had sown in Germany had yet to be reaped – so the idea of a sailing ship being able to avoid the many extra days that it might take to get to London, and her cargo being transhipped more securely by rail instead, was very attractive both economically and strategically. Such was the strategic benefit of avoiding the Straits of Dover that schemes had been advanced in 1825 to 1828 to build a ship canal to connect London and Portsmouth, one of which we should note was proposed to take a route through Guildford. None of the schemes could be financed because they would cost too much, but when the railway Bill had gone before Parliament both the Admiralty and the War Office had spoken up for it: the Army, with more foresight than could have been imagined, noted how strategically valuable Southampton would be.[9]

The amount of existing horse-drawn coach traffic along the rail route was known and the number of vessels by-passing Southampton on their way to London was capable of rough calculation: so, that part of the existing traffic, which might be substituted by a railway was capable of estimation. One of the other methods adopted to measure how much goods traffic might be substituted was to consider the trade in those most essential commodities for sustaining life as it was lived in the 1830s – foodstuffs and coal. Agricultural products, particularly grain and livestock, were an

---

[8] A line from Greenwich to Southwark had opened in December 1836, built by the company which would become the South Eastern Railway of which we will hear more, but the Southampton railway was of a wholly different character.

[9] Southampton was chosen by the War Office as the port of embarkation for troops going overseas in the late 19th century. During the South African War it was heavily used and, of course, from the very start of the Great War.

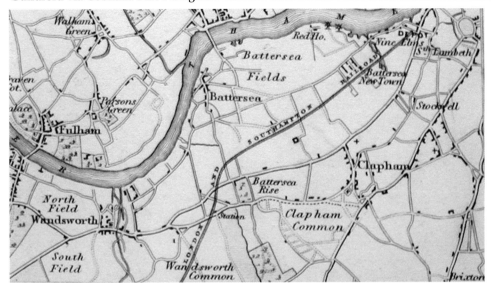

1.4 *Part of a map by Blackwood dated 1842 showing the London & Southampton Railroad running through fields at Clapham station (there is no junction yet!).*

important part of the economic case: 17 farmer-landowners said they would take shares in the company to the value of their land given up for it because they considered that the railway 'would be importantly advantageous to the agricultural interests of the country through which it will pass'. As we shall see the farming interest was a substantial driver for the New Line, and without it, the line would not have been built.

The price of coal on the route of the railway was up to twice the prevailing rate in Southampton: the railway could take some of this premium, being the cost of cartage. Calculations showed that the population that lived within 10 miles of the prospective route was 135,000 and estimates were made of the quantity of coal that would be consumed in a year in that 20-mile swathe. They then looked at how the coal got to where it was burned from where it had been mined: canals had been the great leap by which the exponential economic impact of the Industrial Revolution had reached such levels as then existed. By observing from which canal or river wharf the 10-mile population had

to pay a carter to fetch their coal, the estimates of revenue-substitution by freighting to a nearer railhead could be made: it was reckoned that the annual revenue from coal haulage would be £40,000. Similar calculations could be made for other commodities being brought in by canal or cart.

The Southampton trade prospered: within a year of the line opening, several large steamship companies were calling there routinely and it captured the mail traffic previously handled from Falmouth. In 1841 the South Western Steamship Company was formed to ply between Southampton and France: this was the beginning of a substantial tourist trade for the railway. Queen Victoria, the monarch who gave her name to the age, had seen the work in progress near Esher on a visit to *Claremont* and she graced the railway soon after her accession with her patronage. So much was the LSWR used by the Queen, that Sam Fay called his history of the railway, *The Royal Road*. The Queen will reappear in our story in relation to her love for *Claremont* in Esher and the Crown lands in Oxshott through which the New Line was built.

Chapter 2: The early railways of Guildford, Leatherhead and Kingston

2.1 *A view of Guildford from an engraving by J&P Howard, 1842. The view is from the meadows on which Guildford railway station was built on land sold by the 3rd Earl of Onslow. The telegraph station with semaphore arms in use can be seen at the top of the picture.*

Guildford's early railways

We now have an understanding of how Guildford missed out from having a direct main line to London when the railways came but we must examine its early railway history together with that of Kingston and Leatherhead: the histories of both Guildford and Leatherhead are linked with that of Portsmouth, so we must briefly cover that town too. Guildford was an important town – the most important in west Surrey – and was the centre of local agricultural life. With its strategic position in a gap in the North Downs giving it a key place in road communication, it being a staging post for the Portsmouth coaches, it could not be kept long from being the significant railway town that it became. Guildford enjoyed cheap coal since the River Wey Navigation opened in 1653, and that transport artery had been the basis of the town's wealth ever since: timber, iron, flour and gunpowder were shipped out; coal and corn brought in, all by one man leading his horse pulling a barge from the Thames (a trade which continued until the early 1960s). During the years leading up to 1834, when Parliament passed the Southampton Act, annual traffic on the Wey Navigation

to and from Guildford was around 60,000 tons. In 1836, while the Southampton railway was under construction, the Mayor of Guildford chaired a meeting in the town to discuss the idea of a railway.

Cheap coal in Guildford, advantageous to them that it had been for so long, counted against the people of Guildford when the railways came to Surrey: the directors of the London & Southampton Railway were not yet interested in the town, because Portsmouth was a much more lucrative prize, both for its trade and the cheapness of construction of a railway to it. There was a practical limit on the new railways that could be built simultaneously; the resources of capital, engineering skill and labour were limited and new projects had to be prioritised: each new project had to be shoe-horned into the spaces allowed by the various restraints, not the least of which was parliamentary scrutiny.

Although a line to Guildford had been considered by the London & Southampton in 1838, it remains something of a mystery how the company neglected Guildford for so long when a connection to Woking needed a line of only six miles. But the Portsmouth harbour trade would yield more revenue than Guildford. If there had been a master plan for the railways, Portsmouth would have had a direct line to London through Guildford: this is what it eventually got in 1859, but not before the machinations of a handful of railway companies had all given their stir of the pot.

Portsmouth

Portsmouth was plainly an important town: the population in 1831 was 54,000; there was the naval base to which stores were taken from London via the Wey Navigation and the 1816 Wey and Arun Canal, and some commercial trade. With Southampton about to have its rail connection to London, it is scarcely surprising that Portsmouth wanted its own railway. Gosport, a town of 14,000 inhabitants was just across the harbour from Portsmouth, and only 16 miles from the main line of the London & Southampton Railway: no matter, said the company, that Portsmouth would be approached, somewhat perversely, from the west, and from the wrong side of the harbour; no matter that the resulting mileage would be much more than a direct route. Portsmouth was a particularly attractive target because it could be reached easily and cheaply by building a small branch off the existing Southampton line. It would be a longer route to Portsmouth from London but it could be realised at much cheaper capital cost than any other scheme. This short term solution to Portsmouth's need for a railway would never have survived into a master plan, but on these simple economics rests the explanation of why Guildford had to fight for itself to get a railway, and how the line, which was built through the town to Portsmouth, when it was eventually built, was an afterthought and not built to main line standards.

Parliament approved the Bill for the Gosport branch even as the main line to Southampton was being built. In 1839 the company had the insight to acknowledge that its name was an affront to the sensitivities of Portsmouth people and took its new name, the London & South Western Railway (LSWR), which was both more descriptive of the company's wider ambitions and durable enough to serve with great utility until the grouping of 1923, by which the company became one of the three important components of the Southern Railway. The branch to Gosport opened in 1842.[1]

But Guildford deserved its railway and even if relegated at first by the LSWR, it was to become an important railway junction. With Woking only six miles away, the Guildford Junction company was given parliamentary approval in 1844. At about the same time, three competing schemes were put up to supplement the long LSWR route to Portsmouth via Gosport and the ferry: two of these schemes were opposed strenuously by the LSWR; to a third it gave its grudging support. This was the proposed Guildford, Chichester and Portsmouth Railway. However, of the three schemes for Portsmouth's railway, the only one to get through all its stages in Parliament was that proposed by what was to become the London, Brighton & South Coast Railway (LB&SCR), which had opened a railway to Brighton in 1841. This also was perverse, because it meant Portsmouth's second railway route to London was even longer, at 95 miles, than the LSWR's back door route. Until 1859, Portsmouth was served by the LB&SCR's long route (opened 1847) connecting with Brighton and the LSWR's long route, which at least now entered the town through the front door by an eastern extension via Fareham, instead of obliging passengers to use the ferry.

Meanwhile the Guildford Junction company had, not unnaturally, extended its thoughts south of Guildford – to Chichester, which was on the LB&SCR's long route to Portsmouth. The LSWR was approached and it found it politically convenient to buy the Guildford Junction company as a way of spiking the guns of a 'Portsmouth Direct' initiative, which would have damaged its own Portsmouth trade. Thus, in 1844 the LSWR acquired the branch from Woking, and the single track from Woking to Guildford Junction (it was doubled two years later) was opened on 5 May 1845. Guildford had entered the railway age. The station was built in a field on the west bank of the Wey Navigation:

---

1 This event marked the beginning of the end of the semaphore telegraph line connecting the Admiralty to Portsmouth. On 1 January 1848, a new electric telegraph, which was laid along the LSWR tracks to Gosport, with submarine cable from thence to Portsmouth, was commissioned. This made redundant the semaphore stations, three of which were sited near the New Line, one at Hinchley Wood, now a private house; one at Chatley Heath near Cobham and the other on Pewley Downs in Guildford: the one at Pewley Downs, also a private house, can be seen still from the New Line; the one at Hinchley Wood probably could when the railway was new, but is now obscured by tree growth. The Chatley Heath station, now preserved by Surrey County Council, is open to the public.

the 3rd Earl of Onslow, who as Lord of the Manor of Woking had objected to the Southampton railway, owned the field. It was his nephew – the 4th Earl of Onslow – who was to become the central character of the story of the New Line. The view from the station site as it was in 1842 has been captured on an engraving (see page 7), in which the banks of the river are seen to be open with the town beyond, and above it on Pewley Downs, the semaphore station, arms signalling to its correspondents at Chatley Heath and Bannicle Hill, near Witley. The ownership by the Onslows of this navigable riverside-site was not without significance to this story: the 2nd Earl had been a significant force behind the building of the Wey and Arun Canal and had sold land from his large estate for its construction.

Once Guildford was established as a railway town by its connection to Woking, its strategic position helped its railways grow quickly. Within four years, in 1849, the LSWR had opened a branch to Farnham; the South Eastern Railway (SER) opened the cross-country route between Reading and Redhill (now principally used for a service between Reading and Gatwick Airport) and the LSWR completed an extension of the line from Woking to Godalming. It was not until 1859 that through trains ran from *Waterloo* to *Portsmouth* via *Guildford* after a bitter row with the LB&SCR, following which the Surrey town achieved its status as a major railway interchange.

The *Railway Mania*

The year of Guildford's birth as a railway town coincided, as it happened, with a period that was labelled as the *Railway Mania*. 'Throughout 1845 surveyors were overrunning the country in all directions ...' and 'engineers, lawyers and newspaper proprietors also reaped a rich harvest ... Tradesmen left their counters and merchants their offices to gamble in ... [railway shares] with other speculators in the open street.' So wrote Sam Fay looking back on the period over 30 years later. 'As the mania spread, stock markets were opened in provincial towns, where, as in London, vast concourses of men bought and sold in a state of such furious excitement that a betting ring at our largest race meeting fails to supply its parallel.' Newspapers were crammed with prospectuses for new railway companies, many of which would be competing for the same business. Certainly, the LSWR had been very successful, but the market for railways was moving on: of course the main lines generally were making a lot of money, and the entrepreneurs who laid them only had to open them to see the cash come in at

2.2 *A recreation of the 'Reliance' coach leaving the Lion Hotel in Guildford for London. When Woking station opened the London coaches went there to connect with the railway.*

REVIVING THE GLORY OF THE ROAD," THE "RELIANCE" COACH LEAVING THE LION HOTEL, GUILDFORD, FOR THE VICTORIA HOTEL, LONDON.

2.3 Guildford High Street, looking west c1880.

The Philip Hutchinson collection

undreamed of levels. But no rational analysis would allow these early successes to be extrapolated for ever: there were limits to the incremental growth of traffic, but only the shrewd could see it happening: like all foolish booms before and since – the dot.com bubble of 2000 can be cited – rationale was not allowed to get in the way of a good story while it lasted. Thinking had moved on – it was no longer about linking great ports and cities to London: now the thought was that every sizeable village should have its railway, and indeed that is more or less what Surrey got. As Bevan observed in his *Tourists' Guide to Surrey*, 1887: 'Owing to its vicinity to the metropolis, no county … is better off for travelling facilities than is Surrey. [The railway companies] … supply almost every village with a railway and frequently with two.' He was writing after the New Line had opened, and after the mania had turned to a cruel bust, and at a time when the hurdles of justification for a new railway had been raised to a higher level of rationalisation – at least it had been so raised by professional railway managers, if not by the more amateurish promoters of railways. We will explore how the proposal to build the New Line was not subjected to a financial appraisal of a character that should have been informed by the stupidity that preceded it during the mania.

As R A Williams tells us in the first volume of his *The London & South Western Railway*:

> The post-mania depression hit South Western staff hard. In 1849, a rigorous 'economical enquiry' began, wielding its axe heavily on clerks. Many guided shaky pens while anticipating three months' notice, while survivors could rejoice only to suffer reduction of earnings common to all staff …

No railway manager who had lived through this period could allow his company's existence to be jeopardised by spending shareholders' money on an uneconomic line: it was this doctrine which drove all the many successful essays by the LSWR in stamping out proposals to add new branches to their profitable network, and it was received wisdom in 1880 when proposals that led to the building of the New Line emerged, not to build new branch lines.

Kingston

It is probable that the depression which followed the mania contributed to the continuing neglect of Kingston's need for a railway; neglect which had started when the town had been avoided by the

2.4 Kingston, the largest town in Surrey with considerable river-borne trade, yet having a second class railway service, hoped that by the Guildford, Kingston and London Railway Bill, it would have a main line railway connecting it to Guildford via Fulham, on to the City at Mansion House: it was not to be. This photo of the coronation stone, Griffin Hotel and market place in the distance is from 1903.

London & Southampton Railway in 1834. There must have been some good reason why the first main line railway in the area should avoid Kingston and be driven through a deep cutting to the east of the station that we now know as Surbiton – a cutting requiring the removal of 500,000 cubic yards of clay. It is said that Kingston strove to keep the railway away from the town in order to protect its coaching business, and although there is no primary evidence to support the story, the anecdotal evidence strongly supports it; unfortunately, the relevant minutes of Kingston Council are missing and no contemporary record of the circumstances has come to light.

W D Biden, who wrote *The History and Antiquities of the Ancient and Royal Town of Kingston-upon-Thames* in 1852 talks of the directors of the South Western Railway being 'compelled by the opposition of the town of Kingston' to divert the intended route. F S Merryweather was active in civic affairs, but not at the relevant time, and was Mayor for a period; in his 1887 book, *Half a Century of Kingston History*, he wrote:

… Kingston grumbled and fought against … [the railway] with the obstinacy of old conservatism. It was … [however] flushed with a fatal and barren victory. Its Corporation had beaten off the Railway! Hurrah! The precincts of the ancient borough were preserved from the defilement of the iron road. The proposed Kingston station had been forced right away to Surbiton hill.

Writing a year later in 1888, Rowley Richardson in his *Surbiton: thirty-two years of local self-government 1855-1887* puts it like this:

Although no authentic record is obtainable of the measures adopted to prevent the line approaching the town, and although the earliest plans for the formation of the railway now procurable show only the route actually taken, there is no doubt that the people of Kingston, sharing in the general prejudice, were frightened at the prospect of their trade being destroyed and their property ruined by the substitution of the railway for the stage-coach.

Richardson surmises that the intended line of the railway, as first cast, was to maintain the level ground

2.5 Passenger (in a hurry). 'Is this train punctual?'
Porter. 'Yessir, generally a quarter of an hour late to a
minute!' (From Punch)

at the foot of Wimbledon Hill and Coombe Hill, and go more or less straight to Kingston. Richardson recalls the story that Lord Cottenham, through whose land (on the present site of Atkinson Morley Hospital) the line would have run, took offence at the intrusion. Whether Cottenham made common cause with Kingston is unknown but the railway company considered it more prudent to avoid any confrontation.

There are two pieces of new evidence. We heard in Chapter 1 that the promoters of the Southampton railway were to hold a meeting in Kingston in order to garner support for the line: evidently, from the above accounts, there was no support, only opposition. In 1860 a Select Committee of the House of Commons was told by the Solicitor to the LSWR that when the Southampton line was originally projected, he had heard that 'the people of Kingston did petition, as a great many towns in the Kingdom did, to drive the railway from them'.[2]

The other new evidence tells us that the story was seared as if by a branding iron into the fibres of the

corporate memory of both Kingston and the LSWR. Even over 40 years after the event, the directors of the LSWR still had their own corporate scar-tissue over the episode: this is the story. In 1879 a deputation from Kingston, including Frederick Gould, the Mayor, a man who is to become a major player in our story, went to see the directors of the LSWR and their General Manager, the lofty Archibald Scott – a man who will return, centre-stage. Their mission was to seek major improvements in Kingston's train service. They wanted faster trains: 'It takes 55 minutes from *Kingston* to *Waterloo*' they complained: 'I have a mare in my stables which would do the distance in the same time',[3] grumbled the Mayor. Knowing that Kingston's service was bad, which it was, but that Surbiton's was excellent, at least in terms of frequency and speed, one of the directors, seeking to get on to the front foot but with a slap that was hardly appropriate, observed that:

> Kingston compelled the company to go a mile and a half away from the town hall, and then as soon as the railway came through Surbiton, Kingston was not satisfied until it had a station of its own.[4]

Recovering from this diversion, one of the delegation pointed out that the event was from 45 years previously. A director replied: 'Yes, but everybody must suffer for their ancestors'. If the *Surrey Advertiser*'s report is accurate – its source must have been the Kingston men – the reader will not be surprised that the corporate body of Kingston reacted with such anger that it was, in due course, to become one of the key players in the story, strange though this seems, of how the New Line came to be built and a bitter enemy of the LSWR.

In fact, whatever Kingston did in 1830 – embrace the railway or reject it – its status as a coaching town was doomed and by rejecting the railway when it was first offered the town's prospects for having a main line railway were reduced to zero. Because Kingston is central to our story we must consider, briefly, the later railway history of the town after it had rejected the main line. Kingston had to wait until 35 years after

---

[2] Evidence given in May 1860 by W R Drake to the Select Committee of the House of Commons, which was considering the London South Western Railway (Kingston Extension) Bill.
[3] *Surrey Advertiser*, 9 August 1879.
[4] *Ibid.*

2.6 *This section from the map shown on page 3 shows the route of the South Western Railway passing well to the south of Kingston.*

Surbiton before it got its own station – even Hampton Court[5] only had to wait 11 years – and that Kingston got a railway at all was no thanks to the LSWR but to competitive threats of the same nature that gave us the New Line. It really looks as though the LSWR had given up on Kingston because, evidently, its proposal in 1859 to make a branch to Kingston from its own Richmond-Windsor line at Twickenham was only promoted 'after opposition railways were constantly being projected from the north of London to join the southern railways' and in the process threaten the LSWR monopoly.[6] But as if to add insult to Kingston's injury, this railway was to terminate on the north bank of the Thames at Hampton Wick. Gould, the Mayor was very unhappy about this, and he appears to have had some influence[7] on the LSWR's decision to bridge the river, which it later did and Kingston's railway station opened in 1863. He also told a Select Committee[8] that there had been a scheme for a Kingston to Brighton railway, which the LSWR had declined to support; this confirmed the town's relegated status. Kingston's anomalous position in railway terms was painful to the town's self-image; it was an important town and its branch railway arrived in the town by the back door: it was paying a heavy price for what was either its folly, or this combined with Lord Cottenham's intransigence. Its branch line was upgraded to a loop in 1869 when the town was connected to Wimbledon. This is not to say that Kingston was then supplied with a good service; on the contrary there was a considerable amount to complain about such as having to change trains at

Wimbledon on the way to *Waterloo*; bad punctuality and dirty and infrequent trains. Although there was some diversity in the destinations that could be reached via *Twickenham* with the North London Railway, such as *Moorgate* and *Ludgate Hill*, the trains were painfully slow. 'Where are the cheap fast trains?' demanded a correspondent in the *Surrey Comet* in 1864.

For those men who were in public life in Kingston in the 1870s it was only by complaining to and about the LSWR that anything could be done: when the opportunity came for a new railway to serve Guildford, Kingston and London to be operated by a competitor of the LSWR, it is obvious that their support for it should be open-armed; the town of Kingston is to become a major player in the story of the New Line.

---

[5] At a meeting of the members of the LSWR on 8 August 1837, before the line opened, it was reported that 'a considerable traffic in passengers will at once arise from the proximity of the line to Hampton Court': the tourist guides of the day extolled the pleasures of a day out at the Palace, and in due course the branch line was built to accommodate the tourists; the commuters followed later.
[6] By James Bell's evidence in May 1881 to the Select Committee of the House of Commons on the Guildford, Kingston and London Railway Bill.
[7] By his own evidence in May 1881 to the Select Committee of the House of Commons on the Guildford, Kingston and London Railway Bill.
[8] *Ibid.*

2.7 The first railway station at Guildford: engineer John Wolfe Barry described it in 1881 as 'quite unfitted for modern requirements'.

Leatherhead

Leatherhead like Guildford ended up with a choice of routes to the capital. It was inter-company rivalry that provided the oxygen for the multiple routes into the capital from those towns. While leaving out a considerable amount of detail concerning the inter-company rivalries, this briefly is the story of how Leatherhead achieved the status of having two routes to the capital. Leatherhead will become a part of the story of the New Line to Guildford.

The promoters of the London to Portsmouth railway – the one which the LSWR did its best to frustrate – were active in advancing schemes to approach London through Dorking, Epsom and Leatherhead. The first in the field was the LB&SCR; their route from *Victoria* to *Epsom* opened in 1847. The LSWR's route to Epsom and then Leatherhead connected with their main line in 1859 at what is now Raynes Park taking a route through Ewell. Once the line to Leatherhead had been opened the LB&SCR extended their line to Dorking, Horsham and Portsmouth, while the LSWR service from *Waterloo* terminated at *Leatherhead*.

Criticisms of Guildford station

The railways brought winners and losers, and scarcely any aspect of life avoided the whirlpools of economic revolutions: some predictable, others quite unexpected. The LSWR prospered, enhanced as it now was by services to Portsmouth, Salisbury, Exeter, Ilfracombe, Plymouth, Bournemouth and Weymouth, as well as the overseas traffic, all of which could be picked up from Guildford, or more usually, Woking. In the years 1845 to 1865 the railway status of Guildford, pushed and pulled as we have seen by the great forces of the era – the market and competition – had been developed and was now to be stable for another 20 years. Competition had given Guildford passengers access by rail to other parts of the country, which could be matched by very few non-main-line towns, then or now, and the LSWR direct service to *Waterloo* was timetabled at about 55 minutes for the faster trains.

In the first place Guildford station had been designed as a terminus but now, having grown by stages without any rationale that might have been applied if only one company operated from it, the station was notorious for its muddle: trains for London left the station in opposite directions, with passengers being advised not to board a train without checking with the staff. Muddle was not the only complaint: it was thought by Guildford's MP, Denzil Onslow, to be dangerous. He explained in 1881 that the pillars supporting the canopies were too near the platform edge and the platforms themselves were too low: the station 'is very old and a miserable piece of patchwork' and 'I do not know any station in England which is more dangerous'. This echoed another view, which was that 'It was a disgrace to the county town'.[9]

He was not speaking just of the passenger station: the goods yard was also inconvenient and dangerous. His cousin Lord Onslow knew a bit about goods traffic at Guildford, for his two-way farming produce and supplies business through Guildford amounted annually to 300 tons. He had had a long battle with the LSWR over the approach to the station, which was 'quite the worst approach in England'.[10] Evidently the

streets round the station were very narrow; goods wagons were shunted into the road causing horses to rear up: the evidence of contemporary critics of the station facility at Guildford being sub-standard both operationally and from a safety point of view was overwhelming. Onslow's correspondence with the LSWR was aimed at getting improvements made. When asked by Counsel whether the matter was settled, his tart reply was that 'It had been settled by their refusal to do what was requested'.[11] The LSWR had cause to regret not being more placatory of Lord Onslow for he was a powerful man. In a move designed to embarrass the LSWR, Denzil Onslow asked a question in the House of Commons:[12] would the President of the Board of Trade, he asked, 'send an inspector to view Guildford station … in order that he may report as to its dangerous condition?'.

By the late 1870s the complaints of the Guildford people were essentially about the state of the station and its location, while those of Kingston complained about the paucity of the service; both communities wanted a choice of London termini. The Leatherhead people, with a choice of *Waterloo*, *Victoria* and *London Bridge*, were complaining about their inability to communicate with Guildford. Everyone complained about the late running of trains and, except for the race-goers themselves, everyone complained about the races.[13] When the railways first came the benefits were so overwhelming that they overcame complaint: the system was now almost complete and had grown old. As well as expectations changing, so had the nature of the demands for travel. The legions of the railway age had been marched until almost every conceivable change on society had been wrought.

NECESSITIES OF LIFE

2.8 'Yes, my lady. James went this morning with the hunters and I've sent on the heavy luggage with Charles. But I've got your pencil-case, the bicycle, your ladyship's golf clubs and the hunting crop and billiard cue, the lawn tennis racket, the bezique cards and markers, your ladyship's betting book and racing glasses and skates and walking-stick – and if I've forgotten anything I can easily wire back for it from the first station we stop at.' [Inspired by the Countess of Lovelace?] (From Punch)

[9] Evidence to Select Committee of the House of Commons, Guildford, Kingston and London Railway Bill, May 1881.
[10] *Ibid.*
[11] *Ibid.*
[12] Hansard: 28 February 1881.
[13] The LSWR milked the demand from racegoers for railway travel for all it was worth. Race meetings were held at many locations on the LSWR network (Sandown Park, Ascot and Epsom to name only three) and the special trains that were laid on from *Waterloo* made a mockery of the timetable and caused great resentment among the non-race-going public who were severely inconvenienced.

2.9 An early 20th century view of the rebuilt Guildford station.

2.10 Town Bridge, Guildford, c1880.

Chapter 3: The influence of London

3.1 *The opening of the main line station at what became known as Surbiton, and its ease of access to London combined to induce considerable growth in the second half of the 19th century; this early 20th century photograph of Surbiton shows a scene which was already 30 years old.*

London, the global city

The story of London is part of the story of the growth of Surbiton, Kingston, Leatherhead and Guildford and as we will see later, the New Line. *The Times* observed in 1850: 'Thirty years ago, not one countryman in a hundred had seen the metropolis. There is now scarcely one in the same number who has not spent the day there.' The numbers of rail journeys made increased dramatically. As Sydney Smith, the essayist, had said in the 1850s:

> Man is become a bird; he can fly quicker and longer than a … goose. The mamma rushes 60 miles to her conjugating and declining grammar boy. The early Scotchman scratches himself in the morning mists of the north, and has his porridge in Piccadilly before the setting sun … Everything is near, everything is immediate – time, distance, and delay are abolished.

All this, together it must be said with the inconveniences discussed in the previous chapter, was being achieved by private enterprise, operating in a period when *laissez-faire* was policy, sharpened by a competitive environment that became aggressive. Whatever excesses the *mania* brought about, they are in any event scarcely applicable to London. That great world-city, London, the centre of a United Kingdom, with a globally accepted single currency, Sterling; already the most powerful trading force through its commercial fleets, the fruits of Trafalgar allowing it to capture much of the globe's trade; the greatest entrepôt in the world, and the centre of trading in and the handling of the world's commodities: 'a man in Boston cannot buy a cargo … in Canton without getting a credit in … [London]', so an official committee was told. London was a capital with an incomparable network of European and imperial connections; it had financial sophistication in money, exchange and capital, it being the supreme banking centre in the world and of insurance too; the home of a great power at the epicentre of geopolitics; at the head of an Empire whose tide was rising to its full flood of development; the cultural heart of England: how could London, at the centre of all these things, fail to be the magnet drawing

3.2 Rich residents of Surrey, many of whom had moved out of London, found that they could combine the pleasures of country living without foregoing their favourite London venues; this postcard dates from 1908.

in all those would-be participants to its unique position in the world, now made the greater by the electric telegraph, no longer limited only by the reach of the railways, but expanding under the seas and oceans.

London's appeal as the capital

Southampton was the town from where our railway story started, but whatever trade London lost to that port was nothing compared to the astonishing exponential scale of its endemic growth, aided by the web of railways seeking out the most important city in the world. London's docks may not be part of this story but their wider impact on London's growing wealth certainly is. This was London's explosive century in which its population grew decade after decade until by 1901 it equalled that of the next 18 largest cities in the British Isles.

Even by 1851, London had a working population of over a million; about a quarter of England's traders, government employees, professionals and transport workers lived there, as well as 40 per cent of those in the law, banking and insurance, and two thirds of those in fine art, entertainment, literature and science. The further growth of London from mid-century was phenomenal: the agricultural depression, which we will hear of in the next chapter, supplied the ever-

growing demand for labour, in addition to net migration into London from overseas and further afield in Britain. For young women, London's vast numbers of domestic service jobs beckoned, and for men the capital's position as the world's largest centre for skilled and unskilled labour held exciting prospects.

London and the attractions of Surrey

The county of Surrey has been long-recognised as being blessed with great beauty: the contrasting scenery offered by the North Downs; the views; the farmland; the valleys; the Thames and its charming tributaries, the Wey and the Mole; the woods; the hamlets and the villages; the heaths and the commons: all these contributed to the celebration of a rich inheritance. When all these attributes are combined with close proximity to London it is scarcely surprising that Surrey should have been so popular with those who wanted to combine their affairs in London with a life in the country. From the time of the Tudors, there was a growing tendency for the rich City merchants, lawyers and courtiers to migrate to the less crowded countryside, south west of the capital with its cleaner air. We can call in evidence of this the great country seats which sprang up in our part of the county even before the railways came: *West Horsley Place*; *Clandon Park*; *Hatchlands*; *Ockham Park*; *East Horsley Park* (later

3.3 The importance of Surbiton station grew in the 19th century, leaving Kingston as a railway backwater; this early 20th century view, showing an earlier track layout, shows the crossover giving access to the up lines.

Horsley Towers); *Cobham Park*; *Pains Hill Park* and of course that most celebrated local country house, *Claremont*.

Even as the south western suburbs were covering some hitherto rural areas with densely built terraced housing on small plots, in places further out such as Esher, Cobham and Weybridge residential development was often more spaciously laid out, the houses detached and more substantial. Witnesses to Select Committees on railway Bills praised the beauty of the countryside of central Surrey; thanks to the Metropolitan Green Belt of the late 1940s and 1950s, much of it survives today to be admired from trains over the New Line, though blighted in places beyond the railway by road traffic and its associated infrastructure.

Railway communication, unfettered by cost considerations for the upper and upper-middle classes, had allowed whole districts to become covered by country houses with large gardens occupied by people able to afford their own carriages to transport them to and from the station. Many of these people spent time in London, either in the arts, politics, business or the professions but commuted from the country whether daily or less frequently. For the relatively few who could afford it, to work or play in the metropolis while domiciled in Surrey could be a minor form of paradise. Not only was it attractive for the participants, but also all those places served from *Waterloo* were the private dominion of the LSWR. They were making money out of the inner suburban lines as well as those reaching

further out and they were not going to allow any other railway company to steal any part of their business, not if they could help it.

London and Surbiton's expansion

Much has been written about Surbiton, the first railway suburb in Europe. In the 1880s, Edward Walford[1] described how 'New Kingston' rose mushroom-like with the opening of the railway station. Evidently, the 100 acre Maple Farm came onto the market and was bought by an entrepreneur from Kingston: unlike many from the town, he could see the way the wind was blowing, for it was he that had the vision for the new town. Although the process was not without a stumble here and there, a remarkable new railway town emerged. *The Times* noted the phenomenon at an early date: in its issue of 22 October 1840 it observed:

> Nothing in the history of railway improvements has been more extraordinary than the creation of this singular new town. On the spot where, last harvest two years, a large crop of oats was reaped, now stand rows of handsome houses, terraces and villas …

The 1838 station named *Kingston*, was a small rustic affair on the south side of the cutting near the Ewell Road bridge. Its 1845 successor, on the present site on land given by the first developer of the new suburb, was also called 'Kingston' until 1863. The original

---

[1] *Greater London: a narrative of its History, its people, and its places* (two vols, 1883 and 1884).

project for a new settlement here failed, although not before Victoria and Claremont roads had been laid out. Much of the land intended for the new town fell into the possession of mortgagees. Richardson describes the town at this point 'as having the appearance of a neglected, uncared-for suburb – partly country, partly town-like – with many of the houses and villas in an unfinished state'. The later gentrification of what was at first called *Kingston New Town*, then (somewhat inelegantly) *Kingston-on-Railway* before becoming Surbiton appears to have followed the Surbiton Improvement Act of 1855 by which it was separated, administratively from Kingston. In the 1860s and 70s the Surbiton Improvement Commissioners pressed the LSWR for improvements in the station facilities for both passengers and goods, particularly in respect of 'the means employed in receiving and despatching cattle'.

The popularity of Surbiton improved after a line connecting *London Bridge* with *Charing Cross* was opened in 1864 from which date, by changing trains at *Waterloo* (there was no underground) a commuter could get to London Bridge; a link to *Cannon Street* station in the City opened only a little later in 1866. Walford notes, 'the green fields and lanes of Norbiton and Surbiton have given way to innumerable villas' of handsome and substantial architecture and had by the 1880s become a favourite residence of merchants, 'whose charming residences add to the attractiveness of the place'.

Three notable authors took up residence in Surbiton for a while: William Makepeace Thackeray wrote *Vanity Fair* while living in rooms in the 1840s; Thomas Hardy moved into Hook Road in 1875, from where he wrote *Far from the Madding Crowd*; while Richard Jefferies (*Nature near London*) moved to Douglas Road in 1877. Anyone who worked in London, or needed to be close to it, such as authors for their literary contacts, found Surbiton ideal. The population of this affluent upper middle class suburb had grown to over 7,000 in 1871 and one or more servants lived in nearly one half of all the houses; these were mostly young girls from the farming districts seeking domestic employment including 150 of them employed as nursemaids; there were over 400 men employed as gardeners; these men were part of the drift from the land to the towns. Ten years later the population was over 9,000.

The same thing was happening in East Molesey. The branch line to *Hampton Court* opened in 1849 just one year after the opening of *Waterloo* station and 14 years before *Kingston*. It was built because of the popularity of Hampton Court as a tourist destination for Londoners, but the attraction of East Molesey for residential development for commuters was established. The influence of the railway when combined with the influence of London had a dramatic effect on land values: land which in 1839 changed hands for £10 per acre in Surbiton was fetching an incredible £1,000 per acre by 1853; while in New Malden land which fetched £40 per acre in 1839 sold for twice that in 1850. These steps in land values would not have gone un-noticed by the landowners who are part of this story. Sitting side by side with the influence of the pull on land values, which was exerted by London's influence, the supply of agricultural land for development increased after the mid 1870s because a severe agricultural depression severely blighted the value of land in its traditional use. We must examine the causes of this depression, for it is part of the story of the building of the New Line and the building development that followed it.

3.4 Head Barmaid. 'These tarts are quite stale, Miss Hunt. Would you mind taking them into the second-class refreshment room?' (from Punch)

Chapter 4: Agriculture in depression

4.1 Arable farming on the American prairies, which had been opened up by the railways, was conducted on a scale unknown on British farms: there are 20 horses in the team in this picture.

London's commodity traders

The period from 1875 was marked by a severe collapse in agricultural land values and a spirited attempt by two major landowners, the Lords Onslow and Lovelace, to promote a railway to run across their estates. To have a proper understanding of how it was that agricultural landowners came to be the dominant force pressing for a railway, and were successful where many had failed before, it is necessary to understand both how the depressed condition of farming came about and the intensity of its impact. What happened in the 1870s is that the hitherto inviolate economic law, which held that there was an inverse relationship between low yields and high prices – a law that by and large had avoided ruinous collapses in farm incomes – was mysteriously suspended: the forces of the globalisation of trade, which had been forged from the power of steam, were to be released by events overseas.

All readers will have their consciousness of how the world is changing; in their own lifetimes, they will be able to recall real permanent change. Older readers may sense that the rate of change has accelerated: the concept of globalisation is now on every lip, brought about by the new communications revolution made possible by satellites and microchips. In the 1870s people were caught up in what were to them changes which were just as bewildering: the impact of steam power applied to railways, other machinery and ocean-going ships was now compounded by a new revolution – the electric telegraph. The dramatic economic impact of the railways, although well advanced here at home, and not yet influenced by the internal combustion engine, was still wreaking its enormous influence on change in the new continents of North America and Australasia. The merchants in London, who as we have already seen were prospering, could now order their cargoes from Chicago and New York, or from Auckland and from Sydney by undersea cables. Thanks to the electric telegraph cargo owners would know when their ships sailed, where their captain was instructed to sail to, and by calculation, when the cargoes would arrive. In becoming a leading centre for world trade in commodities, London prospered, but the ratchet of tightening competition for the British farmer was soon to cut swathes through their incomes.

Free trade

The doom of the 'High Farming' period in England was at hand. It had seen the efficiency gains that had been

21

4.2 A shepherd driving his sheep home from Guildford market; c1910.

gathered by new tools and implements; by a more disciplined approach to drainage and by the discovery of artificial fertilisers: these benefits had already been reaped. Steam had revolutionised ocean-going cargo transport, and the railways had opened up the continental space of North America. The economic impact of these global changes could not fail – did not fail – to bring dramatic change in the economic circumstances of Britain.

Agriculture's relative decline was inevitable simply through the expansion of industry and commerce – the growth of London's share of world trade in currencies, commodities and money being, of itself, relevant to what was happening in Surrey because it was close to London – but agriculture was vulnerable also to the endemic free trade policy which allowed the importation of foreign wheat. The farmers, as well as consumers, had benefited from the Industrial Revolution: mechanisation had allowed productivity gains, and of course the industry was a double gainer from the railways, which allowed fertilisers, coal, machinery and building materials to be brought in more cheaply and the crops delivered more economically to their markets. This was the way the world went round, with agriculture being a sort of balancing pond: good harvests increased the money supply and trade increased; poor harvests brought the reverse.

For the consumer, everything looked fine. By the third quarter of the 19th century industrialisation abroad allowed an increasing range and volume of foodstuffs into this country at ever-lower prices; access was now possible to continental products such as bacon, butter and cheese, aided by new railways there and by new ports and ships. It was argued that the sacrifice of agriculture was a small price to pay for industrial supremacy, and high living standards. In fact the price was high.

In a book written during the Great War, and in the context of a food crisis caused by war conditions, A D Hall wrote a review in *Agriculture After the War* of what had befallen British agriculture:

> The history of British agriculture for the last 40 years has been one of continuous decline from the point of view of the gross production from British soil ... the most marked change has been the steady conversion of arable land into grass. The process was brought about in the earlier part of the period by the great fall in prices of the 70s and 80s when arable farming as then practised ceased to be remunerative on the heavier and poorer soils; meat and milk maintained their values but the only way for a farmer to obtain a profit was to reduce his labour bill and take the small but comparatively certain return that the land would yield under grass. The number of men employed in agriculture has declined

with the ploughed land: 100 acres of arable will employ as many as four men, while 200 or 300 acres of grazing can be looked after by one man.

Although this review was written with the benefit of hindsight, it correctly places the commencement of agricultural decline as pre-dating the Onslow/ Lovelace initiative for a new railway. We must examine what Hall was referring to when he spoke of the "great fall in prices of the 70s and 80s", for this period is relevant not just because it saw the eclipse of farming in Surrey but also because it gave the impetus to landowners to recover their losses by considering any possibilities.

The fall and fall of grain prices

After a good harvest in 1874, a succession of cold and wet summers spoiled the crops for several years from 1875: 1878 was bad; the winter of 1878/9 saw a 16-week long frost in some parts of England, but the harvest of 1879 was 'the worst of the century'. Yields fell, but remarkably, the price of what was harvested did not rise: on the contrary, prices fell. The scale of price collapse would have been catastrophic enough if it had been cyclical, but the old paradigm was shattered: from their first fall there was no recovery in prices for 20 years: the falls kept coming and lasted for a period longer than the collective memory of the farmers: the catastrophe had no precedent and it became clear that something had changed.

It was the great rise of cereal farming in the USA, and the huge volumes of exports that it produced, which changed the world. During the Civil War the Union government noted the strategic importance of railways, not just politically but militarily as well. Like the British government before it, that of the USA took care not to be involved in either the construction or the running of the railways. However, while Westminster was concerned only with the protection of private interests and took no role for itself in the laying out of the railway map, it was quite different across the Atlantic: at every level of government – federal, state and local – transportation development was a public sector issue. From this thought process came the inspiration for the coast-to-coast railway financed not with government cash but with the one commodity that the government had in astonishingly large quantities – land.

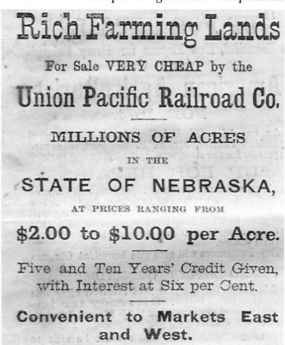

Rich Farming Lands

For Sale VERY CHEAP by the

Union Pacific Railroad Co.

MILLIONS OF ACRES

IN THE

STATE OF NEBRASKA,

AT PRICES RANGING FROM

$2.00 to $10.00 per Acre.

Five and Ten Years' Credit Given, with Interest at Six per Cent.

Convenient to Markets East and West.

4.3 This advertisement appeared in the July 1874 issue of American Agriculturist: *it was typical of the period when the new railways opened up the mid-West of the USA.*

By the so-called *Louisiana Purchase* of 1803 about 800,000 square miles of territory were acquired by the US government for a few cents an acre. The railways that opened up the prairies were financed by land grants covering over 130 million acres in a wide belt on either side of the new railway. To give some idea of scale, the land grants covered land around 400 times greater than the acreage in agricultural use in Surrey at the time.

Unlike the promoters of the Southampton railway, who looked to traffic substitution for much of their early revenues, those who built the prairie railways needed to create a market by converting a wilderness into cereal farms for which the railways needed farmers: the bait was cheap land

Advertisements started appearing in the USA beckoning entrepreneurs to go west and become farmers by buying land suitable for grain crops at very low prices and often on deferred terms. The land-rush that followed created such a huge new food source, that

23

4.4 *The movement of horses became a very important part of the LSWR's freight traffic. Landowners such as the Lords Onslow and Lovelace would become part of this market. These former LSWR horseboxes were photographed at Esher goods yard in the 1950s.*

The John Field collection

it could not possibly be consumed in the home market: it had to be exported, and to where else but to Europe.

The agricultural expansion in North America had been made possible by the power of steam; the same force allowed grain to be shipped across the Atlantic at ever-reducing cost. An improvement in marine steam engines had allowed the expansion of ocean-going cargo vessel capacities with a consequential reduction in freight rates. The cost of sending grain from the USA to Britain had already fallen by 50 per cent when the harvest here was ruined in 1879.

Save our farmers

Agriculture represented such a large proportion of our national production that when farm incomes declined, a general trade depression ensued. The matter came on the agenda of Parliament but the crisis was not peculiar to Britain: the competition from across the Atlantic was

4.5 *This haymaking scene is probably on land that was previously under the plough: the absence of machinery, in stark contrast to the scene on the North American prairies, is evident.*

4.6 The harvest, c1880: a view looking north across the A31 Farnham Road, which is to the front of the hospital to which casualties among the navvies building the New Line were taken.

The Philip Hutchinson collection

affecting the whole continent of Europe: an avalanche of grain was crossing the Atlantic. As Sir Robert Ensor, in his *Oxford History of England* tells us: 'By 1879 every country west of Russia faced the alternative – to put a tariff on wheat or lose the best of their wheatfields'. In Britain, where there was an aversion to tariff barriers to trade, the government did nothing to protect the farmers.

Lord Onslow did not blind himself to the long-term nature of the problem. He had correspondents in America and was well informed. Some of his tenants were already handing back their farms, unable to pay the rent: 'a good deal of my land has been thrown upon my hands' he told a Select Committee of the House of Commons considering the Guildford, Kingston and London Railway Bill in May 1881. He realised that prices were 'so low that their was no margin for profit' and that after allowing for interest on the capital invested in building improvements, the return earned by his tenant farmers on working the land 'was zero'. A correspondent in the USA had convinced him this was no short term affair: in a suggestion of what today would be called 'set-aside' his correspondent told him '… it is a race [as to] which country puts its land out of cultivation first – yours or ours'. In order to help his

tenants Onslow started making remissions of rent charged to his tenants by reference to a benchmark price of wheat.[1] On his own farm, which was principally arable, he observed in 1881 that he was 'endeavouring to make it dairy' in an attempt to staunch his losses.

While the blizzard of competition was sweeping in with the Atlantic gales, Britain was playing to its strengths: the production and export of high added-value manufactures, and the skills of the City of London would see Britain continuing to prosper. The very journals that carried the advertisements for prairie land carried pages seeking to sell British agricultural machinery. The prevailing political consensus allowed foreign imports of cheap food, which provided the Sterling for overseas customers to buy our industrial goods. There were plenty who would deride this policy of free trade, but its stout defenders won the day. The *Surrey Comet* had a view: it sounded odd thought their editorial of 1 November 1879, 'after years of experience of the benefits of free trade, to hear the pleas for protection for particular trades'.

---

[1] *Surrey Advertiser*, 12 January 1885.

The harvest catastrophe of 1879

As already noted the process of the collapse in farm prices had started in mid-decade; while the harvest in 1878 was bad, that of 1879 was a catastrophe. A cold and bitter winter had been followed by an unseasonal spring: it had already been a 'summer without sunshine' when the deluge came in August. A local farmer in the Wey valley wrote to the *Surrey Advertiser* noting that the heavy rain had kept him indoors and that from his windows he could see:

> the submerged meadows of my neighbour's farm where in spite of repeated efforts to get it in for nearly a month, stand the hay-cocks, reduced to little more than manure.[2]

The Thames was reported as being eight feet above normal at Molesey, and all its Surrey tributaries were in flood. In August a most frightful hailstorm brought down acres of glasshouses, only recently erected as a relief from the collapse in grain prices.

The bad harvest was no localised affair: in an editorial the *Surrey Comet* of 16 August 1879 intoned: '... we fail to imagine how a revival of trade can possibly ensue upon a generally deficient European harvest.' 'Only on the American continent is a good crop of wheat expected.' Because of America 'we shall not starve' wrote a correspondent, but 'with the prospect of winter, with depressed trade … it behoves … [everyone] to prepare for a trying season'.[3]

The *Surrey Comet* noted in its editorial of 30 August 1879:

> We are beginning to understand how much social comfort and what millions of wealth [agriculture was still the dominant industry] a day's sunshine pours upon our nation. The disasters of our corn fields, our gardens and our orchards – disasters, which if summed up, would present a fearful total, testify to the commercial value of sunshine. The agricultural interests, long depressed, look more gloomy than ever. At a time when the reapers should be tying up the golden sheaves, the rain pours down on corn, green and sickly in its longings for solar warmth.

When the time came for the celebration of the Harvest Festival, the priests were on the back foot when they were leading the 'thanksgiving': one noted that he had been questioned for having a Harvest Festival at all;

4.7 *William Hillier, the 4th Earl of Onslow, as featured in an original 1905* Vanity Fair *print, when he was 52 years old, and looking quite the Edwardian toff; when he promoted the Guildford, Kingston and London Railway Bill he was only 27 years old.*

'Better a fast than a festival' he had been told, because 'the country generally was suffering from such depression'. It was true responded the priest 'that the harvest is something like 25% less …' but thanks to America, 'The poor man's loaf will be as cheap this year as it was last'.

The essential point of all this for our story is not so much the social impact of the wretched conditions into which this catastrophe drove the agricultural interests

[2] *Surrey Advertiser*, 30 August 1879.
[3] *Ibid.*

in the district, but its economic impact – its crushing effect on farm incomes and land values, and the response of the great local landowners, the Lords Onslow and Lovelace, to this threat to their wealth.

The collapse in land values

Rents in Surrey fell by about a third during the late 1870s and 1880s and at their lowest point did not average more than 8s to 12s an acre for the better land. This was a pitiful level. Lord Onslow, in evidence to the Select Committee considering the Guildford, Kingston and London Railway Bill, averred that he expected to get '30 years purchase' if he were to sell farmland. This sounds by today's standards a very full price, but accepting the multiple without question and applying it to the rents applicable to the best land we get a miserable valuation of £18 per acre. There is no need to argue the toss over multiples; we have seen already that farms were being turned back to Lord Onslow for want of his tenants' ability to pay the rent: the pitiful valuations simply reflect the endemic and protracted nugatory farm incomes. The *Estates Gazette* reported that agricultural land values were 'suffering extreme depression'[4] and the Institute of Surveyors said, in a defining statement touching much of the land through which the New Line was built, that 'the present distress on clay farms exceeds, as a rule, any that has occurred for the last 40 years'.[5] In Parliament, a Royal Commission was appointed to:

> Enquire into the depressed condition of the agricultural interests and the causes to which it is owing; whether those causes are of a permanent character; and how far they may have been caused or can be remedied by legislation.[6]

Onslow, who was active in the Lords, must have known this was just a smokescreen, just as he knew because he was in touch with the USA that there would be no respite from the collapse in farm prices: what would be more natural then, than to want to have a railway to your farm, both to economise on cartage to and from Guildford of its produce and imported requirements, and at the same time sell large tracts of land to the railway company for thirty times its productive value in farming use. As the Lords Onslow and Lovelace brooded in that dreadful period in the autumn of 1879, they seem to have agreed they should try to bring a railway into their area. The usually favourable impact of railways on the residual value of land for

4.8 This feature in the July 1874 issue of American Agriculturist *discusses the use of machinery for making roads. The road roller is made by Aveling & Porter of Rochester, England, cost $4,000: the export of high value machinery and the import of cheap food was typical of the British economy of the period.*

development would have been received wisdom for landowners in the 19th century. When the LSWR had decided to make Molesey the terminus for their Hampton Court branch a landowner, F J Kent from Hampton, having early knowledge of this purchased nearly 300 acres paying between £60 and £80 per acre. Whether this was more than agricultural value at the time does not alter the remarkable impact of the coming of the railway, for when it was developed the greater part of Kent's land in Molesey produced nearly £3,000 per acre.

---

[4] *Estates Gazette*: 1 October 1879.

[5] *Estates Gazette*: 1 September 1879.

[6] *Estates Gazette*: 23 August 1879.

4.9 It may have been in The Saloon at Clandon Park where the Lords Onslow and Lovelace discussed what do do about the collapse in land values: this view is from c1950.

These huge increments in value would be even more marked in the teeth of the agricultural depression now gripping the country and the county. The financial incentive for Lovelace and Onslow to get a railway into their land was obvious. Lovelace had been more or less involved in railway projects before, so it would need great cunning, and a deft change of approach, to succeed now where failure had adorned all previous efforts, but times were bad and need is the mother of invention. In the event Lovelace realised over £8,000 from sales of land to the LSWR,[7] as well as having a private siding built for him, an enclosed coal yard and an obligation on the LSWR to plant thousands of 'neat ornamental' trees to give a 'copse-like appearance'. Onslow did dramatically better because considerable amounts of his land were needed in the Guildford area in addition to that for the running tracks through

Clandon: he realised over £52,000.[8] Whatever multiplier the reader may wish to apply to this number to bring it to a modern equivalent it is plainly a huge realisation. We do not know what Onslow did with the money, but what he could have done with it is to buy over 2,000 acres of the best farmland in Surrey at the depressed prices of the time, and still have change – that is the measure of the brilliance of his initiative to bring the railway through his land and the realisation he made from it.

---

[7] LSWR terrier of the Surbiton, Guildford, Leatherhead branch railways, 1886. NA RAIL 411/406.
[8] *Ibid.*

Chapter 5: Railway problems

5.1 By 1884 the volume of traffic on the routes into Waterloo, with the New Line due to begin service in the following year, was such that the tracks were quadrupled: here a Class L12 (Drummond) 4-4-0 No 417 (built 1904, Nine Elms) heads a Down express near Durnsford Road bridge, c1910; note the cultivated fields.

The aversion to monopolies

The success which the railways had undoubtedly achieved in the 19th century came hand in hand with crowds, frustration, dirt and delays: the honeymoon was over and the passengers were now consumers who, in the environs of London, could find plenty to grumble about. For them, it was the LSWR's monopoly that was the root of their travel problems: 'The train service is very bad; we are suffering all the worst evils of a monopoly', said a farmer from Clandon at the 1881 Select Committee, which was also told that Kingston Town Clerk's support for an alternative to the LSWR was because 'we look upon it as our only chance of emancipation from the South Western monopoly'. If only competition could be introduced, the tribulations

of the travelling public would be assuaged, was the general belief; this was the burning issue in the railway towns: an improvement in service was their demand and they used the columns of the local newspapers to voice it.

Competition was the only known antidote to the hated monopolies that the railway companies strove to create and protect. The elimination of competition and the achievement of a monopoly is the unspoken ambition of any business. The imposition of competition among the railway companies was one of the political consensuses of the day, but the concept was then more easily accepted than applied. Where there was no alternative means of transport with which to compete, the concept of competition, helped by the railway companies' anti-competitive behaviour, became a fiction. In large measure, the railways were natural monopolies and calls for nationalisation were made or considered by the Duke of Wellington, Walter Bagehot, Gladstone and others from the 1830s onwards; the *Surrey Comet* opined in 1881 that: 'The time cannot be very distant when the whole system of railway management must be taken into serious consideration of Parliament', while the lament of the *Kingston and Surbiton News* was: 'How this neighbourhood has suffered because the railway company is independent of any kind of public control.' The *Surrey Comet* continued:

> Whether it will come to the State exercising direct control or not, depends … upon the way in which the railway companies regard their duties to the public … Monopolies are always prone to become selfish, and in some railway managements we certainly need some check to this tendency. So many interests, essential to the very life of society, are now connected with our railway systems, that a monopoly which is found to be prejudicial to the public, will not be allowed to become permanent. Certainly the railway management of the present time is open to serious objections, and so far as this neighbourhood is concerned, has been somewhat disappointing.[1]

Complaints against the LSWR

This was not a case of a good local paper taking a lofty view: a correspondent from Thames Ditton wrote a rational critique of the LSWR in 1879:

> As to the carriage accommodation, the compartments are small and low, the seats of each being too close, and the roof a destroyer of hats. The carriages are hot in summer, being of dark colour externally … and cold in winter, foot warmers being almost unknown. The carriages are wretchedly lighted, the lamps only making darkness visible, and are extremely dirty …
>
> As to the stations, the platforms of many are dangerously low, and [with] most of the carriages being unprovided with continuous foot-boards, the difficulties of the aged and feeble passengers are made greater … Few of the stations … are provided with overspan roofs … [merely having] a shed, often only covering one-third of the platform. [At Surbiton] … if it rains the ladies must get wet.[2]

Another complainant wrote about the meagre 2nd class accommodation and the want of mats in the carriages and included the dismissive reply he had received from the LSWR:

You do not … state in what respect the accommodation is meagre. So far as I have been able to ascertain, there is much more 2nd class accommodation provided than is made use of.

With regard to mats. No mats have been taken out of those carriages into which they had been placed. It is not, however, the custom to put mats into the 2nd class carriages on the suburban lines, nor is it necessary to do so.[3]

5.2 WHY TAKE A CHILL?
If your train is not heated, get plenty of foot-warmers, as Algy and Betty did. Sit on one, put your feet on another, a couple at your back, and one on your lap …(From Punch*)*

---

[1] *Surrey Comet,* 8 January 1881.
[2] *Surrey Comet,* 22 November 1879.
[3] *Surrey Comet,* 20 December 1879.

5.3 Impatient Traveller. 'How long will the next train be, portah?'
Porter. 'How long? Well, sir I don't know if I can say to half an inch. About four or five coaches and an' engine, or so.'
(From Punch)

This reply is the more remarkable because Archibald Scott, the General Manager, signed it. Another correspondent calling himself 'Cold Feet' wrote about 'high fares, slow trains, and bad accommodation':

> … but 'mats!' Mr Scott, 'mats!' is the cry from all 2nd class passengers kept waiting in the cold and dreary fog when the train, as usual, is 'late, late, so late', and many a passenger wishes he had you there to see how you liked it, with your feet exposed to a thorough draught from the badly constructed doors.[4]

There is no doubt where the *Surrey Comet* stood in this matter: at about the time Lord Onslow was feeling the pinch down on the farm, the newspaper joined in the general criticism of the LSWR; in the editorial of 20 December 1879 they said:

It would, as a matter of policy, have been wise, had the company shown some little courteous desire to mitigate the inconvenience of this inclement season by at least covering the bare, cold floors of the 2nd class carriages with mats, even if they could not see their way to foot-warmers … High fares and a niggardly disregard for the comfort of passengers, will not tend to develop the many possibilities of good dividends …

Practically everyone thought more competition was the answer, and when Lord Onslow introduced the prospect of a new line to be operated independently of the LSWR, the people of Kingston, Surbiton and Guildford were enthusiastic in their support, and as we shall see, these stories of bad service were to be paraded in front of a House of Commons Select Committee to the discomfort of the LSWR who hated any idea of competition. For the railways it was ruinous competition that was restricting the availability of profit to fund improvement. Most of the railway companies had been through scarring competitive fights with other railway companies: it was now time for most of them to live and let live, which meant accepting the *status quo* in respect of territory: predatory pricing had ruined many railway companies.

Living in peace

An excellent illustration of how the LSWR was living in peace with its previous arch-competitor the LB&SCR is allowed by the evidence given by a witness to the Select Committee, greater detail of which we will hear more soon. The witness explained how he had become frustrated by the LSWR's unwillingness to entertain a new railway from Leatherhead to give a connection to Guildford: thinking that he would be able to needle them into action by smooching with the LB&SCR, who operated into Leatherhead as well as the LSWR, he received an unexpected rebuff: he was told that there was some sort of understanding – plainly it was an anti-competitive arrangement – which precluded one company from interference in the traffic of the other. Anyone who used the railways would be angry about this obvious abuse of their interests. The District Railway would have known about this cosy arrangement, but would have felt no obligation to respect it: they could look with predatory eyes at what was for them a fresh and rich pasture, and be welcomed

---

4 *Ibid.*

by the customers for their trouble. The battleground for a fight was being laid out.

The regulatory regime

Compared with the regulatory regime in which today's private railway industry operates, the scene in the 1870s was a picnic. It is true that the railways had the burden of funding the renewal and upgrading of the basic infrastructure and that the industry knew that the high level of fixed costs was becoming the spectre which would ultimately smother the shareholders' dividends. Paying a dividend at a creditable rate was, however, the benchmark by which the companies were judged at the time: it was a virility test. The LSWR shareholders were well rewarded after the early stumbles in the construction of the Southampton railway were stabilised: the company paid a dividend on its ordinary stock in every half-year from 1839: 6 per cent per annum in the first few years, but rising to 10 per cent per annum and then 16 per cent per annum in 1845 and 46. The panic in the late 40s, following the *Mania*, saw dividends fall to 6½ per cent per annum in 1849, but by 1882, just before the New Line building commenced, 11½ per cent per annum was being paid. The realities of corporate life were harsh, then as now: reduced profit meant reduced dividends; reduced dividends meant capital starvation; capital starvation meant no renewal programme and an inexorable decline into bankruptcy: it was the eternal conflict between capital and consumers. The shareholders would be the first to criticise the building of new lines which did not satisfy a tough hurdle of prospective profit.

The government was by now more hands-on in safety matters, and there was some regulation of freight rates although, according to some critics of the industry, it was not very effective. As to passenger fares, punctuality, cleanliness of trains, speed and frequency, only competition – if there was any – could restrain a railway company from exploiting its customers. The LSWR milked the race traffic over which they had a monopoly and which was giving them very rich pickings – and let their regular customers down badly. As policy-makers have observed over the decades some activities are natural monopolies: before statutory regulation was invented and motorised road transport started to introduce competition into the equation, and draw its veil over railway economics, there was only one way to induce competitive behaviour: it was to give customers a choice.

The prevention of competition was one issue; the avoidance of building uneconomic lines was another. By the 1870s the lessons of the *Railway Mania* had been properly learned and it was plain to the powerful railway companies in general that more railways had been built than were good for the financial health of the industry. Competition as well as hysteria had allowed this to happen, but a well-managed railway company was now in the business of making what it had already pay well. The fixed costs of a line were high and the traffic receipts variable; a certain volume of traffic was essential otherwise the losses mounted. When account is taken of the costs of replacement of fixed facilities and rolling stock, the losses which an under-used railway can accumulate is a horror story: nothing has changed today, except that with today's higher standards and expectations, it is worse.

Waterloo a muddle

As the 1880s approached the LSWR had at least three strategic problems in and around London which could only be solved by massive new investment: the period then as it is today was one of capital rationing; there was just not enough capital available to fund every ostensible good idea for new routes; and quite apart from new ventures there was the whole question of the renewal and improvement of the infra-structure which had been laid down 40 or more years previously, and which had grown haphazardly ever since, much of which was in urgent need of either renewal or upgrading. The bad and dangerous state of Guildford station – it was not the only one – has already been mentioned; the other problems were the geographical disadvantages of *Waterloo* station and the traffic bottleneck in its approaches: all three of these weaknesses were part of the means by which its enemies could make the LSWR seem to be failing to serve its customers.

We saw in Chapter 1 that the route into London had been deliberately kept south of the Thames in order to avoid the additional cost of demolishing valuable buildings: the benefits that had been achieved 40 years earlier had now been reversed. Passengers did not want to go to *Waterloo* – *Waterloo* was nowhere: they wanted to go to the City, to Mayfair, to Westminster or wherever their business took them. The LSWR had successfully built a passenger business but the expectations of those passengers of a railway were growing all the time: when the railway was novel being taken to *Waterloo* was acceptable; but for many *Waterloo* meant a cab or horse-drawn omnibus ride to their destination; the long door-to-door journey times were no longer acceptable.

The LSWR was aware of its problems and the journey to the City had been improved by the introduction of an interchange, which had been provided at *Waterloo* in 1869 whereby *Cannon Street* station could be reached (as well as *Charing Cross*) from *Waterloo Junction* (now *Waterloo East*). But this arrangement and indeed the whole muddle of *Waterloo* came in for stinging but humorous condemnation in 1889 by Jerome J Jerome in *Three Men in a Boat*. The reader should beware of thinking that this very funny piece of comic writing

5.4 Traveller (waiting for a train already 20 minutes late). 'Porter, when do you expect that train to come in?' Porter. 'Can't say sir. But the longer you waits for it, the more sure 'tis to come in the next minute.' (From Punch)

about *Waterloo* is total fiction: the very situations, which Jerome mocks, were described to a Select Committee in 1881: '*Waterloo* is very inconvenient: we frequently do not know what platform to go onto, and have to ask, and we get into the wrong carriages.' *Waterloo* station was plainly a muddle in spite of having been rebuilt in 1879. 'In cold weather there is no more miserable station in Europe than *Waterloo*' was the assessment of Wolfe Barry, the railway and bridge engineer who will take a major part later in our story.

'*Waterloo* lands you nowhere', was a typical assessment but for those needing to get further into the City than *Cannon Street* with its inconvenient change of stations at *Waterloo*, the whole business of getting there was a problem. The underground tube railway did not at that time exist; but the cut-and-cover steam lines of the District and the Inner Circle lines were well developed and now serving *Mansion House*; this was a threat to *Waterloo* and in due course it will come into our story – centre stage.

Waterloo bottleneck

The LSWR's success in generating its passenger business into *Waterloo*, both by the number of services and routes, meant that there were not enough paths on the lines to accommodate the demand for them. There were only two tracks – one each way – to accommodate the traffic which was a mixture of suburban and express workings. By 1881 the LSWR had decided to grasp the nettle and quadruple the track from Hampton Court Junction to Clapham Junction: this radical solution, which the LSWR had doubtless seen coming for years, meant acquisition of more land,[5] excavation of cuttings and widening of the viaducts near London: it was very demanding of capital with very little immediate incremental revenue. In the meanwhile the bottleneck caused heavy problems of unpunctual train running. Complaints about this appeared in letters to local newspapers and were vented at length to the Select Committee considering the New Line: the enemies of the LSWR had found one passenger who had kept a record and gave it in evidence to the Select Committee. A managing clerk in the Solicitor's department of the Board of Trade, his habit was to catch

---

[5] An excellent view of the original two-track bridge side by side with the newer bridge can be seen in Angel Road, Thames Ditton.

the 10.16 train from *Walton on Thames* due to arrive at *Waterloo* at 10.55. For 58 days in 1878 his train was on average 12 minutes late; in 1879, 10 minutes late over 122 days; and in 1880 nine minutes late over 127 days.[6] One is tempted to observe that on some days he must have been so late in getting to Westminster that he was nearly late for his lunch, but the point here is that although it was unusual to have such statistical support, the actuality of witness statements about bad timekeeping are sufficiently numerous and robust for us to be able to conclude that the late running of trains was endemic.

Special traffic apart, the operational restraints caused by there being only two tracks into London to accommodate the main line and suburban traffic were beginning to be insurmountable. Any new railways going through *Surbiton* would only make matters more

BEHIND TIME

5.5 Ticket Collector. 'This your boy, mum? He's too big for a 'alf ticket!'
Disdainful mother. 'Oh is he? Well, p'rhaps he is now, mister; but he wasn't when we started. This excursion's ever so many hours behind time, an' he's a growin' lad!'
(From Punch*)*

acute at *Waterloo*. By the early 1880s the coming of the New Line made it plain that something had to be done, and by 1884 the line between Hampton Court Junction and *Waterloo* had been quadrupled. In the meanwhile the detractors of the LSWR proclaimed the need for more competition for its beneficial effect on 'traffic and fares'.

Goods traffic

We must turn briefly from the passenger traffic of the LSWR to their goods business. The economic revolution, which would be caused by the coming of the internal combustion engine – an event which in its full force would destroy the economics of the railway industry – was still in the future. In the meanwhile, those businesses and farms, which were near a railhead were enjoying the full fruits of the economic benefits of the railway age: those that were not close to a railway were under a severe cost disadvantage because the only means of moving a load was by means of a man, his horse and a cart. Being located close to the nearest railhead or wharf meant that there was a considerable cost advantage in terms of imports and exports from the farms, the mills, the coal yards, the timber yards and any other bulky commodities necessary to the trade of the time. Those who were located a long way from the railhead suffered the extra cost of cartage from their pockets; and when the agricultural depression started, the pain increased. In these conditions it is easy to see how the farming community was at the front of the queue pressing the railway companies for a railway for every village.

It was in the light of the pressures on LSWR to bring about service improvements that they resisted robustly – and with success until they were manoeuvred into building the New Line – many suggestions that they should add to their route mileage. Until the decision to build the New Line was made in 1881, the LSWR had finished the development of railways in Surrey; they successfully defeated a proposed Esher, Hounslow and Southall Railway, which would have brought traffic into Hampton Court Junction. They knew that the system could not cope with any new routes – the capacity was not there – and they killed any proposition that would put unacceptable strain on the tracks into *Waterloo*.

6 Evidence of Mr R V S Smith to the Select Committee of the House of Commons, Guildford, Kingston and London Railway Bill, May 1881.

Chapter 6: Cobham's fight for a railway

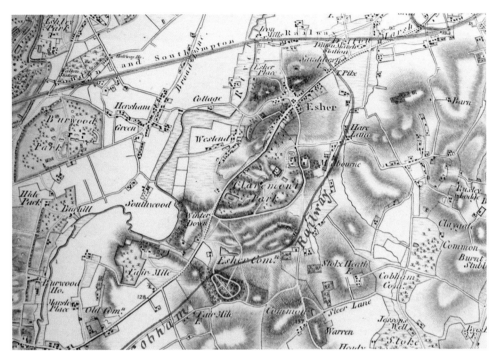

6.1 This map shows the route of James Bell's 1870 Cobham Railway scheme, which was for a three-feet narrow gauge railway. It followed the same route as his 1866 scheme, which was killed off by the LSWR.

In the general area of where the New Line was built there were, in the 15 years or so from the mid 1860s, a plethora of schemes to make connecting railways involving variously Esher, Cobham, Leatherhead, Surbiton or Guildford. Most of them were aborted before they reached Parliament, including one, which was objected to by Lord Lovelace, because 'it came along the foot of the Downs above my house'. Many of these schemes could be derided as part of a plan to provide a railway for every large village; an exception to this would be the scheme to put a railway from north of the Thames through Kingston to Brighton, a railway which if it had been built would have had huge strategic possibilities: although abandoned this railway could not be dismissed as part of the village railway network.

James Bell's first Esher to Cobham railway scheme

But the pressures to over-expand the network, which would have needed a Dr Beeching before the 1960s to pare back the folly, were driven by the macro-

economics of trade at the time: the forces that fought against every more or less hare-brained scheme, the LSWR amongst them, were backed by micro-economic arguments to prevent them happening. Many a scheme was 'throttled by the LSWR' because the burden of an ill-judged investment would permanently impair its value, for new lines that merely were to serve the hinterland of existing routes would generate very little incremental traffic, leaving the costs of building and running the branch line as a net drain on its resources, leading in the long run to ruin: the alternative ruin would come from excessive competition for finite traffic. The arguments in favour of new in-filling lines were often driven by the economics of the movement of goods rather than the demands of existing would-be passengers (except for a rich few) from sparsely populated agricultural districts. In 1881 the cost of cartage from Esher station to Cobham was, at four to five shillings a ton, significant. While this caused hardship the alleviation of it was not what the LSWR shareholders thought their company was about: profit was king, and it would take some bigger vision from an external source to make the LSWR change its assessment of the paucity of revenue that could be achieved from the new lines: put plainly, for them there was no business case for the New Line.

The population of the combined villages Church and Street Cobham and Downside had grown from over 1,600 in 1841 to 2,100 in 1871. It was natural, therefore, that Cobham should have been in the forefront of schemes to get onto the railway map. The problem of Cobham's location, with the natural barrier of the North Downs not far to the south and it lying only about four miles from *Walton-on-Thames* or *Esher* stations, meant that the railway traffic potential was not convincing to the LSWR, who first refused a request for a Cobham connection in 1845. Their capacity on the dual track to London and at *Waterloo* was filling up with trains earning good revenue from the west without adding to its problems with little incremental revenue to show for it. Nevertheless, attempts to get the connection lasted over many years, and Cobham's consistent champion was a Solicitor, James Bell, who practiced in Kingston. For all his great efforts, however, he was unsuccessful in getting a railway into Cobham – we will be considering later the juxtaposition of Stoke D'Abernon and Cobham – but if he had had his way there would have been a railway station in Between Streets which in those days, separated Church Cobham from Street Cobham.

As early as 1866, Bell, had found promoters for a railway to connect Cobham with the main line at Esher and acted as Solicitor to the parliamentary Bill. In the first place Bell prudently went to see the General Manager of the LSWR, Archibald Scott, who told him, disingenuously perhaps, that 'without referring to the directors', he did not see that they had any reason to oppose such a line. Following this encouragement the Bill was deposited at Parliament, but there was a *volte-face* from *Waterloo*. The LSWR wrote to Bell in January 1867 telling him that they had no interest in working a line from Esher to Cobham, even if laid out better, and that they would object to it in Parliament.

Bell's first route to Cobham was flawed because, starting from Esher, it meant crossing too much common land. It is unclear what the LSWR had in mind with their view 'that a better line than the present could be laid out' but a mere branch to Cobham that terminated there would be anathema to them: any business it won would be mostly in substitution for

traffic they already had. Charles Combe of *Cobham Park* was one of the chief promoters of this Cobham railway, but now that the original benign support of Archibald Scott had been reversed they withdrew the Bill rather than incur the heavy cost of fighting the LSWR in Parliament. By merely confronting the promoters the LSWR had won round one.

Two competing schemes for a railway to Cobham

In the next phase of Cobham's story of railway woe, the capacity for duplicity of the LSWR is exposed. In 1869/70 two new schemes emerged for a railway to Cobham both of which were independent of the LSWR, and the promoters prepared to battle it out against each other in Parliament. In the eyes of the LSWR both these schemes were just a nuisance to be swatted away. Queen Victoria also found much to distress her in both proposals, but her objections never had to be aired publicly. Nevertheless, her passion for *Claremont* and its estate caused her to exert considerable pressure on the Hon Charles Gore, the Commissioner for Woods, Forests and Land Revenues, which had responsibility for the management of the Crown lands through which both railways were planned. Her professional servants were placed in the unhappy position of being allied to the LSWR in opposing both Bills, even though they could see plainly that a new railway would enhance the value of the Crown lands. To the satisfaction of the Queen, both schemes were killed off; to the despair of Bell his Bill was killed only after he had been induced by the LSWR to help them kill the other: its own flaws and the Queen's displeasure destroyed Bell's second attempt at getting a railway to Cobham.

The Queen was able, in the event, to stop both railways by the actions of her subjects without opening up what might have been a row over the proper management of the Crown lands. The conflict was between the Queen's private interest and the best interests of the government and the taxpayers who funded it.[1] A pragmatic approach by her professional servants allowed them to play a long game and when in 1880 both Lord Onslow and the LSWR proposed railways through the Crown lands – neither of which proposals affected the quiet

---

[1] Like every sovereign since King George III, the Queen had surrendered the Crown lands to the government at the start of her reign, in return for being granted a Civil List.

6.2 James Bell's proposed narrow gauge railway of 1870 passed within a quarter of a mile of Claremont Park: Queen Victoria was 'much opposed to it'.

enjoyment of *Claremont*[2] – the Office of Woods and Forests took great care to embrace both. However, were it not for the inherent defects of the 1869 schemes, the conflict would have been more difficult to manage.

The legal process followed by both the 1870 schemes put the Office of Woods on formal notice that both railways would pass through the Crown lands (but not *Claremont Park*). Gore wrote to Her Majesty's office:

> I am advised that the construction of such a line would add greatly to the value of the property in my charge, and I am therefore desirous to encourage the construction of the proposed railway, provided the details of the scheme shall prove to be unobjectionable.[3]

The Crown lands in the district at the time covered a vast area including Warren House Plantation and the wastes of the Manors of Esher and Milbourne stretching out to the south incorporating Oxshott Heath and beyond. *Claremont Park*, which was contiguous with the Crown lands, had an unusual status: under the Crown Lands Act of 1866, Queen Victoria had

been granted a life interest. Her office wrote back to Gore:

> Her Majesty cannot but consider that a railway in the position indicated will be in some degree an annoyance and would wish for precise information respecting it before any sanction is given.[4]

There were two schemes, Gore reported: one, which comes within half a mile of the Park, goes for 'more than a mile through the Office of Woods lands and will be very convenient to that estate'; the other scheme (Bell's) was for a narrow gauge railway which would run 'within a quarter of a mile of the Park'. The route as

---

[2] At its nearest point the New Line runs a mile from *Claremont House*. When it was built trains would have been visible from the upper windows of the house and when the wind was in the east the whistle of the engines would have been audible. Whatever her inner thoughts no Royal objection was made to this limited intrusion.

[3] Royal Archives, Windsor Castle: reference PP/Clmont/CSP/ 139.

[4] *Ibid.*

6.3 The consistent flaw in James Bell's various schemes for a railway to Cobham was that they all terminated there, and made no connection to Guildford: this photograph from c1880 shows Castle Arch, Guildford.

The Philip Hutchinson collection

it passed by *Claremont Park* is shown on the map of part of the railway on page 37. The Office of Woods was trying gently to steer Her Majesty into support for the first scheme while disapproving of the narrow gauge, but:

> The Queen is rather unhappy about these rail roads chiefly in consequence of the people who will be about during the making of them, but also on account of their proximity to Claremont and that side by which the Queen goes out walking.

> The Cobham railway [Bell's] is the one Her Majesty really objects to and thinks something might be arranged to get rid of that one …

> What do you think could be done? Claremont [is] close to such a network of railways that it certainly [will] before long be surrounded.

> [Her Majesty's] fear of the Office of Works being left to look into it is that they will look at it in … [terms of pounds, shillings and pence] and not as the value of the place as a Royal residence.[5]

It is as easy to understand the Royal objection, as it is to applaud the reputation of the Office of Woods for its stewardship of Crown property. Fortunately, some of

her loyal subjects were preparing to ride to her rescue, but seemingly for their own self-interest, not hers.

Bell's narrow gauge scheme was on the same course as he had proposed earlier for the standard gauge railway to connect Cobham to Esher. The idea of a narrow gauge railway is quaint:[6] they were not at all common at the time and usually had an industrial genesis, which was absent in the case of Cobham's needs.[7] Bell's low cost scheme was borne out of LSWR's stated view that a standard gauge branch to Cobham was unviable, but he had missed the point for he wrongly assumed that the viability of a narrow gauge railway was assured

---

[5] *Ibid.*

[6] Evidently, a horse-worked narrow gauge railway was operated on the *Claremont Estate* by the Canadian Forestry Corps during the Great War.

[7] The concept was not at all quaint on the Continent: at the time the idea of low-cost light railways, sometimes narrow gauge, known as *chemins de fer vicinaux* were enthusiastically adopted in Belgium and France to serve communities not touched by the national rail networks. Continental space compared with our smaller hinterlands probably explains the difference in approach.

because it was cheaper: he had forgotten the impact on traffic. His Cobham Railway Bill of 1870 would have met the passenger needs of Cobham poorly: they would have had a somewhat slow connection to the main line, but of course, no through trains; and for goods traffic the break of gauge at Esher meant double handling. Bell's hubris was induced when the LSWR started a conspiratorial collaboration with him aimed at killing the opposing scheme for he seriously misjudged that he was being used; the LSWR plan was not to support Bell as a means of killing the other scheme, as Bell thought, but as a means of killing the second scheme first, and when that job was done, to kill Bell's scheme.

The second scheme of these two appears to be much the better: it was for a Surbiton, Cobham and Ripley railway; a scheme which by taking in Ripley, the village on the Portsmouth Road which had been a significant stage-coaching post on the Portsmouth run and still had a population, to include Send and Ockham, of nearly 4,000, would have a higher traffic potential: but at its best it was just the sort of branch line which would offer a convenience to users but not much incremental traffic because most of it would be taken from the main line; and it shared with Bell's scheme the diseconomies of being merely a spur. In fact, the objectors to the railway averred that the intention was to extend the line, ultimately, to Guildford:[8] such a plan could only redouble the LSWR's objection to it. Early in 1870, Bell received an obsequious letter from Francis Burchell, the Solicitor to the LSWR:

> We are advised to attack the Surbiton Bill for non-compliance with Standing Orders [a fatal failure to follow Parliamentary procedures, which were designed to protect private rights] on the ground of no notice given to the landowners within a mile of the line. Can you get the landowners to sign [a memorandum to express their objection to Parliament]? … There is not a moment to lose ….[9]

Taken at face value this letter can only be interpreted as coming from a party who recognised the benefits of linking arms with the other in a mutually compatible fight; Bell was beguiled by the LSWR's bad faith: a month later Burchell wrote to him again:

> I have a Petition ready for signature against the Surbiton, Cobham and Ripley Bill and am about to send it into the district for signature. It appears to me to be better that I should do so by independent means, but I await a suggestion from you …[10]

This was blatant dissemblance: here was Bell being invited to organise the signatures to a Petition against a competing scheme, which the LSWR wanted dead. It was in Bell's interest too, for in this respect his interest and the LSWR's were aligned: a fact that the LSWR was ruthlessly exploiting. We can note here that Wolfe Barry, the prominent and experienced railway engineer had laid out the scheme, which Bell helped the LSWR to kill by helping with the Petition against it: a Petition which proved to be fatal. The land-owner objectors to the Cobham and Ripley railway were incensed by a novel proposal by the promoters to impose a tithe on them: they proposed that all the landowners within a certain distance of the line should pay four percent per annum of its cost as a guaranteed return to its entrepreneurs; this was a revolutionary notion, which would not of itself be anathema to the LSWR. In fact, many later generations of promoters, especially when railways were publicly owned, have struggled to find a way of capturing the increments to the value of private land created by the very railway for which the public was being asked to pay. Because the promoters overlooked a technicality in giving proper notice to the affected landowners the Bill fell stone dead without the intriguing funding arrangement being exposed to a Select Committee: to have heard the arguments articulated would have been fascinating.

Bell and Burchell had acted in concert in organising the demise of the Ripley Bill. Bell could now pursue his own Bill with a lightened load, and he wrote to the LSWR for some help with traffic projections on his line; he was expecting that they would be supportive of him as he had been of them. Was this naïve? The whole story of the LSWR's dissemblance was exposed to the Select Committee of the House of Commons when it was examining the Guildford, Kingston and London Railway Bill in 1881. It suited the LSWR's opponents to expose them as anti-competitive, for having had Bell's help in killing the Ripley Bill, the committee was told that the LSWR had betrayed Bell because not only were they now going to oppose his Bill, but also they would not give him any help with traffic estimates.[11]

---

[8] Royal Archives, Windsor Castle: reference PP/Clmont/CSP/139.
[9] Evidence of James Bell to the Select Committee hearing the Guildford, Kingston and London Railway Bill, May 1881.
[10] Ibid.
[11] Ibid.

6.4 James Bell's plan for a railway from Esher station to Cobham would have taken a route through Hare Lane Green, Claygate and the Arbrook Lane area: in a later photo, c1916, two ladies are seen out walking near the proposed route.

The Paul Langton collection

Bell's narrow gauge railway Bill came before its Select Committee in 1870 as an opposed Bill, opposed not by the LSWR, whose scheming against Bell meant they could not expose themselves publicly, but by other powerful interests who would attack it for its inherent weaknesses. The route the railway would have taken from Esher to Cobham is shown in the map on page 35. Turning quickly south from its parallel orientation with Esher station it would run through what is now part of Sandown Park racecourse, across the Portsmouth Road; through Littleworth Common; through the hamlet of Hare Lane Green, down the side of Arbrook Lane; then across what is now Brendon Drive and up the Rythe valley through Arbrook Woods taking it close to *Claremont Park*, probably to within about three or four-hundred yards. The route would then turn west across Esher Common, and then picking up the line of the Portsmouth Road, run into the space between Street and Church Cobham, probably just to the north of the present Waitrose store in Between Streets, having negotiated a gradient of 1 in 50 on the way, probably in the area of Tartar Hill.[12]

Objections to Bell's narrow gauge railway

A Petition was presented to Parliament in objection to Bell's railway by 13 local landowners who were mostly from Esher and Cobham, including the Lord of

the Manor of Cobham, F J Mount of Poynters [sic] but also from Hare Lane and two others from Claygate. A total of 93 inhabitants of the district objected including the Revd Dr Henry Richards, the Vicar of Claygate, Samuel Duer of *Claygate House* and most notably for the later course of the story, the Revd Frederick Parr Phillips, the Lord of the Manor of Stoke D'Abernon and Rector of St Mary's. The objectors averred that there was 'no need whatever of any further railway accommodation'; they pointed out the weakness of their being no junction with the LSWR line at Esher (on account of the break of gauge) and, most vitally, they exposed the lacuna that not only was there no obligation, either existing or to be imposed, on the LSWR 'to stop their trains at Esher' neither was there any obligation to keep Esher station open.[13] They were probably going too far in averring that 'there is no local traffic in existence, or likely to be created … [by the proposed line]'. The Vicar of Claygate would have later cause to regret being associated with this opinion. The best point of all, however, was that the promoters planned (no doubt in the interests of

---

[12] This steep gradient was a serious impediment to any thought of upgrading the line to standard gauge at any time in the future.

[13] Royal Archives, Windsor Castle: reference PP/Clmont/CSP/139.

6.5 The Manor House, Stoke D'Abernon, c1904; the home of the Revd Frederick Parr Phillips (1818-1903), the Lord of the Manor of Stoke D'Abernon, Rector of St Mary's and opponent of railways.

economy) to cross every road including 'the turnpike [Portsmouth] road, the main arterial communication of the district, and four other highways on the level', and that this was being done 'in opposition to the wishes and feelings of the landowners and inhabitants of the district'.[14] It certainly seems that Bell's scheme was flawed in this respect: disruption to local traffic would have been tiresome.

Twenty-seven petitioners from Esher and Claygate, including the Curate 'in sole charge of Esher Parish', Revd W R Stewart Williams noted:

> the great inconvenience which will arise to the neighbourhood if the projected railway from Esher to Cobham be carried into effect. In addition to [the disruptive effect of several level crossings] the privacy of the Royal property of Claremont and its surrounding woods will be much interfered with. The requirements of Esher and Cobham do not necessitate the introduction of this railway scheme and we trust it may not receive Your Majesty's approval or support.[15]

The Petition contained the usual supplication 'May it please Your Majesty': no doubt it pleased her very much: so much so that a cynic might muse about whether the whole thing had been suggested by an equerry after church one day. A draft reply to the petitioners reads:

Her Majesty considers either one [of the two railways] would be in some degree [a correction to the draft replaces 'some degree' with 'a great degree'] detrimental to Claremont as a Royal residence and more especially the one called the Cobham Railway.[16]

Whether the letter was ever sent is moot, but Gore observed in correspondence that 'The Esher and Cobham Railway is an abominable nuisance': word had come from *Osborne House* that 'The Queen is much opposed to [the railway]' but relief was at hand. The procedure was that the promoters had to prove the preamble to the Bill to establish the need for the railway but Bell's narrow gauge railway Bill was damned by its own words for it suffered the gross indignity of being thrown out before any objections, including the Queen's, were heard. The costs of the petitioners amounted to £507 and enquiries were made as to whether the Queen would make a contribution. Her office had 'not the least belief that the Treasury would sanction a contribution from the Land Revenues to pay the expenses of opposition to the Cobham Railway scheme': in the event the Queen paid £100 out of her private funds.[17]

---

[14] *Ibid.*
[15] *Ibid.*
[16] *Ibid.*
[17] Royal Archives, Windsor Castle: LAW/VIC/37/1.

John Clutton

Because their evidence was never called we can only surmise on the extent of the scorn that the LSWR would have poured on Bell's scheme had they been called to do so. That the case for the Bill was going to collapse was made certain before the evidence of John Clutton, the Crown Receiver and Surveyor to the Office of Woods and Forests for Surrey, was given. As early as 1845 he had been giving evidence to Select Committees: at one there was an incident which gives colour to Clutton's attitude towards the New Line and Oxshott: 'suppose a railway goes in front of an old and hallowed ruin so as to entirely spoil its picturesque effect – on what principle would you compute your compensation?' The inspired reply was: 'I should pray Parliament not to sanction a railway near so beloved a spot, or get a railway station made near it and turn it into building land.[18]

Clutton, who had been advising Gore over the *Claremont* business and probably had settled with Bell the price for the Crown land, would still be in office 10 years later when the New Line was being considered. The following letter from Clutton to Bell dated 17 November 1869 was produced to the Select Committee when the matter of costs was raised:

Dear Sirs

Esher

I went to Esher on Friday as arranged … [and] we went over the ground [of the proposed railway as it affected the Crown estate] You must if you please quite understand that we do not in any way admit that your scheme is one that can in any way be adopted, and I do not desire that you should consider any alteration of the proposed scheme as coming from me. In fact I do not see any way at all to advise that a three-feet line would be of use to the Estate.

Yours Truly[19]

Clutton was laying a smokescreen: the given grounds for objection to Bell's railway was because it was narrow gauge; the reality was that the Crown Receiver had been obliged to find a reason. In giving evidence in 1881, Bell was asked about his narrow gauge project: 11 years after the event he told the committee that his scheme had been thrown out because 'It was too near to *Claremont House* and the Queen objected to it': this was the whole truth. Cobham still lacked its

6.6 John Clutton (1809-96): doyen among surveyors; first President of the what became the Royal Institution of Chartered Surveyors; Crown Receiver and Surveyor to the Office of Woods and Forests for Surrey; veteran of 46 appearances at Select Committees of Parliament.

railway – it was round two to the LSWR – but the Crown had been alerted to what Clutton knew already: what a railway, one day, could do for its Oxshott estate. The significance of this can be considered now.

One of the great benefits of having a monarchy is its continuity quite separable from the sovereign. Clutton could see that a railway to the Crown lands did not have to start at Esher. The same man gave evidence in support of a new line from Surbiton in 1881: at the time there was a choice of two routes but both went through Oxshott. When it was pointed out that there were very

---

[18] *Memoir of John Clutton* (1809-1896): Transactions of The Surveyor's Institute, 1896.
[19] Produced in evidence to the Select Committee on the Cobham Railway Bill, 1870.

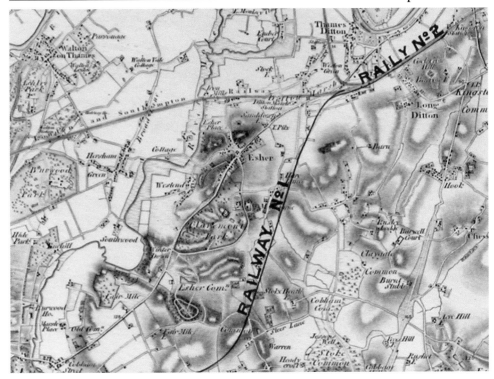

6.7 James Bell's 1880 Cobham Railway scheme was the first to be laid out to start at Hampton Court Junction and take the route ultimately taken by the New Line as far as Little Heath, where it branched north for Cobham.

few houses in Oxshott (to provide passengers for a railway) Clutton was ready with his answer: 'Very few, but we hope to get some if we get the railway.' He could see plainly that there was a general point here about the impact which a railway would have: 'It is a very nice district if we had railway accommodation [to open it up].'[20] As events turned out, the fact that the Crown had helped to kill the narrow gauge railway worked well for its interest. In Clutton's office it was not so important that the realisation of the development value (substantial as it proved to be) might be delayed for a decade or several decades. When two bigger vision schemes were presented to the Crown in 1881, Clutton left the new Select Committee in no doubt that 'Her Majesty has no objection to … [either] route'. That Oxshott got its station is due to Clutton seizing on the benefit of it to the value of the Crown lands. It was to the misfortune of both Bell and Cobham that the Crown had no financial interest in a station in Cobham; it did not matter to them that there was an existing population; Cobham's interest was subordinated to Oxshott's where, perversely, there was no population. The Crown's lack of financial interest in a Cobham railway was a cross that Bell had to bear.

James Bell's Hampton Court Junction scheme

The resilience of James Bell is established already, but there is another episode in his ultimately failed quest to give Cobham a railway; it was not that he could not learn the lessons from each of his setbacks: it was unfortunate for him that he could only learn them one at a time; the big vision escaped him; he forgot about Guildford and he forgot about an alternative to *Waterloo*; these were the big missing ingredients to his schemes. From the first failure, he learned that a railway from Cobham to Esher would be too expensive, so he tried a cheaper narrow gauge railway, to no avail. He learned from Clutton that only a railway that would allow the quiet enjoyment of *Claremont* and would release development land in Oxshott would work for the Crown: his next railway plan would course its way to Oxshott, before bending

---

[20] Evidence of John Clutton in May 1881 to the Select Committee of the House of Commons on the Guildford, Kingston and London Railway Bill.

6.8 Today the station is known as 'Cobham and Stoke D'Abernon' but in this c1910 photo there is no equivocation: the station is at 'Stoke D'Abernon'.

The Lens of Sutton collection

to Cobham: it all seemed so rational but Cobham as a terminus would neglect so many other prizes which could be achievable.

In 1879/80 Bell worked up another scheme to bring a railway to Cobham: a map of part of the route is shown on the previous page. His new route had *Surbiton* as the junction station instead of *Esher*, its up line joining the LSWR's at Hampton Court Junction, while the down line left at Surbiton. It then followed the actual course that the New Line takes before turning north of Little Heath in Oxshott and on to the same terminus site which had previously been selected in Between Streets, Cobham: this was exactly the route which the LSWR was to propose as its own route the following year, the difference being that the LSWR proposal projected the line on to Guildford. Bell's scheme was for a seven-mile branch railway the cost of which to build was £110,000 or just less than £16,000 per mile. Charles Combe was still paying heavily for coal to heat *Cobham Park* and again he supported Bell's proposal but the LSWR was ruthless in its suppression of it. A public meeting was held in Cobham early in 1880 at which a resolution in favour of the railway was adopted. Combe wrote a friendly letter to the LSWR, enclosing a copy of the resolution of the Cobham people, in order to enlist their support for a railway from Cobham to Surbiton, which was considered by the board along with a request for agreement of terms for working the line.[21] How much

consideration was given is not recorded but the suspicion is that it was dismissed out of hand: the Secretary was instructed to reply under advice from the Solicitor and the General Manager (Scott) and his response was out of Goliath's handbook:

> Referring to your letter of 30 January [1880] to the Chairman and Directors of this company, I am directed to state that they have ordered a Petition to be sealed and lodged against the Cobham Railway Scheme in order to enable the company to be heard on the Bill in Parliament.

In fact the Bill failed not because of the malign influence of the LSWR: it failed Standing Orders; it was round three to the LSWR.

Bell's new proposition to the LSWR

It was becoming quite evident that only a group that had power, wealth and vision, which could be ranged against the *status quo* to which the LSWR was so wedded, could overcome that company's hostility to any new railway. Recognising this, Bell wrote to Scott on 24 September 1880: his letter, which was read out to

---

[21] Minutes of meeting of court of directors, of the LSWR, 5 February 1880. NA RAIL 411/6.

the Select Committee hearing the Guildford, Kingston and London Railway Bill in May 1881, is of seminal importance to the story of the origins of the New Line: it is reproduced below.

My Dear Sir

Cobham Railway

Mr Combe [of Cobham Park and a Promoter of earlier Cobham railways] and other landowners suggested to the promoters of this line that they should appoint me the Solicitor ... and I agreed to go into the matter provided I got the assent of all the landowners ... The proposed line starts from Surbiton station and we propose another line in conjunction with this from Cobham to Leatherhead. [This is the first known reference to including Leatherhead in the plans for what we now know as the New Line.] When I first saw you some years ago about the Cobham Railway you informed me the South Western would not, you thought, oppose it but [one of your colleagues] who I now hope will be friendly, induced the directors to withhold their support, I think on wrong grounds but they know their own interest best. I hope they will now support the line, as it must add traffic to the South Western.

I hear that one of the District Railways who come to Putney [Fulham] intend to apply for a line from Putney to Surbiton and then intend to go on to Guildford through Cobham. I know this is a fact because they have communicated with the engineer of my proposed line on the subject. Such a line would be bitterly hostile to the South Western and do it a great deal of damage, it is therefore to the interest of the South Western that the ground should be occupied by a friendly and subordinate line such as the Cobham Railway would be . . . I wish to clear all opposition away and to understand how the South Western Company view the Railway as soon as possible and that is why I write to you and ask you in a friendly way whether you will remain neutral or will support us. I hope they will see that they will support us for the following reasons.

If the District Railway ever gets to Cobham it will be a competing line and this [ie our line] would prevent them.

The promoters of the present line would willingly insert a clause in their Bill that they will never sell the line to any other Railway Company without giving the South Western the first option of purchase – such a clause would render the new line [this is the first known usage of the term 'New Line' [still in currency 125 years later] subject to the South Western.

They would of course be only too glad to submit to any terms as to junctions to [which] the South Western thought right to impose. The line is proposed to run by the side of the South Western from Surbiton station to about Hampton Court Junction [in the space now occupied by the down approach to the Hampton Court flyover] and of course the South Western would have a right to use these metals if ever they determined to make a double line to Hampton Court which they will some time or other have to do.[22]

This is a remarkable document: if it came as news to Scott that the District Railway was interested in operating a railway from Fulham to Guildford – the suspicion is that it did – it must have had a bombshell effect; and if it came as news that Bell was promoting a line from Surbiton to Cobham and now with a link to Leatherhead, this too must have been salutary. Doing nothing was clearly not a viable option for it would be ruinous if the District Railway was able to penetrate the LSWR's area; no doubt the greybeards at *Waterloo* could see the writing on the wall: something was going to happen, and the only way to make it happen suitably was for the LSWR to get their own scheme together, even if it meant accelerating the quadrupling of the tracks between Hampton Court Junction and Clapham Junction. What obfuscation would be perpetrated by the LSWR in smooching with Bell again? Would he allow himself to be deceived again? The story of the New Line must now move up a gear as the pace quickens.

Bell's letter to Scott of 24 September 1880 was brought to the attention of the board at their meeting on 30 September. The shock was so great that the matter was held over until the 14 October meeting, at which the board declined to support Bell's scheme for it had already occurred to them that they should prepare one of their own. On 25 October, Scott reported on a communication he had received in relation to Bell's scheme for the Esher, Cobham and Leatherhead railway and the further extension of the line from Fulham as first mooted by Bell's letter of 24 September.

---

[22] This reference to the branch to Hampton Court still being a single line over 30 years after it was first built is very curious. No reference in the literature has been found to give any support to the notion, which was so plainly stated.

6.9 The Tilt, Cobham, c1910: when the railway was built this area found itself with a convenient station at Stoke D'Abernon.

'After full discussion of the whole question with the General Manager and the Solicitor', the board resolved: 'That it is expedient to take the necessary steps for depositing a Bill for making a line between Leatherhead and Guildford.' There was no question at this stage it should be noted of a line from Surbiton to Guildford – the board would soon change its mind about this – but here we have, at their meeting of 25 October 1880, the board's decision to seek powers from Parliament to build a new railway.[23] At this stage the details of the Guildford, Kingston and London Railway Bill were unknown to the board (the shock was still to come), but the best defence was plainly attack, but the initial response was much too conservative.

Archibald Scott became aware very quickly of the full force of the menace that confronted his company, and the inadequacy of his board's initial response to it. He had 'communications' with the principal landowners by which he learned that the proposed Guildford, Kingston and London Railway Bill would seek powers to take a railway from Guildford, Surbiton and Kingston (not Cobham be it noted) to London completely independently of the LSWR, thus giving a new strategic route to the capital which by-passed *Waterloo*. Only two weeks after the board had resolved to build a railway from Leatherhead to Guildford, at its meeting of 11 November and after 'full consideration' it now resolved:

That in addition to the steps ordered [two weeks earlier] for a railway between Leatherhead and Guildford, the necessary steps be taken for bringing before Parliament a railway from the Leatherhead and Guildford railway to join at or near Esher.[24]

'At or near Esher' turned out to be Hampton Court Junction, for the LSWR could find no better place than the one adopted by James Bell earlier that year. The die from which the New Line was cast was now taking shape and we must consider how it was that the mighty LSWR was induced to build what became the New Line, not for any reasons of its own, be it noted, but in response to an attempt at the penetration of the district covered by their monopoly.

---

[23] Minutes of the court of directors, LSWR, 25 October 1880 NA RAIL 406/6.
[24] Minutes of the court of directors, LSWR, 11 November 1880. NA Rail 406/6.

Chapter 7: The alliance against the LSWR monopoly emerges

7.1 In 1880 Charles Combe, the notable owner of the Cobham Park Estate, decided to join Lord Onslow's Provisional Committee for his Guildford, Kingston and London Railway Bill, a scheme which routed the railway through Stoke D'Abernon: this is a late 19th century view of Combe's house at Cobham Park.

The Dominic Combe collection

The events of the year that immediately followed the harvest catastrophe ensured that 1880 was to be the natal year in the history of the New Line. It was the year which saw the combination of several forces that when united would fuse together the opportunity with the circumstances in which an attempt at a competitive penetration of LSWR territory could be made. As it turned out this new combination was the catalyst which when stirred in a large pot produced a modest new railway – the New Line to Guildford – but in fact its members were trying for something much more ambitious: if this new alliance had been entirely successful the railway service in this part of Surrey would have been closer to that in Middlesex and Buckinghamshire in what became known famously as Metro-land, where the interests of the shareholders of a railway company were aligned with their interests as property developers: it was not to be, but it was so close. In this chapter we consider how the alliance between the landowners, James Bell and the District Railway, albeit kept at arms length, was struck and consider how there came to be two competing schemes which were, ultimately, deposited with Parliament.

The landowners

The Guildford, Kingston and London Railway Bill was presented to Parliament in November 1880. The Chairman of the Promoters was the Earl of Onslow; another Promoter was his neighbour, Earl of Lovelace who was Lord Lieutenant of Surrey, and also a major landowner whose estates included land at Horsley, Ockham and also to the east, near Surbiton.[1] Apart from them having the same economic interest in having a railway through their land, they both sat in the House of Lords where Onslow at least became active. They

---

[1] Unlike Lord Onslow, whose estate remains today in large measure intact, in spite of considerable sales for building, especially round Guildford, the Lovelace Estate was entirely broken up. As we shall see much of the land that was developed in Horsley was Lovelace land. The building boom of the 1930s saw another large sale, but because the Second World War intervened, much of the Lovelace land that was sold for development in the 1930s was included in the Metropolitan Green Belt, as was the final tranche of land sold in 1957 and the Onslow land which was not sold.

7.2 *The Earl of Lovelace, a substantial landowner in Surrey, became a Promoter of the Guildford, Kingston and London Railway Bill in 1880; this view of his seat in East Horsley, is from c1898.*

7.3 *Polesden Lacey, occupied in 1881 by Sir William Farquhar, one of the Promoters of the Guildford, Kingston and London Railway Bill.*

7.4 *Fairmile Court: the seat of Frederick Keays. 'There are a good many gentlemen residing in Fairmile who are professional gentlemen engaged in business in the City.'*

had collaborated on other railway schemes, but in 1876 they promoted the West Surrey Railway Bill which proposed a railway to connect the LSWR lines at Guildford and Leatherhead: this Bill failed Standing Orders before the LSWR's objections could be considered. Previously, Lovelace had been 'friendly' to the Surbiton, Cobham and Ripley proposal of 1870 (the one Bell had helped the LSWR to kill) because it would have opened up his estate at Ockham: it can be fairly said that Lovelace had been friendly towards any railway proposal which was going to increment the value of his land. He maintained good relations with the then Chairman of the LSWR, Captain C E Mangles, who was on visiting terms with Lovelace at Horsley, which probably gave him a good insight into how difficult it would be to get the LSWR to brook any competition or put their hand into their shareholders' pockets to build an uneconomic new line.

Between them, the Lords Onslow and Lovelace owned the first seven miles of the land through which their railway was to run from Guildford. Next along the route was the Crown whose estate, if not contiguous with Lovelace's, because the Manor of Stoke D'Abernon intervened, amounted to another three miles; a meeting of the landowners through whose land the proposed railway would run between Guildford and Surbiton would require a very small room, for the only other major landowner was the Banks estate in Thames Ditton and Long Ditton; householders in the Guildford area being effectively disenfranchised by the cost of petitioning Parliament. From Surbiton to Putney, the significance of which will become plain, the dominating land holding was the estate of HRH Duke of Cambridge: the proposed railway went through four miles of his land. Both the Duke and the Crown were careful to distance themselves from the promotion of the railway, but the reader should not doubt their enthusiasm for it because it would open up property development districts on their land. Plainly, the Guildford, Kingston and London Railway was to be a landowners' line born of their own private interests: if Parliament thought they could finance the scheme and if they over-ruled any objections – only one landowner on the entire route objected – then Parliament would grant the powers; that was the way it worked. In introducing the Bill to the Select Committee that considered it, Counsel for the Promoters, who were 'noblemen and gentlemen', said that the proposed new railway was 'pre-eminently a local line' having 'its origins in the wants of the locality', and that rarely had a scheme come before Parliament 'which had been so generally promoted and supported by the district … it was intended to serve'.

In casting around for allies, which gave truth to Counsel's sweet words, Onslow found two other prominent local men in the district to join him as Promoters of the Bill: Sir Walter Farquhar, who lived at Polesden Lacey, and Frederick Keays of Fairmile Court, Cobham. Farquhar, who had collaborated with Onslow and Lovelace in 1876 in the failed West Surrey Railway Bill, had a long history of involvement with railways: evidently, in 1857 he was active in getting the line in from Epsom to Leatherhead. He had tried to get other schemes going round Leatherhead, but in 1880, no doubt like Onslow and Lovelace, he wanted a railway to ease the harsh farming economics on his estate and to raise cash from the sale of land to the railway company. Having hit the *Waterloo* buffers with his earlier attempts, he explained to the Select Committee that: 'The LSWR would not help us so we helped ourselves.'

The other Promoter, Keays, owned property in Surbiton as well as at Fairmile and he was a daily traveller to London by train from *Esher* to *Waterloo* and then on to St James' Square; he shared the commuting habit with several upper middle class professional people living in the Fairmile district of Cobham and earning their livings in the City. They travelled to *Esher* station, almost certainly in their own transport, but a daily horse omnibus to and from Cobham served the station as well. The benefit of a new line, were it to be built, would be that they would be able to travel more conveniently from *Oxshott* instead of *Esher*: here was the voice of an influential group, which was 'fed up with the LSWR', but whose interests alone it was absurdly uneconomic to serve. One has to have some sympathy with LSWR's fight against the 'every village has its railway' syndrome.

A Provisional Committee had been formed, and from this group would have been formed the board of directors of the new company had the Bill in its then form been approved by the Select Committee. Apart from Onslow, Lovelace, Farquhar and Keays, their number included several other notables, including Lord Foley (5th Baron) of *Ruxley Lodge*, Claygate. Foley was more notable for the low profile that he adopted,

but his landholdings in Claygate ensured his attention, although, as we shall see, it was his brother who became the property developer.

The District Railway

As the year 1880 opened, the gloomy prospects for agriculture following the catastrophe of the 1879 harvest were staring the landowners in the face. Something else happened in 1880 – something that is always a powerful driver of corporate change – a new player emerged in the market. On 1 March 1880 a southern extension of the District Railway from West Brompton reached the Thames at a station called *Putney Bridge and Fulham*. The contractors, Lucas & Aird, had built it; theirs is a name of which we shall hear more, and there was a Thomas Lucas, a business partner of Aird on the Provisional Committee of the Guildford, Kingston and London Railway. By a new railway reaching the river suddenly the scene was set for the landowners to cock a snook at *Waterloo* and form a strategic alliance to break the monopoly of the mighty LSWR. The new kid on the block was the District Railway.

The early developments of the underground railway system of London that we know today are of central importance to our story. The Metropolitan District Railway (often shortened to District Railway) began as an offshoot of the Metropolitan Railway only to become its deadly competitor. The Metropolitan had opened the world's first underground railway from *Paddington* to *Farringdon Street* in 1863, extending this to *South Kensington* at the end of 1868; from therethe line was simultaneously continued round to *Westminster* as the Metropolitan District Railway and this was further extended eastwards to *Blackfriars* in 1870 thus forming the beginnings of the Inner Circle line, eventually completed in 1884 with operation shared by the two companies. The District Railway had been managed since 1871 by the autocratic, devious and combative James Staats Forbes of whom we shall hear more.

The District Railway's suburban extensions

We must reckon it to be inevitable that a railway company whose initial objectives were to move people around the metropolis should look outwards to the rich pickings to be had from more distant commuters.

7.5 Staff of the District Railway pose in 1876 with a Mansion House-bound locomotive.

London's Transport Museum

We should note that the District Railway was an impoverished company largely because the construction costs of underground urban railways were so cripplingly high: Forbes reckoned that it had cost, in today's money, about £70 million per mile from *South Kensington* to *Mansion House* but that the early traffic receipts from the extension to *Mansion House* were disappointingly low: a longer reach into the new residential districts was needed. An extension to *Hammersmith* was promoted independently in 1873 and leased to the District in the following year when it opened for traffic. The financial arrangements are relevant to our story, for the operating company did not have the credit to build the line itself, but paid heavily to use it. The District reached *Richmond* in 1877 over LSWR tracks from *Hammersmith*, and *Ealing* in 1879, using the same LSWR line from *Hammersmith* to *Turnham Green*. The 1880 extension to the Thames at Fulham was to become the seminal event that allowed the prospect of the deep penetration beyond the suburbs and into the LSWR's heartland in Surrey to become a reality. Sir Sam Fay was to observe that this was the period when the District 'cast eyes upon the fair and rich traffic district of the South Western suburban system': they certainly did,[2] and it is central to our story, and had they had the resources to promote an extension from *Fulham* themselves the story of the New Line would have been very different.

The traffic figures for the Inner Circle and the western extensions of the District were given in evidence at the Select Committee hearing in May 1881, which considered the Guildford, Kingston and London Railway Bill. On the Circle Line Forbes claimed fabulous numbers while on the Hammersmith extension the first full year saw 2.4 million journeys rising to 2.76 million in 1880; the newly opened Fulham extension was already producing an annual volume of over 800,000 journeys. 'An enormous traffic is drawn from these western extensions', preened Forbes:

> and I think I know that district [Fulham to Guildford] pretty well, and what can be done with it; and my calculation is that the results there will quite equal if not surpass any other [of my extensions].

In a wounding jibe at the LSWR which brought laughter to the committee room, Forbes said that Scott, the General Manager, 'was South-Western to the back-bone [a charge Scott would not have denied] and he

---

[2] The District's mood at this time was bullish; the ordinary shareholders had received their very first dividend - one half per cent – for the first half of 1878, nothing in the second half. The following years saw a peak average of one per cent in 1880, but nothing at all was paid on the ordinary stock after 1882.

7.6 Surbiton was already a popular town for its railway to Waterloo; if the Guildford, Kingston and London Railway Bill had been approved as drafted Surbiton would have had a new strategically diversified access to London via Fulham to Mansion House; this view of Surbiton's second station shows the Southampton Railway Hotel.

thought there was only one place in London – *Waterloo* – but that was not so'. Warming to his brief, examining Counsel asked:

> 'Looking at the character of the populations of Putney, Roehampton, Wimbledon, Malden, Kingston and Surbiton [he wisely stopped there because any traffic from further west would have been little], do you believe you will develop a similar traffic counted by millions that you have done on the other side of the river?'

And with a response in the same key, Forbes proudly asserted that 'I have not a shadow of doubt that the same results will follow, and probably in a greater degree'. This was the second time the Select Committee had heard the powerful rationalisation of Onslow's

scheme: the General Manager of the District Railway, John Bell [not to be confused with Cobham's Bell], had explained that the railway that was proposed would allow the dense population in the areas that they already served to communicate into Surrey without having first to go round the moon to get to *Waterloo*. Moreover, because his system connected with the Metropolitan's lines into North London, a convenient route would be offered also from those parts to the LSWR system.

It was important for the Promoters of the railway to keep the District Railway perceived as being at arm's length because of their poor credit rating – under cross examination Forbes was revealed as presiding over a very weak, unstable company. In accordance with what seems to have been the party line, Forbes denied being either directly or indirectly involved with the promotion of the Guildford, Kingston and London Railway Bill: 'I heard, of course, through the usual channels of information [Wolfe Barry?] that some such object was afloat.' Naturally, he conceded that the District was very happy with it, but he was not asked if he had in his back pocket a draft operating agreement. He had plainly given it some thought, for he gave this assessment:

> We have two trains an hour running from *Mansion House* and all those important intermediate centres: because every station of the District is the centre of a large ... population, those two trains now ending their journey at Fulham can equally well end it somewhere more distant – they cannot traverse that district between Fulham, Surbiton or lower down without affording the public enormous additional accommodation.

Forbes had a vision of his trains running from *Guildford* via *Surbiton* to *Mansion House* and gave eloquent testimony to the economic gains which were available from the extension: it was self-evident that an extension, at least as far as *Surbiton*, would create significant incremental traffic, and Forbes had said that not only was 'It perfectly practicable', but also 'very advantageous to the public and the District Railway.' The LSWR did not need to hear this from Forbes in May 1881: the portents had been plain from Bell's letter of September 1880. Forbes made an interesting point, as if to assuage his competitive threat, when he said that he did not think that the extension 'will do them [LSWR] much harm because the result of these extensions [of the District Railway] has been not abstraction from neighbouring companies but the creation of a vast amount of new traffic' which did not exist at all before – something which today we call the M25 effect.

Who would wish to argue against this? It must have quite drained the colour from the corporate cheeks of the LSWR, who were in the room to hear Forbes proudly proclaim his traffic expectations from deep inside LSWR territory. Readers will know that the line for which Forbes ached was never built, but was this the moment when a despotic voice in *Waterloo* cried: 'This line has to be stopped: whatever the cost!'? We can only surmise, but stopped it was, as we will see, and the cost to the LSWR was the building of the New Line which, until Bell's latest approach they had tried to prevent. An alliance had been struck, which was

sufficiently powerful and its timing serendipitous, to cause the LSWR to modify its position.

The alliance

Piecing together the evidence given by many of the key players at the May 1881 Select Committee hearing we can place the order of the key events and how the players in Onslow's alliance joined it. Wolfe Barry was the engineer to the Districts' line to Fulham and of the proposed line to penetrate the LSWR territory to Guildford, but this was not his first involvement in the Cobham area. He had been the engineer to the proposed Surbiton, Cobham and Ripley railway in 1870 – the one James Bell helped the LSWR to kill and to which Lovelace was 'friendly' – and later had been consulted on the subject of new rail communication by people from Stoke D'Abernon, the Fairmile district of Cobham (where Keays came from) and Ashtead, where there was a proposal to connect with Guildford, so plainly he knew the district. He knew that all the

The Dominic Combe collection

7.7 Charles Combe (1836-1920); Promoter of the Guildford, Kingston and London Railway Bill, owner of Cobham Park.

7.8 A steam hauled District Railway train at Earls Court station looking east, 1899.

London's Transport Museum

conflicting interests could only be reconciled within a compromise: he also knew that the District Railway, although they certainly had the will, did not have the wherewithal themselves to cross the Thames at Putney and penetrate Surrey.

Wolfe Barry testified that it was the summer of 1880 before the directors of the District Railway had the least notion of the proposed Guildford, Kingston and London Railway: even so we can be certain that Wolfe Barry knew before. We have seen that when Bell wrote to Scott with his important letter of 24 September, he had heard of the proposed railway, but presumed that the LSWR had not. This suggests only two possible conclusions as to the initiators of the Guildford, Kingston and London Railway – either Wolfe Barry (perhaps in concert with Lucas & Aird) or the landowners with the Earl of Onslow at their head. Barry denied it was his initiative by his testimony that 'the initiation of this line came entirely from the country' which is supported by Onslow's claim that when the line was made to Fulham, he saw 'the means of getting in to London independently of the big companies'; he had got so 'fed up with the LSWR' that he 'promoted the new initiative to get the railway in'.

It is no coincidence at all, that Wolfe Barry was the engineer for both Forbes' extension to Fulham and Onslow's protraction of it to Guildford: if you are a landowner wanting a railway, the first port of call before trying to finance it is an engineer to lay it out; equally, if you are an engineer looking for business, and your impoverished client, the District Railway, can not raise the money for a new project, you go looking for someone who can. If Wolfe Barry was not obfuscating it is perfectly clear who made the first approach: Onslow. Perhaps he invited Barry round to the House of Lords for 'a cup of tea'; however it happened, Onslow must have made it plain that he wanted a railway through his land and he wanted to be liberated from the LSWR monopoly. Wolfe Barry, fresh from the opening of the District railway to Fulham could offer the golden solution: a railway from Guildford through Surbiton and Kingston to Putney, to connect with Fulham and ultimately, *Mansion House*. This, let it be noted, is the explanation of why the railway goes through Onslow's 1,500 acre-farm; and why there was a station on the farm. If Onslow's Guildford, Kingston and London Railway Bill had been passed without amendment, the deal that Onslow had made for one fast train a day from Clandon would have come into play – this did not happen, but it shows that Onslow was calling the shots.

James Bell joins the alliance

We must now explore how James Bell became a convert to the Onslow strategic alliance: we left him in the previous chapter with his fourth Cobham Railway scheme where he was trying to get the LSWR to be friendly towards it, but having alerted them to the Guildford, Kingston and London scheme with which the District Railway's name had been associated. On 20 October 1880 the Secretary to the LSWR wrote with their baleful reply: '... the Directors are unable to accept your proposal for the assent of this Company to the scheme for a railway from Surbiton to Cobham and Leatherhead.' Evidently, anxious over the delay in any response from the LSWR to his proposal – always an ominous sign – Bell had had a meeting with Scott, during which it had become clear that he was going to be opposed. The conversation between Bell and Scott 'became rather warm' – we can take this to be code for 'they had a row'! In the course of it, according to Bell's evidence, Scott said some highly intemperate and inflammatory things: to suggest that: 'A tramway along the Esher road is quite good enough for the Cobham people' was not the sort of statement which looks good when written in a transcript of evidence – Scott was lucky that the proceedings finished without him being examined on it – but to observe that: he would 'no railway to Cobham on any terms' suggests contrary to his reputation that he was unhinged, for even as he spoke, the LSWR was preparing a Bill for a railway to *Guildford via Cobham* using Bell's route as laid out by Wolfe Barry from Hampton Court Junction to Cobham.

After this appalling episode, and on the very day of the LSWR's terminal letter to Bell was written, but before he had received it, 'the Promoters of the Guildford, Kingston and London Railway called' upon Bell. These were Burchell, Solicitor to the LSWR, who was well-known if not well-liked by Bell, and R Peregrine Birch, an engineer also well-known to Bell. Evidently, Birch had approached Combe, the Promoter of Bell's scheme seeking his permission to go through his land in Cobham. Combe had naturally referred him to Bell and the obvious idea of fusing the two schemes was put to Bell, who at the time was obliged to confide that he had offered to act in concert with the LSWR. Before October was out, however, Bell and Combe gave up their Cobham railway and threw in their lot with Onslow: 'We thought unity was strength', said Bell, 'and I abandoned my line and supported theirs. We knew we had to fight the South Western.' Before the final breakdown came, the correspondence between Bell and Scott, which showed how he had tried and tried to work with the LSWR, is most revealing of Bell's understanding of the dynamics of

the possibilities for economic development when the new line was built, and of how arrogant the LSWR could be.

In a letter to Scott of 20 October 1880 – a letter which shows some signs of despair and agitation of his mind even before the interview with Burchell and Birch – Bell observed that he had heard about a proposed line from Leatherhead to Walton – a line which Scott thought Bell misinformed about – but which Bell thought 'one of the most absurd and useless lines ever contrived'. He continued:

> The Surbiton & Cobham line on the other hand will develop the largest building properties in the neighbourhood and the most beautiful building sites. It is supported by the Crown, through whose property it goes for nearly three miles, all of which property is to [be] let on building leases. It is supported by Mr Banks [who owned land in Thames Ditton and Long Ditton] through whose property it goes for a mile and all his property contains most beautiful sites and is about to [be] let on building leases. It is, therefore, not so much Cobham that we look to get traffic for although the traffic from Cobham where it is brought into contact with a first class station site [Between Streets] would be very considerable, it is the intermediate neighbourhood between Surbiton and Cobham which in the next 10 years will be large enough to pay enormous dividends as it is the most lovely building neighbourhood on the South Western near London. The country through which this line goes will have a railway before long, it is of such great building importance, and I do therefore trust that the South Western Railway will not oppose this line. I do not care about their supporting it if they do not oppose it. I offer them such terms they will have complete control over the line and in effect will make the line a part of their system, and it will greatly add to the traffic on it.[3]

By these statements Bell marks himself as the first to canvass to the LSWR the great traffic potential from the future residential development of Cobham, Oxshott, Claygate and, 50 years later, Hinchley Wood. But he was wasting his time with the LSWR whose attitude could be parodied as: 'Thanks very much Mr Bell; well argued. Yes, we'll have some of that but, oh sorry, there is nothing in this for you.' Bell had no proprietary rights to his vision: it was not possible to 'own' the idea of a route, but the LSWR plagiarised his ideas

---

[3] Evidence of James Bell to the Select Committee hearing the Guildford, Kingston and London Railway Bill, May 1881.

7.9 Cobham's station has been variously named over the years; this photo is from the 1950s.

shamelessly. They had probably decided to do so well before receipt of Bell's letter, which continued:

> Of course it is not my wish to threaten any one but the Cobham people are determined to have a line ... to Surbiton and if they are disappointed in this I shall put myself at once in communication with the District Railway and see if we cannot get this line through Cobham. Do not take this as a threat for I do not mean it as such, it is only because the Cobham people are determined to have a railway to Surbiton – they want still to travel by the South Western line, but if they are rejected they must take their own course.

Scott took notice of the three days Bell had given him, but his obfuscating reply was aimed at delaying the falling of Bell into the arms of Onslow and the District Railway. Moreover the reply was not only in contradiction of their previous refusal, it came from the pen of the man whose lips had uttered the 'tramway' jibe and that he would have 'no railway to Cobham on any terms'. The same man now wrote to Bell:

> I have to acknowledge your letter of 20 October. You will no doubt have received from our Secretary a letter conveying the resolution of the Board upon the subject of the proposed new railway from Surbiton to Cobham and Leatherhead. It is to the effect that they do not see their way at present to support or approve of the proposed line [it was a snub], and indeed the scheme is

not now before them [which scheme? Bell's or the one stolen from him and shortly to have an LSWR wrapper on it?] in a sufficiently mature state to justify the Board in coming to any other resolution. You will however please understand that the Board have *not* decided to oppose the scheme – in fact they have not at present sufficient before them to enable them fully to form a judgement upon the scheme: you have therefore been entirely misinformed when you state that the South Western Directors will oppose your Cobham Line.[4]

Scott closed his letter by pouring scorn on the Leatherhead–Walton line notion, and he took a po-faced objection to the tone of Bell's letter. Bell responded:

> The reasons you gave me for not supporting a line to Cobham, which would increase your business, you could not go before a Committee in opposition to a line supported by every landowner in its course. You know from me that your Company will have a serious fight this session and that it is most clearly in your interest to prevent any hostile line getting in to Cobham, Guildford and from there to Portsmouth and Southampton. [This is an allusion to the Onslow scheme.] If you undertake to support my line at once, for no time is to be lost, you will at any rate stop any other line at Surbiton [and] we could carry it through

---

4 *Ibid.*

[from there] together. I shall certainly seek support elsewhere now for I offered you everything I could offer you, and you have declined it. I cannot now be satisfied with mere negative support: you must undertake to assist me by your evidence.[5]

This letter shows that not even yet has Bell decided to throw in his lot with Onslow: it also shows that there were in fact two sets of landowners – one which Bell was leading to his Cobham scheme – another which Onslow was leading through Stoke D'Abernon: if Bell joined Onslow, Cobham's interest would have to be sacrificed, and naturally after 15 years of trying on its behalf, Bell was reluctant to abandon all his previous efforts. If the LSWR had embraced Bell's scheme in October 1880 as its own, it seems very likely that the New Line to Guildford would have gone not through Stoke D'Abernon but Cobham because the schism between the interests of the two different landowning groups would have had more force. In the event, as we shall see, it was only the Revd Phillips who put up any fight against Onslow's scheme, which went through Phillips' land in Stoke D'Abernon.

Scott's further reply reveals that they had a scheme of their own being hatched:

> I understand you to state that you are acting for, or in concert with landowners in the Cobham district; if so, I think it would be well if the landowners in that district were to reserve themselves, and not come to judgments until they have the necessary material for forming a correct opinion upon what may best suit their interests. So far as we know of the matter your scheme had not been matured, and at all events we have only had an outline of it; it is therefore too early before plans have been prepared for any of the landowners to be able to judge properly of any railway scheme. If it be the case that you are acting for any landowners in the Cobham district I venture to think that it would be prudent to reserve your judgment upon any railway scheme *and if possible, to believe that your proposed scheme may not be the very best that can be devised*.[6]

The words italicised for emphasis here are a cloak for the LSWR's reinvention of Bell's scheme and, later, serving it up with a projection to Guildford via Ripley as their preferred route for a Guildford via Cobham railway. Bell's scheme suffered only one major fault when reviewed at *Waterloo*; it could not be any good because 'it was not invented here'. The 'Wags of Waterloo' as *Punch* christened them made bitter enemies by this act of arrogance – they could have said

to Bell: come and join us, and bring your Surbiton to Cobham landowners with you – and if they had they would have probably made the District Railway's hopes unattainable. Whatever, this marks the end of Bell's fourth attempt to get a railway to Cobham; it is perverse to record that the fifth attempt was put forward by the LSWR in a competing Bill to Onslow's, but Onslow's forces were too strong: even at the fifth and final attempt the LSWR itself failed, as we shall see, in its attempts to get a railway into Between Streets.

For Bell the process of ditching the LSWR was a hard decision, but ultimately he had been diminished too much and both he and Combe changed sides and threw in their lot with Onslow, Bell becoming a Solicitor to the Bill, and Combe a member of the Provisional Committee. The ultimate alliance of all the landowners included every one except the Revd Phillips of Stoke D'Abernon: ultimately, his was the only voice among the landowners to speak against Onslow's route. At a meeting of landowners in October 1880 (the month that Bell was being dangled on a string by Scott) Phillips had framed the issue, in the way in which Scott had counselled Bell that they should: that no support one way or the other should be given to either until both schemes were out in the open. Phillips was reported as saying:

> Let us see what the LSWR (the company in possession of the district) are going to propose, and let us see what the new ideas are, and then make up our minds.[7]

Wise though this appears to be, it was not practical politics because the suggestion did not accommodate how things worked: two different routes were being formed behind closed doors to suit the private interests of the protagonists; routes which the two opposing parties – Onslow's landowners' group and the LSWR – thought could be commended to Parliament on their merits, even if compromises had had to be made here and there and, equally, even if all the objections had not been headed off. It was not for the people to decide which railway they wanted: it was for Parliament, and if there were two schemes to consider, Parliament would decide which. By October 1880, Onslow's plans were crystallised and he was not interested in any other

---

[5] *Ibid.*
[6] *Ibid.*
[7] *Ibid.*

7.10 The west entrance (carriage drive) to Clandon Park c1910.

route than the one through his land in Clandon; a route which would take the line through Phillips' land in Stoke D'Abernon. From conversations with Bell and others, Onslow knew that the LSWR had a spoiling plan in hand, and if the Guildford, Kingston and London Railway Bill was to be heard in the 1881 session of Parliament, only a few weeks were available to give the landowners the required statutory notice and to deposit the Bill, its associated plans and schedules of affected interests in land; all of the costs of this process were borne by Onslow's landowners' group and the

Guildford, Kingston and London Railway Bill was deposited at Parliament on 18 November 1880.

Even as Phillips counselled his forlorn 'wait and see' policy the LSWR was briefing its Parliamentary Agents and their Bill for a competing scheme was deposited in Parliament only a week after Onslow's. The guileful LSWR, having at first thought their power was unbreakable, had caught up with the game: defeat for their opponents would not be easy; a duel would have to be fought out in Parliament.

Chapter 8: Two competing schemes

8.1 Town Bridge, Guildford, c1885, after the reorganisation of the approach to the main station was completed.

In November 1880 the two competing schemes came into the public domain for the first time. We must now consider them and how the various public sector bodies reacted to them as a prelude to how the battle lines were to be drawn when the fight in Parliament took place six months later. In this connection we shall explore in this chapter the corporate responses of the major towns affected by the proposals – Kingston, Guildford and Surbiton – and consider how the two schemes had different approaches into Claygate; in the following chapter we will consider the public spat over Wimbledon Common; but first we must describe each of the two lines that were proposed.

Onslow's *Blue Route* and the LSWR's *Red Route*

The railway proposed by the Guildford, Kingston and London Railway Bill was identified as the *Blue Route*, parts of which are illustrated on the map on page 111: this was we might call the deep penetration route starting from the south western edge of London's nascent urban and largely underground railway and proceeding through the 'sparsely populated agricultural district' on its hamlet-hugging route to Guildford – a route which the promoters insisted, for their own reasons, went through Oxshott, Clandon and what we know as London Road, Guildford, but which was indifferent to the needs of Cobham.

The railway proposed in the London & South Western Railway Bill, known as the *Red Route*, which is also illustrated on the map on page 111, was a minimalist, low cost response that had no strategic component: whereas the *Blue Route* brought diversification and choice in how to enter London, which was a feature of many of the other railways south of the Thames, the *Red Route* had no component east of Surbiton and it was simply a duplication (plus a connection to Leatherhead) of the existing route from Surbiton to Guildford via Woking. The essential feature of the *Red Route* was that it took in Cobham as Bell's scheme had done, and reinforced *Waterloo* as the point of entry to London; in this feature it proved to be

8.2 A section of Lord Onslow's Blue Route *showing the entry and exits to and from Surbiton: to the east the line was planned to go to Fulham via Kingston (Fairfield).*

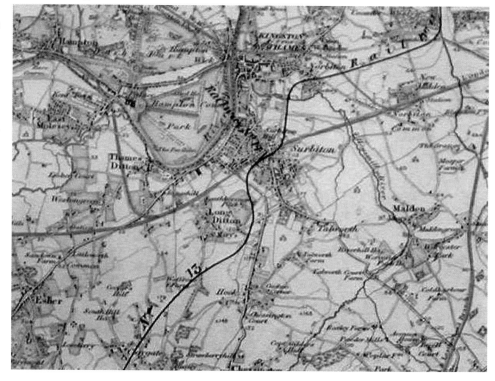

8.3 A section of Lord Onslow's Blue Route *showing the route through Stoke D'Abernon and the junctions for the spurs.*

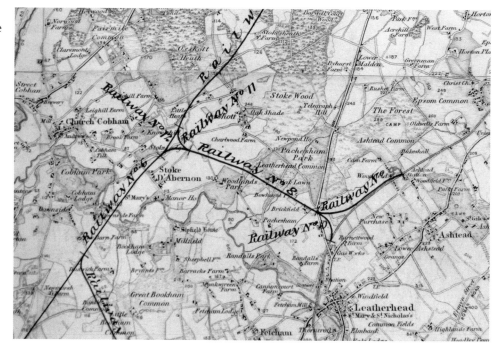

the most vulnerable to attack and unfavourable comparison with the *Blue Route*. A branch to Leatherhead was common to both schemes, but only the *Blue Route* added to the diversification of routes into London. The agricultural district which lay between Surbiton and Guildford was sparsely populated but the LSWR, having decided on Cobham took their railway nearer to the greater concentrations of settlements at Ripley, Ockham and Send. Onslow's *Blue Route* west of Surbiton was driven only by farm economics and the Crown Estate's long view of residential development potential in Oxshott. In the long run the passengers would come to live near the railway because it was there, but the economic case at the time for Onslow's railway west of Oxshott was pretty thin. In contrast, on the London side of Surbiton it was so visionary that one can only regret that some version of it was never built.

Taken as a whole from Fulham to Guildford, the *Blue Route* was a compromise between two sets of incompatible economic components – the farms in the country to the west and the prospective urban sprawl around Putney, Kingston and to the south of Surbiton, the precedents of which had already been set by the District Railway with their extensions to Hammersmith, Richmond and Ealing. The LSWR was able to expose this inherent weakness, which had not been thought through by railwaymen: if the London end of the line was about mass transit of people into London, how was this to be reconciled with the heavy concentration of goods traffic, and only a handful of passengers, at the country end?

The LSWR's *Red Route*, put together at the last minute in desperation, was nothing more than an attempted spoiler, and probably considered at *Waterloo* to be making the best of a bad job; it borrowed much from Bell's efforts by taking his route from Hampton Court Junction to Cobham: the changes which the LSWR made to Bell's abandoned scheme were the elevation of its status from a spur to a through route to Guildford and the bringing in of Leatherhead into the system. As readers will be aware, neither the *Blue* nor the *Red Route* was built as proposed: the New Line that was built (which is illustrated on the map on page 111 along with the proposed *Blue* and *Red Routes*) was the best compromise between the two competing schemes in their respective courses between Surbiton and Guildford. The reasons for the compromise will emerge, but for the present we must stick with what was proposed because those were the schemes that

were fought over in Parliament.

The *Blue Route* was a 31-mile railway from Putney to Guildford via Kingston and Surbiton; in addition to the direct route to Guildford, there was a branch to the south between Oxshott and Stoke D'Abernon to join up with both the LSWR and the LB&SCR tracks at Leatherhead; and a branch from near Downside to Bookham. At Guildford, although the line connected with both the LSWR and the SER, allowing through working to the Farnham line from Guildford and the Reading-Dorking line, the much despised station at the bottom of the town was not to be the terminus for passenger trains: instead a new station was to be built in the upper part of the town, at what is now 'London Road'. At Fulham the *Blue Route* would allow access to the District's line to *Mansion House*, with or without an interchange (this unknown – would there be through trains from *Guildford* to *Mansion House*, or not – was a continuing weakness of the scheme). Once access had been gained to the underground network (there were no tube railways yet) the web of railway systems round London would be opened up.

The LSWR's *Red Route* was, naturally, fully integrated with its existing system in the manner of the New Line, but Onslow's *Blue Route* was not: Wolfe Barry explained that the principle he had followed at Surbiton station was to lay out his railway side by side with the LSWR 'without touching it, or interfering with its levels' so that no junction would be formed: 'Passengers would be put down by our line' and communicating by a subway those 'who wanted to go along the LSWR line to the West of England' would be able to reach their platform 'which is nearly at the same level'. For all those passengers on the other route who were coming up the line and who then wished to go down the main line, the arrangements proposed were the same as we have today. For passengers coming down his line from the District system, Wolfe Barry thought the interchange being offered at Surbiton would provide 'a very convenient route' which would allow them access to the LSWR main lines without having to go to *Waterloo*: to achieve this benefit would have required the LSWR's active cooperation, which could not be guaranteed. Naturally, Wolfe Barry put his arrangements at Surbiton in their best light, but because necessarily the design had been done independently of the LSWR, they were flawed: there would be no connection with the LSWR system which was a lost strategic opportunity because it meant that

8.4 The ridge of Oxshott Heath, which in 1880 belonged to the Crown and being far enough from Claremont, it marked the point where John Clutton would allow a station to the south of it; this almost treeless view is from c1903.

Blue Route trains from the country could never serve *Waterloo*. After leaving Surbiton Wolfe Barry took his line along the cutting on its north-facing side up a gradient of 1:100 so that a bridge could carry it over the main line. Space was allowed for the planned upgrade of LSWR's metals from their existing two tracks to four.

The proposed stations on the *Blue Route* were, after starting at the new one at Guildford: Merrow (which was never built, although there was a big public goods yard); 'West Clandon' (for Lord Onslow); 'either West or East Horsley' (for Lord Lovelace)[1], 'Downside' (for Charles Combe of Cobham Park); 'near Stoke Road at Stoke D'Abernon' (for nobody); 'at the south-west corner of Oxshott Heath' (for the Crown Estate and the Fairmile phalanx); 'Claygate' (for Lord Foley) on an unidentified site probably somewhere near Church Road; 'Long Ditton at St Mary's road' (conveniently for Lord Lovelace's development land); 'Kingston near the Fairfield'; 'New Malden, Roehampton, and Tibbett's Corner' (all convenient for part of the HRH Duke of Cambridge's development land at Coombe Wood); 'Putney and then to Fulham'. The station at Roehampton was to be placed almost opposite the Robin Hood gate of Richmond Park, 'which would be a great boon to the London public'.

The LSWR's *Red Route* from Hampton Court Junction to Between Streets in Cobham via Oxshott showed more vision than Bell's for although they saw the point of serving Cobham, they saw no point in stopping a railway there: they proposed a projection on to Guildford[2] passing near Ockham, and close enough to Send and Ripley to serve them both; even Bell would have to concede it was a better way of bringing Cobham on to the railway map. In striving to serve Cobham, the LSWR found the same restraint as had Bell: the Crown would brook no railway that ran too close to Claremont and which did not serve their land in Oxshott, so it had to take an anomalous deviation to the north through Little Heath. The other advance on Bell's scheme was the inclusion of Leatherhead, not quite as it was ultimately to be included when the New Line was built, but the concept of including that town in a system in a more coherent way than was proposed by the *Blue Route*, led to its ultimate provision in the final compromise. The *Red Route*, in its own reticent way, was a rationalised tidying up of the LSWR's existing area monopoly, which although it could be built for modest cost, was unlikely ever to do as well for its shareholders as it would for the landowners who

---

[1] Lord Lovelace was an each way winner: if the Guildford, Kingston and London Railway Bill had been thrown out and the LSWR Bill passed, Lord Lovelace's land in Ockham would have been served by a railway.

[2] It is entirely conceivable, but no evidence has been found to support it, that the LSWR had in mind the strategic benefits that the New Line achieved in being a relief line by duplicating its facility between Guildford and Surbiton.

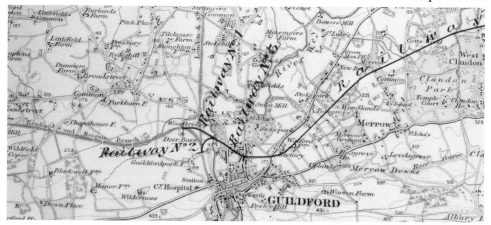

8.5 *A section of* Onslow's Blue Route *showing access to the Guildford main line station, and the Farnham line.*

would benefit from it. We can take this opportunity for making a remark about economics: an over-arching feature of the *Blue Route* was that the greatest part of all the risks and responsibilities of the project lay with the landowner Promoters – the very group who would reap the greater part of the benefits – a very neat relationship which would have found few critics among rational observers.

A second station in Guildford

In promoting a second station in Guildford to be operated in competition with the LSWR, Onslow was going with the grain of local thinking in Guildford: the town was prospering but the reason for its existence – the river crossing in the gap in the Downs – came with the steep hills in the approaches to the town from both west and east. First the Wey Navigation, then the railway had provided the means of transporting the goods on which the town's wealth was based, but the hills were a problem: they were a natural restraint on building development and in the days when everything which had to be taken to or from a wharf or railhead needed a man with his horse and cart, the growth in trade caused severe congestion in the bottom of the town around the single river crossing and the nearby railway station.

Guildford, by its importance as a civic and business centre, was a destination town for railway travellers as well as the town of origin for many other railway users. Civic pride ensured that the Town Council members were delighted with the *Blue Route*: as one member explained:

Guildford is a major local centre, the capital town of Surrey, the business centre of all of the lower part of Surrey and a considerable part of the upper. It housed the headquarters of the Surrey Constabulary, [and] the Assizes …[3]

There were several strands to the town's warmth towards Onslow's new railway and second station; a great attraction was the fact that it gave a better diversity of routes into London than the town already had, and it introduced more competition. The existing opportunities for travel to Guildford were by the LSWR from *Waterloo*, or by the SER from either *London Bridge*, *Cannon Street* or *Charing Cross*: Onslow's route could get them in from the West End of London at a fare, Guildford people assumed, which would be competitive with the LSWR's fare from *Waterloo*, which at that time was 10/- return, first class. This was considered very expensive compared with the SER fares to London of between 6/- and 7/-.[4] This grumble, however, did not stand analysis: the SER's pricing policy was using the only competitive weapon that it had, for how else but on price advantage were travellers between Guildford and London going to be induced to take a slower train on a 10-mile longer journey than the LSWR could offer? No: although the competition was welcome there was something much more powerful in what the *Blue Route* offered Guildford.

---

[3] Evidence of D McCluer Stephens to Select Committee hearing the Guildford, Kingston and London Railway Bill, May 1881.
[4] *Ibid.*

63

Lord Onslow wanted a station to be built in the upper part of the town to serve an expanding suburb; he needed to rub salt in LSWR wounds over the deplorable state of *Guildford* main station; and he also needed to gain the corporate support of the town to his scheme. Onslow wanted a station in Guildford for both passengers and goods that was completely independent of the LSWR; to be owned by the Guildford, Kingston and London Railway and operated (probably) by the District Railway. The contortions of the railway's route round Guildford, and the extra engineering cost that went with it, were the price to be paid for putting another station into Guildford in spite of its topography: as it turned out the only thing Onslow did not get from his wish-list was to be rid of the LSWR.

We have already heard about the state of *Guildford* station: the engineer of Onslow's line, Wolfe Barry, describing the existing station in measured terms, thought it 'quite unfitted for modern requirements' – an assessment with which the LSWR could only concur – for even as the criticism was being made, the LSWR was seeking powers to take land to effect the enlargement and improvement of the station,[5] which was completed by the time the New Line was built. Wolfe Barry thought the station very inconvenient because 'it was on the wrong side of the River Wey'.[6] The whole question of circulation at the bottom of the town, and the constraints on it caused by the single river crossing and the approach to the railway station was a major contemporary issue. The only way to get goods to and from the station was by horse and cart and the steep hills on the approaches from east and west made this awkward; what the critics were actually saying was that a new station at the top of the town would make life easier for all those who lived on the east side of the town, but this was a muddle of several issues – the single river crossing, the bad station design and the topography of the town. The first two of these problems were soon to be eased: the second river crossing opened in 1882, financed by the Town Council and greatly to Onslow's benefit, while he also went to considerable expense in connection with the formation of the new approach to the station,[7] which was itself rebuilt in 1884.

The enemies of the LSWR found many traders willing to testify that the station was built in an awkward place, and that they would like another one in the upper part of the town. To criticise the safety and operational convenience of Guildford station was legitimate but the criticism of its location, built on land sold by Onslow's father, was a bit harsh for there was nowhere else for it to go: Guildford being a hilly town, and railways liking the level ground which comes with rivers, the station was naturally placed in the gap between the Downs. The reorganisation of the station and its approach could scarcely be done independently of the new Onslow Bridge, but because those critics who had a hidden agenda found it expedient to censure the LSWR for the general difficulties and congestion at the bottom of the town, they took the brunt of the criticisms that were not wholly their fault or responsibility; nonetheless the mud stuck and ultimately the new *London Road* station was the result.

The LSWR's *Red Route* took the least-cost course, further to the north – a route which would avoid the 'S' bend approach and take the line into their rebuilt station, the location of which they accepted no criticism. We can cite the experience of the Wey Navigation in support of the LSWR on this point. The town of Guildford had thrived on the canalisation of the Wey for over two hundred years: the wharves that brought the trade were within yards of the railway goods yard, and were still conducting a good business in spite of it. Anyone looking at the issue objectively could see that the main station was where it had to be – at the bottom of the valley on a route that minimised the tunnelling through the North Downs, and was cheek by jowl with the river and near the heart of the town. To argue that it was 'inconvenient' was to make a relative judgment that missed the essential truth – the development pattern of Guildford was changing. The LSWR was slow to realise that the need for a new station in the upper part of the town was not just about the state of their station or whether it was inconvenient or not: a competitor had spotted the demand for a second station and the LSWR was obliged, because of their selection of a route into the town, to defend both the location and the convenience of their station. In the face of the evidence ranged against them, this was a tall order.

---

[5] Evidence of J Dullen to Select Committee, considering the Guildford, Kingston and London Railway Bill, May 1881.
[6] Evidence of J Wolfe Barry to Select Committee, considering the Guildford, Kingston and London Railway Bill, May 1881.
[7] Invoice for Lord Onslow's Solicitors' charges: Surrey History Centre, 5337/2/103.

8.6 The last cattle market to be held in North Street, Guildford, 9 June 1896.

Part of the convenience argument was about the agricultural interests and the traffic in goods. All those farms which lay to the east of the town, of whose interests Onslow was the champion, would have easier access to a goods yard at the top of the town for their imports of manure and other materials and for the dispatch of their produce and livestock to market: the avoidance of the steep hill down to the main station would be a considerable asset when transporting heavy loads, or driving large herds or flocks for transportation to Smithfield (where the killing took place) or to more distant parts. Of course, Onslow had no difficulty in finding tenant farmers who were enthusiasts for his line, which would be 'very useful to farmers up the line to Surbiton'. A member of the Town Council put the farmers' case more objectively: Guildford had:

> a very large cattle market, which was increasing week by week. It is the market town for Merrow, the two Clandons, the two Horsleys, Effingham and Bookham. There is a lot of traffic for stock and grain.[8]

A butcher from Putney considered Guildford's market one of the best in the county.

At this time steam power had arrived on the farms; it was used for driving machinery and for ploughing from anchored points along the edge of fields: naturally the delivered price of coal affected the economics of these innovations; but the evidence which was given about coal economics was just a part of the 'railway for every village' argument: it was as likely to find a tenant farmer opposed to a railway conveniently placed for him as it was to find a resident of the Fairmile district of Cobham drinking in the White Lion and discussing the prospects for the price of wheat with those whose lives still followed the plough. The more telling evidence from a farmer was that 'several farms are unlet':[9] proof that the agricultural depression was still biting in 1881, and that any railway close to a farm would bring economic relief to it. To the penetrating analyst, the farming case for a new station at the top of the town, as opposed to Merrow or Ockham, where

---

[8] Evidence of D McCluer Stephens to Select Committee, considering the Guildford, Kingston and London Railway Bill, May 1881.
[9] Evidence of A Wells to the same committee.

they were also being offered one, was a bit thin, but it did not stop the point being driven home.

The passenger market was quite different, for the top end of the town was developing fast in spite of the 'inconvenient' location of Guildford station. The reason for this phenomenon was that Guildford was prospering and all the land at the bottom of the town had already been developed: a member of the Town Council explained that:

> the area around the existing station is land-bound. In St Mary's [parish] there has been scarcely any building for 20 years. [The parishes] of Stoke and Holy Trinity is where the development is taking place.[10]

8.7 Henry Peak, Surveyor to Guildford Urban Sanitary Authority at the time of the expansion of the town served by London Road station: 'the present station is so exceedingly badly placed because there is so much haulage attending it'.

8.8 The expansion of Guildford in the mid-18th century took place in the Parish of Stoke-next-Guildford: the new London Road *station served the residents of houses such as this villa in Stoke Road.*

Guildford was growing and with no land available in the ancient heart of the town, aspirants for it had to look further afield.

Residential growth in upper Guildford

Well before there was any talk of a new station at *London Road*, substantial residential development had taken place in the 1850s in the parish of Holy Trinity. This was largely on high green fields above the town beyond Sydenham Road and towards the semaphore tower, where an area of land almost as great as the existing town was developed. Henry Peak came to the town at the time of this expansion and practiced as an able surveyor/architect and grew to great prominence

---

[10] Evidence of D McCluer Stephens to the same committee.

8.9 *Birthplace of P G Wodehouse in Epsom Road,*
Guildford, built before the coming of the New Line.

in the town. He was appointed Borough Surveyor in 1864, and shortly after, Surveyor to the Guildford Urban Sanitary Authority, ultimately becoming Mayor and writing his unpublished memoirs.[11] He laid out the roads and services of the new township of Charlotteville, and from Peak's memoirs we know that the market then was men of substance who might build a villa at the then huge cost of between £3,000 and £5,000 and at the same time erect 20 or 30 artisans' cottages, the rents from which would subsidise his handsome home. In due course, the residents of these houses would provide a market for rail travel, the new *London Road* station being conveniently located for them.

Because of his position in relation to the sanitation of the town, through Peak's office went all plans for domestic building expansion; he was intimately involved in every aspect of the development of the

town over the seventeen years that preceded the proposed new railways. Since his appointment over 700 houses had been built in Guildford with an annual value ranging from £12 to £250. When Peak gave evidence to the Select Committee, this expansion was continuing in the area towards the top of the town in spite of 'the general depression in 1879',[12] which had followed the harvest catastrophe of that year.

With the restraints on building opportunities in the old parish of St Mary's, the 12 per cent rise in Guildford's population in the 10 years to 1881 had been largely in the parish of Holy Trinity, but the greatest expansion was taking place in the parish of Stoke-next-Guildford. Nightingale Road, on the edge of Stoke Park had been laid out in the 18th century, and was first known as New Road. (York Road, a product of the new station, was not laid out until 1897.) In mid-century, as development in Chertsey Street took place the area between the Stoke Road extension of it and Woodbridge Road began to be developed: Peak refers to Dapdune and Markenfield Roads.[13] Kings Road was already developed when in due course the New Line bridged it. In the 1870s came an extension to Markenfield Road, and Onslow, Queens and Park Roads. Villas were being built along London Road; P G Wodehouse was born in a well-established house in Epsom Road in 1881; Waterden Road connected the two and Christian worship commenced at Christ Church as early as 1868, with a new church consecrated in 1874. By 1881 the population of Stoke at 6,700 was rivalling Guildford's 7,500, Stoke's having grown by 50 per cent in 10 years.[14] The process by which Stoke and Guildford would join up was already inexorable: 'Guildford is so popular a neighbourhood that even now without this railway, building is going on' and houses were continually sought after in 'one of the prettiest parts of Surrey.' This growth was set to continue, said the same member of the Town Council for there were 'acres and acres cut up for building purposes in the upper part of the town'. And he

[11] Memoirs of Henry Peak: Surrey History Centre, Woking: 6517/1 *et seq.*
[12] Evidence of Henry Peak to Select Committee, considering the Guildford, Kingston and London Railway Bill, May 1881.
[13] Memoirs of Henry Peak: Surrey History Centre, Woking: 6715/6.
[14] Population figures given in evidence to Select Committee, considering the Guildford, Kingston and London Railway Bill, May 1881, by F Smallpiece, Town Clerk of Guildford.

forecast with remarkable prescience 'I should think Merrow will soon be joined to Guildford'.[15]

Plainly, Guildford was undergoing great change. Speaking at a time when the second river crossing was being planned,[16] Wolfe Barry gave an engineer's view of why Guildford now needed two stations: he explained that the Onslow team had decided to locate a new station in a middle position between the upper and lower levels. We have already heard the catalogue of criticisms of the LSWR station at *Guildford*: when Peak referred to it as being 'in a very inconvenient position, even after the new bridge is put across the river', he was thinking not so much of the convenience of residents in the new houses being built, but of the convenience of the contractors building the new houses – and in terms of the haulage of materials to the building sites. Not only would the new station at *London Road* save about 50 feet of vertical haulage, it 'will be considerably closer to all the ground which has been opened up [for building], and which is likely to be opened up for many years to come'. The man's knowledge could not be gainsaid, and his eloquent and calm testimony must have carried much weight, not least with the LSWR, whose representatives were present to hear him say:

> I speak of Guildford, and I say most decidedly, that we are very, very anxious that ... [the new station should be built]. When I say 'we', that is the general opinion of the town. I am mixing with people every day, and I know the feeling of those who have a great many building materials [to move]; and as the Surveyor of the Board, I have had for some years to order many hundreds of tons of building materials, and it is exceedingly awkward indeed at present – the present station is so exceedingly badly placed because there is so much haulage attending it.[17]

There was some building taking place on the west side of the river but Peak knew that this was only – and could only be – a small fraction of what was happening in the east and north of the town. Wolfe Barry, in his evidence, showed that what was happening in the west was off the point: so far as the western end of the town was concerned, the LSWR, he said, were welcome to it: any traffic coming from 'the other side of the River Wey ... can be accommodated by the existing line which is on that side of the river'.[18] The 'firm conviction' of Guildford's MP, Denzil Onslow, was that the new station at *London Road* would 'enhance the value of house property in the neighbourhood of the station in the parish of Stoke'.[19]

The strong case for a station at London Road

The evidence given in support of the new station at London Road was among the most robust that the Onslow team mustered. No one before Onslow had considered the significance for transportation – of people and goods – of the development that was going on at increasing distances from the valley station: when *London Road* station opened in 1885 it was going with the grain of development; a trend that already existed was now allowed to accelerate: the market was demanding to be served by a new station. Given that the *Blue Route* had to go through Clandon, which it had to in order to serve Onslow, it was astute to accept the extra engineering cost to place a station where there was demand for one. In the face of Peak's evidence, it would be ungracious to make the link between the chosen site for it and the fact that Onslow owned the land on which the station was built. That the LSWR overlooked the changing shape of Guildford can be attributed to one or both of two factors: the greater priority given by them in taking the line to Cobham (like Bell) and taking the more natural, northerly approach to Guildford; and the desire to avoid the materially greater engineering costs of taking the line through Onslow's deep cutting and the 'S' bend into Guildford.

Wolfe Barry had noted the expansion of Guildford in the Stoke Road area 'before we selected the position of the station; and I think we may say that the position has been almost unanimously approved of'.[20] The station was to be built in 'Foxenden Field on the London Road' which had 'an entrance from the Stoke Road':[21] this appears to describe the location of *London Road* station as ultimately built by the LSWR near Foxenden Road. As can be seen from the section of the plan on page 107, which was drawn shortly after the station was built, access from the Stoke Road area was via Nightingale Road, to 'give communication from the main Portsmouth Road running down into the station yard'.

---

[15] Evidence of J Dullen to the Select Committee, considering the Guildford, Kingston and London Railway Bill, May 1881.
[16] Evidence of J Wolfe Barry to the same committee.
[17] Evidence of Henry Peak to the same committee.
[18] Evidence of J Wolfe Barry to the same committee.
[19] Evidence of Denzil Onslow to the same committee.
[20] Evidence of J Wolfe Barry to the same committee.
[21] Evidence of John Dullon to the same committee.

In the decision to provide a new station Onslow, as a major landowner in the town, showed considerably more vision than the LSWR in terms of the exploitation of the economic impact of the new railway. This is a major discussion for later when we consider the development land that was opened up by the New Line, but in fairness to the LSWR they and the other railway companies were prohibited by law from holding surplus lands (this was a corollary of Parliament granting them compulsory land purchase rights) and so were not in a position to benefit from the increment in land values which had been created by their investment in a railway. The Select Committee heard from several witnesses about the economic activity going on around where the new station was to be built, and were no doubt impressed by the evidence of it which made the case for a new station stand on the merits of its location, without relying on the poor state of the old station, or its supposed inconvenience, as a reason for building a new one.

Looked at from Guildford's perspective, the LSWR's *Red Route* offered them much less than Onslow's *Blue Route*. Many operational issues had been quietly overlooked, such as the fact that journey times from Guildford to Westminster and the City were likely to be very long, but the new station and the diversification of the access to London were very seductive. Onslow had recruited the town of Guildford, oblivious as it was of snags that had not been thought through, as a corporate supporter of his landowners' alliance, with the Mayor becoming a member of the Provisional Committee of the Guildford, Kingston and London Railway. In view of Onslow's importance in the town as a landowner, it is scarcely surprising that the 'Corporation and the population' were 'decidedly' and 'strongly' in favour of his line: it is not surprising either that the LSWR yielded to the evidence in its favour in the compromise on the route of the New Line and to build a new station at *London Road*. This, however, was in the future; for now the corporate shoulder of Guildford was pressing on the Onslow wheel.

The voice of Surbiton

The corporate voice of Surbiton came from the members of the Surbiton Improvement Commissioners. The townspeople had one of the best train services, so their complaints about the LSWR were confined to those we have heard of already: dirty, dark, unpunctual trains, which vanished on race days, but when they ran they took them only as far as *Waterloo*, which was not where they wanted to go. If any one wanted to go to *Guildford*, there was a train via *Woking* to do the job; the station at *Guildford* just had to be tolerated. The LSWR's *Red Route* did not really offer much to Surbiton: a new route to Guildford through a 'sparsely populated agricultural district' was unlikely to get much attention from the town. In fact, one of the great benefits of LSWR's scheme would be that Surbiton's train service to *Waterloo* would become of the highest standard because the additional traffic would make the quadrupling of the line between Hampton Court Junction and Clapham Junction impossible to postpone any longer. This, of course is what actually happened: the New Line and the quadrupling came together, and this opened up the opportunity for a large increase in the amount of traffic, whether fast, semi-fast or stopping from *Surbiton* to *Waterloo*.

In fact the only favourable reaction to the *Red Route* in Surbiton was as a result of the negative view taken by some property owners in the town of the *Blue Route*: the *Red Route* involved the rebuilding and configuring of the station, but unlike the *Blue Route*, it involved no disturbance to the built fabric of the town. Surbiton, with its growing population of commuters, was more likely to be the station of origin for passenger journeys than a destination, and with the focus being on London the *Blue Route* promised an alternative to *Waterloo* and a connection to the north London railway systems. To any objective analysis it was absurd that the *Blue Route* did not integrate fully with the LSWR's railway at Surbiton – what was proposed was an interchange involving a change of train, like that at Wimbledon today, but it had been designed in spite of the LSWR, not in conjunction with them. The *Blue Route* had a serious design problem at Surbiton: somehow and somewhere the line had to cross the old London and Southampton main line: the landowners' line bridged it, whereas a railwayman's line would form a junction somewhere and a *dive-under* so that the strategic integration of two systems could be achieved. It was received wisdom at the time that 'Every fresh railway that you connect with another system the more traffic you get'.[22]

---

[22] Evidence of J Knight, General Manager, LB&SCR to the same committee.

Because the *Blue Route* made its own route into Surbiton, independently of the LSWR, it allowed some property owners to object to it for the wrong reason: 'it was likely to spoil the beauties of Surbiton' because the railway would 'cut up the neighbourhood'. There were sufficient numbers within the Commissioners' ranks to relegate such narrow thinking – reminiscent of Kingston's folly in 1830 – to wider visions: one Commissioner spoke for many when he said that he was satisfied:

> that private residents and those engaged in mercantile pursuits in London would, one and all, desire that the Commissioners should give them all the facilities they could get for approaching the metropolis ...

> The present railway was all very well a quarter of a century ago, but it was not very well now. It did not give them all they wanted. It did not drop them in London at all, but left them on the Surrey side of the river, and it was quite time to give their support to another company, who would give all the facilities they required.[23]

If this assessment owed anything to the Onslow influence, and it certainly seems to, the source was probably the engineer, Wolfe Barry, who had taken the trouble to attend on some of the Commissioners to brief them on the attributes and benefits of the *Blue Route* and to seek their support for it. The Chairman had had an interview with the Traffic Manager of the LSWR as well as with Scott, the General Manager, but the drift in Surbiton was more towards getting local improvements to the *Blue Route* rather than supporting the *Red*: the Commissioners narrowly rejected an amendment to a resolution giving no more than conditional support to Onslow. By a narrow majority the Commissioners adopted a resolution by which a Petition to Parliament in favour of the Guildford, Kingston and London Railway Bill should be sealed. A Petition in the town in favour of the LSWR's *Red Route* obtained only 170 signatures.

This resolution having been passed, Surbiton joined the Onslow alliance and the Chairman of the Commissioners, Rowley Richardson (the historian of whom we have already heard) became a member of the Provisional Committee. The Commissioners called a public meeting on 4 March 1881 so that ratepayers and residents from outside the immediate area of the Improvement Area, but who were concerned about the railway service, were able to express their opinions on the matter. At that time the population of the Improvement Area was over 9,400 in 1,600 households having grown from 7,600 in 1,300 households in 10 years. Included on the platform at the crowded meeting in the Lecture Hall in Maple Road were the Mayor of Kingston, Frederick Gould; Wolfe Barry and Birch, engineers to the Guildford, Kingston and London Railway; and James Bell, the erstwhile champion of railways to Cobham but who was now working for the Onslow team and supporting the *Blue Route*. There were no representatives of the LSWR in attendance: the meeting did not give a balanced presentation of the merits or demerits of the alternative schemes; it was designed to reinforce the Commissioners' unqualified support for the *Blue Route*. The resolution moved was:

> That this meeting is of the opinion that the projected Guildford, Kingston and London Railway will be of the greatest advantage to Surbiton and neighbourhood, and trusts that no objection of a purely sentimental nature will be allowed to destroy the great material advantages that will follow if the railway is made.[24]

Ignoring realities and tiresome detail, Wolfe Barry noted that the railway would give passengers direct communication with the City as well as linking with all the important goods lines in the country. It was said that there was no real opposition to the new railway except by the shareholders of the LSWR; their line, said the Mayor of Kingston, as if to damn it by its moniker was 'a shareholders' line': in this district 'we have been cruelly deceived, owing to the company not having kept its pledges'. The Mayor, no doubt recalling the bruising received at the hands of Scott and the Directors two years earlier, asserted that 'the existing railway monopoly has been prejudicial to the interests of this neighbourhood, and can only be remedied by a competition such as that now proposed'. After a general vituperation of the company, its attitudes, its high fares, its stations and its late and dirty trains the meeting was led, with only three dissentients, to approve the motion and support the railway which would give them 'access to all parts of the County as well as to London'. This was an empty remark: both schemes gave access to the sparsely populated agricultural district between Surbiton and Guildford. Bell had changed sides, so he had to keep quiet about the fact that the *Blue Route* he was now favouring by-passed Cobham

---

[23] *Surrey Comet*: 18 February 1881.
[24] *Surrey Comet*: 5 March 1881.

The voice of Kingston

Kingston 'was suffering all the worst evils of a monopoly' and its position in relation to the *Blue Route* was unequivocally in its favour: here at last was the town's opportunity for deliverance from the LSWR. In January 1881 the Editor of the *Surrey Comet* wrote a leader that showed the imprint of Gould, the Mayor. The Editor spun a story which invited public support for an act by the Council which Gould had already decided was right in order to prevent the dissembling and obfuscation which had characterised his recent experience of the LSWR: the *Surrey Comet* offered 'for the serious consideration of the Council … that they will, as a condition of their support and approval of the Guildford, Kingston and London Railway, … [require] some representation on the directorate'. The Council of Kingston upon Hull had recently been given power, evidently, to both invest in the equity and be represented on the board of a local railway affecting the economic interest of Hull. Secure in the existence of a precedent for this unusual step, the *Surrey Comet* argued the case. No lesser person than Gladstone had already advanced the idea of state intervention, claimed the paper: 'ought we not to draw some lesson from our experience, and avail ourselves of this opportunity … by which the public interest of our district may be protected against … a new and untried monopoly?'[25] The paper continued:

> If Kingston and Guildford, as large and important towns … each had the power to nominate one of the proposed nine directors, it would tend greatly to secure attention to the wants and convenience of the public, and give confidence in the management.

Although Guildford gave its corporate support to Onslow's *Blue Route* it did not seek these extended powers as did Kingston, but if it were to succeed in establishing the principle of the town's direct participation in the promoting company 'it will share with Hull the honour of leading a reformation in railway management' claimed the *Surrey Comet* but speaking Gould's words one suspects, because it was he that took the high profile public stance in advancing Kingston's cause in relation to the new railway. The great worry for Gould, however, was that Onslow might get his Bill and then, having secured the building of a railway through his land, sell out leaving Kingston hanging out to dry:

> It would be very vexatious … to find that the company had sold their railway to some … existing monopolists, who might refuse to give our town … the facilities which the promoters so temptingly promise.[26]

Plainly, the numerous indignities suffered by Kingston at the hands of the railway companies were still well to the fore: as it happened, the worry proved to be prescient, for this is more or less exactly what happened: in the great compromise that was to come, Kingston had no place at the table where it was hatched, and in due course the town was left with the second-rate railway which it had been destined to suffer ever since the London & Southampton railway had been made unwelcome 50 years earlier.

The Guildford, Kingston and London Railway was 'in every respect a promising scheme [which will] open up new and beautiful residential localities, and … [provide] increased facilities to large centres of population like Kingston and Guildford'. Here was a clear open-armed signal to the opposite numbers in the then County town and economic competitor to make common cause with Onslow against the LSWR: 'this neighbourhood has suffered in the past because railway companies are independent of any kind of public control, [so] ought we not to draw some lessons from our experience.'[27]

Gould's briefing was good and he got what he wanted. A committee of the Council was set up to consider and report on the Bill which Onslow and his chums had deposited in Parliament; it had an interview with the engineers to the *Blue Route*, including H M Brunel,[28] and the Solicitors, Burchell and Bell. The brief report of the committee to the Council put a very agreeable gloss on the benefits to Kingston which would flow from the new railway: assurances were given by the professionals to the Kingston committee that:

---

25 *Surrey Comet*: 8 January 1881.

26 *Ibid*.

27 *Ibid*.

28 Henri Marc Brunel was the second son of the celebrated engineer, Isambard Kingdom Brunel. He is noted for a partnership from 1878 with Wolfe Barry with whom he designed the Blackfriars Railway Bridge in central London. Their other works together included the docks at Barry in South Wales. Among the pupils articled to Brunel and Wolfe Barry was Alexander Gibb (later Sir Alexander) who like Wolfe Barry became President of the Institution of Civil Engineers and a notable engineer of his age.

the 'New Line' [as they called it, but not to be confused with the New Line as built] will afford direct communication with the Great Western, the London and North Western, and consequently the North London and the Midland Railways and also (though less direct) communication with the Great Eastern Railway.[29]

Moreover, the representatives had assured them that the railway 'will offer every facility for the conveyance of goods'. The whole question of the conveyance of goods on an urban underground railway was a source of vulnerability on the Promoters' part when the Select Committee examined the scheme. Equally was the assurance, repeated in the committee's report, that 'it is estimated that trains will accomplish the distance between *Kingston* and *Mansion House, without change* [report's italics], by fast trains in 44 minutes'. If these assurances had been made by a railwayman, no doubt some qualification would have been added, for the Guildford, Kingston and London Railway Company did not have, and as we will see could never obtain access to the tracks of the Inner Circle underground railway: the District Railway was in control of the track; they were not a Promoter of the *Blue Route*, and by giving this publicly-aired assurance the actual Promoters of it had compromised their negotiating position with Forbes of the District Railway who would exact a high price. What was worse, however, was that by putting this assurance into the public domain, Onslow's group, none of whom were railwaymen, had blundered into the exposure to the LSWR of the fact that the absence of a contractual settlement of the interface between an urban underground railway and a feeder line, both in separate ownerships, was a serious lacuna: it was one of the biggest weaknesses of the scheme and the LSWR took great care to ensure that the weakness was exposed.

All this, however, lay in the future; the trap was obscured behind the honeyed words of Gould's report. In introducing the Bill to the Select Committee, Counsel fleshed out some of the *Surrey Comet*'s hopeful words: it was no wonder, he said, that those who had been frustrated by the LSWR 'had long since endeavoured' to improve the local service and

they would have obtained it had it not been for the fact that this was a sort of neutral territory lying between the LSWR and the LB&SCR, who practically had partitioned it between themselves with a view of maintaining the monopoly they possessed, and had consequently poured cold water upon any such proposals.[30]

The LB&SCR actually petitioned against Onslow's scheme because they alleged that

... rival interests may be introduced into the district disturbing the relations now subsisting between ... [us and] the LSWR and SER in a manner injurious to the companies and without advantage to the public.[31]

Sensing that he was on to something, Counsel for Onslow outwardly intoned that he supposed that the nature of the relationship is that 'neither invades each other' and 'the arrangement is that you should be loyal to each other in the case of strangers coming into the district'. The General Manager J P Knight, of the LB&SCR denied that his company's understanding with the LSWR 'forbids you to do anything but look with indifference or coldness' upon Onslow's scheme for a railway competing with the LSWR. 'It has always been understood' said Knight,

that the district between Leatherhead and Guildford belongs to the LSWR; that is to say that if any accommodation is required ... [between the two towns then] the LSWR should take the initiative in supplying it.[32]

This was just the sort of anti-competitive behaviour that Gould was determined to combat, and why Onslow's initiative in promoting his scheme was so welcome. Evidently the Kingston Council had concurred with Gould and resolved unanimously to promote the scheme; to petition Parliament in its favour; to invest a substantial £10,000 in the equity of the promoting company, and to have the power to appoint a director of it. According to Gould, at one of the largest meetings he had seen in Kingston for many years, the action of the Council was unanimously endorsed; the crowded meeting was 'unanimous' in its support of the *Blue Route*.[33]

---

[29] Report of committee on Guildford, Kingston and London Railway Bill to Kingston Corporation, 1881, Local History Room, Kingston Museum.
[30] Counsel's introduction of the Guildford, Kingston and London Railway Bill to the Select Committee, reported in *Surrey Comet*: 28 May 1881.
[31] Included in the verbatim record of proceedings of the Select Committee during cross-examination of J P Knight, General Manager of LB&SCR.
[32] Evidence of J P Knight to Select Committee, considering the Guildford, Kingston and London Railway Bill, May 1881.
[33] *Surrey Comet*: 10 September 1881.

8.10 Kingston's status as a port was never properly integrated with the railway system, and much of the river-borne traffic from the London docks by-passed it for handling in Guildford on the Wey Navigation instead; this view near Canbury Gardens is from 1905.

Kingston's river-borne traffic

Gould claimed a point in favour of the agricultural district being opened up to Kingston: 'The trade of Kingston did not lie between it and London' he was reported as saying and not in the direction of Richmond and Twickenham, 'but lower down the county towards Guildford, just in that tract of land which the line would open up'. Although he had to be careful to disguise it, Gould was making a competitive point against the County town. What Gould was saying was that Kingston's wharves were closer to London and the source of coal and other heavy cargoes: there was no import of any scale into Guildford through the Wey Navigation that did not pass Kingston on the way, and Guildford's exports which involved both a rail-lift and a river journey could be more economically shipped from Kingston. The businessmen of Kingston were concerned about the cost of freight: a miller in the town complained about what he thought was discriminatory pricing. With an eye to sourcing his grain from where it was cheapest he thought the *Blue Route* would be an advantage 'because it would place the district in communication with the northern [railway] lines'. He thought that 'the requirements of the district have

entirely outgrown the facility afforded, if not the capacities of the South Western system'.[34]

As for the passenger market, Kingston was a growing town in spite of its poor train service: its population in 1881 had increased by a third in 10 years to over 33,000 (Guildford's was 14,000). It would appear that the river was still a great economic asset to the town, but one can only sympathise over the town's second class status in railway terms: a heavy price indeed was still being paid for the reaction to the London & Southampton railway 50 years previously.

More passenger grumbles

Every complaint that railway passengers had was attributed to the LSWR, and as we have seen, Kingston's complaints were many, well-justified and aired in the *Surrey Comet*. The abuse of the LSWR in print took on a particularly ironic and sharply critical vein: a rancorous journalist in *Punch* observed of the *Wags of Waterloo* that:

---

[34] Evidence of J Marsh to Select Committee, considering the Guildford, Kingston and London Railway Bill, May 1881.

8.11   *THE SLOW TRAIN*

On Southern lines the trains which crawl
     Deliberately to and fro
Make life a burden; of them all
     This is the slowest of the slow,
Impatiently condemned to bear
What is indeed an awful bore,
t've seemed to be imprisoned there
          Three days, or more.

                    (From Punch*)*

It is evident that the directors must be great rabbit fanciers, for the number of hutches scattered over their system is enormous. It is only by experience that the traveller ... finds out that these hutches are not for rabbits, but for human beings, and that they are known technically as 'Country stations'.[35]

Punch returned to the theme in the following year: the LSWR 'has, after its dear old doddering fashion, ... succeeded in disgusting the great majority of its passengers by its creepy-crawly trains and its rabbit hutch stations'.[36]

Because the LSWR had the local monopoly, it was axiomatic that everything that was disagreeable about train travel was, just like today, their fault, and there was no shortage of people prepared to throw mud, some of which was bound to stick. *Punch* had not invented their jibes. A witness had an estate at New Malden, 'a rapidly increasing place', which was 'entirely dependent on the LSWR' and their station 'waiting room would only hold about 12 packed pretty closely together' when 50 might be waiting to go to London.[37]

According to Gould, travellers from *Kingston* to *Waterloo* returning via *Surbiton* were charged extra fares in spite of pledges having been made, it was alleged, that return tickets would be available over both routes. This concession by the LSWR was apparently never made but the appearance of the LSWR's competing scheme coincided with some improvements to *Kingston* station, which according to Gould were more than he 'had ever seen ... during the last 20 or 30 years'.[38] This and other attempts by the LSWR to assuage the wrath of Kingston, including putting on an additional early train,[39] cut no ice with a town whose patience was too stretched.

The benefits to Kingston of the *Blue Route* were self-evident: at last it would be on a through route to central London and the town's leaders gave it their utmost support. The *Red Route*, on the other hand, had nothing to commend it to the people of Kingston; moreover, the company at whose door was laid the blame for all Kingston's railway woes since the 1830s was promoting it. Because the town's enthusiasm for the *Blue Route* was the greatest, so was their despair when, ultimately, it was compromised.

Two routes through Claygate

The position of Claygate was quite unlike any of the other villages on the two proposed routes to Guildford. In Claygate both routes went through the village – one, Onslow's *Blue Route*, through its heart and the other, the LSWR's *Red Route* at the west edge of the village. That Claygate got a railway at all was nothing, perhaps surprisingly, to do with its brickfields – they were not mentioned at the Select Committee, neither in the context of Claygate nor Oxshott – neither was it due to Lord Foley's influence: Claygate got a railway because of its lucky geographical position. Among the numberless possible ways in which any railway could be laid out, one certainty was that *Surbiton* would be the interchange station; to this can be added another certainty: there would be no railway at all that did not serve the Crown land at Oxshott – John Clutton for the Crown saw to that – and there was no way of building

---

[35] Quoted in *Surrey Comet*: 30 October 1880.
[36] Quoted in *Surrey Comet*: 28 May 1881.
[37] *Surrey Comet*: 28 May 1881.
[38] Evidence of F Gould, to Select Committee, considering the Guildford, Kingston and London Railway Bill, May 1881.
[39] Evidence of J R Gover to the same committee.

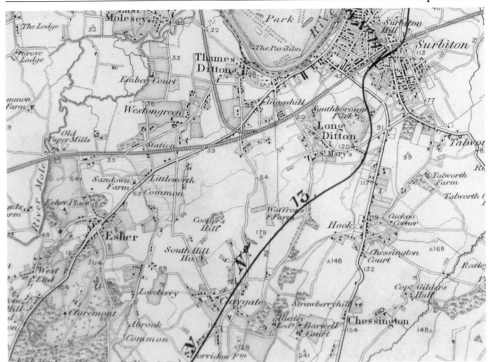

8.12 This map shows part of the Blue Route: the southerly bias of the route from Surbiton can be seen, taking it through Southborough Park, near The Waffrons farm (through land on which Surbiton Golf Course was built) and on to Claygate through the heart of the village very close to the church, and through Horringdon Farm.

a railway to Oxshott from Surbiton which did not go through Claygate.

When it came to be built the New Line took its course from Hampton Court Junction as laid out in the LSWR's *Red Route*; it integrated fully with *Surbiton* to give an interchange station for the main lines to the west. Economy was achieved by avoiding the need to build a new track bed between *Surbiton* and the Junction. Arthur Pain, acted as engineer for Bell's Cobham Railway of 1879 and he identified the valley of the Rythe, a river which rises near Oxshott and flows near the Junction as the best place to leave the main line. By taking this route, which held the level ground at the foot of Telegraph Hill, further cost advantages were gained by the LSWR over the *Blue Route*, which needed deep cuttings for its own route out of Surbiton.

Wolfe Barry defended the Onslow route at the Select Committee by explaining that a large estate called Southborough Park had been put up for auction in 1880 for development and between Southborough Park and Claygate lay a large tract of land owned by Lord Lovelace: 'our line will be in close contiguity to it' and this is 'where the land is ripe for building'. This beacon

of light in the Onslow team's thinking shows their certainty of the umbilical connection between London-serving railways and residential development. The land through which the *Blue Route* was laid out became part of Surbiton Golf course 15 years later. This and other land in the area, between Claygate, Long Ditton and Hook was saved from development by the outbreak of war in 1939 preserving Claygate from being enveloped by London's centrifugal expansion.[40]

Onslow's plan was to enter Claygate by crossing Claygate Lane, Red Lane and Church Road; then to cross the present recreation ground until finally rejoining the as-built New Line route somewhere to the south of *Horringdon* (*Horridon*) *Farm* having crossed Vale Road on the way. A map showing the route from Surbiton to Claygate is shown above. While it is true that the LSWR route ran a little to the west of Claygate – causing a shift of the village in later years – the *Blue Route* with its many bridges would have been intrusive to the village centre and the church.

---

[40] *Hinchley Wood: the Origins of a 1930s Settlement*: Howard Mallinson, 2002.

8.13 Ruxley Lodge, c1918; seat of Lord Foley a member of the Provisional Committee of the Guildford, Kingston and London Railway, but strangely low key in its advocacy.

The vicarage was so close to the line of the *Blue Route* that it was within the so-called 'limit of deviation' – representing the practical limit of where the centre-line of the railway may be built under the powers granted by its Act of Parliament. Remarkably, the Vicar found in this fact no cause for objection: it was the more remarkable that he was a member of the Provisional Committee for the new railway. The vicar said he was concerned about the empty houses in Claygate, some of which were his own and on land required for the railway; this temporary housing surplus was probably due to the agricultural depression, but any railway would have brought with it the prospect of finding tenants: the route of the railway was immaterial to the issue. His objections to the same railway that Queen Victoria had objected to was aired at the new Select Committee, leaving in doubt the wisdom of his being called as a witness for he did neither harm to the LSWR nor advanced the cause of Lord Foley who, although he was a member of the Provisional Committee of the Guildford, Kingston and London Railway, surprisingly adopted a passive role in the whole affair: he gave no evidence in its support. Foley was a patriarchal figure in Claygate; his estate around *Ruxley Lodge* extending over Winey Hill into Chessington was large and although Onslow's railway did not run through any of his land, it would be better served by it than the LSWR's, and no doubt he was very pleased to be part of the agitation for a railway. It was his brother, the Hon Fitzalan Foley (later 6th Baron Foley), who demonstrated his enthusiasm for the railway – any railway – by buying land contiguous with the one that was built and after parcelling it up for development, building on it.

Chapter 9: Cobham or Stoke D'Abernon and other skirmishes

9.1 *Street Cobham, c 1914; in the White Lion Hotel (centre) was held a public meeting in January 1881 in which the two schemes for new railways to Guildford were debated.*

In this chapter, a prelude to the Select Committee hearing of the evidence on the two schemes for new railways to Guildford, we consider some of the skirmishes between the protagonists which preceded the set piece confrontation that was to come in Westminster. Before discussing the dilemma of whether it was Stoke D'Abernon or Cobham that should have a railway, we must consider an issue which although vital at the time, was ultimately sidelined by the final compromise over the routes of the proposed railways.

Wimbledon Common

When the Guildford, Kingston and London Railway Bill came before the House of Commons on 31 March 1881 the greatest protector of Wimbledon Common in Parliament – Sir Henry Peek, the Member for Mid Surrey – moved that it should be thrown out. His tone was patrician and officious, brooking no scope for compromise, and his attack brought upon himself a caustic public attack from Frederick Gould, the Mayor of Kingston – the town, of all those which supported the Bill, which had the most to gain from it and whose participation in the promotion of it was the most earnest. The Promoters of the Bill recognised that fierce

opposition could be expected over interference with commons, which then as now were a subject of huge public concern, but they sensed 'dirty tricks' by a campaign of mischievous disinformation and issued a public statement by the engineer, Wolfe Barry. His report explained that thanks to the cooperation of HRH Duke of Cambridge a deviation could be made, including a deep tunnel under Putney Heath, to assuage the concerns of the Conservators of Wimbledon Common, through which a cut and cover solution had been proposed. Wolfe Barry suspected obfuscation in the deliberate placing of difficulties in the way of achieving this compromise (any role by the LSWR in this is obscure, but it was claimed by Gould) but because everything depended on Parliament and the need to submit to its dominion over procedure, Wolfe Barry led the Promoters, at great cost to their project, to the pragmatic decision to abandon all idea of making any part of the line on the surface of Wimbledon Common. Wolfe Barry also made explicit the resolve of the Promoters to preserve the existing size of all commons through which their railway ran by the substitution of new land to replace that taken by the railway. Wolfe Barry's 8 February 1881 published report contained a specially produced map which

9.2 Street Cobham, c1904; a delivery is made by a cart which has probably come from Stoke D'Abernon station.

demonstrated how his railway was laid out to avoid the many commons on its route.[1]

Another objection raised by the Conservators was the risk of death or injury that might be suffered because the National Rifle Association used part of the Common for firing practice. Wolfe Barry proposed a solution to this objection, to the entire satisfaction of all, by proposing a bund alongside the exposed part of the railway to provide a bullet-proof screen. Notwithstanding the elimination of this objection, Peek was not without one friend: a cantankerous Member 'heartily' seconded Peek's attempt to throw out the Bill because 'they should teach Railway Companies a lesson' and make them sort out their problems before troubling Parliament.[2]

Lord Onslow had a particular supporter in the House in Denzil Onslow MP: playing to the Guildford grandstand he announced that: 'I have in my hand a Petition in favour of the Bill signed by the Mayor and Corporation' which claims support for the line came from every part of Surrey through which it passes. His strong support for the Bill was founded on its attack on the LSWR's 'monopoly of the railway accommodation in this district'.[3] Another Member caught the mood of the House when he said that he supported the Second

Reading irrespective of its merits because he thought they were wholly 'unfitted to dispose of a project of this kind, without first sending the Bill before a Select Committee, which alone was capable of dealing with the questions'. It may be thought remarkable that this needed to be said at all: the very next day the LSWR's Bill, which included their competing scheme, was sent to Select Committee without a division,[4] but the Guildford, Kingston and London Railway Bill had excited considerable interest and because of the great air of expectancy which was abroad in Westminster – the Lords Onslow and Lovelace had no doubt been active – it was suggested 'it might possibly surprise the House that instead of it being a great railway measure, it was a very small Bill indeed, simply for the purpose of constructing what was called 'a landowners' line'. It was a small railway and 'it affected a not very populous part of the county of Surrey': so assuaged the House referred the Bill to a Select Committee by a majority of 226.

[1] Guildford, Kingston and London Railway Bill, Report of Mr John Wolfe Barry, 8 February 1881. Surrey History Centre, Woking: Onslow papers.
[2] Hansard's Parliamentary Debates, 1 April 1881.
[3] Ibid.
[4] Hansard's Parliamentary Debates, 2 April 1881.

The *Surrey Comet* was briefed by Gould, the Mayor, who was convinced of dirty tricks, but writing with some restraint the Editor said it was a 'miserable result' for in spite of 'all the efforts made by the LSWR to whip up their parliamentary friends' Peek had found only 48 MPs willing to vote the Bill out. The newspaper agreed that it was a matter of general regret that Sir Henry Peek 'should have used the vote and influence delegated to him by his parliamentary constituents in a manner so at variance' with Kingston's interests.[5] Gould's essential complaint to the *Surrey Comet* was that Peek had disregarded Kingston's long-standing affliction 'with all the worst evils of a railway monopoly' and just when 'an opportunity had been presented … to remedy this evil and give us all the advantages of a healthy competition' the town had been let down by Peek's unnecessarily lofty, uncompromising and pedantic attitude.[6] Gould reminded Peek that after one of the largest meetings of the inhabitants of Kingston ever held the actions of the Corporation had been unanimously endorsed and generally supported in Surbiton and Kingston and various petitions and several deputations to the government have left no doubt as to public feeling in the matter.

Gould asserted that Peek had been doing the work of the LSWR but as his bile took charge of his pen he made an error of exaggeration: he averred that all the landowners affected by the Guildford, Kingston and London Railway Bill supported the Bill: as we shall see one large landowner, had in fact petitioned against it. Peek was well-enough informed to counter Gould's error: 'Some half dozen with a good deal of land to develop are undoubtedly warmly in favour', he allowed 'but if enquiries be made at Ripley, Stoke D'Abernon, and other parishes, a very different story will be told' he said.[7]

As the thoughts of the combatants turned to the Select Committee, Gould who was one of the most staunch allies of the Guildford, Kingston and London Railway Bill, could at least be satisfied that the arguments about the route from Fulham to Surbiton were settled, but there was indeed a different story in Stoke D'Abernon: the Lord of the Manor of Stoke D'Abernon; the Revd Phillips had petitioned against the Bill. It is one of the great ironies of this story that both these men – the one doing his best to bring the railway in: the other to stop it going through Stoke D'Abernon – were destined to failure at the hands of the same powerful force: railway politics.

The Revd Phillips objects to Onslow's railway

The proposed route of Onslow's railway threatened to bisect Phillips' property in Stoke D'Abernon and his opposition to it became spirited and was well funded. The very idea of a railway through Stoke D'Abernon, as opposed to Cobham had never been proposed before. Phillips asserted in his Petition against the Guildford, Kingston and London Railway Bill that:

> There is no local traffic in existence, or likely to be created to justify the cost of the proposed railways, and there is no reasonable prospect of the promoters being able to show such a probable return on the necessary outlay as to induce parties to subscribe the necessary capital to enable the promoters to complete their undertaking.[8]

If Phillips had no vision for or wish to see the residential development that many of the other landowners expected to flow from building the line, he was oblivious to the strategic benefits that Forbes of the District Railway predicted for the new railway. Phillips' most telling point was the one on which Onslow's case was the weakest: none of the Promoters could give any comfort that the required capital could be raised, and if it was, whether the railway would make any sort of return for its shareholders. Phillips considered Stoke D'Abernon 'a retired, picturesque, and peaceful spot' but he was characterised by Wolfe Barry as one serially opposed to railways, whose only interest was to retain 'the rustic simplicity' of his Manor. Like Queen Victoria, Phillips wanted no more than the quiet enjoyment of an idyllic estate, but the Queen had John Clutton fighting her corner and he had stitched up the Oxshott pivot around which the railway would be built and set on its course for Stoke D'Abernon

It was in the nature of railways at least initially to spoil the environments in which they were built: the assessment of whether they yielded economic benefits to outweigh the scars is the test, and 120 years later, Stoke D'Abernon (today no longer including Oxshott)

---

[5] *Surrey Comet*, 2 April 1881.
[6] *Surrey Comet*, 9 April 1881.
[7] *Surrey Comet*, 30 April 1881.
[8] Quoted during the giving of evidence by William Grover to the Select Committee considering the Guildford, Kingston and London Railway Bill, May 1881.

appears, at least to an outside observer, to have retained some of its charm. An interesting point is whether Cobham would have suffered scarring if the LSWR route had been built. At the time no one drew attention to the environmental damage that would be done by a railway that permanently separated Street and Church Cobham either by a level crossing in Between Streets or high on an embankment.

Phillips' aversion to a railway through Stoke D'Abernon and by implication a preference as a lesser evil of one that went through Cobham had some substance: in 1881 Stoke had a largely peasant population of 400 while Cobham's population of about 2,300 was about two-thirds the size of Leatherhead, and which was supported by a diversified economy. Reflecting Cobham's mercantile as well as rural scope, Bell and Combe had been trying for years to get a railway into Cobham, and both, having become exasperated with the LSWR's obfuscation, were now in the Onslow camp. The local railway political scene had changed: pragmatism overcame perversity because the LSWR was now proposing a line through Cobham while the previously unsuccessful advocates of such a plan were extolling the benefits of a line which by-passed it. Combe had been with Onslow and Lovelace on the West Surrey Railway Bill, and because he was allied with them again, he was obliged to relegate Cobham and speak up for the Stoke D'Abernon site for a station: it was a juxtaposition that he would never have taken up 'if the South Western had met us in any way'.[9] Thus did Combe, the largest landowner in Cobham, and Phillips the largest landowner in Stoke D'Abernon, become in conflict with each other over the best route and station site for what became the New Line.

Combe was not the only person to be embarrassed by having to kick over the traces of his previous position: the reader will recall the patronising attitude towards Cobham's need for a railway expressed by Archibald Scott, the General Manager of LSWR only a few months previously: 'A tramway along the Esher road is quite good enough for the Cobham people' and 'no railway to Cobham on any terms' had been his haughty assessment. It was fortunate for Scott personally and the LSWR generally that these intemperate remarks, which had the potential to make them look extremely foolish, were never examined in public now that the LSWR was seeking to do the very thing that Scott had said he would never do 'on any terms'.

The Fairmile phalanx and *Mansion House*

Combe's unlikely attitude to the route for the new railway was not a singular one. Frederick Keays of Fairmile Court was induced to give explicit support to the Stoke D'Abernon route and, more remarkably, to give evidence against the LSWR's plan to put its station in Cobham. It is perhaps less remarkable that Matthew Arnold, the poet who lived at the time near Pains Hill, Cobham, and who was on visiting terms with Combe, did not go through Keays' mental contortion of arguing in public that a line that gave a station in Stoke D'Abernon was preferable to one that offered a station in Cobham. The difference between Keays and Arnold, both of whom travelled to London from *Esher*, was that Keays was in it for the money: he was a Promoter of the Guildford, Kingston and London Railway Bill, and he was the champion of a significant group who lived in the Fairmile district of Cobham – a Fairmile phalanx – who were 'professional gentlemen engaged in business in the City coming up every day'.[10]

Keays claimed wrongly that 'all the people of Cobham were in favour of the Onslow scheme': it was a statement in which hyperbole triumphed over substance, and being unsupportable was turned to LSWR's advantage: Keays had to concede that he had been present at the large meeting at the White Lion Hotel in Cobham in January 1881 when Phillips of Stoke D'Abernon moved the resolution:

> That this meeting, having had under consideration the scheme of the Guildford, Kingston and London Railway in connection with the District Railway is of the opinion that the interests of the neighbourhood cannot be adequately served by the proposed ... [railway] and that both as regards passengers and goods such a railway would fail to serve the requirements of Cobham and district. That the railway proposed by the LSWR affording both Church and Street Cobham direct and convenient access between the district and the LSWR main line at ... Surbiton would best serve the interests of the vicinity.[11]

[9] Evidence of Charles Combe to the Select Committee considering the Guildford, Kingston and London Railway Bill, May 1881.
[10] Evidence of Frederick Keays to the Select Committee, considering the Guildford, Kingston and London Railway Bill, May 1881.
[11] Quoted by Counsel cross-examining F Keays at the same committee.

9.3 *The Cricketers at Downside Green, Cobham, c1960s. The Guildford, Kingston and London Railway considered building a station at Downside. The LSWR, having been obliged to build Cobham's station in Stoke D'Abernon, abandoned Downside as a station location. In 1888, when Effingham Junction station was opened, it became the nearest station to Downside.*

For the articulated substance of Keays' denial of the benefit of a railway station in Cobham we have to look to the seductive influence of the District Railway. His unspoken thought, but an open secret, was that the patrician residents of the Fairmile district wished to keep the railway, with its dirt, noise and trade, at a distance. Keays supported the Guildford, Kingston and London Railway because he believed – according to his evidence he had been told by Forbes himself – that he was going to be able to get a train all the way to *Mansion House* – direct. We have already heard that Forbes had made it crystal clear that the Guildford, Kingston and London Railway could never be given access to the Inner Circle railway: either Forbes had misled Keays or allowed him to deceive himself but on the evidence Keays defied the evident will of the Cobham people to have their own railway station on the misunderstanding that direct trains would run into *Mansion House* from *Guildford*.

J A Radcliffe was also a vocal member of the Fairmile phalanx; he was a Solicitor practising near Charing Cross and also a member of Onslow's Provisional Committee. He pointed out the benefits of Onslow's railway for those businessmen who had to use the omnibuses that run from *Waterloo* to the City which were 'full every day'. He thought that the proposed LSWR station in Cobham 'was entirely useless' because

it interfered with the roads and 'does not put us into communication' with London's urban railway system.[12] 'It is far better' he said, 'for persons coming to the West End, to be landed at *High Street Kensington* or *Victoria* than at *Waterloo*. It is far better for a City man to be landed at *Mansion House* than *Waterloo*.'[13]

Radcliffe was not alone in neglecting the very long journey times that would have been unavoidable when a feeder service from the country came up against an urban railway system to which there would be no access without a change of train. This oversight in defending Onslow's railway allowed him to be gently chided by LSWR's Counsel. With piercing theatre he suggested that: 'You have to its faults been a little blind, I suppose' while to another enthusiast for Onslow's railway, a farmer from Clandon, came the inevitable dismissal: 'Cobham has been left out in the cold.'

Onslow's legal team knew that they would have to defend the avoidance by their line of Cobham, the town whose interests had been so strongly advocated over many years. They called in aid Arthur Pain, who had been the engineer for Bell's final unsuccessful Cobham

---

[12] Evidence of J A Radcliffe to the same committee.
[13] *Ibid.*

9.4 A District Railway train at the West Brompton terminus in 1876; trains similar to these operated from Fulham to Mansion House and, if the aims of the Guildford, Kingston and London Railway Bill had been fulfilled, would have taken passengers into the 'Inner Circle': there was a mistaken idea that through trains from Guildford to Mansion House would operate but access to the Inner Circle was strictly controlled.

London's Transport Museum

Railway Bill. Pain, who lived in Surbiton, was now a serious supporter with Bell and Combe of Onslow's railway by which 'I can get all round London'. He conceded that the quadrupling of the LSWR's tracks to *Waterloo* would allow a considerable improvement in their service 'but *Waterloo* is the neck of the bottle': there were only four tracks outside *Waterloo* at the time and until the bridge over Westminster Bridge Road was widened, the delays caused by having to find a path for the race specials would continue to be endemic, argued Pain.[14] The problem for the LSWR was that their main line trains arriving in *Waterloo* had to have their carriages shunted back to Clapham Junction, whereas the District's shuttle service was continually rolling with no shunting required. Pain's analysis was right: the shunting problem at *Waterloo* – the use of scarce track paths by empty stock movements – was one that could only be solved by more investment (and ultimately electrification).

Residential development opportunities

In giving evidence in support of Onslow's railway through Stoke D'Abernon, Pain had to justify his previous espousal of the Cobham scheme; he liked the straightness of the Onslow line – the LSWR's line had

been dubbed the 'wiggling worm' because of the deviation it had to make to take in Cobham. He justified the reversal of his previous preference because 'at that time it was a line from Surbiton to Cobham, and not through to Guildford'. He conceded readily that the LSWR line would accommodate the people residing in Church and Street Cobham but taking 'the question of the district as a whole; and the future probable extension of it' he had no hesitation in saying that the area between, Stoke D'Abernon and Oxshott was where the building would take place: 'it is the highest land and remarkably well situated for residences around Fairmile' whereas the undeveloped land near the Mole valley flood plain in Cobham and Stoke D'Abernon was unsuitable for development. In Pain's view there was 'no district around London so fine' as the area between Fairmile and Oxshott.[15]

Of all the remarks made in the debate over whether the route should go through Cobham or Stoke D'Abernon, some of which were absurd, shallow or blatantly partial, this was one of the most sagacious. Looking at

[14] Evidence of A Paine ICE to the same committee.
[15] Ibid.

9.5 *The compromise over the route settled the need for an embankment across the River Mole flood plain near Downside; this view is from c1883; the unsuitability of this area of land for development and land on the west bank of the Mole opposite Church Cobham was one reason advanced for Cobham's station to be in Stoke D'Abernon.*

the map today, the built area to the north of the railway between Stoke D'Abernon and Oxshott Heath merging in with Fairmile is practically filled, as Pain predicted, with substantial houses – only Knowle Hill and Little Heath have been spared development. The foresight shown by Pain was probably the most penetrating analysis of the benefits of a route through Stoke D'Abernon. This was Onslow's good fortune because we can be certain he had not conceived of this benefit before his engineer drew a line between his farm at Clandon and Oxshott. When it came to the time for compromise over the route which the New Line should take the LSWR may have found in Pain's analysis sufficient reason to accept Onslow's Clandon route.

There was one major practical snag to implementing the solution advocated by Pain: much of the required land was owned by Phillips, the petitioner against the Bill. Pain's view of this was worldly: to focus on the small population in Stoke D'Abernon was to miss the essential truth for it was the fact that there were three million people in London, continually growing and wanting to extend outwards. It was the centrifugal forces of London's expansion that would create the demand, 'You have to consider the future as well as the present' and of the man who was the defender of 'rustic simplicity' he said:

I have seen a good deal of opposition by the owners of estates to railways, and when the railway is made, they are the very first to take advantage of it, and I cannot believe that Phillips, with that valuable estate, would not take advantage of it.[16]

If John Clutton, the highly experienced, astute but aloof Receiver of the Crown Estate, heard these words we can imagine his knowing nod. Clutton thought Onslow's the better of the two routes because it opened up a new strategic route into London, but as both of them went along the southern edge of Oxshott Heath 'which belongs to Her Majesty the Queen' and were well clear of *Claremont* and opened up the Crown lands for development, he was as unconcerned with how the railway got to Guildford from Oxshott, 'an uninhabited district', as he was about how it got to Oxshott from Surbiton. While Clutton had no interest in the games that the lawyers liked to play in their theatre, equally, he had no interest in being the judge of whether it was Cobham or Stoke D'Abernon which should have a station. When asked about the impact on the two-and-a-half-miles of Phillips' land which the railway would traverse, Clutton's wistful reply was that: 'Its value will go up' noting that it was better to have a station and a

---

[16] *Ibid.*

9.6 *Cobham Stud: an early 20th century photo. An objection was made to the LSWR's proposal to take a railway into Cobham because it would pass near the stud and 'frighten the horses'.*

line than just a line. When Clutton was pressed: 'What is best: Cobham or Stoke D'Abernon for a station?' he regarded the question as hopeless: 'To do what?' he had countered for like Pain, he knew it was the wrong question. But it was a matter on which Clutton was able to make a telling point against Phillips. Clutton with dramatic understatement but in the sure knowledge of the impact of it on the Crown's land in Oxshott, said it 'will do no harm' to Phillips' Stoke D'Abernon Estate.[17] In Claygate, Lord Foley's younger brother the Hon Fitzalan Foley, would have noted these comments on the development impact of the new railway, but probably hoped the word would not get round before he had bought up some land in Claygate for development without paying a development premium. For the present, however, it was not clear where Claygate's railway would run.

It will frighten the horses

While Phillips' estate in Stoke D'Abernon would benefit from the railway, Combe asserted that part of his estate would suffer actual harm if the LSWR scheme were to be built. Combe wanted cheap coal and other imports for his estate, without being troubled by the

railway which gave it to him: the LSWR route after 'wiggling' to Cobham had to regain its direction for Guildford and in doing so intruded. He needed a rationalisation for his objection, the essence of which was his selfish desire to have a railway, but in someone else's back yard – the Revd Phillips' for example. He had a stud farm on his land and did not want a railway 'running up alongside the paddock full of mares and young foals'.[18]

His manager backed up Combe's problem with the horses: this was Richard Bell (not to be confused with the James Bell) whose evidence was at least as interesting as it was persuasive. The stud farm, which occupied 200 acres of Combe's *Cobham Park Estate*, maintained anything from 200 to 300 horses at any one time and in the course of a year they would consume between 800 and 1,000 quarters of oats, which of course had to be brought in by a horse and cart from the nearest railhead. He also bought a lot of straw from Winchester. The stud was, he claimed, 'the largest

[17] Evidence of John Clutton to the same committee.
[18] Evidence of Charles Combe to the same committee.

84

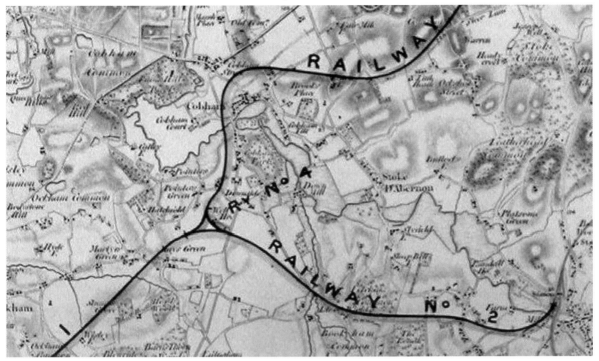

9.7 *The LSWR's* Red Route *showing clearly the diversion to allow it to take in Cobham causing the sobriquet of 'the wiggling worm'.*

trading concern in Cobham' to which a large number of visitors was attracted including 600 people who 'come from West London for the yearling sales', for whom a station at Downside, which was under consideration on Onslow's railway, would be very convenient being perhaps only half-a-mile from his paddock.

In the event, Combe got neither a station at Downside nor in Cobham: the station at Downside which Combe expected was never built, but for different reasons a station at *Effingham Junction* was opened in 1888. The evidence of Combe and his stud manager was directed at stopping the LSWR coming to Cobham and in favour of Onslow's railway going to Stoke D'Abernon, which would mean the introduction of competition for the LSWR, in the criticism of which he was articulate. Combe's opposition to the LSWR gave him something of a pyrrhic victory because with the Downside station being dropped, he ended up with having one of the most awkward journeys to *Stoke D'Abernon*, which was between two and three miles from *Cobham Park* on the wrong side of the River Mole and the station at *Stoke D'Abernon* was only two miles closer to Combe's needs

than the nearest railhead on the main line (albeit with some intervening hills). Bell the loyal manager thought this a price worth paying because if the LSWR route had been adopted it would have been fatal to the stud because 'it would frighten the horses'.[19] It is not recorded what John Clutton thought of all this: had his opinion been asked he might have suggested to Combe that he welcomed a railway and a station and turned *Cobham Park* with its 1,000 acres into the sort of estate that Clutton had in mind for Oxshott.

A straight line or a wiggling worm?

The last word of the professionals on the issue of Stoke D'Abernon or Cobham must go to Wolfe Barry who gave his assessment of the merits of both: he conceded the obvious that the LSWR proposal served the people of Cobham better but he considered that 'to prolong the distance for all time between Guildford and Surbiton, merely for the sake of accommodating the then small

---

[19] Evidence of Richard Bell to the same committee.

9.8 An early 20th century view of Warren Lane, Oxshott.

houses in Cobham's settled districts was unsound compared with serving the important properties at Fairmile (and in his mind) at Oxshott. A map of the LSWR's deviation to Cobham – the so called 'wiggling worm' – is shown on the previous page. The deviation to take in Cobham, which was made inevitable by the imperative of taking the Clutton determined route through Oxshott, is plainly anomalous, as an inspection of the map confirms.

As Wolfe Barry explained:

> The point that everybody has to consider … is the south-east corner of Oxshott Heath … which is under the control of Her Majesty and no line will be allowed which goes further to the westward than the line which has been selected at that point; therefore that is the point by which we are all tied … therefore we drew the line in a pretty straight direction pointing from the south-east corner of Oxshott Heath … The LSWR apparently have been in some way led astray by the local lines that have been suggested in former years to serve Cobham, and they have deviated their line to the west of Cobham and then they have come back again to join the main line of communication between Guildford and Surbiton.

There we have it: the interests of Queen Victoria and the Crown lands dictated where the line had to leave Oxshott, and Cobham could not be reached without the 'wiggling worm' deviation. Certainly, conceded Wolfe Barry, Cobham would have been included on Onslow's line if it were possible but 'you can buy gold too dear'.[20]

---

[20] Evidence of J Wolfe Barry to the same committee.

Chapter 10: The Select Committee of May 1881

10.1 The typical scene at a Select Committee railway hearing. (A sketch by Harry Furniss (1854-1925) reproduced in The Graphic, *20 July 1889, and House of Lords Record Office memorandum No 85.)*

The Guildford, Kingston and London Railway Bill together with its attendant maps, estimates and drawings of the route with a key to the landholdings that were affected by it, were lodged in Parliament in November 1880. Because the Bill was opposed, not least by the Petition of the LSWR and their own deposit of a competing Bill with its associated annexes, the two Bills were grouped and were considered by the same Select Committee of Members of the House of Commons during a 13-day period in May 1881.

A gladiatorial contest

These Select Committees attracted considerable public attention at the time and because the evidence given to them was written down its availability is of considerable value to historiography. In the event, as we shall see, the Committee hearing the evidence on Onslow's Bill did not have to pronounce on it because the LSWR took the view that a compromise involving them building the railway which they did not want, but which in the process shut out the District Railway from deep Surrey, would be an infinitely better result than if

Onslow's Bill were to be passed and their own to fail; equally, Onslow needed to compromise because his scheme contained fatal flaws specially west of Surbiton. The evidence on the LSWR Bill was never heard – the compromise preceded it – but the evidence given to the Committee on the Guildford, Kingston and London Railway Bill, some of which has already been discussed, gives us a colourful and revealing insight into the circumstances and opinions prevailing in our part of Surrey at the time.

The advocates who were appointed to represent the promoters and the petitioners were often leading Queen's Counsel, and they conducted themselves as if they were in Court. There were no juries: the judges were the Members who were parliamentarians bringing to the hearing whatever baggage or benefits their experiences of life had either been burdened or blessed. The scene in the committee room, with large numbers of be-wigged Counsel and their juniors and attended by their clerks, instructing Solicitors and parliamentary agents, resembled a small courtroom with proceedings conducted in the normal judicial

10.2 The atmosphere in the committee room was gladiatorial: maps of Lord Onslow's Blue Route *and the LSWR's* Red Route *hung on the wall. (A sketch of a similar case by Harry Furniss (1854-1925) reproduced in The Graphic, 20 July 1889, and House of Lords Record Office memorandum No 85.)*

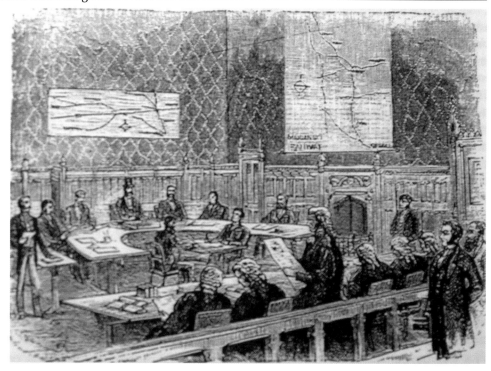

adversarial style. The process, second nature to the lawyers, had been described as a merry game which goes on for weeks, 'and the result is that the lawyers and their agents amass fortunes, and shareholders go mourning for their dividends'.[1] The prospect of 'mourning for their dividends' was certainly true in this case for the LSWR shareholders: it was damage limitation time for them because their best interests, as Archibald Scott, their General Manager had made plain, were thought to lie in building no new railway. The District Railway shareholders might be the gainers from the LSWR's loss; while the Promoters of the Guildford, Kingston and London Railway Bill – those who owned the huge swathes of land through which the right (for them) railway might run – had hundreds of thousands of pounds in cash hanging on the result.

The atmosphere was gladiatorial: the contest was between the landowner-promoters of one Bill, some of whom were 'noble Lords' in the very Palace where the fight was on, against the LSWR's Bill, a successful railway company which everyone loved to hate. The theatre for the gladiators' contest was dominated by two large maps which were placed on the wall behind the witness box; one showed Onslow's *Blue Route*; the

other the LSWR's *Red Route* (see page 111). Neither of the two routes, which were the subject of the Committee's patient consideration of the evidence, is wholly recognisable with anything that was actually built, but an important point is that both routes passed through Oxshott for reasons that have already been explained. Below the witness box sat the shorthand writer, impassively recording Counsels' questions and the witnesses' replies. The Committees usually rose at 4 pm, the shorthand notes were reduced to a transcript of the proceedings some hours later, and copies – each copy was produced simultaneously by dictation from the master copy – had to be delivered to the parties by 9 am the following morning. It was only when all the key players on a particular side of the argument had read the evidence that an informal partisan conference could be held around 10 am, in order to prepare for a Committee sitting at 11 am; thus all this work on processing the evidence was done overnight.

---

1 *The Graphic*, 20 July 1889; quoted in *Witnesses before Parliament: a guide to the Database of Witnesses in Committees on Opposed Private Bills 1771-1917; House of Lords Record Office Memorandum No 85.*

The process of giving and recording evidence was considered very important: as one Parliamentary agent said in 1862, the evidence in writing was needed, first:

> … to enable the Solicitor for the Bill to review the evidence which is given day by day in order to enable him to get up the evidence which he shall call in support of the Bill; and then, as it regards the opponents, to enable the Solicitor for the parties opposing the Bill to direct his case as to the evidence which he shall call in answer to that which has been given for the promoters, or to give instructions to Counsel for the cross-examination or re-examination of a witness whose evidence may have been … [already given].[2]

Counsel would stand before the witness, who would be alternately confident, when examined by one friendly to his interest, but more guarded when clever cross-examining Counsel contrived to ensure that witnesses had to perform mental headstands, some of a character we have already observed, to maintain a point of view which even a schoolboy could see was contrived to be adapted to the witness's personal interest. When necessary the witness was provided with a long stick so that, for example if he were a landowner, he could indicate where his property lay. A succession of witnesses was asked whether he thought the *Blue* or the *Red* route would give 'the best railway accommodation' to the districts served by the competing lines: how much ice this cut with the Select Committee in this case is not recorded but the proceedings must have had an influence on the promoters of the competing schemes because of the compromise which emerged.

Strengths and weaknesses

The task which confronted the legal teams which represented the two Bills was to expose the weaknesses of the other side's position, while limiting any damage which might be done by having their own exposed: at the same time the strengths of their own case had to be demonstrated with what was hoped to be blinding clarity, while exposing the shallowness, so they hoped, of the opposition's claimed strengths. We have already heard how John Clutton, a veteran of a huge number of appearances in front of Select Committees, held the process in disdain, but it was the way things were: the very Parliament which was to decide the fates of the Bills lived and breathed by debate, by points scored, by rhetoric, by fine speeches: in Parliament substance gave way to performance – everything depended on the lawyers. The choice of witnesses to bring in support

10.3 Some witnesses, imbued with a familiarity of Railway Bills garnered from many years' professional work, gave their evidence with confidence and clarity. (A sketch by Harry Furniss (1854-1925) reproduced in The Graphic, *20 July 1889, and House of Lords Record Office memorandum No 85.)*

was the lawyers', a choice that had to be tempered to a judgment on whether they might quail under cross-examination. The whole plan depended on a scrutiny by each legal team of the strengths and weaknesses of their clients' case. We should do the same: on page 91 is such a statement. In compiling this retrospective statement – no contemporary version of it has been traced – all those strengths and weaknesses that are common to both schemes have been omitted because they do not have any impact on the adversarial analysis.

As can be seen, the longer list of the strengths of the *Blue Route* is attended by a long list of weaknesses, many of which have already been discussed: the ill-defined interface with the District Railway at Fulham and the financial weakness of that company; the alleged damage to the Commons at Wimbledon and Putney – damage which was ultimately conceded to be nugatory; and most recently we have examined the neglect of Cobham. The fact that none of the promoters

---

[2] Witnesses before Parliament: *a guide to the Database of Witnesses in Committees on Opposed Private Bills 1771-1917;* House of Lords Record Office Memorandum No 85, *p 10.*

10.4 *Lord Onslow's* Blue Route *involved heavy engineering costs in the London Road area; this view looking east, c1884, shows the deep cutting and the viaduct carrying Cross Lanes over the railway.*

was a railwayman, nor an experienced entrepreneur has been exposed in the preceding pages. Also, Onslow and his friends, although ground-breaking in their initiative, have already shown themselves to be somewhat amateurish, and more examples of this will be revealed in this chapter: amateurs or not, what must be said is that Onslow had taken on the power of the LSWR monopoly, and if he was to measure his own success, as he was entitled to do, by succeeding in bringing the railway to his farm in Clandon, then his accomplishment is established: that he succeeded in doing this while risking none of his own capital, save for the costs of the Bill, while at the same time banking a considerable sum for the sale of land to LSWR and pocketing the increment to his land holdings, specially round Guildford, then the final outcome was for Onslow a triumph. This can be asserted even though the Fulham to Kingston and Surbiton railway was never built.

Guildford, Kingston and London Railway – Lord Onslow's *Blue Route*

Strengths

- A brilliant conception offering the possibility of a new strategic route into central London
- Strong corporate support from the towns of Kingston, Surbiton and Guildford
- Provided a second station for Guildford
- Strong support from every landowner along the route bar one
- Would open up large tracts of land around Kingston and Putney for development: the experience of the District Railway, with their earlier extensions to Hammersmith and Ealing augured well in this respect
- Opened up access to Wimbledon Common and Richmond Park to Londoners

Weaknesses

- The strategic conception blurred by uneconomic spurs and branches, with too many junctions
- Promoters were neither railwaymen nor experienced entrepreneurs; they had no knowledge of railway economics or management
- Ill-defined interface with District Railway; through trains from *Guildford* to *Mansion House* not feasible without further expenditure by the impoverished District Railway
- No estimates of traffic receipts made
- At £41,000 per mile, the construction costs were very high
- No certainty that the capital requirement could be met in the market
- District Railway financially unstable
- No station in Cobham
- The operational restraints at the London end were incompatible with a rural railway, ie high volumes at one end, low at the other

The LSWR's *Red Route*

Strengths

- Low budget (£17,700 per mile)
- Promoter established, successful and financially robust railway company
- Gave Cobham a conveniently-sited station
- No difficult engineering

Weaknesses

- By including a convenient station for Cobham, the route was made more tortuous, increasing journey times
- No strategic addition to the railway network – simply an infilling scheme
- No new competition
- No new station for Guildford
- No substantive third party support

The reader may recall the strength of the economic analysis that was made and exposed to the Select Committee considering the original London & Southampton Railway Bill. One might have imagined nearly 50 years later, and with a nascent accountancy profession emerging, the process would have become more refined: not a bit of it. Not a scrap of evidence was produced to begin to demonstrate any economic return or any trace of viability of the *Blue Route* and, moreover there is no explanation of why this was so. We might suspect that it was because it was feared that to give traffic estimates for the outer section beyond Surbiton that would be high enough to give a return to shareholders would expose the promoters to ridicule. The New Line itself was a dubious economic venture, which even though cheaper to build, was much more likely to be a drain on LSWR resources than a contributor to them. The serious economic impact was on land values, but as we shall see, the growth in the population served by the New Line was very slow; it took a combination of electrification and a favourable climate for residential development around London to cause traffic levels to rise but that was almost half a century in the future.

Many members of the Provisional Committee of the Guildford, Kingston and London Railway were called to give evidence. A complete list of the committee's 26 members follows:

The Earl of Lovelace#*	The Mayor of Guildford*	W Standford Hodgson Esq
The Earl of Onslow#*	The Mayor of Kingston*	C Durant Hodgson Esq
Lord Foley	Colonel Parratt	T Farmer Hall Esq
Sir Walter Farquhar Bart #*	Colonel Boileau	James Paine Esq
Charles Combe Esq#*	J L Du Plat Taylor Esq	F L Soames Esq
Frederick L Keays Esq#*	The Chairman of the Surbiton	Dr Stedman*
T Lucas Esq	Improvement Commissioners*	Revd Dr Henry Richards, DD*
Henry Farquhar Esq		Arthur Bowles Esq
The Revd Prebendary Mount		E Boycott Jenkins Esq
		J A Radcliffe Esq*
		G Gouldsmith Esq

# Denotes Promoter of Guildford, Kingston and London Railway Bill.
* Denotes evidence given to the Select Committee considering the Guildford, Kingston and London Railway Bill, May 1881.

Members of the Provisional Committee are made to look foolish

Sir Walter Farquhar was one of those landowner promoters who revealed by his evidence that he was hopelessly ignorant of railway economics. He made himself look foolish, when having asserted his confidence 'that the line will make money' he had to concede that he had no idea of the population which the railway was serving. He just took it 'to be axiomatic that a line into London from our county would have traffic *ex necessitate*'. This was nothing more than a further promulgation of the 'railway for every village' argument, which the LSWR was determined to avoid for pretty sound economic reasons.

Sir Walter does not deserve to be singled out as the only ignorant amateur: of the others, there were plenty who gave illustration to the lack of financial appraisal and LSWR's Counsel exposed them with relish: consider this sequence of Charles Combe under cross-examination:

Counsel: Have you and the other promoters taken any pains to get information as to whether the line is likely to pay?
Combe: I have not.
Counsel: Do you know anyone who has?
Combe: I do not.
Counsel: You are a member of the Provisional Committee. You will have some day to frame a prospectus – upon what basis are you going to ask the public to find the money for the line?
Combe: I shall not frame any prospectus.
Counsel: You will not undertake to tell the public that it will pay?
Combe: No.[3]

---

[3] Evidence of Charles Combe to the Select Committee considering the Guildford, Kingston and London Railway Bill, May 1881.

If this were a work of fiction and not history, the above exchange might not survive the editor's sceptical review: here was a serious point of weakness; Combe's reply gives vivid colour to the charge of amateurism, which was endemic among the Promoters and their friends.

Edward Upperton had been Mayor of Guildford five times: he was a strong supporter of the *Blue Route*, and so 'decidedly was the population of Guildford'. He was a farmer (with a tenancy from Onslow) and also a member of the Provisional Committee. He faired no better than Combe in the witness box as this exchange shows:

Counsel: Have you taken the trouble to find out where the traffic is to come from on this line that will make it pay?
Upperton: No.
Counsel: Have you any idea of the population between Guildford and the next important place along the line, Surbiton.
Upperton: No; I have not the least [idea].[4]

Cross-examining Counsel could not restrain himself from intoning: 'If someone [else] finds the money to pay for this expensive line, you will be very glad to have it?'

Another member of the Provisional Committee was Dr Arthur Stedman, a GP from Great Bookham, who considered it a 'very beautiful neighbourhood, one of the best in Surrey, and very suitable for residential purposes'. His instinct – he had taken no steps to ascertain the likely traffic – was that 'a line of this kind will encourage building in the neighbourhood and that will make traffic'.[5]

No viability tests

The essential point was how much in operating losses would be racked up before the incremental traffic arrived? In a more enlightened age, or with a more professional approach, some respectable accountant would have been engaged to opine, independently, on all the prospective traffic forecasts and operating costs, which should have been a key part of the demonstration of viability: Onslow's lawyers failed to stop up this lacuna and the LSWR lawyers, and those of the other railway company petitioners against the Bill, made hay. It was a graphic example of the amateurism which characterised Onslow's scheme.

Denzil Onslow, the Guildford MP, was similarly, but more forgivably, ignorant about how many potential passengers lived between Guildford and Surbiton: to the question 'What traffic will there be between Guildford and Kingston?' the MP thought it was 'difficult to say in a time of agricultural depression' – and then in a remark which was almost Cluttonesque, he said the line 'would pass through what has been no doubt a large agricultural district – *what it is to be in the future we do not know* [author's italics]'.[6] He knew that there was a considerable amount of business in manure from London, but conceded that there would not be enough traffic at first to pay a dividend on a cost of £41,000 per mile 'but later with good management, it will pay a fair dividend'. This was the closest any witness came to averring any sort of viability and this from a gentleman who was not on the Provisional Committee and from whom there could be no reasonable expectation that he should have an opinion at all. Even Lord Onslow himself wasn't able to say how the money was to be raised: 'I have not given it my personal consideration but I have every confidence it will be' was his inadequate reply.

The question of what the traffic receipts might have been achieved by Onslow's *Blue Route* must be separated into the passenger and goods markets. Taking the market for passengers that already travelled to London, this would be merely substitution of the LSWR's existing traffic receipts, which is valid from Onslow's point of view. We can allow a good deal of substitution business from the LSWR's passengers who usually travelled from *Surbiton* (population 9,400 in 1881) and perhaps an even higher proportion from *Kingston* (34,000); and *London Road*, Guildford would no doubt have grabbed some business from the main station (population of Stoke 6,700). That much having been allowed, one must but remark on the great paucity of population that was available from the 'rustic simplicity' of the villages and hamlets between Surbiton and Guildford. The total population in 1881 of the parishes of Long Ditton, Claygate, Stoke D'Abernon (including the hamlet of Oxshott), the Horsleys, the Clandons and Merrow was nearly 6,000: if we add in

---

[4] Evidence of ET Upperton, to the same committee.
[5] Evidence of Dr Arthur Stedman to the same committee.
[6] Evidence of Denzil Onslow MP, to the same committee.

10.5 It was through Lord Onslow's intimate knowledge of how Guildford was growing that he proposed a second station at London Road in spite of the difficult engineering that had to be overcome: the LSWR agreed in the compromise; in this view of c1884, the Down platform of the station is visible through the arch together with deep cutting and the tight entry curve.

Cobham, in spite of its distance from a station on the Onslow line, we get to a total market for travel in the hamlets and villages, including women and children, of not much more than 8,000 souls. All this was exposed to the Select Committee, more with acclaim than apology: 'it is a great residential district, with a great many resident landowners', agreed Lord Lovelace, but there are in West Horsley and East Clandon 'mansions vacant for want of a railway':[7] there seemed to be a great reluctance when talking the market down, to attribute any causal effect on void properties to the severe agricultural depression affecting the district at the time; depression, it seemed to the landowners, was for 'want of railway accommodation'.

Lovelace had already agreed that a railway was necessary 'for communication between the districts for men who take part in public affairs': laudable though this activity was, aimed to make it sound as though we were dealing with an area teeming with population, Lovelace's local friends involved in public affairs could scarcely have made up a cricket team. He explained

that: 'The greater part of the rural population is clustered along the main road – one of the great roads to the west in the old coaching days, the Upper Portsmouth Road': with this statement was swept aside the proper Portsmouth Road and the claims of Ripley, Send and Ockham (population 2,400) to be served by a railway; this was a group of villages whose populations exceeded those of the Horsleys, the Clandons and Merrow combined. All this is very unconvincing as to the existence of a sufficient existing passenger market to support the *Blue Route* west of Surbiton.

There was, of course, the matter not just of the existing population with its 'rustic simplicity' but of the expansion of the passenger market – an expansion which would be driven by the coming of a new railway line – but this expansion was not a matter on which the choice of route was going to be a deciding factor: the stimulus of a railway to residential

---

[7] Evidence of Lord Lovelace to the same committee.

10.6 The cutting on the approach to London Road station, looking east c1884, with the Cross Lanes viaduct in the background.

development in an area which was already under the economic influence of London, and where land values were suffering from the agricultural depression, was going to happen anywhere, leaving aside the flood plains, where building land was made available: it was not about a *Red* or *Blue Route*; it was about whose money would be used to release the increment in land values. The LSWR had been saying for years: 'Not ours.' The prospect of the increment in land values was one on which the Hon Fitzalan Foley was quick to latch, for soon after the route was settled he bought large quantities of land that would be opened up by it. This is a subject for later, but for the present we may note that Fitzalan's elder brother, Lord Foley, gave no evidence to the Select Committee and no contemporary report of the brothers' attitude to either of the proposed railways has come to light. No prospectus for the railway was ever issued, so we cannot know how the weakness of the passenger market, and its dependence for any sort of economic volumes on future residential development would have been exposed to public view.

High traffic potential east of Surbiton

As to the passenger traffic east of Surbiton, the potential, when looked at from this distance was enormous. The empirical evidence of the fast success of the District's Ealing, Richmond and Hammersmith extensions to their inner London underground railway allows an easy extrapolation for its potential between Fulham and Surbiton, taking in east Kingston on the way: the need to respect the sacred ground of the commons does not cause one to recede from the generality of this, for there was plenty of non-common land available for development. Development took place here in the 20th century and would probably have happened the sooner if Onslow's railway from Surbiton to Fulham had existed. This part of the analysis shows how Surbiton was a key factor of the economic landscape: it was already a dormitory town for London; Onslow's railway would have been a vibrant influence to the connection of the town to London in the direction of Putney, but only Forbes (and the dominant landowner, HRH Duke of Cambridge) could see this

95

with prismatic clarity, and its potential impact on the feasibility of the railway through the attraction of prodigious passenger numbers was never written down: it was, of course, in the interests of the LSWR to conceal it, so the fact that the point never came before the Select Committee was a serious error on the part of the Onslow legal team.

We have, then, from the above a scenario in which east of Surbiton the passenger market was potentially strong, while to the west towards Guildford the passenger numbers were small with a potential for growth which paled when compared with that market which Forbes had his eye on for the District Railway. We must now consider the goods market.

The goods market

The route, which any new railway might take from Surbiton to Guildford, would supply the economic benefits to the farms that lay within 'horse and cart' distance from a goods yard that was built on it. The Onslow legal team majored on the benefits to farming that their railway would bring, not realising that to any objective analysis, the undeniable benefits would flow to whoever was close to the railhead: if one farm gained another might lose; the benefits to farming of a new railway were very great specially in the teeth of the depression, but it was a zero sum comparative analysis – the benefits would flow to someone whatever the route. Notwithstanding this the Onslow legal team hammered away on the benefits to farmers and as a result, they got into a tangle, which the LSWR cross-examining Counsel was able to exploit.

Onslow was confident that the agricultural case for his railway was robust: if the LSWR had not intervened with their own scheme it would have been more convincing, in spite of its flaws. If only a railway were available, thought Onslow, he would be able to send his farm produce, now tending towards dairy products since the collapse of grain prices, into the London markets directly instead of sending it via *Guildford*. Although Onslow genuinely believed that there was an advantage to him here, his notion was exposed by the LSWR as an absurdity: did Onslow really suppose that his milk and his cattle would meander into London via Putney and then the District's underground railway system, with a little dock loading facility at *Mansion House* where a horse and cart could deliver to the brokers' doorsteps? And what about manure, which was a major import to

the farms by tonnage: 'Is your Lordship not aware that they cannot take it – manure is prohibited from being carried on the underground lines?' Onslow conceded that he did not know if there was any existing cattle traffic on the underground: there certainly wasn't and a serious flaw in his case was being exposed. Onslow explained that the goods traffic coming from London was more than just coal and manure: there was 'wine and things of that kind' and processed cattle food. Counsel for the LSWR, not wanting to separate a man from his wine, even though one would imagine that one train-load per month would probably keep the whole district in surplus, persisted on the theme of where Onslow thought all these goods were going to be loaded. His trite answer 'at the depot' was exposed to mean Earls Court, which Counsel pointed out, was 'thickly populated with the best class of houses': 'Do you seriously think that the inhabitants of Earls Court would stand the establishment of a manure depot in their midst?' Onslow was in trouble; he was on the back foot, on the wrong wicket.

The Onslow team had brought in a whole succession of traders who said they wanted a goods facility on his line to London. William Williamson was a member of Guildford Town Council, an estate agent, upholsterer and antique dealer trading in the High Street, and with connections across the oceans in America, Australia and Africa. Every week he sent a van load of goods to the West End, and the scores of peers and MPs with whom he did business could 'more easily get to his showroom' on the *Blue Route*, but he was made to look very foolish when Counsel extracted from him his assumption that the District Railway would somehow offload a single van of antiques for his customers in Belgrave Square.

Onslow meanwhile persisted in the defence of his position which was beginning to border on the absurd: Counsel pointed out that everything which Onslow wanted his line via Fulham to do in relation to goods was at that moment being 'done by the LSWR via their Wharf at Nine Elms'. At this stage Onslow would have done better to have stopped digging for there was a huge void opening up before him – a void that might easily swallow up his bold plan. Instead, he embarked on a ludicrous denigration of Nine Elms as a location for a wharf: 'it is on the wrong side of the river'; 'it is not in the City' and 'it is inconvenient for goods to and from the Pool of London'. The LSWR had managed to expose what Forbes knew very well, but kept mute

10.7 The high engineering costs of taking a railway through Oxshott was common to both Lord Onslow's and the LSWR's route; this view of the viaduct carrying Warren Lane looking east towards Claygate is from c1884; the Mole valley watershed is at this point: the approach to the station is at a gradient of 1:100 in each direction.

about: a riverside wharf integrated as was the LSWR's with access to the rail network was exactly the right place for a freight facility.

A confusion in relation to the different markets being served

The whole question of a railway from *Guildford* to *Mansion House* can now be seen as being schizophrenic: east of Surbiton it was about people, while west of Surbiton it was about agricultural goods, coal and Lord Onslow's wine. If there was only one reason why Onslow was bound to compromise with the LSWR, here was it: the Guildford, Kingston and London Railway was in a muddle about its markets. Between *Surbiton* and *Fulham*, and on to *Mansion House*, the market which would be created by the railway was for mass-transit of workers into London: between *Surbiton* and *Guildford* the traffic would be more languid; it would be a mixed traffic line with small but growing passenger levels as low-density development took

place; but the goods market was never going to be a money-spinner or, unlike the commuter market, offer any growth. Not only did the Guildford, Kingston and London Railway suffer from this conceptual muddle, the promoters clung to the myth that they were going to offer passengers a through route from *Guildford* to *Mansion House*: the LSWR lawyers exposed the impossibility of this because access the Inner Circle would be denied. Even if this problem were to be overcome – if Forbes were the operator he would overcome it – there was no way in which fast or semi-fast trains could be run from *Guildford* on a dual track to be shared with stopping trains: this was the experience of the LSWR who were at the time quadrupling their tracks from Hampton Court Junction to *Waterloo*.

The high costs of the *Blue Route*

The estimates, to include construction costs and land, to build the *Blue Route* presented to Parliament totalled

£1.3m consisting of the following elements:

	£000s
Permanent way including junctions and sidings	225
Cuttings and embankments	144
Tunnel under Wimbledon Common	119
Bridge over Thames	58
Other bridges	68
Temporary works	51
Culverts and drains	17
	682
Stations	123
Land	495
	1,300

The estimates included a general contingency on the works costs of 10 per cent but some judges thought the line could not be built for £1.3m; in any event the parliamentary costs, which would have been heavy, were not included. The Guildford, Kingston and London Railway Bill proposed a share capital of £1.3m plus borrowing powers of £430,000, the total of which would have been insufficient to meet the £2m that one witness thought the cost of the whole enterprise would be, to include over-runs. Whatever the railway might have cost it was plainly going to be a large sum, even in 1881 £s. The expenditure actually incurred in the construction of the 76½-mile London & Southampton Railway nearly 50 years earlier and before steam shovels were available, amounted to 'only' £1.55m: there was patently something exceptional about the *Blue Route* estimates.

At £1.3m the average cost for the 31½ miles was £41,000 per mile, compared with about half that for the total costs incurred on the Southampton railway in the £s of 50 years earlier. The costs per mile of Onslow's railway were sharply different for the Surbiton to Fulham section (£81,000) than they were for the country end (£29,000). The bridge over the Thames and the tunnel under the common were obvious exceptional costs, but even by eliminating those items and their associated temporary works, the rest of the costs still averaged about £55,000 per mile, of which land amounted to £32,000, and the high cost of this reflected the higher value of urban land which would have had to have been acquired in Surbiton, Kingston and Putney. Thus, it was not so surprising that the extension of the line from Fulham across the Thames and through a tunnel on its way through Kingston to Surbiton should be expensive – the underground railways had cost horrendous sums per mile – but the point was that

no monetary estimate had been made of the revenues which such a quasi urban railway might achieve, analogously with the District extensions to Hammersmith, Ealing and Richmond: it was a point of considerable weakness to have exposed the high costs without a forecast of high revenues which might (we do not know whether they would) have supported them. Equally, it was obvious to all those who studied the figures that the economics of the line to Surbiton were quite different to the economics of the Surbiton to Guildford section, and from this reality came the compromise which recognised that the two parts of the line were different.

Too many 'stumps', branches and level junctions

We should not allow this exposure of the relative cheapness of the country end of Onslow's line to beguile us into thinking that the cost for the line and its branches between Surbiton and Guildford was good value: on the contrary, the average cost per mile of Onslow's railway west of Surbiton was £29,000, which was 66 per cent more than the LSWR estimates, which were just over £17,000 per mile. The LSWR was very experienced at procuring engineering work at market prices, but the Onslow team would have found it difficult to resist the soft prices that their own contractor/collaborator had put into the estimates. There were, however, more important factors that contributed to the very high cost. The *Blue Route* came in for much criticism at the Select Committee for its excessive number of junctions and branches. Considerable damage was done to the *Blue Route* case by the evidence of J P Knight, the General Manager of the LB&SCR. The junctions with other railway companies' lines, at Guildford and Leatherhead, were all to be built on the level, which would introduce conflicting train movements, some of which would have a very disrupting effect on the existing traffic including 'special trains [that] are run for the Queen going to Osborne and Admiralty trains'.[8] The excessive number of junctions, all on the level with their huge potential for conflicting train movements, was a serious weakness that was eloquently exposed to the Select Committee.

---

[8] Evidence of J P Knight, General Manager of LB&SCR, to the same committee.

10.8 This early 20th-century photograph shows a barge being manoeuvred on the Wey Navigation, with the viaduct that connects the New Line to the main line at Guildford in the background: the LSWR's preferred route into Guildford would have joined the main line further to the north.

A former railway manager witness was vitriolic in his criticism of what he called the 'stumps'[9] or branches: here the LSWR legal team had alighted on a serious weakness; cross-examining Counsel had great fun at Sir Walter Farquhar's expense over the branch line on the *Blue Route* to Great Bookham (he lived at Polesden Lacey): with his best sense of theatre, Counsel, taking care to ensure that everyone could hear, suggested that 'It looks like a branch to serve your house': it was a cruel, stinging quip. It was no use protesting that Counsel had exaggerated; the hunter had found his quarry: not only were the branches expensive, with their junctions and stations, but also their low revenue potential was pitiful and had been exposed like a museum exhibit.

The high cost of cuttings and land for Onslow's railway

We have already heard how the *Blue Route* involved significant excavation of cuttings as it took its hilly route from Surbiton through Claygate (instead of going up the Rythe Valley from Hampton Court Junction) as did both the *Red Route* and the New Line; naturally there was a price to pay for this; the estimated cost of the earthworks on the *Blue Route* west of Surbiton were nearly £2,500 per mile higher than the New Line. (Both the *Blue Route* and the New Line estimates include the heavy costs of earthworks near Oxshott and London Road stations.)

There was however another more significant reason why the costs per mile of the *Blue Route* were very high: it was a landowners' line and it seems they were being very generous with themselves over the amount to be paid for their land. East of Surbiton the *Blue Route* land was to cost on average £1,451 per acre, while west of Surbiton it was £973. The total estimated cost of land west of Surbiton, where the biggest landowners were Onslow, Lovelace, the Crown and Phillips, was an astonishing £258,000. While some of the land in Guildford would have had buildings requiring demolition, much the greater part of the land was farmland which, as we have already heard, was fetching as little as £12 an acre in the agricultural depression: it is impossible to escape the conclusion that Onslow and the other promoters were, in the modern vernacular, 'taking the Mickey'. The LSWR estimate for the cost of land for the New Line was £230 per acre: less than a quarter of the generous amounts the landowners proposed to pay themselves.

---

[9] Evidence of S J Mason to the same committee.

The Promoters did themselves no favours by their opportunism in their extravagant land pricing: the *Blue Route* estimates came under the professional scrutiny of railwaymen; and it was not just the LSWR: Onslow's brave initiative had brought forth Petitions of objection from the SER, the LB&SCR and the GWR all of whose interests were affected at the interface of junctions with their railway systems, and if the truth were told none of those railway companies, any more than the LSWR, were too keen on a new operator or the outward expansion of the District Railway.

The high cost of Onslow's railway west of Surbiton

The *Blue Route* received a particular mauling from one witness on account of the costs of the line: not, be it noted, the costs of the Fulham to Surbiton section – an experienced railwayman could see that the additional costs might be supported by a material traffic generation, albeit not specified – but the costs of the section west of Surbiton, combined with the expected paucity of traffic which it might generate. This witness had been called in support of the LB&SCR's Petition against the Guildford, Kingston and London Railway Bill and great damage he did to it. He thought it was 'absurd to suppose that the line … could pay' when it was to cost £41,000 per mile. To do so, the witness calculated that the line would have to earn £5,300 per mile per annum: he set about demonstrating the absurdity of the line making anything like this level of profit by quoting from the Board of Trade returns for all the railways that operated out of London south of the Thames. By combining them (LSWR, LB&SCR, SER and the LC&DR) including both goods and passenger traffic, he computed that their combined earnings per annum were 'a little less than £5,000 per mile'. This comparison, which showed that the *Blue Route* would have to be more profitable than the whole railway network south of the Thames, in order to pay its way, was being generous to Onslow's scheme, explained the witness, because the network average had to carry the costs of the *Cannon Street* lines of the LC&DR and SER, which because of their metropolitan and suburban character, had been 'very expensive' to build.[10]

The fatal flaw, and a compromise is suggested

Onslow's team must have looked mortified as another thrust went home: the same witness demolished any remaining doubt that the Select Committee might have about goods on underground railways: 'the District Railway cannot compete with other railways for goods'. The damaging evidence became a cataract that no force could resist: having demolished Onslow's rationale for goods traffic, there was worse to come: in relation to his passenger market rationale the witness uncloaked the fatal flaw: if trains stopped all the way from *Guildford* to *Mansion House*, they would take all day; if they ran fast they would cut out from the market those who wanted a service between *Guildford* and *Surbiton*.[11]

In view of all that had been said, and written here, about the need for more competition in order to make the LSWR service better, there was a certain irony in the fact that it was the witness supporting the Petition of the LB&SCR, with whom the LSWR had a cosy 'no-competition understanding', that should have so undermined Onslow. It was the amateurish weaknesses of his scheme which were its undoing, even before the LSWR witnesses were called. The proceedings of the Select Committee were coming to their premature end. Sir Edmund Beckett QC, Counsel for the LSWR offered his witness this observation:

> … commercially, would it not be a great deal better if the company [Onslow's] were *bona fide* wanting to find the money and make a good line [from Fulham] to be without the Surbiton to Guildford bit?

'Yes' agreed the witness 'it is the piece of their line which could never pay': the tendon of the Achilles heel of Onslow's *Blue Route* had been severed; irretrievably. Nemesis had struck; from now on the possibility of a Fulham to Surbiton railway would have to be looked at independently of a new line from Surbiton to Guildford; the great burden of weaknesses that lay behind the Guildford, Kingston and London Railway Bill had overwhelmed the vision that characterised a noble attempt at a new strategic railway concept. The LSWR and their industry friends had killed the Bill: the cost to them, a railway they did not want and which 'could never pay', was the New Line from Surbiton to Guildford via Cobham – a euphemism for Guildford via Stoke D'Abernon!

---

10 *Ibid.*
11 *Ibid.*

Chapter 11: The New Line is born of a compromise

11.1 *The Select Committee that was hearing evidence on the Guildford, Kingston and London Railway Bill in May 1881 came to a sudden halt when a compromise was suggested; this is a modern view of the Palace of Westminster where the proceedings took place.*

The gladiators call a halt

The gladiatorial scene at the Select Committee continued its daily process: the combatants, Onslow and his friends on the one hand, and the LSWR on the other, were fighting for the death of the other's Bill, only one of which or neither of which could Parliament spare life – unless. Here the allusion to an ancient contest breaks down because this was a civilised affair and there was a third party intervention; to the great relief of many, but not to the satisfaction of all, good sense was allowed to take over and the duel was abated. The Onslow team had fired off all its artillery – the LSWR had not at this stage been examined on their Bill – but the counter-questioning of the LSWR and particularly their friends in the industry had done considerable damage to Onslow's not altogether well-planned defences. On of the 10th day the proceedings took an unexpected course from the start: no more evidence was offered and Sir Edmund Beckett QC, announced that negotiations were taking place, without making it plain between whom, which might result in a compromise proposal being put.

The previous day at the Select Committee had been a very bad one for Onslow, the faults in his scheme being

cruelly exposed to the light; it was a succession of witnesses from the railway industry who had uncovered its many lacunae. The objective assessment that the Surbiton to Guildford part of the line was 'the piece of their line which could never pay' was nearly fatal but it was not Onslow's Counsel who announced that negotiations were taking place. Sir Edmund Beckett was leading Counsel for the LSWR (and it may be noted, also for the petitions against the Guildford, Kingston and London Railway Bill by the LB&SCR and the West London Extension Railway); it was he who stood up first to announce that peace talks were in progress. Was it Onslow or the LSWR that was the first to call on the other to suggest a deal?

Why? it should be asked did Counsel for the LSWR suggest to the witness on the previous day that there was commercial sense in separating the Surbiton to Guildford portion of the railway from the Fulham to Surbiton piece? This was the moment when the LSWR had conceded that they could accommodate a scenario in which the Fulham to Surbiton part of the line should not be put to death. Why was the announcement coming from the LSWR side – why not from Onslow's? Suppose the day before his bad day Onslow had invited the Chairman of the LSWR, the Hon Ralph

H Dutton (Chairman 1875-92), to attend on him at the House of Lords and said over a cup of tea: 'Why don't we stop fighting each other and split the line: you do the bit from Guildford to Surbiton and we will do the bit from there to Fulham.' If such an event had happened the LSWR would have sensed a plea for mercy from a man who knew he was doomed. This scenario has probably no credibility, except for the part that Onslow knew that he was on the ropes. If such a conversation had taken place it is more likely that Dutton would have suggested that Onslow should 'return to Clandon Park', using whatever turn of phrase was in common currency in the tea-room of the House of Lords.

This had been the response of the board of the LSWR even before the Parliamentary fight had begun. In a letter of 11 March 1881 the Solicitors acting for unspecified 'landowners' had suggested an arrangement between the promoters of the Guildford, Kingston and London Railway Bill 'so as to avoid a parliamentary contest'. This was repeated in a letter of 6 April, with which was enclosed a letter from the secretary of the Guildford, Kingston and London Railway 'on the subject of the proposed arrangements for avoiding of a parliamentary contest' – a proposal rejected by the board who, sensing the possible need for nimbleness, appointed the Chairman and three others as a committee to watch the Bill 'with full powers to act in an emergency'.[1] If the LSWR were winning the argument in Committee, why should they compromise when they had refused to do so before the fight started? In all the circumstances, it seems unlikely that the approach started from the LSWR side: none of their behaviour, before, at the time or later was at all consistent with their leaning over backwards to save the Fulham line. The compromise probably came about by an intervention by Forbes of the District Railway, who was about to become a player in the story – centre-stage.

The District Railway is now a player

On that first morning that the Select Committee was told that negotiations had already taken place Sir Edmund Beckett said that the parties 'had pretty well arranged between themselves what portion of each line should be taken': 'the difficulty', he said, was that their were 'some independent landowners who were opposing parts of each scheme'. It would be better, thought Sir Edmund, for there to be a short adjournment.

On this basis the parties could come back to the Select Committee having sorted out exactly what lines were to be built by whom in 'a kind of jointly-promoted line', and if they had not been able to reach an accord with any landowners who still held out against either railway, 'they would be entitled to be heard'.

In concurring with all this, it was Onslow's Counsel, Bidder QC, who blew the gaff on the role of Forbes: 'we understand', he said, 'that there have been negotiations between the two companies' – the LSWR and the District – 'and a certain proposal' which had been made by those companies, 'has been laid before us as a joint proposal' of theirs. Bidder, recognising that half a loaf was better than no bread, acknowledged that:

> It is a proposal that we have entertained very favourably, and, subject to its receiving the sanction of [this] Committee is one that when it is put into shape will probably meet with the approval of all parties: and under those circumstances I agree … that we should be allowed a reasonable time for adjournment in order that the matter may, as I think it will, take a definite shape, and come before you for approval of its terms.[2]

So, there is no room for doubt that there had been an intervention, almost certainly initiated by Forbes, which was to save the day for Onslow's Bill. One thing had changed, and this was probably greatly to the relief of Onslow: the District Railway had come out of the closet and were now to be, explicitly, one of the principals behind the Fulham to Surbiton railway. This raises the question about the veracity of Forbes' evidence, given only three days earlier be it noted, when he had averred that he was 'neither directly nor indirectly' involved in the promotion of the Guildford, Kingston and London Railway Bill: it would be ungallant to be accusatory. We know from other evidence what others thought about him and the attitude of the District Railway. In his history of the LSWR, which was published a year later in 1882, and written with a railway industry insight, Sam Fay saw nothing to doubt about Forbes' intentions. Since the accession to the Chairmanship of the LSWR by the Hon

---

[1] Minutes of meeting of court of directors, LSWR, April and May 1881. NA RAIL 411/7.
[2] Bidder QC, quoted in the minutes of the Select Committee hearing the Guildford, Kingston and London Railway Bill, May 1881.

11.2 Nightingale Road, Guildford was laid out before the New Line was conceived: although the railway ran in a cutting at the bottom of the gardens, the occupants of these houses would have found London Road *station very convenient.*

Ralph Dutton, Fay tells us, the greater part of its affairs round London had consisted of projects for improving access to *Waterloo* and 'contests and arrangements with the District Railway', who, 'tired of burrowing like a mole in the bowels of the great city, cast their eyes enviously upon the fair and rich traffic district of the LSWR suburban system'. This was an allusion to the District Railway's extensions to Hammersmith, Ealing and Richmond, but says Fay, in 1881, an onslaught was made upon a new quarter of the LSWR's territory.

> A company [Onslow's] closely in league with the District, was formed for the purpose of carrying a line from Guildford through Kingston to Fulham. ... As the

> LSWR opposition, assisted by the Wimbledon Common Conservators [whose opposition had been eliminated] was unable to stay the progress of the Bill, an arrangement was made with the promoters ....[3]

Fay makes the whole project sound like a Forbes initiative (the District Railway did nothing without Forbes being at its heart) from the beginning: if this was true then he was particularly lucky in having Onslow for a partner to give him cover and if Fay was right then Forbes was a perjurer. Not being a railwayman, Onslow's role in the action may have been downplayed by Fay, who was very close to the LSWR local action at the time: for some nine years after he had started working for the LSWR he worked on the railway in Kingston. What Fay has to say on the subject cannot, therefore, be lightly averted, but his relatively junior position at the time probably exposed him to the received industry wisdom and gossip rather than the ear of Forbes, or the Chairman or General Manager of the LSWR. The relationship between Onslow and Forbes, and quite when it started, remains obscure: if Forbes was in the scheme from the beginning, as Fay would have it, why should he go on oath to deny it? The unanswered questions are a canvas on which Forbes' known devious mind mingled in its mists of obfuscation and dissemblance overlaid with optimism.

The landowner objectors do not like it

We must return to the landowner objectors (there were minor ones on the Leatherhead branch in addition to Phillips at Stoke D'Abernon) to whom all of this no doubt came out of the blue. Counsel for Phillips was alert, however: he wanted to ensure that the line was to go through Church Cobham and Street Cobham and not through Stoke D'Abernon. An adjournment was granted and when the Select Committee reconvened two days later the parties had to concede that they had not been able to tie up the loose ends, least of all Phillips' objection, which was becoming the central issue. The problem now was whether further delay would cause the Bills to be lost to parliamentary procedure: the last day for a Second Reading in the House of Lords loomed. There was plainly a serious risk that all the effort and money that had been expended to date – the dimension of it would have had a chilling effect on those who stood to have to write it off – might be wasted.

---

[3] *A Royal Road*: Sam Fay (1882).

11.3 Christ Church, Waterden Road, consecrated in 1874 to serve the expanding area of Guildford before the New Line and the station at London Road was built; this view, taken before the completion of the tower, is from c1885 after which the parish expanded further.

The Philip Hutchinson collection

Counsel for all those parties that were not part of the negotiations naturally felt at risk and not caring 'whose fault it is – whether the LSWR or the District Railway, or both of them, probably both' Phillips' advocate said: 'We have as serious interests to consider as the railway companies themselves. They have brought it upon themselves going on for six months fighting and now they ask us to swallow anything that they may give us.' If Counsel smelled a rat, a stitch up even, then events proved him right. A short adjournment was granted until the following Monday morning. Galvanised as they were by the spectre of the total collapse of their venture, Onslow's team and the LSWR's had to work together with Forbes' – the District Railway had been promoted in the space of a few days from an onlooker to a central figure in the scene – and reshuffle all their respective interests so that a united front could be shown, quickly.

Heads of Terms are agreed

Onslow's team arrived with the LSWR's at the Committee with the whole deal parcelled up with metaphorical string: it was Onslow's Counsel who announced to the Select Committee that the time allowed had sufficed to complete the arrangements. He proceeded to recite the Heads of Terms that had been settled between himself, the LSWR and the District Railway.

Phillips' Counsel wanted to be able to call the witnesses that the LSWR would have called to defend their decision to take their railway through Cobham – a decision which the LSWR had dumped in the negotiations of the last 48 hours – in order to pursue Phillips' objection to the Stoke D'Abernon route. This was the last chance for Phillips; there were no more cards to play and there were no trumps in his hand. With the Chairman's impatient words: 'The Committee is not prepared to hear any further evidence in support of Phillips' case.' The room was silenced with an unbending finality with which all residual opposition to what became the New Line collapsed. All that remained now was for Phillips to be bought off. As well as receiving over £8,000 for the land required by the railway and for the realignment of Blundel Lane east of where the station would be sited, Phillips procured road improvements and widening, which later gave space for a small development of shops to be built near *Stoke D'Abernon* station (Plough Lane at the time).[4] The best testament however to his residual strength was that as a consolation for the failure of the purpose of his Petition – to save Stoke D'Abernon from the railway – he obliged the LSWR to reimbursing him

---

[4] Terrier of the Surbiton, Guildford, Leatherhead branch railways, 1886. NA RAIL 411/406.

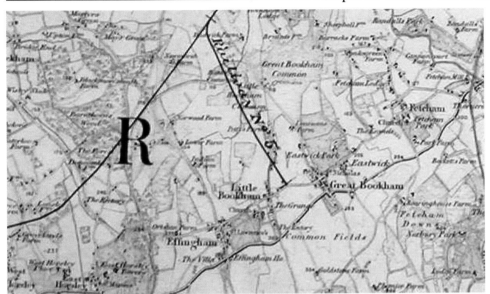

11.4 *Part of the map of Lord Onslow's* Blue Route *showing the 'stump' to Great Bookham.*

for his entire costs of the fight amounting to the considerable sum of £1,236.[5]

The Heads of Terms that had been thrashed out over the weekend and presented to the Select Committee were incorporated in the Act of Parliament that duly authorised the Fulham to Surbiton Railway. The legalities were organised such that the Guildford, Kingston and London Railway Bill became the Kingston and London Railway Act, 1881 while the New Line was authorised by the South Western Railway Act, 1881. The company, which was to operate the Fulham to Surbiton Railway, was known as the Fulham Company and the deal was that the District Railway and the LSWR would operate jointly its line as laid out in the Onslow plan. For its operational convenience the LSWR was authorised to be able to construct junctions with their existing railways at Norbiton and Putney.[6]

As to the west of Surbiton, this was to become a LSWR affair and Onslow abandoned everything to the company against which he had hoped to compete. The engineers drew up new plans for the New Line informed as they were by the evidence which had been given as to the strengths and weaknesses of the *Blue* and *Red Routes*: parts of each line were abandoned while the few parts which were common were retained (see map on page 111). Onslow gave up the expensive part of his line to be cut through the hills south of

Surbiton and through Claygate village: the Vicar of Holy Trinity and the Lord of the Manor, Lord Lovelace would be disappointed by this but the Vicar was not invited to the meeting and Lovelace, whose land at Horsley would be opened up, could see that if he did not give up this part of the *Blue Route*, he would have no line at all. It was much more sensible not to drive a railway through the Thames valley escarpment, but to go up the Rythe valley from Hampton Court Junction. Onslow also gave up his 'stumps' and branches, by which Sir Walter Farquhar of Polesden Lacey would not get the 'branch to [his] house'.

If Onslow was bending in the compromise that led to the New Line, then so was the LSWR: their deviation to Cobham was ditched and the line would now make a straight shot at Clandon. This was a great achievement for Onslow, for apart from the failure to introduce competition for the LSWR, he had achieved what may have been his prime goal. His greatest triumph, perhaps, and the one which yielded him the most cash, was the decision by the LSWR to accept the additional

---

[5] Minutes of meeting of court of directors, LSWR, 21 July 1881. NA RAIL 411/7.

[6] Readers who wish to consider further the development of the story east of Surbiton should consult: *The London & South Western Railway Volume 2: Growth and Consolidation*, R A Williams, 1973, in chapters 1 and 2.

11.5 Frederick Gould, Mayor of Kingston-upon-Thames 1853 and 1880: a robust but ultimately unsuccessful champion of a new railway from Guildford to London via Kingston.

engineering cost of taking the railway through *London Road* station. This, as well as for Onslow in the cash he raised from the sale of development land, was a triumph for the future development of Guildford.

The branch of the *Blue Route* that gave a direct connection to the SER's Reading line north of Guildford was abandoned in order to keep the New Line budget down. Onslow's reason for this junction had been so that goods trains could be brought up from the direction of Reading – there had never been any talk of running through passenger trains from Reading – independently of the LSWR.

Instead of Onslow's stumps and branches, the LSWR's version of the integration of Leatherhead into the New Line was adopted; a branch through Bookham to Effingham Junction would connect that town. This gave operational flexibility to the LSWR and choice to the passenger, offering the latter alternatives to *Waterloo* via the LB&SCR, as well as giving *Guildford* its connection to *Leatherhead* for the first time. It should be noted that a deviation in the route of the Leatherhead branch to the position as built was allowed by Parliament later in 1881.

All things considered the design of the New Line went a long way towards eliminating the negative features of both the *Blue* and *Red Routes*, while retaining many of their combined strengths. The Fulham to Surbiton railway was never built, but it is beyond the scope of the present account to pursue that; we must simply say that the District Railway, true to form, found it impossible to raise its share of the capital required and the LSWR allowed the Act to run out of time, even after an extension was granted. If this was death by deliberate neglect it is a cause for regret, because leaving aside monopoly issues, the railway network would have been greatly incremented by Kingston being linked into the underground system. Instead, the LSWR built the railway across the Thames from Fulham to connect not Kingston but Wimbledon, giving us the familiar railway, which is now operated by the District Line of the London Underground system via *Putney, Wimbledon Park* and *Southfields*.

The *Surrey Comet* is not happy

In the meantime as the news of the negotiations was breaking the *Surrey Comet* did not like what was happening. The Editor had his reporter at the Select Committee hearing when the adjournment was sought, and he was also present in the House of Commons the same evening to hear the motion by which the Committee was given the power, if they saw fit, to consolidate the two Bills. 'We would rather the Bill did not pass at all, than that it should be passed embodying this compromise' wrote the Editor: 'Kingston ought at once to bestir itself' because it is not too late for 'a vigorous and well organised opposition, to defeat it'.[7] During the weekend adjournment when Onslow, Forbes and Dutton were in their huddle from which emerged the final compromise, *Surrey Comet* readers were being informed that 'the public have been deceived and duped', and the House of Commons 'ought to be fully informed of the altered condition of things' so that they the public may see how they 'have been sold'.[8]

---

[7] *Surrey Comet*: 28 May 1881.
[8] *Ibid.*

106

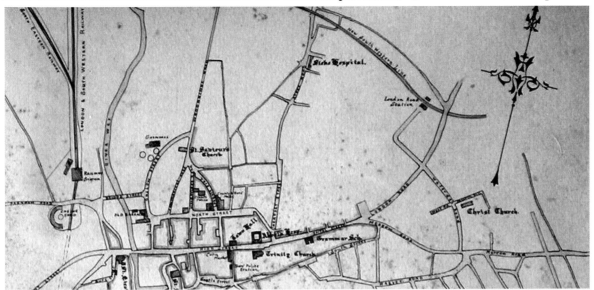

11.6 A plan of Guildford drawn shortly after the New Line opened in 1885; London Road station, Nightingale and Waterden Roads are shown, which together with the area around Christ Church had already been developed, but York Road, which connects the London and Stoke Roads is not yet laid out.

Anticipating this sell-out for Kingston, the *Surrey Comet* Editor wrote:

> It is incumbent upon the Mayor, who, in spite of all his astuteness has been outdone by the promoters, to call a public meeting at once and prepare a strong Petition against this consolidated Bill. … a consolidation which robs the new scheme of all its competitive elements, and leaves the public to the tender mercies of a still stronger monopoly.[9]

The LSWR retains its monopoly

As things turned out – with the Surbiton to Fulham railway never being built – there were even more important things to worry over, but it was the reinforcement of the LSWR monopoly that really rankled. When the details of the deal, which had been stitched up behind closed doors, became known and the conclusion reached that all hope of influencing events had been lost, the *Surrey Comet* said that 'these branch lines of the LSWR will only rivet the chains of the present monopoly more grievously upon the inhabitants' of the district through which they will pass.[10]

In his obsession with the loathing of monopoly the Editor of the *Surrey Comet* was no doubt reflecting

public opinion at the time, but there had not yet developed an acceptance that there was something naturally monopolistic about operating a railway at a local level: the notion of watchdogs, passenger councils and the other modern systematic methods of regulation of monopolies did not exist; competition was the only known antidote to the abuse of monopoly power. In due course, but unknown at the time, the railways in and around London were soon to be exposed to competition from electric tramways and motor buses in urban and suburban areas and from the latter in country districts, whilst the wealthy were buying motor cars. In the district we are considering and in others, the railways fought back with electrification. By the *Surrey Comet*'s logic it was better to have no railway at all in the area than one operated by the LSWR. This, the reader will recall, is exactly where the LSWR was coming from, but it seems that it was public opinion that was more flawed than was the LSWR's. Only six months earlier the *Surrey Comet* had been saying that it was a subject 'of annoyance, if not surprise', that a large portion 'of the most beautiful

---

[9] *Ibid.*
[10] *Surrey Comet*: 4 June 1881.

part of Surrey' should have been left 'almost totally unprovided with railway accommodation'. Within so short a distance from London it would be 'difficult to find an area richer in sylvan and scenic beauties, than that fair tract of diversified and picturesque country lying south-west of Surbiton and stretching through Cobham to Guildford' said the paper and yet 'Nothing has been done to develop' the area's 'capabilities as a residential district'.[11]

The *Surrey Comet* blinded itself to how the New Line had emerged and was caused to be built. Left to itself, the LSWR would have no more built the New Line than it would have built (or allowed to be built by others) a branch to Cobham off its main line. And yet the mighty organisation had been forced to go against its instincts and build the very railway, which was unlikely to pay a dividend for many years, if ever.

Lord Onslow goes public

The *Surrey Comet* was, of course, a Kingston paper and its reference to the New Line as a branch line 'riveting the chains of monopoly' was as much consideration that the inhabitants of Cobham received; inhabitants whose interests had been swept aside in favour of Stoke D'Abernon in spite of the unhappy Lord of the Manor, the Revd Phillips, whose objections to the railway going through his land had been ignominiously dismissed. If the *Surrey Comet* found no room for any joy in the outcome, Onslow felt he had some explaining to do, quickly. On the day after the seminal event in the history of the New Line had occurred – the deal that had been cut with the District Railway – Onslow addressed himself to his Guildford constituency through its newspaper, the *Surrey Advertiser*.

If his letter was triumphal, he was perhaps entitled to adopt such a tone: a 'main line' was to be built between Guildford and Surbiton he announced and in Guildford there was to be a new station (*London Road*). He took the opportunity to say that Guildford's original station was to be upgraded (to which the LSWR had agreed quite separately from the compromise). He specially noted that the finance for the railway 'was not at risk of the markets' for it would be built from LSWR's pool of resources. This must have been a notable escape for Onslow, for he was spared the almost inevitable embarrassment of the market giving his own scheme the financial cold

shoulder. Onslow conceded that there would be no new company to compete with the LSWR as far as Surbiton (which was the *Surrey Comet*'s gripe) but from there trains will go 'to all parts of the District system; booked tickets from *Guildford* would allow travel into the City with a second change at *South Kensington*': there was no more talk, it should be noted, of the fiction of through trains to *Mansion House*. As he wrote, Onslow had no more idea that the Fulham section of his railway would never be built, than anyone close to the scene could have had but he was genuinely pleased that the underground railway system was to be opened up to travellers from west Surrey, and an alternative to *Waterloo* offered.[12] Onslow felt no necessity to tell his audience that he had had to give up the fast train from Clandon that the Guildford, Kingston and London Railway was contracted to provide: at this stage in his battle this totem of his dominion was expendable.

If the arrangements suited Guildford people, it was a different matter in Kingston where the *Surrey Comet* Editor was like a dog with a bone, and special criticism was reserved for Onslow who had now befriended the LSWR. There had been on the part of those who had estates to open up for building purposes between Surbiton and Guildford nothing but 'a miserable disregard for anything but their own interests' and 'seem to have embraced the offers of the LSWR with eager gratitude, and have troubled themselves little or nothing about anything else' As to Onslow's relief about the finance, 'Until this amalgamation was thought of', said the Editor 'we never heard a word about the possibility of there being any difficulty in raising the capital.'[13]

Some of the criticisms of Onslow were fair, but it was not fair to criticise him for ceding control over the New Line to the LSWR: on the contrary, the evidence suggests that Onslow's Guildford, Kingston and London Railway Bill was heading somewhere for defeat; if not defeat in Parliament, then defeat in the market. Onslow's greatest achievement was to overcome the possibility that the New Line should not be built at all – why? Lord Onslow and his friends needled the LSWR into building the New Line by

---

[11] *Surrey Comet*: 27 November 1880.
[12] *Surrey Advertiser*: 4 June 1881.
[13] *Surrey Comet*: 11 June 1881.

11.7 Of the two routes that were promulgated for a railway from Surbiton to Guildford there was only one place of congruity where no compromise was necessary: Oxshott. Both sets of Promoters knew that a fair distance from Claremont had to be given, but not so much as to deny the Crown lands residential development opportunities: this view, from c1884, looking east towards Claygate shows the entrance to the large cutting that was required to penetrate Oxshott's ridge.

introducing the spectre of a pervasive virus, in the form the District Railway, which would eat its way into the profitable business that it had around Surbiton district. It was 19th century competition policy at work, and work it did.

The criticism that came from the direction of Kingston (Gould continued to simmer for some time) was divorced from some harsh realities. Onslow and his friends had been staring into the abyss of failure, where the cost of losing the fight would have been very heavy. There is an aphorism in currency today to describe a situation where a speculator recognises that he might lose everything, but may recover something by giving way to what he can not control: *Get what you can get*, seems to cover what Onslow was thinking when things were going badly in the Select Committee. There was, however, no balm from Kingston for Onslow. The Editor was returning to the old sore: in first offering Kingston a release from the worst evils of the LSWR monopoly – the effect of which the town had old scar-tissue – Onslow's biggest crime was to give the monopoly back to them.[14]

As it happened Kingston suffered further not through the absence of competition – it was the District Railway and LSWR jointly that was to operate the trains from Kingston into the underground system – but through the inability of the District to organise its share of the finance. There was no one more entitled to disappointment at the turn of events of 1881 than Frederick Gould, the Mayor of Kingston. When all the dust of events of the year had settled, Gould gave an account of how he had been 'sold down the river by the tripartite compromise'. In the final analysis the compromise which was cobbled together was a deal done by railwaymen – such was their muscle – and there was no place for the Mayor of Kingston to get in the way of these powerful interests. Even Onslow and Lovelace had had to bend with the wind that was blowing from the railway companies' boardrooms. Ultimately, Gould's efforts came to nothing: no one did more than him to try to recover Kingston's position in railway terms so lamentably relegated by earlier townsmen in 1830.

Onslow retains his land deal

There was one feature of the compromise that Gould did not expose: by the final clause of the Heads of Terms of the great compromise:

The LSWR [is to] take over and observe all agreements made by the promoters [of the Guildford, Kingston and London Railway Bill] … and any landowners upon the line between Ockshott [*sic*] and Guildford.[15]

The handsome deal that Onslow had done to sell his land in both Clandon and Guildford to the railway at very generous prices had been preserved. There was no secret that a deal had been done – the Select Committee was informed of it – but the terms were not exposed because the Chairman of the Committee did not wish to pursue the point.[16] Such was the scale of the cash that Onslow banked, it would have made a good story for those riven with envy. Shortly after the New Line opened Lord Onslow was appointed Governor of New Zealand, an office that evidently bore heavily on his wealth.[17] There is further evidence that can be cited of the recycling of Onslow's gains into the community, an example of which is the subsidy granted to the Onslow Village Association, years later, when the next Lord Onslow sold 646 acres 'at a tithe of their market value – receiving £57 per acre against the £200 per acre of its true value'.[18]

As the summer of 1881 rose to its zenith, and the minds of the contractors who would build the railway turned to mobilisation, it had found Lord Onslow and his friends with a certain sense of deliverance, and restored finances. Whether the Revd Phillips ever gained any composure over his defeat is unknown but for Mayor Gould there was no solace (and even more disappointment later as the District Railway failed to deliver). Forbes was still, no doubt, aglow at his prospective penetration to Surbiton, unknowing in his confidence that it would never be. As for the LSWR, they had at least the comfort of having kept any influence which Forbes was to have to the east of Surbiton and they had retained total operational independence west of it, and would now build the line they had not wanted (but be thankful years later that it provided a welcome relief line for the Woking route that it duplicated).

---

14 *Surrey Comet*: 28 May 1881.
15 Schedule to the Kingston and London Railway Act, 1881.
16 Evidence of Lord Onslow to the Select Committee considering the Guildford, Kingston and London Railway Bill, May 1881.
17 Private information.
18 E R Chamberlin, *Guildford*: 1970, p 45.

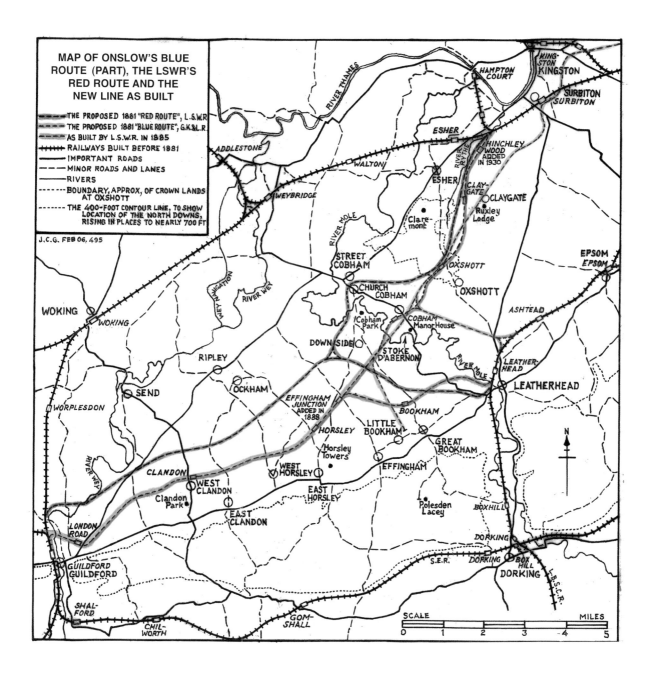

MAP OF ONSLOW'S BLUE
ROUTE (PART), THE LSWR'S
RED ROUTE AND THE
NEW LINE AS BUILT

THE PROPOSED 1881 "RED ROUTE", L.S.W.R.
THE PROPOSED 1881 "BLUE ROUTE", G.K.& L.R.
AS BUILT BY L.S.W.R. IN 1885
RAILWAYS BUILT BEFORE 1881
IMPORTANT ROADS
MINOR ROADS AND LANES
RIVERS
BOUNDARY, APPROX, OF CROWN LANDS
AT OXSHOTT
THE 400-FOOT CONTOUR LINE, TO SHOW
LOCATION OF THE NORTH DOWNS,
RISING IN PLACES TO NEARLY 700 FT

J.C.G. FEB 06, 495

111

The Mary Roome collection

This SR S15 Class 4-6-0 (Maunsell, based on a Urie design) heavy freight locomotive No E828 (built 1927, Eastleigh) hauls an excursion (the latest steam outing on the New Line) on the Down line out of Claygate on 9 November 1996.

This agricultural scene (2005), looking south-east across the New Line between Claygate and Oxshott came in for special mention by Professor Abercrombie in his Greater London Plan of 1944: 'no further development should be permitted' was his stern injunction.

Looking east across the New Line south of Claygate with Ruxley Towers in the background (2005).

An Up Guildford via Cobham train pulls into Claygate station with Loseberry Farm in the background (2005).

A fast Up Portsmouth service passes through Oxshott station (2005).

The sharp curve between Guildford and London Road stations (2004).

The sharp curve on the Up side of London Road station (2004).

A 4-VEP unit runs into Claygate on the Down line after a heavy snowfall in December 1981; these units were replaced in the mid 1980s by the then new Class 455 units.

The Michael Baldock collection

One of the first workings of the new Class 455 units runs into the Up platform at Effingham Junction (c1984).

The Michael Baldock collection

Sunset on the Slammers: one of the last slam door trains on a Down Portsmouth service passes between the backs of houses in Gordon Road, Claygate and Loseberry Farm, marking the limit of development controlled by the Metropolitan Green Belt (2005).

The view from Telegraph Hill, Hinchley Wood looking towards Roehampton, showing how the furthest reach of the builders in the 1930s was ultimately protected by the Metropolitan Green Belt (2005).

The ballast from the old track bed is removed during the works to lay continuous welded rail at Claygate (July 2005).

An Up Portsmouth – Waterloo train at Claygate; the rail ready for the continuous welded works can be seen between the Up rails (June 2005).

The jointed rails have been removed and are carried away in preparation for the works to lay continuous welded rail at Claygate (July 2005).

A Down Guildford via Epsom service comprising refurbished Class 455 units pulls into Horsley station (December 2005).

A Down Guildford via Cobham service makes an unusual manoeuvre: due to engineering works all services terminate at Surbiton and the trains reverse out of platform 1, fouling all lines until the Down line is rejoined west of Surbiton (4 March 2006).

A Down Guildford via Cobham service approaching Stokesheath, looking towards Claygate (March 2006).

The old jointed track is cut up in wagon lengths to be taken away prior to the laying of continuous welded rail at Claygate (July 2005).

The new track bed having been laid, the new sleepers are hoisted onto it in sets; part of the works prior to the laying of continuous welded rail at Claygate (July 2005).

A Class 455 unit with an Up service starts the descent from the summit of the New Line at Horsley (2005).

The railwayman's cottage at the former Sheath Crossing, Oxshott (2005).

A refurbished Class 455 unit at the Up platform at Clandon, 27 December 2005.

A Weymouth train comprising 'Wessex' stock passes through Clandon on 27 December 2005, having been diverted from the main line.

An Up Guildford via Cobham service comprising refurbished Class 455 units pulls into Claygate station (March 2006).

An Up Guildford via Cobham service at Oxshott with the viaduct carrying the Esher-Leatherhead Road in the background (March 2006).

Guildford via Cobham

Part 2: Impact

Chapter 12: The New Line comes to life

12.1 Looking Up the line from Cross Lanes bridge towards the entry to the London Road cutting; the farm land on either side of the cutting was developed after the railway came.

With powers sought by the Guildford, Kingston and London Railway Bill subsumed into the London South Western Railway Act, 1881 (which covered other minor LSWR interests) the Solicitors for the LSWR set about acquiring the necessary land for the New Line. With Onslow, Lovelace, the Crown and now with Phillips, the reluctant vendor, accounting for much the greatest part of the holdings, there were just a few other agricultural interests to secure between Oxshott and Hampton Court Junction and on the Leatherhead branch, while in Guildford there were some fragmentary holdings to acquire where settlement had already taken place in Stoke. Edward Ryde, LSWR's notable surveyor, travelled over the district conducting negotiations in relation to these land transactions, meeting surveyors acting for vendors, considering tenants' rights, negotiating prices and going to arbitration over the price of some Lovelace holdings.[1] Although Lord Onslow was able to assert the contractual rights granted in the compromise negotiations, the whole process took until 1885.

Lucas & Aird

The contractor for the New Line was Lucas & Aird, the hugely successful partnership of Sir John Aird (1833-

1911) and Charles Thomas Lucas (1820-1895); names that resonate among the who's who of great Victorian entrepreneurs.[2] The same partnership had been the contractors for the District Railway extension to Fulham, and it is almost certain that as a way of promoting their business and getting into a favourable contracting position it was Aird in conjunction with Wolfe Barry who made the introduction between Lord Onslow and James Forbes of the District Railway: it is

---

[1] Surrey History Centre, Woking: 1262 (series). Edward Ryde's remarkable journal records these activities including his attendance on LSWR during the Select Committee hearing of May 1881. Also of interest is his reference in 1884 to using the telephone to conduct business (1262/41).

[2] Lucas had been in partnership with his brother and their major works had included Covent Garden Opera House and the stations and hotels of Charing Cross, Cannon Street, Liverpool Street and York. In association with others they were contractors for the District Railway; for the East London Railway they tunnelled under the Thames. In 1870 the Lucas brothers took into partnership John Aird and the firm of Lucas & Aird was formed. Aird and his father had been large infrastructure contractors and started railway contracting in the 1860s and the firm became hugely successful and a massive employer of labour.

12.2 One of the giant steam shovels used during the construction of the New Line.

by no means absurd to suggest that the very idea of the Guildford, Kingston and London Railway may have been Aird's or a combination of him and Wolfe Barry. Certainly Lucas & Aird had a good deal more than an understanding with Onslow. A huge amount of behind the scenes support work for Onslow such as logistical evaluation, measurement and costings got them into the position that when the LSWR took over the project west of Surbiton, the extra-contractual obligation that was felt towards Lucas & Aird ensured that the firm was given the work to build the line but with the LSWR as their client. These contractors of the late Victorian age were very influential people, and Sir John Aird amassed a huge fortune; he will reappear in our story.

Engineering the route

When planning a route, railway engineers in general try to stay within a river basin for as long as its course is compatible with the destination. Broadly, this achieves the desired economies in line construction costs, for when a line has to penetrate a new river

system, leaving aside general undulations in the land, it often means that deep cuttings or tunnelling are the only way to avoid excessive gradients. As we have seen, when the great railway promoters drove their main line out of London to Woking in 1838, they had in mind a route through Basingstoke: Guildford and its direct route to Portsmouth was an afterthought. As a result, the route that the old line takes to Guildford is not the most direct: the New Line is one mile shorter. Operationally, however, the original, and what we can call the main line to Guildford, is quicker: the reason for this is that in the whole of its route from *Waterloo* to *Guildford* the main line is either in the Thames valley or following the Wey valley and consequently there are no gradients to remark on, it having been possible to maintain a level by the combination of cuttings and embankments. We can say with some certainty, therefore, that if the original main line had been driven to Guildford on its way to Southampton (as it might have been) it would not have taken the New Line route because the gradients would have been too severe for the steam locomotives of the period.

12.3 The south elevation of the seven-arch viaduct over the River Wey at Guildford under construction; a temporary railway from the Woodbridge Road depot can be seen on the line of the present footpath and footbridge.

Unlike the main line, which was laid out to economise on engineering costs and for fast running, the New Line, as we have seen, was laid out by reference to other factors, with the only concession to engineering costs being the LSWR's preference for taking the line up the Rythe valley from Hampton Court Junction instead of Onslow's route through the hills south of Surbiton. The extra engineering cost of taking the line tightly into London Road station was accepted because it was thought, and the notion was right, that extra passenger traffic would be generated by having a second station in Guildford compared with a more northerly and cheaper route. Having had both ends of the route set for their own reasons – one for cheapness, the other for traffic – and the decision to go through Oxshott being made effectively by the Crown's servant Clutton, the engineering difficulties that this presented just had to be accepted. These were a seven-arch viaduct over the Wey near Guildford station and gradients to cope with two summits on the line where the watersheds of the Mole and Wey valleys are crossed. These two tributaries of the Thames drain the land to the south of

the North Downs and by a curious geological feature, on their northerly route to join the Thames both rivers have found (or made) gaps in the ridge formed by the Downs. Somewhere or other any route from Surbiton to Guildford has to cross these rivers and the route that was given to the engineers was the one they had to work with. Although the main line has to cross these rivers too it does so at points where the tributaries are close to their confluences with the Thames, where the surrounding land is flat: the Mole near Esher and the Wey near Weybridge. By taking a route much closer to the North Downs the engineers were forced to tackle the problem of going over the watersheds into the Mole valley at Oxshott and the Wey valley at Horsley. Fortunately the heights involved were not of an order that required tunnelling but the engineering difficulties were overcome by the combination of some deep cuttings and steep gradients.

The corporate knowledge of Lucas & Aird was rich in railway engineering. The industry had had 50 years of experience by the 1880s of building tens of thousands of

12.4 *View of the Lucas & Aird depot at Woodbridge Road, Guildford looking west; Stag Hill, the site for the future cathedral and university, is in the centre of the picture.*

12.5 *The site of London Road station, looking Down towards Guildford main line; the formation of the Up platform can be seen on the right.*

12.6 Looking along the Down approach to London Road these bridges, which were probably for agricultural access, have been demolished subsequently; the men appear to be reinforcing the cutting sides with chalk boulders.

miles of railway and the 16½ miles of the New Line plus 4½ for the branch to Leatherhead was a small job to which all the experience and mechanical development within the industry could be applied. Having figured out where the spoil from the three deep cuttings could be employed in embankment construction, the contractors started work in March 1882 on the section from Hampton Court Junction to Horsley. The section from Guildford to Horsley was started in August 1882 and the branch to Leatherhead in September 1883. Depots for the storage of equipment and materials were established at Downside, Leatherhead and the Woodbridge Road area of Guildford. The superintendent for the works was C J Willis while Sir John Aird's son, Charles, assisted him. Evidently difficulty was experienced in finding foundations for the viaduct over the Wey, but the smaller viaduct over the Mole at Leatherhead presented fewer problems. At the peak of construction activity some 1,200 men were engaged, but an unusually high level of employment of mechanical plant – something that was to become normal in civil engineering work – achieved considerable economy in the number of navvies used. Aird had been involved in

the development of the steam navvy, which pre-dated the New Line. These monster machines were awesome in the dimension of their spoil grabs which were levered on huge jibs operated by cables the straining of which was accompanied by great belches of exhausted steam. Five such leviathans were engaged in the works, each one being capable of doing the work of 50 men when presented with a good face of earth to work. The use of mobile mechanical plant, including temporary railways, had become endemic in the civil engineering industry, for the only available alternative was a horse and cart and men with picks and shovels. Such was the overall scale of Lucas & Aird's operations that they were the owners of a fleet of over 100 locomotives for use on contracts, 12 of which were engaged in the New Line works hauling 100 ballast trucks loaded with spoil from the cuttings and hauling them to the 500 tipways where the embankments were fashioned. Later in the works these temporary trains would carry the sleepers, ballast, chairs, rails and fishplates for the assembly of the permanent way.

The five-arch viaduct over the Mole at Leatherhead necessitated a diversion of the river and once work got

133

12.7 The cutting on the Up approach to Clandon station.

under way on the railway the whole four-mile length of the branch was completed in not much over a year. The Leatherhead branch had the exceptional feature of a short tunnel, more of a wide bridge, under Bookham Common. This was not required because of topographical conditions but because of a requirement to mitigate as much as possible disturbance to the common, the point which Wolfe Barry had publicly emphasised. The station at Bookham was built on the edge of the common and the LSWR had been obliged to create roads across it to give access from Little and Great Bookham, which were some distance away but which grew to meet the railway. The early maps of some cartographers show the station name to be *Bookham & Effingham*, but although the station was relatively convenient for Effingham – more so than Effingham Junction when that station came to be built – the station was always called *Bookham*.

In previous times the role of the navvies who were engaged in building the railways of Britain had been etched, not without justification, with tales of debauched drunkenness. Much had been learned at this late stage in the building of railways, not just in terms of the employment of mobile plant but also in the management of very large numbers of itinerant men on construction sites and who were, while living in temporary accommodation, vulnerable to all the human weaknesses: the contractors of the New Line tolerated no drinking of alcohol on the job by the men. Although this did not eliminate accidents – the work was inherently dangerous – it kept them down to less shameful levels compared with the disgraceful and wanton sacrifice of life that had been endemic in the industry. The fatalities through accidents on the construction works of the New Line were about 10 but the incidence of non-fatal injuries was unreported; of those that were suffered they were in the greater part treated at the new Royal Surrey County Hospital at Farnham Road, Guildford, presumably after much distress on the long journey to reach it.

12.8 Boxgrove Road c1885 looking north towards London Road in the distance.

12.9 The same view in 2005, the bridge having been rebuilt.

12.10 Looking north up Merrow Lane with New Inn Lane, Burpham, to the left c1885; the road to Merrow Sidings is on the right before the bridge.

12.11 The same view in 2005.

The New Line opens but the Fulham to Surbiton line stumbles

Three years after the work had started the New Line was ready for the Board of Trade Inspector, Col W Yolland RE, to give sanction for opening. Together with LSWR officials he left *Waterloo* on a special train taking them down to Guildford via Cobham and back via Bookham and Leatherhead.[3] A general meeting of LSWR shareholders was held soon after this inspection trip and it was observed that Col Yolland had said he had 'never seen better work'. At the same meeting it was further remarked that the line 'would open up a beautiful country for building'.[4] The inspector being satisfied, it was announced that the line would open for passenger and goods traffic on 2 February 1885. In the four years since the Guildford, Kingston and London Railway Bill had been separated into two parts, the LSWR had kept its bargain with the New Line, but powers granted by the Kingston and London Railway Act, by which the Fulham to Kingston line was to be built as a joint venture between the LSWR and the District Railway had not been exercised. The project was in the final year before its ultimate collapse brought about by the expiry of its parliamentary powers later in 1885 – an event accompanied by much hand wringing in Kingston, causing the Editor of the *Surrey Comet* to write:

> Whether [the LSWR], who became masters of the situation, ever had any real intention of constructing the line [from Fulham to Surbiton] is very doubtful. They certainly opposed it from the first, and when it was found that opposition was vain, they managed by the golden opportunities of their powerful influence, to get their rival [the District Railway] fairly under their control, and to merge the 'independent' line [the New Line] into their own system. After lengthy procrastination they are now about to apply … for powers to abandon the [Fulham to Surbiton] project …[5]

Thus, the events that flowed from the Guildford, Kingston and London Railway Bill of 1881 were the opening of the New Line in 1885 and in the same year the final abandonment of its more grand initial objective.

Newspaper reports of the opening

It seems scarcely credible that a newspaper of the standing that the *Surrey Comet* had achieved should not report the opening of the New Line but that otherwise encompassing organ greeted the event with silence.

The first newspaper report was in *The Times*, which in noting the forthcoming opening of the New Line had also remarked that 'it passes through some of the most picturesque parts of Surrey'.[6] Could it be out of pique, and knowing that the writing was on the wall for the demise of the Fulham line, that the *Surrey Comet* had carried no story on the opening of the New Line? It seems an unworthy suggestion but the contrast with the other local newspaper coverage at the other end of the line could not have been starker, and how could something be worthy of a note in a national newspaper but not be covered in a local one? In their first issue after the opening of the New Line the *Surrey Advertiser* announced their long coverage of the event, albeit in somewhat overstated terms, with:

> The much-talked of and long-desired new railway … is now *un fait accompli*, the constructive operations having been completed, and the line opened without ceremony on Monday [2 February 1885]…[7]

If it had been 'much talked of' and 'long desired' there is not much evidence of this being a general sentiment: the privileged few would perhaps agree and the nugatory approach taken by the *Surrey Comet* is in contradiction. Nevertheless, the report of the *Surrey Advertiser* was buoyant, favourable comment being made on the finishing of the works by the sowing of grass and clover on the banks, while between Merrow and Clandon on Lord Onslow's property, the side facing Clandon Park had been planted with a variety of trees, 'and each side of the whole length of the line is alive with vegetation, which gives a pleasing finish to the land contiguous with the metals'.

Although there was no formal ceremony to mark the opening of the line (unlike when it was electrified 40 years later) considerable interest in it was shown in Guildford where 'nearly a hundred' passengers gave a loud cheer as the four-coach train started from the platform. It seems that most of these were there merely to enjoy 'the novelty of the thing' for when they got to *London Road*, which was as far as they had booked, they got off and either walked home or waited for the return train, the latter being delayed by the indignity of its

---

[3] *Surrey Advertiser*: 24 January 1885.
[4] *Surrey Advertiser*: 24 January 1885.
[5] *Surrey Comet*: 21 November 1885.
[6] *The Times*: 1 January 1885.
[7] *Surrey Advertiser*: 7 February 1885.

The Avril Gilbert collection

12.12 To mark the event of the centenary of the New Line (2 February 1995), Claygate Dramatic Society turned out in force.

loco failing temporarily. According to the report 'near neighbours to the line left their houses with their children and gave a hearty cheer' and doubtless the more numerous greetings came from the 'farm labourers, at their work', putting down their tools to welcome 'the great civilizer [*sic*] of the 19th century'. Unfortunately the reporter gives no account of the greeting that the first train received at each of the stations, but with the peasants in the fields, their children in school and few other residents there may have been little activity. Interestingly, the reporter observed the only industries along the route, in addition to agriculture, were 'wood-chopping and fencing', with no mention of brickmaking but with some prescience he thought that this would change because it was expected that the line 'will give a great stimulus to building operations in the localities' – in due course it certainly did.

Writing at the time of the New Line opening in *The South Western Gazette*, and echoing much that had been said at the Select Committee and elsewhere, Sam Fay

opined: 'It is a beautiful country which certainly in time will become a favourite residential district for City men'. The use of the words 'in time' strikes a chord, carefully chosen perhaps to subsume the view that there was no realistic chance of the line making money until the commuters had come, and as we will see this took some time. The *Surrey Advertiser* had a sense of this too because in a separate piece, as if to qualify the reporter's enthusiastic reporting of what may have been LSWR rhetoric, it said:

> It is not to be expected that the new line will all at once be thronged with travellers, but it will not only be a means of transit for passengers and goods, but a feeder of settled population from other and congested districts to places along its route.[8]

In this assessment we can say that the *Surrey Advertiser* was, in due time, wholly correct. In the meanwhile the LSWR had to run an unprofitable railway.

[8] *Surrey Advertiser*: 7 February 1885.

12.13 Bridge over Ripley Road, East Clandon looking north, c1885; the contractor's loco is hauling wagons loaded with chalk and other spoil to form embankments elsewhere.

12.14 The same view in 2005.

12.15 Bridge over The Street, West Horsley, looking north, c1885.

12.16 The same view in 2005.

The inaugural timetable

The inaugural timetable for the New Line, which was advertised the week before it opened, [9] is set out below.

Up

Guildford	7.12am	8.11am	8.35am	9.16am	12.20pm	2.14pm	4.33pm	4.44pm	6.29pm	7.05pm	8.10pm
Surbiton	8.09am	...	9.32am	...	1.17pm	...	5.30pm	...	...	8.02pm	9.07pm
Leatherhead	...	8.52am	...	9.57am	...	2.55pm	...	5.25pm	7.10pm	...	...
Waterloo	8.37am	9.41am	10.00am	10.44am	1.45pm	3.46pm	5.58pm	6.19pm	7.58pm	8.30pm	9.35pm

Down

Waterloo	6.45am	7.25am	10.20am	11.27am	2.32pm	2.55pm	4.30pm	5.20pm	6.20pm	7.38pm	8.50pm
Surbiton	7.11am	...	10.46am	...	3.00pm	...	...	5.44pm	6.46pm	...	9.16pm
Leatherhead	...	8.17am	...	12.16pm	...	3.41pm	5.17pm	...	...	8.24pm	...
Guildford	8.09am	8.59am	11.44am	12.58pm	3.58pm	4.23pm	5.59pm	6.42pm	7.44pm	9.06pm	10.14pm

Note: Timings for intermediate stations were not given.

The 11 trains up and down each weekday, six via *Surbiton* and five via *Leatherhead*, had journey times for the whole distance which were a grindingly slow 85 minutes via Surbiton and 90 minutes via Leatherhead, an average speed of not much more than 20 miles per hour, with *Guildford* to *Surbiton* being run at an average speed of a mere 18 mph; the gradients were perhaps taking their toll.

For those travelling to the City, the journey from *Waterloo* would have to be continued either on foot, by courtesy of the horse or by changing stations for *Cannon Street*. The 8.35am from *Guildford* departing

Oxshott at about 9.10am and arriving at *Waterloo* at 10.00am may have been all right for those travelling to the House of Lords, but for those with any business to do much before 11.00am there was effectively only one up train. For the return journey there were two evening trains via Surbiton with the last one being at 8.50pm. With the service being so slow and the overall journey times so long, it is perhaps not surprising that passenger traffic was light for many years, discouraging residential development.

---

[9] *Surrey Advertiser*: 31 January 1885.

12.17 In 2005 a Down train crests the summit of the New Line east of Horsley station, and is about to pass under the now closed (and overgrown) bridge with Lord Lovelace's former right of way.

141

12.18 This view shows considerable activity in the excavation of the deep cutting on the Up side of Horsley station looking towards Effingham Junction; the temporary bridge was later replaced by a permanent one for access for Lord Lovelace from Horsley Towers to his estate; although still existing, the bridge is now unused, the land having been developed.

Paucity of traffic

One of the first impacts of the coming of the railway was the immigration of the railwaymen needed to operate the stations and signals. With a staff, incredible as it seems today, of ultimately perhaps six men per station to include the men for the intermediate signal boxes and crossings, and with most being the head of a household, there were over 20 houses to be built to accommodate them. The stationmaster moved into the house on the premises while terraced cottages were built near the stations to accommodate the other staff.

With this level of staffing, the paucity of traffic and the infrequent trains, it is perhaps easy to accept that the line was not paying its way. As for the staff they had time to kill between trains and it is said that they played cricket while waiting: there is an unsourced story in Claygate that a passenger, finding he had a long time to wait for a train, joined in a game and being put on immediately to bowl, was informed that the stationmaster facing him 'had been in for a fortnight':[10] whether apocryphal or not, it illustrates the scarcity of business being conducted on the railway in its early days. The character of the railway in those late 19th century days is beyond any living memory today but an eye witness of the opening of the line, a resident of

Claygate, recalled 'that the carriages were very small and the engine was a real 'puffing billy' with only four wheels and a tall smoke-stack'[11] (presumably a reference to the 4-wheel coaches and Adams or Drummond 0-4-4 tank locos).

In 1881, the last census year before the railway opened, the total population of the parishes served by the New Line (excluding that served by *London Road*) was 6,900. It was a population spread around the 39 square miles of land in the census area at a density of 177 people per square mile – about a third of the density for England and Wales as a whole in 1881 and about one tenth of the density today, in spite of the Green Belt. If an average household size of 5.3 is assumed (this was the actual figure in Claygate in 1881), then the 1,300 dwellings needed to accommodate the population of the New Line parishes would be distributed at the astonishing low density of about one dwelling per nearly 20 acres. The Revd Phillips was accused of wanting 'to retain the rustic simplicity of Stoke D'Abernon'; plainly at this low density of inhabitation 'rustic simplicity' was an

10 *Claygate, Surrey*: Claygate Village Hall Association, 1953 (also known as 'The Golden Book'), p 43. The author is grateful to Mr Sam Collins for lending me his copy of this rare book.
11 *Ibid.*

12.19 *The bridge over Ockham Road looking north, with Horsley station to the right, c1884.*

12.20 *The same view in 2005.*

12.21 *The River Mole has been bridged and the loco, which is hauling ballast trucks, appears to have time to pause for the photographer, c1884.*

12.22 *A Lucas & Aird works train pauses for the photographer at an agricultural access bridge east of Effingham Junction.*

12.23 Looking Up the line from east of Cobham station towards the bridge carrying Stoke Road over the railway.

12.24 Looking Up the line towards Oaken Lane bridge, Claygate; the contractor's loco is on light duty and the men look as though they are checking the gauge of the track which looks ready for operational use, c1885.

12.25 Although the quality of this photograph is not good, it is exceptional because it is one of the rare images of the land on which part of Hinchley Wood was built in the 1930s: the view is taken from the lower slopes of Telegraph Hill; the spire of Esher church can be seen on the horizon, while to the left of that in the middle distance can be seen the reconfigured Oaken Lane and the bridge carrying it over the railway; the onlooker seems to be looking towards Oaken Lane brickworks, Claygate.

epithet which could have been applied to the whole area of the New Line hinterland formed by the interstice of the North Downs and the Portsmouth road, the more so when account is taken of the fact that one third of the population of the New Line parishes lived in Cobham, leaving the other districts with an even lower density of habitation.

As we have seen the New Line was built against the better judgment of Archibald Scott and his directors at the LSWR to keep the District Railway out of Guildford and anyone who benefited as a result of its being built, apart from the protagonists, was just fortunate. The 'sparsely populated agricultural district' as it had been referred to at the Select Committee, could not generate passenger traffic, Keays and the Fairmile phalanx apart. Scott had wanted to take the railway to Cobham where at least there was known demand, but even that had been abandoned: around *London Road*, Guildford was the only area in the entire length of the New Line where

people lived in any numbers. No doubt Keays and his friends at Fairmile would now be making for *Oxshott* station but this traffic, which was low volume anyway, was simply displacing journeys that used to be made from *Esher*: Scott's reluctance to go to the expense of building a line to serve such an under-populated area seemed to be entirely justified; there was a well-known aphorism in the industry at the time: 'feeders' to the main system can all too easily prove to be no more than 'suckers'.

'Rustic simplicity'

Let us consider what 'rustic simplicity' might have meant in 1885. Industry scarcely existed in any of the villages in the area. Brickmaking was only a desultory local affair made more viable by the coming of the railway but not a reason for its coming. John Earley Cook bought Knowle Park (later to be used as the Schiff's Home of Recovery, offices then for residential

12.26 The 'rustic simplicity' of the district was slow to abate; this scene of a farm labourer with his wagon on Claygate Common was typical of the period and well into the 20th century.

use) in 1855 and 10 years later secured 30 acres of land, most of it from the Crown, at Little Heath. Cook's minor brickworks in Little Heath was one of the luckiest beneficiaries of the building of the New Line. Cook was on good terms with the Revd Phillips of St Mary's and they shared a dislike of railways, for they had acted in concert in opposing James Bell's narrow gauge scheme. In spite of the obvious benefit to his brickworks there is no evidence of his support for Onslow's scheme – why did he not give evidence to the Select Committee in its favour? – perhaps it was in a gesture of solidarity with Phillips, but when the LSWR proposed their own railway on the same route past his brickfields he was on an each-way winning bet. He must have been delighted when without the slightest influence from him, the New Line was laid out adjacent to his brickworks (as we have seen, the route went through Oxshott because of John Clutton's influence) and he sold land for the railway to the LSWR for over £1,000 and was given a siding to his works near Cook's Crossing named after him.

This minor activity apart, life in the early years of the railway followed the same pattern as it always did. Leaving aside Cobham, where its position on the turnpike to Portsmouth had allowed trade to develop, most of the rural population would earn their living from some association with the land or with the great estate houses of Onslow and Lovelace and the others.

Perhaps one half of all the households were of land-labouring families – 53% in Claygate, and for them the rhythm of the year had followed the plough, now less in use because of the depression rendering crops less economic than pasture. A few would be yeoman farmers; the rest of the men, leaving aside the families in the great houses and their butlers, stewards and other domestic staff, would be more or less skilled workers such as shepherds, thatchers, carters, blacksmiths, wheelwrights or carpenters; a quarter (67) of the female population of Claygate in 1881 was in domestic service. Each village would have its baker (the Mole mills ground flour) and dealers in meat and game; there would be a general self-sufficiency within the villages, with most households growing vegetables, keeping chickens and perhaps a pig and bees, and in season making jams and jellies. All the skills needed were available within the village and the horse was king. The rhythm of the day starting as the men led out the teams of horses through narrow lanes rutted with cartwheels and trampled by hooves to do their day's work in the fields. On the Downs the shepherds kept their own company, mending enclosures, doing their best to abate the tithe exacted by foxes; in the coppices the woodmen gathered their harvest, fabricating it to the needs of the village; wisps of smoke located the charcoal burners while the roadmen cleared the ditches. Life went on punctuated from time to time by the birth of a new heir in the mansion, or the death of the master. The boys growing up in these indigenous families would expect to do the same as their fathers, and where the depression prevented it they would leave for the towns. The girls would go into service, where the opportunities had expanded beyond the local Lord's estate by the growth of the middle and upper-middle classes in Surbiton, Kingston, Leatherhead and Guildford.

That the railway came at the same time as the ruin of agriculture was not a coincidence – as explained in Chapter 4, the depression begat the railway – but its coming did little to relieve the rural poverty among the

12.27 *A photo from 1953 taken from the Bookham branch, showing the remaining earthworks at Effingham Junction for the unbuilt spur to create a triangular link to the Cobham line.*

The Lens of Sutton collection

agricultural labourers. In her account of village life in the 1880s Flora Thompson[12] suggested that 'even the poor enjoyed a rough plenty' but cheap food was the currency which was funding the export of our manufactures – poverty within the rural poor manifested itself not in hunger but in the absence of shoe leather, the donning of cut-up hessian sacks in the fields to keep out the rain, and a total absence of luxuries. The railway brought more news of the towns, of opportunities of employment or of advancement. Only the new century brought any respite to agriculture and for a quarter of a century the decline in rural trade and employment was unabated. By then the new forces were bringing newcomers to the villages; business magnates at first and later the commuters. While the seeds of destruction had been sown for the villagers, it was not until the 1920s and 1930s that their numbers were overtaken by newcomers, the so-called 'daily breaders', who used the railway to go to work; but at first there was a sort of harmony, a co-existence which will be well illustrated by the Oxshott story in the next chapter.

A journey on the New Line

As a reference point for the physical changes that were to come let us take an imaginary journey from Surbiton to Guildford in the very early days of the railway, using this opportunity to point out the characteristics of the grades on the line. Leaving Surbiton, our imaginary train has taken the slow down line, for the track was quadrupled as far as Hampton Court Junction in 1883-4, partly in anticipation of the completion of the New Line. The villas of Surbiton are spreading to the west with impressive new housing growing by the year. Ahead on the far side the driver can see the tracks turning off the main lines to the right taking the branch line to Hampton Court off on its embankment, and we will shortly be leaving the main line ourselves. As the driver prepares to accommodate the lurch of the locomotive, as its front bogies take the points to go down the New Line, both up and down tracks of the New Line are side by side (they were not separated until 1908) as they leave the main line which maintains its direction to the west.

Going down the New Line will require a change in the way the locomotive was driven down from *Waterloo* with its easy gradients. The driver knows his engine; he has an intimate relationship with her – always feminine – for he knows every part of her personality when she

---

[12] Flora Thompson: *Lark Rise to Candleford*, 1945.

12.28 The bridge over Stoke Road, Guildford, looking south to the town; the view today is barely recognisable, not least because of the construction of a pedestrian tunnel through the abutment on the left.

is in steam. He knows how strong she can be; when she needs coaxing and how to respond to her peccadilloes; how she will always give as well as the pressure in her boiler will allow. But the relationship of the driver with his locomotive is only one of the two vital relationships on the footplate. The fireman knows at one remove the qualities of the engine and her ways, but he knows too that when he is working as one with the driver, their teamwork will bring out the best in her. Always alert to the water level in the tender – no supply would be available on the New Line until Horsley – alert even more to the pressure gauge, he knows how much the approaching gradients on the New Line, even though they are short, will take out in pressure what only coal can put back.

As his train turns away from the main line the driver can see an *Esher* train halted on the up slow line where the signal is holding a path clear for an up train on the New Line which will have to traverse all the metals in a conflicting movement to join the up slow line. The line here is less than a mile from the Thames and is carried on a high embankment in order to equalise the level with the deep Weybridge cutting further down the main line. The New Line, quickly loses this height

on a grade of 1 in 132 down to where Hinchley Wood station will to be built in 1930: a grade which in the opposite direction will present starting difficulties for an up train which might be held at the signal waiting for the main line to clear. The train is carried over a rough track that is Claygate Lane, previously a route to the port of Thames Ditton out of Claygate, now rendered redundant by its goods yard. This is the same Claygate Lane of which in *Nature near London* Richard Jefferies wrote in 1880 that 'the first stroll of the year should be taken' in order to observe the beauty and natural history of the district.

Our train is now travelling on its climb up to *Claygate* through farmland: *Manor Farm*, Thames Ditton in view on the left, then *Couchmore Farm* on the right, while opposite is Telegraph Hill with its signal station tower coming into fleeting view. As *Claygate* is approached some activity can be seen in Oaken Lane brickfield; as Hare Lane is bridged some of the original big houses of Claygate can be glimpsed, including *Loseberry House* opposite the goods yard which is on the down side as the station is approached. Just before the goods yard below the embankment is the row of cottages in Hare Lane built for the railway workers, while away to the left further on can be seen the *Foley Arms* across the fields and *Ashbourne* next door, both of which will be discussed in the next chapter.

When *Claygate* station comes into the driver's view, a hand bell having been rung on the platform to announce its imminent arrival, he peers through his glass as he feels the engine take the curve on the approach. He knows where to close the regulator, so the power is shut off. The staff on the platform, long in their wait, can now be discerned; a glance at the signal at the end of the platform shows it is 'off' already: only the business of the platform will delay the journey. It is time now, after a moment's coasting, to start applying the vacuum brakes to the whole train, gently feathering the control to keep regular the rate of deceleration: not too slow, or we will overshoot; not too fast or the passengers will complain, and even worse, make urgent a squirt on the regulator to give some momentum back, with the tell-tale puffs to announce that a misjudgment of distance has been made. But the driver knows his spot on the platform and brings his locomotive to a slow halt, inch perfect, and with the lessons of the hardest part of driving well-learned, the urgency of the business of the platform commences.

The driver is grateful for the level track at *Claygate*, deliberately fashioned out of the 1 in 100 incline in to the station to facilitate a good start before having to take on the 1 in 110 grade out of the station, which is called *Claygate for Claremont*,[13] not for the benefit of Queen Victoria, for she had ceased to visit the house, but probably reflecting a desire by the LSWR to emphasise its connection with Royalty. Soon after the station a level crossing is passed (which will be replaced by a bridge when Claremont Road is laid out) allowing agricultural movements into *Loseberry Farm* on the up side.

After climbing out of *Claygate* and after a brief downhill stretch past *Horringdon Farm* on the left and *Arbrook Farm* on the right, one of the tough climbs for the engine is encountered for the track is graded at 1 in 100 for over a mile. The grade is no worse than 1 in 100 because the cutting, which yielded over 300,000 cubic yards of spoil, at *Oxshott* station has been cut to a depth of 45 feet. The grade has taken some toll of the boiler pressure but the fireman knows the route: he has been coaling the fire since before he left the main line, not too much at once, for that would cool the fire – coaling at the back at first; then at the front and the sides,

distributing an even supply of new coals thinly to the fire bed – venting the fire to increase the temperature at which the fire is burning, until the coals can no longer be seen, the fire now licking the edges of the firebox door, the colour whitening into an opaque mass of burning gas, heating the steel tubes in the boiler, turning the water within them into steam to be stored, pent up for the job still to be done.

As the Claygate farms are left behind the scene gives way to Clutton's woods and forests and as we approach Oxshott the coppicers can be seen at work. The track at Oxshott station is also on the level built at the summit forming the watershed of the Mole valley. The station is called *Oxshott and Fairmile* (reduced to *Oxshott* in 1913) in recognition of the Promoter, Frederick Keays and his little phalanx of travellers to the City from the Fairmile. The station sits in its cutting, deeper on the down side and as we draw away and looking to our right the splendour of Oxshott Heath comes into view with some railway cottages newly-built and followed soon by the goods yard nestling in the forest which now reaches to both sides of the track, the deep cutting having receded. On the up side a third track has appeared which will shortly turn off into Little Heath brickworks siding. From Oxshott it is downhill all the way at various grades the steepest of which is 1 in 95 until the Mole is reached in two miles. As we emerge from the forest of Oxshott into farmland again we can observe how Blundel Lane had to be reconfigured to allow for the railway. Arriving in Stoke D'Abernon under the newly raised Stoke Road, the Revd Phillips' Manor House and St Mary's church can be seen less than half-a-mile away on the left across the Mole flood plain. The station has been called *Cobham* in spite of the fact that it was in Stoke D'Abernon, a fiction no doubt influenced by the LSWR's failed attempt to get the New Line into Cobham. In due course Cobham would grow to meet the station in a continuous spread of residential development but for the present it is in a field surrounded by Phillips' farmland with an improved Plough Lane (later Station Road) giving access to the station and goods yard on the up side of the country end of the station.

On this occasion there is an unusual frenzy of activity at Cobham station for sometimes a big group comes

---

[13] Esher had been the station for *Claremont* hitherto, its name boards announcing the fact. On some maps of the period cartographers continued with the name *Esher & Claremont Station* even after *Claygate for Claremont* had opened.

12.29 Clandon station under construction, looking Up the line towards Horsley.

down to the stud farm of Charles Combe, and uses the Plough Inn as a refreshment room. Suddenly the commotion on the platform is reduced as any departing passengers climb aboard: the alighting passengers make eye contact with a porter to help them on their way; others make for the exit, ticket in hand ready to be given up. The last of the doors slam after the scramble aboard, the stationmaster reaching for the final one that has been left open by the lady more intent on settling her skirts around herself; slamming it shut and turning to the guard, green flag in hand, a shrill whistle accompanies the flag waved excitedly to the driver, looking at the familiar scene from his cab, while having his own moment of calm. The fireman has been attending his fire, the blast of heat being like a furnace as he opens the firebox door. The driver, noting that the signal is off and he is now clear to go, winds the valve gear cut-off up to the maximum length of push on the piston; a sharp tug to open the regulator and in a little while, once clear of the departing passengers on the platform, opens the cylinder cocks setting off a blast of steam gushing forward, driving out all the condensation from within the cylinders which has accumulated while the engine was at rest.

On leaving *Cobham* station (renamed *Cobham and Stoke D'Abernon* in 1951) the Mole is soon crossed, the flood plain being traversed on an embankment. Soon the track starts its toughest climb on the whole line; for over three miles until the summit of the line is reached

after the long cutting at Horsley, the track climbs at various grades the steepest of which are two stretches of about a mile each at 1 in 95. Towards the end of the first of these sharp inclines on the left can be seen the unfinished work on a track bed bending away towards Leatherhead. Effingham Junction was to have been a triangular junction and some of the earth works for it were made at the time of the original construction.[14] The station – the only one on the line, bar *Hinchley Wood*, never to have a goods yard – was built in its cutting in a field at the edge of Effingham Common

---

[14] The LSWR may have had in mind a roundabout route: *Waterloo*-to-*Waterloo* via *Surbiton, Claygate, Oxshott, Bookham, Leatherhead* and *Epsom*. Why the loop was not made is uncertain, but there is something slightly odd about a pair of routes (*Waterloo* to *Guildford* via *Cobham* and via *Effingham Junction*) that start at the same terminus; follow the same route for eight miles; then run a separate course for 12 miles or so before coming back together again for the last eight miles. The effect is rather perverse: the stations on the up side of *Effingham Junction*, where being nearer London the demand is higher, have a less frequent service than those at the country end. Because the triangular junction was not built any attempt to get from the New Line at points north of the junction required (and require now) a change of train and direction: *Effingham Junction* station was built as an afterthought probably because the loop was abandoned with the new station allowing the reversal to be made to connect for Leatherhead without proceeding unnecessarily as far as *Horsley*.

12.30 This 1904 photograph illustrates how isolated was Effingham Junction station; the railway cottages are on the right.

The Stephen Spark collection

nearly two miles from Effingham village and opened three years later than the others on 2 July 1888.

The original six stations of the New Line were all designed to a common architectural design, with the main facilities on the Up or Down side whichever suited the site. A spacious stationmaster's house, large entrance canopy, waiting rooms (general and for ladies), ticket hall, staff rooms and well-ventilated gentlemen's toilets were included in the standard brick structure, the effect of which is aesthetically pleasing.[15] On the platforms the decorative canopy stanchions are also attractive, picked out as they are today in various colours. Evidently, the staff quarters in the station buildings were dank and unappealing, the structures having been built without a damp-proof course. It is unrecorded when stationmasters ceased to be, but ultimately the British Rail Property Board let the houses to railway tenants, while in the 1990s these were sold with their sitting tenants. Ultimately many of the stationmasters' houses became occupied by private owners. At Claygate, the owner has developed the site into The Station Master's House, a restaurant which exploits the extended ground floor area of the original house.

The fabrication of *Effingham Junction* station, which like *Hinchley Wood*, has nothing in common with the original stations, was built on an awkward site essentially of timber distinguished by its vernacular simplicity. Today the station feels more open than the others and when it was built it must have been the loneliest station on the line. The track leading over the bridge heading from the station to Effingham village was not upgraded to the status of a road for many years. At first there was just a terrace of railway cottages (later demolished to make way for the car park extension) and the expanse of the Common at the approach to the station.

The track has been running straight since the Mole was crossed and now approaches the long cutting at *Horsley* by an extended incline. An excellent view of this gradient can be seen today from the London end of

[15] Staff who have worked on the New Line report a family atmosphere, with many of the staff having been or being popular local personalities. Typically, the staff would have been familiar with the regular customers and exchange pleasantries and perform minor acts of service. The New Line appears to have been a special favourite of many former staff members that the author has spoken to, whether as station staff or guards. Today, it is only the booking office clerk who provides any human interface with the customers, but the family atmosphere still characterises many of the relationships between today's customers and their man at their station.

Horsley station. In the days of steam it must have been a remarkable sight to stand on the platform and to be able to see an engine come into view many minutes before it was due and watch it puff and strain its way for two miles to *Horsley*. Our present day electric trains take the gradients on the New Line in their stride, passengers being oblivious of them: but even so, the route is slower than the mostly level or gently graded main line even though the *Guildford via Cobham* route is one mile shorter. Today, just as in the days of steam, some Portsmouth or Guildford expresses are timetabled to take the New Line: of the three current daily trains from *Waterloo* non-stop to Guildford via Cobham the fastest is booked at 34 minutes: while this may sound fast compared with the stopping services that we are used to, it is actually a pedestrian average speed of only 45 mph for the whole journey from *Waterloo* including the much faster working on the main line before the train joins the New Line. There are no equivalent journeys on the old line today because all main line services to Guildford call at Woking: even with this delay, fast trains are quicker on the old line than the new, with the fastest booked time to Guildford via Woking being one minute less than the New Line at 33 minutes. The New Line is slower not just because of the gradients: there is another factor soon to be discussed – the sharp curves near *London Road* and *Guildford* stations.

Back in the days of steam the long haul to *Horsley* station was a great test for driver and fireman alike. The fireman's job was done well before the climb started: through faith in his fireman the driver will know that when he starts the climb the boiler pressure will be high enough to take the climb, and still have some in reserve when *Horsley* is reached. The two men on the footplate have each done their work almost wordlessly for the noise in the cab is great, responding to the unspoken drill and instincts, sharing the attention the locomotive craves, each in his own way, to make a single attendant to her whim. Water is available at *Horsley* and will be taken on board if required but normally the facility was available for the occasional train from Leatherhead that terminated and turned round at *Horsley*.

One of the reasons why the cutting at *Horsley* could not be made deeper in order to ameliorate the gradient is because sufficient height had to be maintained to carry the line on its bridge over Ockham Road. Today the long cutting keeps from view the substantial residential development that has taken place. When the line was built the station was quite isolated being over a mile from East Horsley and much more than that from West Horsley. The area around Horsley today is a very good example of the settlement coming to meet the railway at the station, with its goods yard on the down side at the London end, but for many years it stood in its emptiness convenient for few but Lord Lovelace. The station was called *Horsley, Ripley & Ockham* disguising the fact that it was convenient for none of those places: it was shortened to *Horsley* in 1914.

Only five miles after it was first entered at Oxshott the Mole valley is traversed, for the summit at *Horsley* marks another watershed; having now entered the Wey valley, the New Line crosses undulating land but runs generally downhill, sometimes at 1 in 100, until the river itself is reached at Guildford in seven miles. Three miles after Lord Lovelace's station at *Horsley* is Lord Onslow's at *Clandon*. The habitation then as now at West Clandon follows the north/south orientation of the road between Send and the Downs. The population was less than 400 when the New Line opened and a large proportion of this would have lived on Lord Onslow's estate: *Clandon Park* was just a mile away to the south. East Clandon (population less than 300) was oriented round the Epsom road and none of it was convenient for the station. As the line is now nearer the North Downs sheep are more in evidence and run away from the noise of the engine in their fright. In the first place the station was named *Clandon & Ripley* (*Clandon* from 1910 and later *Clandon for Newlands Corner*), evidently unconcerned that *Horsley* was also for *Ripley*. This again was probably influenced by the fact that the LSWR wanted to take their *Red Route* nearer to Ripley, but the reality was that the station was built in fields and was convenient only for Lord Onslow's farm. Just over a mile from *Clandon* station and the trees planted for Lord Onslow's screen, is *Merrow* sidings on the down side.

The contractors had to tackle a third deep cutting in addition to those at *Oxshott* and on the climb up to *Horsley*: that at *London Road* station is also deep enough to allow the descent down to Guildford station to be restricted at its steepest to 1 in 100. The excavations uncovered some intriguing mammalian remains: parts of the legs, ribs and skull of an extinct mammoth were found along with the perfectly preserved tusk of a young mammoth. The excavated material from this cutting and the long one at *Horsley* yielded over 650,000 cubic yards of spoil.

12.31 The occupants of these working class houses in Kings Road, Guildford were probably too poor in 1881 to make an effective complaint about the intrusive proximity of the New Line as it was driven through from London Road station to the main line.

The great depth of the cutting and the half-mile diameter sharp curve on the up side of *London Road* station must have been awesome, as they are now in their verdant setting, to those who saw them in their early raw state. Later, the awe of the same folk, if watching cricket at Woodbridge Road might have turned to puzzlement as the trains, on an equally tight reverse curve, inscribe a semi-circle round the ground, their wheels riding up on their screeching flanges as the centrifugal force exerted by the curve found its release. Some would have known that there was a more forgiving route into the town to the north, the one actually proposed by the LSWR, but Lord Onslow had won the argument: a new station was to be built at the top of the town and the result was the steep climb up from the main line station; the 'S' bend contortion and the deep cutting, the extra cost being borne as the price for the railway reaching for customers in the developing part of the town.

London Road (renamed *London Road Guildford* in 1923 to avoid confusion with its namesake at Brighton) was unique as the only one of the original stations which was sited within an existing built-up area. There was more development to come, induced directly by the railway so that the settlement became contiguous with it and the goods yard on the down side at the Guildford end, but Nightingale Road was there before the railway as was Waterden Road and Kings Road, one house in which, although avoiding demolition, was left within a few feet of the track. When the railway came many hundreds of people already lived within easy walking distance of the new station and it would be nearly 20 years – more in some cases – before the same could be said of any of the other stations.

Before the tree growth came and which now restricts the view a little, in the early days of the New Line the passengers between *London Road* and *Guildford* stations were given a magnificent view of the town as the railway described most of a circle around it: looking across the rooftops to the downland above the town to the south the semaphore signal station could be seen high upon it on its lonely sentinel spot. It is still there today but it is no longer lonely, the town having expanded up to it and beyond to the edge of Pewley Down.

After a while the screeching of the wheel flanges abates as the curve relents and we join the main line and then soon draw into *Guildford* station, which has now been completely rebuilt by the LSWR in response to the severe public criticisms. The reader will recall that it was the bad state of Guildford station that had put the LSWR on the back foot when opposing Lord Onslow's proposal for a new line. There had been nothing in mitigation which the LSWR could offer and in the end they were obliged to find the capital to rebuild the station and construct the New Line, both of which projects were a drain on resources. It is interesting to muse on the possibility that if in 1880 the LSWR had bitten the bullet and done what they would have to do sooner or later – build a proper station at Guildford – they may have been able to fend off Onslow's assault on their monopoly because both Onslow himself and many witnesses at the Select Committee had given persuasive evidence about the need for and benefits of a second station in the town. In private reflection some of the senior LSWR personnel might have rued the times when they put off rebuilding a station which at the time was accommodating 4,000 passengers a day. It is unfortunate that the traffic figures on the New Line are missing but it would appear that the LSWR shareholders were to pay a high price for keeping the District Railway out of Guildford.

Chapter 13: ... and then what happened?

13.1 One of the first edifices to appear as a result of the coming of the New Line was the Foley Arms in Claygate, which opened as the railway came in 1885; this view, looking west along Hare Lane, is from c1909.

To give in answer 'not much' to the question: 'What happened after the railway came?' would be only a degree too trite; as we shall see the impact of the railway was slow to gain its impetus, with not much at all happening in the first five years after the New Line opened. In this chapter we will look at the development that took place in the period to 1901, that being the date of the decennial census, and which also marks the point by which the changed character of the expanding settlements of Claygate, Oxshott and Cobham had been established and from which time the pace of development quickened. We will examine them separately later.

Early changes in Claygate

The district round Claygate was described by a travel writer in 1876 as 'closely agricultural but the neighbourhood is pleasant and buildings are increasing'.[1] The coming of the railway was the direct cause of a particular edifice to be built in Claygate of which many residents, 120 years later, have cause to be grateful – the *Foley Arms*. Through the opportunism of

at least two entrepreneurs in acquiring land which was in loose hands and aided by its being the closest to London, Claygate was the first of the 'new' villages to be developed. Unable to resist the gravitational force exerted by the railway, and aided by the determination of the Hon Fitzalan Foley (the younger brother of Lord Foley) to become a property developer, land deals were done which were to shape Claygate in the next two decades into the basic plan that it has today. Although the *Foley Arms* is plainly named in honour of the family, and indeed both Lord, and Fitzalan Foley were vocal supporters of it, it was built by a man who was no less shrewd than them about the impact that the coming of the railway would have. William Limbrick[2] had been the owner of the *Prince of Wales* public house in West End, Esher along with its associated brewery; in 1881, the same year that the New Line was authorised by Parliament, Limbrick sold out his interest to Watney,

---

[1] *Handbook to the Environs of London*: James Thorne, 1876, p 113.
[2] The author is grateful to John and Gil Salter for drawing his attention to William Limbrick and his story.

155

13.2 *Ashbourne was one of the first houses built in Claygate in response to the coming of the railway; William Limbrick developed it as well as the Foley Arms, (2006).*

Combe[3] & Reid, but being alert and fresh into cash, he recognised that the New Line would bring new opportunities for trade.

In 1884, Limbrick who had built *Ashbourne* on the plot next door to the *Foley Arms* in Foley Road for himself, applied to the local Justices for a full licence for 'a new hotel about to be built near the new railway station at *Claygate*'.[4] The application, which was opposed by the landlord of the *Hare and Hounds*, was granted but it was not confirmed at Surrey Sessions, where the objections continued on the somewhat feeble grounds that the railway had not yet opened. Just when the *Foley Arms* did open for business is not clear, or whether it opened as a hotel without a licence; but by the time the trains came on 2 February 1885 the *Foley Arms* presented itself, isolated on a constricted corner of Hare Lane, with an edifice so bold (and substantially unchanged today) having a view, if not from the garden then certainly from its windows on the upper floors, of the railway station which begat it across a field.

The question of the Foley Arm's licence continued and a newspaper report[5] into the affair gives one of the few contemporary accounts of the changes, or lack of them, made by the coming of the railway. At a hearing in March 1885, the Solicitor who represented Limbrick was none other than James Bell, whose brief was of a more work-a-day character than his pioneering efforts to bring railways to the district. Limbrick's application was supported by 'every influential resident' of the village, including the vicar, the Revd Dr Richards (he who was so keen to see the railway come through his land). Part of the case pleaded was that the railway had now opened giving rise to the need for accommodation: an auction sale attended by 60 people had been held in the 'hall' (still in use today) of the recently opened *Foley Arms*. In opposition to the application, which had again been granted locally, but which was now up for confirmation at Surrey Sessions, it was stated somewhat strangely that 'nothing new had occurred during the past year to warrant the licence being granted'. A nearly equally divided Bench

---

[3] This Combe was the same family as Charles Combe of Cobham Park.

[4] *Surrey Advertiser*: 4 April 1884.

[5] *Surrey Comet*: 14 February 1885.

13.3 Brickworkers' cottages, next to The Griffin public house, Common Road, Claygate, c1914.

The Paul Langton collection

evidently agreed and the application was refused. One witness was the agent for the Hon Fitzalan Foley, who announced that Foley had been acquiring land 'for building purposes', including the Fee Farm Estate, in transactions amounting to £35,000, and that since then 'several thousand pounds' had been spent on road making.

Even though the Bench was not impressed by Foley's land buying, the reader should be. To have spent £35,000 on land acquisition may not sound a lot, but let us attempt to convert it to the currency of the day: when the agricultural depression was at it worst the best farming land in Surrey was fetching £12 per acre; even if we assume that Fitzalan Foley was generous and paid or was obliged to pay £100 per acre, then even on this assumption he would have bought about 350 acres of Claygate – about one eighth of the parish – for development. (This illustrative number is not documented but is given to show the large scale of Foley's land purchase.) The witness at the licence hearing was talking about *future* housing development and 'was unable to show' that development had taken place in 'the neighbourhood of the *Foley Arms* during the past year'. From this account we can see that

in Claygate, even though Foley was quick off the line, the changes that were to come were slow to appear, and apart from laying out the roads and some housebuilding in the 1890s, most of Foley's development activities took place in the new century. Bell's witness was able to talk about the coming of the railway but he said nothing about the scale of any impact, emotional or real, it had had when it opened less than a fortnight before. On the footing that it was in Foley's interest to talk up the impact, it rather suggests that Claygate's entry into the railway age was, shall we say, undemonstrative.

The story of the *Foley Arms* illustrates the slowness of the pace of change. It is curious that the stamp of approval given by the vicar and the Foley brothers did not carry the day with Surrey Sessions. Whether in frustration or not is unrecorded, but in 1888 Limbrick sold the *Foley Arms* to Young's Brewery: a move which no doubt delighted Fitzalan Foley, whose development agenda it advanced, as much as successive generations of residents of Claygate, not least the present one. It is most likely that Young's used the goods yard at *Claygate* to deliver its beer from Wandsworth. With the *Foley Arms* and the railway facilities being an anchor, a

13.4 Elm Road School, Claygate opened in 1886; it was probably the increase in jobs in the brickworks, brought about by the building of the railway, that caused the school roll to expand. Note the fields at the end of the road; this view is from c1914.

row of shops in The Parade opened around 1897 to serve the increasing brickworkers and the embryo new settlement on the east side of the railway, created by Fitzalan Foley.

The building of *Ashbourne* by Limbrick added to the stock of large houses that already existed in Claygate. It would appear that even before the railway came the isolated character of the place (it is still on the way to nowhere) was attractive to those families who were rich enough to have their own transport to take them to a railway station. An advertisement in 1867 describes 'a freehold villa residence' in Claygate, with '7½ acres, lawn, stable, paddock, fish pond and two cottages'; it was promoted as being one-and-a-half miles from *Esher* station and two from *Thames Ditton*.[6] After the railway came to neighbouring Esher about 25 such houses had been built in Claygate, providing work for the brickfields, explaining the increase in population – each household had its entourage – and providing the sites for higher-density housing development when Claygate's popularity grew in the first half of the 20th century. If the people living in these houses were rail travellers then no doubt they would have been pleased

to substitute their journey from *Esher* by one from *Claygate*; a point in total justification of Archibald Scott's disinterest in building the New Line.

There had been brickfields in Claygate recorded in Tudor times but the coming of the railway, or rather the building activity it stimulated, gave the brick industry a sustained boost. The capacity of the Claygate brickfields was only ever small, and the inadequate transport links before the railway came probably ensured that they were only ever used in local construction; some writers have suggested otherwise but the evidence for this is thin; more reliable is the recollection of a J Sims, who was born c1870 who 'remembers taking many loads of bricks to Hampton Court for repair work'.[7] Nevertheless, before the railway brickmaking in Claygate seems to have been

[6] Information from an unpublished dissertation by John King: *The development of a commuter village. A case study of Claygate, Surrey.* Held in Esher Library.
[7] *Claygate, Surrey*: Claygate Village Hall Association, 1953 (also known as 'The Golden Book'), p 41.

13.5 One of the first impacts of the coming of the railway was the immigration of the railwaymen needed to operate the stations and signals; these former railwaymen's cottages are in Hare Lane, Claygate (2006).

desultory, with occasional stimuli as another big house was built: in the 1881 census there are only 11 men recorded as brickmakers in the three brickfields, with perhaps some additionals noted simply as labourers. Unlike Oxshott, where the railway came to the brickfields, in Claygate there was never any rail link to the sources of production. As a result there is no evidence of any shipment of bricks out of Claygate by rail (probably because the double handling would render it uneconomic) until the famous and high added-value Claygate Fireplaces began to be made in the 1920s.

Even if there were few exports of raw bricks, the building activity within Claygate itself ensured sufficient local demand to bring an expansion to the industry. For example, in the period to 1885, bricks were required for the building of the station, the *Foley Arms*, *Ashbourne*, railwaymen's cottages in Hare Lane and the bridge over Hare Lane – sufficient for employment in the industry to expand. In the 1890s, housing for brickworkers and other lower paid workers had been constructed in Elm, Common, Coverts, Vale and Station Roads and at the northern end of Gordon Road. More housing was built in Vale Road after 1905. By the testimony in 1947 of John Wellbelove, a notable maker of Claygate Fireplaces, when he worked as a boy in that brickfield in 1888 there were 30 brickworkers.[8] It is probable that it was the sustained expansion of employment in the brick

industry in the 1880s that caused the increase in the school rolls at Claygate's elementary school: in 1885, shortly after the railway opened, the foundation stone was laid for the new school in Elm Road which opened in the following year.

Even as the railway was being finished the young Fitzalan Foley – he was 32 years old when the railway came – had laid out his Foley Estate: his first plan involved building on *Loseberry Farm* land as well as on the east side of the railway. The farm was owned by John Peter Robinson (founder of the department store) who lived in and owned *Loseberry House*. Robinson, who died in 1895, had been either unwilling or unable to sell *Loseberry Farm* to Foley. Thus frustrated Foley's development took place on one side of the railway only: it was a fortunate escape from urbanisation and in due course the farm land entered the Metropolitan Green Belt. The modified Foley estate comprises Foley Road and Fitzalan Road (both named after himself), Beaconsfield Road (after Disraeli who died in 1881 when the Guildford, Kingston and London Railway Bill was in Parliament), Claremont Road (after the house), Albany Crescent (after the occupant of Claremont – the Duchess of Albany) and Gordon Road (possibly after the General whose death in Khartoum was announced as the railway was opening).

In order to control the type of development covenants were placed on the land to restrict the use to residential and to impose minimum values for developed houses. In order to develop Gordon Road, Foley had to get rid of the level crossing which had provided a right of way for agricultural movements to *Loseberry Farm* at a point where the shallow cutting more or less peters out: it was replaced by the bridge over the railway at the end of Claremont Road (giving more demand for bricks) in about 1895.[9] The magnificent three-storey semi-detached houses at the north end of Foley Road were built in the 1890s and by 1901 some of the middle class detached villas (with accommodation for a maid on the third storey), had been built in Foley Road, Gordon Road and Albany Crescent. The bigger of these houses, which had six or seven bedrooms, some with tennis courts, have not survived, the biggest *Caprons* being demolished to make way for several smaller houses in the 1930s. *Rowan Brae* in Gordon Road, now occupied

---

[8] Reported in the *Surrey Comet*, December 1947.
[9] NA, RAIL 411 406, p 134.

13.6 *Several of these large, magnificent semi-detached villas, which were among the first houses in Claygate after the railway came, were built on land laid out by Hon Fitzalan Foley in Foley Road in the 1890s; this view is from 2005.*

as a school, was one of two that were occupied by stockbrokers in 1901. Foley's estate took off much slower than might have been expected: the sale of a plot of land in Gordon Road for £50 is known to have taken place as early as November 1885,[10] but the 1891 census does not record anyone living in the road. Some purchasers bought double plots for their own good reasons: unhappily when these were sold from about 1970 onwards the eclectic architectural styles that were used made no concession to the ordered elegance of much of the original Foley estate, and most of the earliest big detached houses have now gone.

It appears that some of the early houses were built by Fitzalan Foley himself either to stimulate demand or as investments or both, because when his landholdings were broken up for sale in 1919 (he died as the 6th Baron unmarried and childless in 1918, his brother, Henry, having died childless in 1905), his estate was the owner of 14 houses in Gordon Road, four in Foley Road and four in Albany Crescent.[11] The market for houses seems to have changed considerably after Foley started his development: although the railway station was a common factor as demand changed, the need for

provision for stabling became redundant. Several of the houses that Foley owned when he died had stabling in the grounds (the coach house of *Caprons* has survived converted to domestic use) as well as garaging, while many of the smaller detached villas which were built in the early 20th century in Gordon Road were built with no garage but had sufficient space for a carriage but certainly not for a horse.

As can be seen Claygate was changing, albeit slowly: the grinding agricultural life employed fewer men and the old families, some living on their private means since before the railway came, were not yet gone; the brick industry was enjoying a revival and the newcomers with their domestic servants had started to arrive, setting a pattern which would characterise the next phase of the development of the village. As the century turned Claygate, the revived industrial village with new housing appropriate to it and Foley's

---

[10] Copy of conveyance held in Esher library.
[11] Auction catalogue, *Ruxley Lodge and the Claygate Estate*: 19 October 1919, kindly given to the author by Mr Michael Breckon, lately of Billinghurst, estate agents.

Claygate designed for newcomers from the middle classes whose living came from London, were each growing as a result of their mutually sustaining stimulus – the railway.

Change comes via the goods yards

In the early days of the New Line the goods yards along the line, all in their isolated verdant settings, became a new centre of activity. In addition to the yards at every station, generally identifiable today by the car parks, there was a public facility at Merrow, which was associated with a brickworks. The freight train making its daily bucolic journey, dropping off a few wagons at each lonely yard, would bring forth the carters to finish the distribution to the farms or the parcels from London to the few wealthy homes. A milk train ran daily: starting from Guildford shortly after nine in the morning, it would collect the churns delivered from the farms, and wend its way to each station on the line until, job done, it would arrive at *Waterloo* after 11.00am where the onward distribution would be completed.

Livestock coming to and leaving the farms would no longer have to be in the charge of drovers all the way to and from the markets: now they could be taken to the station; the movement of locally reared animals through the goods yard would have been commonplace. Within its overall system and beyond it, the LSWR used to run timetabled cattle trains by which movements over long distance could be made, and on the New Line special wagons would be included in mixed goods trains, either to join one of the special trains or to be taken to Guildford. Every week on market day a special train would run to take animals to Guildford's cattle market and later in the day would return to distribute those newly purchased to their new owners' farms. Horses too could be dispatched round the country: those rich enough to keep their own stables would be able to send their favourite horse, even with a carriage, to a holiday destination and then send it back again. Manure as fertilizer for the farms could now be imported by train and straw sent back to the London stables, where the horse population was immense. The sand extraction in Oxshott Woods is said to have started in the late 19th century; the local demand may have absorbed production; the goods yard at Oxshott was probably too far away to be sufficiently competitive for a wider trade to have developed.

The roads to the new stations had to be improved and widened to make way for the newly created horse-drawn traffic: at the turn of the century the Claygate blacksmith was shoeing 20 horses a week. In 1893 Young's gave up a portion of their land at the *Foley Arms* to allow the widening of Hare Lane. Coal merchants sprang up and ultimately considerable trade developed in the more populous villages: Lord Onslow needed his wine delivery, but others would be equal beneficiaries of the newly improved economics of distribution. Practically nothing came into the villages nor left it except via the goods yard, carters finding new business by converging on the station when a train was due, with passengers as well as parcels to be carried. As well as building the *Foley Arms*, Limbrick was the first goods agent at *Claygate* and as the railway arrived he purchased some horses and carriages to let out for hire. The embryo of the taxi service that exists today had started life. While all this activity was taking place on the New Line it will be plain that much of the railway business was in substitution of traffic that was previously handled on the main line: hence 'feeders' can become 'suckers'.

Little demand for housing south of Cobham

Under the influence of Limbrick and Fitzalan Foley, Claygate's early expansion was significant, even if slow. Generally, if change was slow in Claygate it was slow and slight around the stations elsewhere. East Clandon, the estate village of *Hatchlands* (built in the 1750s), was always quite distinct. When in 1888 the house and its large estate were sold, the catalogue referred to the benefits brought by the coming of the railway to the economics of its farms. Here was the opportunity for residential development to take place soon after the railway came, Foley style, but it didn't happen. We can take this as a good indicator that there was no demand, actual or latent, for someone like Foley to buy the land and lay out a new estate: it was an idea ahead of its time at that relative distance from London with the slow trains. In fact *Hatchlands* was bought and was owned continuously by the same family through most of the rampant development years of the 20th century, until it was given to The National Trust in 1945; this suggests that the maintenance of the *status quo* was more important than profit to the family that did buy it in 1888. Along with the *Hatchlands* estate came much of East Clandon

13.7 By the end of the 19th century Church Cobham is well developed; this scene is from c1904, with Church Street on the left.

village: ownership was the surest way of keeping control and this must explain why the village, more than any other, resisted any ambition to develop it and as a result still retains its *olde worlde* charm today: for its close range to London it is a remarkable village.

As we shall see, Oxshott was available only to the very rich and its development plan as conceived by the Crown's shrewd advisers was fulfilled more coherently and consistently than Foley's development of Claygate: Clutton knew about land and development value – Fitzalan Foley was an enthusiastic amateur. While development in both Claygate and Oxshott was slow, the wide selection of new property available much closer to central London probably choked off, at least in the early days, any demand much further out. London was still the centre of gravity, but distance from it counted because of the journey times and the poor service and they seem to have put a brake on change. In the early days of the service, the timetable might have been satisfactory, if slow, for Lord Lovelace travelling from *Horsley* or Lord Onslow from *Clandon*, perhaps only travelling in one direction each day, but for Frederick Keays and his Fairmile chums, and other early commuters the service frequency from *Cobham*, *Oxshott* and *Claygate* was pretty unappealing, and it

only took them to *Waterloo* which was not where they wanted to end up. There is little doubt that had Onslow's line been built to take passengers into *Mansion House*, even with a change of train somewhere, the attractions of the district would have had a faster appeal to commuters.

'The New Line cluster of villages' defined

A useful measure of change is to consider how the populations altered in each of the villages through which was built the New Line: a measure that will suggest the impact on them that the railway may have had. It is, however, dangerous to attribute the growth in population after it opened solely to the effect of the railway: certainly until quite well into the 20th century any great influence of the motor car can be discounted, but there are many other factors than the railway which have an effect on population change. There was already in existence a secular trend of growth in the districts we are concerned with – in every decennial census of the 19th century the populations of the relevant parishes was greater than it had been 10 years earlier. There is a danger, therefore, of muddling the effects of several factors and attributing the aggregate to one cause only.

13.8 *A tree-less view of the viaduct at Oxshott from the Heath; this photograph is undated but the brickwork looks very fresh; behind the trees on the high ground is the Warren Estate.*

Population changes are the result of a multitude of inputs, some of which may be pulling in different directions. The population statistics for 1881, 1891 and 1901 would have contained within their general increases the opposing effect of the new trend of rural depopulation and the drift to the towns exacerbated as it was by the late 19th century agricultural depression. The increases in the population of a particular parish might mean that as well as an absolute increase in newcomers, who were more likely to use the train than the indigenous population, there might be a hidden further increase in newcomers masked by the drift of artisans and labourers to the towns, to the army or their loss to emigration overseas. Cobham, in this respect, may be different: its population may indeed have increased when the agricultural depression came because of the drift to the towns, it being the most economically diversified parish.

Until the railway came the vast majority of the indigenous population would not need to travel out of their parish to work; gradually but inexorably these people were either not replaced when they died, or

they left through economic reasons until ultimately, save for those in domestic service, much the greater part of the working population would travel to work – by train at first, then by bus, car or train. The process of converting the villages of the New Line into dormitories began as the century was closing, but the measurement of this change of mix is too difficult – the very process of the production of high class housing, led to a demand for artisans, gardeners and domestic servants.

Equally, there are also difficulties of where to put the limits of boundaries for an attempt to measure the impact of the railway. How to treat the population change in the parish of Send and Ripley in this respect is a good example of the difficulty; the southern parts of the parish would have come, more or less, within the orbit of the new station at *Horsley*, but those living in the northern parts would still have *Woking* as their nearest station and the coming of the New Line would have passed them by, notwithstanding the fact that theirs was a station called *Horsley, Ripley and Ockham*.

163

The parishes for our analysis start naturally with those suggested by the names of the stations, giving the Clandons and the Horsleys, Stoke D'Abernon (including Oxshott) and Claygate. The Bookhams and Effingham can be grouped as one to include them in the analysis: Cobham has to be included in spite of its distance from its station, but to have included Send, Ripley and Wisley would have stretched the point; while the figures for population change at Ockham, even to the present day, have no materiality for present purposes. Thus to arrive at aggregates, all the parishes on or near the New Line after Thames Ditton in the east are included but not Merrow in the west: Merrow was increasingly under the influence of Guildford and will be discussed in the context of that town to which it was tending towards annexation. Although the New Line bisected Thames Ditton, until *Hinchley Wood* station was built it had no impact on it. Thus defined, we will call these villages 'the New Line cluster of villages': they are the parishes of the Clandons and the Horsleys, Stoke D'Abernon, Cobham, the Bookhams and Effingham and Claygate, the early impact on which has already been considered.

Population growth: 1881-1901

We do not know how many of the 6,900 population of the New Line cluster in 1881 was engaged in the rustic life described above, except to assert that it was a huge majority. We can also assert that this huge majority had, in 1885, no reason except as a means of leaving the land for ever, to leave their parish, let alone be able to afford railway travel if they wanted to make use of it. The aristocracy in the form of Lords Onslow and Lovelace; the upper middle classes from the Fairmile district of Cobham and the likes of Matthew Arnold would make their commuting journeys to London but the numbers travelling each day must have been very low and have included few of the indigenous population. This remained the case for the rest of the 19th century; for the first 15 years of its life, the change in the villages which were going to provide passengers for the railway was too slow to make it viable.

The total population of the New Line cluster of villages had grown by only 1,200 in the 50 years before the railway opened; by how much would it grow in the future? Scott no doubt hoped for the best, but feared the worst. What did happen to the population in the 15 or 20 years after the opening? If we add in to the analysis the parishes of Merrow and Stoke next Guildford in order to capture the effect that *London Road* station had we find that the aggregate population grew from just over 14,000 in 1881 to 23,000 in 1901 – an acceleration in the rate of increase previously in evidence to which we can safely say the railway contributed. But of this increase of 9,000, 6,000 of it is explained by the combined growth of Stoke next Guildford and Merrow. We have already seen that the population of Stoke was on a sharply rising trend before the railway came, and there was in existence from a Guildford town councillor the prediction that Merrow would soon be joined with Guildford; plainly the development around *London Road* station after the New Line opened was in part induced by the newly improved convenience of the nearest railway station for large parts of the Guildford population. By the turn of the century much of the new development around and induced by *London Road* had been completed. As for Merrow, we have observed elsewhere that its population grew in every decennial of the 19th century but it accelerated by more than doubling in the 20 years to 1901; it would be surprising if the New Line had not influenced this, even though Guildford itself was growing by its own impetus.

Focussing on the New Line cluster of villages, the total population rose by 2,700 in the 20 years to 1901, the distribution of which is shown in the table below.

New Line cluster of villages
Population growth: increase to 1901 compared with 1881

	No	%
Cobham	1,581	68
Claygate	592	75
The Bookhams and Effingham	255	14
Stoke D'Abernon (including Oxshott)	163	40
The Clandons and the Horsleys	109	7
Total	2,700	39

From 1899 the owner of *The Spectator*, Meredith White Townsend (1831-1911) lived in the *Manor House* at Little Bookham, while maintaining a house in Harley Street, and like Matthew Arnold in Cobham before him, he found the railway connection made it possible to escape the rigours of London life while retaining access to it. So far as the Bookhams, Effingham, the Clandons and the Horsleys are concerned this seems to be a rare example of the railway attracting successful London people, for unlike Claygate, Oxshott and Cobham there is no evidence of any organised attempt at exploitation of the railway by development in the 19th century. Unless something very strange happened within the

View of Oxshott from Heath Hill

mix of the populations it would seem that the railway scarcely touched the rustic character of these outer villages in the 19th century. Claygate's hesitant growth has already been discussed, but the crude numbers in the above table may exaggerate the population growth trend because of boundary changes to include Hare Lane Green, which may have been responsible for some of the increase in 1901. Apart from this the Claygate expansion can be attributed to the stimulus to the trade of the brickfields; the early incoming families on Foley's new estate, with their domestic servants, and the nascent retail area near the station.

While the dominating figures in the above table are those for Cobham and Claygate, plainly something is stirring in Stoke D'Abernon to challenge its rustic simplicity. In 1886 the grand house at *Woodlands Park* (now an hotel) was built by one of the Bryant family who had made their fortune with matches, and the domestic staff brought in to run the mansion numbered about 20. The railway made the location ideal for those with new-found industrial wealth and the genre had a big influence at the other end of the parish.

Oxshott presents particular measurement difficulties: parts of the Oxshott of today were in the parish of St Andrew's, Cobham which used to extend to the

borders of Esher and include the significant Crown development of Queens Drive, while generally much of Oxshott was in the Revd Phillips' parish of St Mary's, Stoke D'Abernon. Phillips owned most of the land in what we now know as Stoke D'Abernon, and he was able to limit development; but in what we now know as Oxshott, the Crown, under the shrewd management of John Clutton, owned most of the land and he was keen on exploiting the effect of the railway for residential development. The statistics show that there was a 40 per cent increase in the population of Stoke D'Abernon (including Oxshott) in the 20 years to 1901; this understates the population increase because some of it was captured in the Cobham numbers. Whereas nothing other than *Woodlands Park* happened in Stoke D'Abernon in the immediate years after the railway came, Oxshott saw the permanent shaping of its character, which remains discernible today. Domestic staff came in great numbers to the new large household formations in parts of what we know as Oxshott, and they represent a good proportion of the 40 per cent growth in the overall population in the official statistics for Stoke D'Abernon; they also added significant numbers to the population statistics which were collected for Cobham, but with a much smaller proportional effect.

165

13.10 Englefield, Oxshott, was one of the early houses (built 1890s) to exploit convenience for the station and proximity to Oxshott's charms; this view is from 2005.

Oxshott, a 'new town'

We must go back to the Oxshott before the railway came. A considerable refocussing of the mind is necessary to conceive of what the place was like as the agricultural depression hit in the late 1870s, and few of the general remarks already made about village life apply to it. There seems to have been only one substantial house in Oxshott before the railway came: *Oxshott Lodge*, formerly *Oakshade House* stood in isolation on the track to Leatherhead. In addition, a scattering of meagre cottages numbering perhaps a little more than a couple of dozen was associated with a small number of poor farms where livings were eked out in forestry and tending pigs: whatever arable farming that the ungiving land allowed gave way to husbandry and when the depression came, the peasants of Oxshott must have been living in grinding poverty. Communication by road was difficult: Leatherhead, from where the mail was delivered, being more easily reached than Esher or Cobham. The road to Esher was only upgraded from nothing more than a track well after the railway came. The peasants, who

had been living out their lives in a poor isolation that was reinforced by the distance to St Mary's and its inaccessibility in winter, had been rescued from their endemic illiteracy only by their caring Rector and Lord of the Manor, our railway-hating Revd Phillips. Saddened by the poverty and ignorance that he had found after he had bought most of Stoke D'Abernon, Phillips re-endowed the Royal Kent School, which had closed some years before through the loss of its patronage, and in time brought the children, if not the adults, to the borders of literacy.

This was the scene, to which can be added some desultory brickmaking, which Oxshott presented in 1885, but the restraints that Phillips placed on development in Stoke D'Abernon could not be applied to Oxshott where the Crown was keen to see the building of a high-class residential district. The period in which very large houses with stabling and extensive grounds were built for very rich and successful families started about 1890 and the pattern established in Oxshott lasted until the Great War closed that chapter of social history.

We have already noted that the way in which the railway arrived on the doorstep of Oxshott's brick industry was a fluke, as indeed were the deposits of clay themselves, but it was no fluke that the production of this industry should find its outlet in the building of approaching 20 mansions in the 15 years after the railway opened. Under John Clutton's guidance the Crown's policy was to dispose of sites in large plots, almost invariably on leasehold terms, and in spite of poor road communication the railway attracted several notable members of London society to supplement their London facilities with gracious living in the country.[12] This trend, although recognisable with what happened in Claygate in the early years of the 20th century, was in fact of a more elevated character, giving rise to a sustained and recognisably different type of

---

[12] The research for this book has not covered the role of the electric telegraph, which was already endemic in business houses, nor later the telephone which as the railway came was used in the richer family homes, in encouraging or supporting the concept of living in say, Oxshott, and conducting business in London. The expectation must be that as the 20th century approached, telephone traffic between London and the Oxshott and other mansions, unconstrained probably by cost, must have become material to the London aspect of the family lifestyles.

Illustrative map showing main features of Oxshott c1899

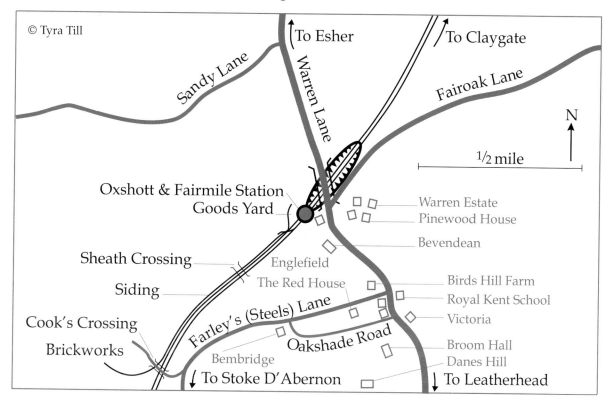

settlement: where Claygate showed some of the characteristics of an industrial village, Oxshott was more of a 'new town' in glorious surroundings which the rich incomers could fashion in their own mould. Although Claygate had no Lord of the Manor as a patron, it did have Lord Foley to fill that role; Oxshott, however, needed patronage, which came in plurality.

Danes Hill, Broom Hall, and *Bevendean* were just three examples of the several great houses that were built in the late 19th century in Oxshott. *Danes Hill,* which is a substantial mansion remaining in use today as a well-known school, was built around 1890 for a family with industrial wealth, which already knew Oxshott by its leasehold interest in farmland. Successive owners, until it was requisitioned during the Second World War, have been in the original mould cast in Oxshott by the Crown: rich, upper middle-class and locally caring. *Broom Hall,* also off the Leatherhead Road was built in 1898 on a seven-acre plot; it was a mansion with

substantial land, which like many of its genre, was demolished and redeveloped in more recent times. Above is given a sketch map of Oxshott at about 1899, showing the location of some of the larger houses that had been built to that date in relation to the station.

Bevendean was of particular note: the New Line contractors Lucas & Aird built the 23-bedroom mansion in 1898; lavishly equipped it was set in its own parkland bordering the railway to the north, and Sheath Lane and Farley's (now Steels) Lane: cottages were built in the grounds for the estate workers, the total indoor and outdoor staff numbering about 30. The house was built for Basil Ellis, who became a notable Oxshott philanthropist, whose wife was a daughter of Sir John Aird: Ellis himself was a partner in associated firms of Lucas & Aird. Another daughter of Sir John had married George Neill Abernethy, the owner of *Broom Hall.* Whether Aird discovered Oxshott himself when inspecting the works in progress of the New Line,

167

13.11 *Pinewood House, on the high ground of the Warren Estate, near Fairoak Lane and Warren Lane, was built c1890 for a City financier; this view is from 2005.*

or was told about it by Clutton is unknown but a new mould had been cast: the special characteristics of Oxshott as a location for a grand home for incoming successful and rich families had been established.

William T Bishop, an associate of John Clutton – it can not be a coincidence – lived in *Bevendean Cottage* near the entrance to the estate in Warren Lane, and was involved in later dealings by the Crown when the estate was broken up in the 1930s to provide the low-density housing in Goldrings Road and Holtwood Road. The freehold of the land on which stands *Englefield* was conveyed in 1890 from the Crown to R Ashford Dash, who was also an associate of Clutton. It was unusual for a freehold title to be given by the Crown but the conveyance is interesting also for its restrictive covenants: the land was to be used only for a hotel or a large house with a contemporary build cost of, respectively, £1,500 and £1,000.[13] Nothing has been heard of the hotel and Oxshott, unlike Claygate, Cobham and Horsley remained without one. *Englefield*, which when it was built was next door to the entrance to *Bevendean* in Warren Lane, borders the top of the railway cutting: the house remains today and must

have been since it was built one of the finest houses from which to commute, being within yards of the station but so secluded from it by the depth of the cutting that there is no detraction from the country house feel by any awareness, at least since the steam trains stopped, of its proximity to the railway.

The *Warren Estate*, at the junction of Warren Lane and Fairoak Lane, which at the time was no more than a track, comprised four mansions with steep drives to their elevated aspects overlooking the railway, now obscured by trees, and broad vistas to distant hills. The proximity of these large houses to the railway, but proof against intrusion by the height of the land gave them like *Englefield*, an idyllic combination of exclusiveness and convenience. Perhaps the most notable of these (some have been demolished for redevelopment) was *Pinewood House*, now a Grade II listed building, built around 1890 for a City financier.

---

[13] Land Registry document: The author is grateful to Mr S Mellstrom for access to this document.

13.12 Loseberry House was one of the mansions built in Claygate before the railway came; its position was so near to the LSWR Red Route (and the New Line as built) that it had special protection from the normal 'Limit of Deviation' allowed to a new railway (2005).

13.13 Oxshott station, from the viaduct, c1911, Englefield to the left, Oxshott Heath to the right.

13.14 Pausing for a photograph, c1904, this passenger, probably from Cobham, is headed for Stoke D'Abernon station.

Nearly a mile in the Esher direction, *Copsem House* was built around 1900, shortly after Queens Drive had been laid out on Crown land, while development in the *Birds Hill Estate* had been commenced already. Development of what was ultimately upgraded to a road from its beginnings as no more than a track – Oakshade Road – began in 1897 with the development of, notably, *The Red House* near the *Victoria* public house and, on a much smaller scale, *Bembridge* in 1898 at the other end of the road opposite the future site of the church: both these houses survive.

This small account gives ample illustration of the considerable building activity that was stimulated by the railway in Oxshott in the last 10 years of the 19th century. That there was no immediate building after the railway opened – nothing of note appears to have been built before 1890 – is consistent with the general theme that there was no group of people clamouring for a railway, but once it was there a sophisticated few recognised the minor form of paradise that had been opened up in Oxshott with its exceptional Heath and forests. Always able to take the long view, there is no evidence of a public marketing of land by the Crown in this period: it is highly probable, therefore (and it would be in the style of Clutton), that it was marketed

in an exclusive way: directly but circumspectly by Clutton in London to his favoured network of successful people – Oxshott was too good for wide exposure, lest it lost its exclusivity.

The first retail businesses started in the High Street in 1895 and Barclays Bank arrived in 1899. The building of the mansions and their associated cottages, and the shops stimulated the setting up of a number of local building businesses in Oxshott in the 1890s and the building activity gave a major boost to the brick industry, which as in Claygate brought with it a need for housing for the brickmakers. So began the existence within Oxshott of a thriving group of artisans: none of the new owners of the mansions was short of cash, and the houses and the estates generated considerable demand for skilled labour. Each of these groups in their own way was dependent on the other: the rich families, some members of whom would travel to London by train, were always willing to support the provision of the local facilities which were needed, while the artisans who first built their properties, then kept them in order. Side by side and in the space of less than 20 years these two distinct social groups were to turn a poor hamlet into a thriving nuclear village.

13.15 With Cobham's station destined to be in Stoke D'Abernon, it must have been a great time to be a carter; a sketch by John Swain.

Cobham

By 1901 Cobham had a population of 3,900, an increase in 20 years of nearly 1,600 or 68 per cent; it was three times bigger than Claygate, five times bigger than West Horsley and it dwarfed any of the other cluster villages. With the exception only of the Tilt neighbourhood, all the settled areas of Cobham were a long way from the station. Cobham depended on trade, and there can be no doubt that trade was given a boost by the coming of the railway, with the economics of the milling and brewing industries being improved by the increase in the population. Following a change in ownership in 1888 Cobham Brewery entered a period of buoyant trade. Even though the railhead was at some distance, suddenly the delivered price of coal came down, giving a boost not only to domestic and trade users but to the Cobham Gas Light & Coke Company: in 1899 street lighting was introduced, and employment in that industry increased. Equally Cobham's own minor brick industry near Knipp Hill was boosted by the increased building activity. *Painshill Park* was extensively rebuilt in the 1880s. In 1892 the road from Cobham towards the station was improved to reduce the incidence of flooding. In the 1896 Epsom Derby there were five runners bred from Combe's stud farm and the yearling sale in that year was so popular that a special train was run from *Waterloo*. A village hall was opened in 1888 and in 1894 the inaugural meeting of the Parish Council was held there. In 1886 a parish library opened and in 1899 a rudimentary fire service started, through the patronage of Combe. If the railway stimulated much of this considerable private and corporate activity in the period to 1901, then it is a reminder of how much was Cobham's need in the years of the many abortive attempts to bring it in.

The exclusive Fairmile district received a boost from the railway because it was now closer to Oxshott than to Esher, and this also would boost retail trade in Cobham and give employment to former agricultural labourers as gardeners. As a place where employment could be found, Cobham would have pulled in those agricultural workers who were victims of the depression on the farms. While it seems unlikely that commuters (other than the Fairmile phalanx) would be attracted to Cobham in preference to Claygate, because of the difficulty of getting to the station, it seems a reasonable hypothesis that a boost to trade was brought about by the railway.

171

13.16 West Clandon was slow to be changed by the railway; this is an early 20th century view.

Cobham is the furthest out from London in our village cluster where the population increase to 1901 had any significance, and even today it marks the point where farmland and forestry become the dominant scenes until Merrow is reached. (The exception to this being the delightful two miles that separate Claygate from Oxshott, where cattle and sheep can be seen grazing on both sides of the track.) Of course, as we have explored already, development can only take place where land is made available for it. In Cobham two very important estates came onto the market at a moment that allowed the great expansion to take place. In 1880, 144 acres of 'undulating meadow and arable land' came up for auction in the first spring after the catastrophe of the 1879 harvest, when it had been remarked that it seemed perverse to offer a thanksgiving to God for the ruined crops: *Eaton Farm* sold for a pitiful £8 per acre, and gave its name to Eaton Park Road, and Eaton Park. It was noted to be 'about four miles from *Esher* and *Leatherhead* stations' and 'admirably adapted for sub-division for building purposes'. When the New Line came this land became more valuable because it was very convenient for Oxshott station. Frederick Keays had built his *Fairmile Court* in about 1879, having moved from a suburban villa in Uxbridge Road, Surbiton, and his phalanx was

obviously attracted to the location more for its exclusiveness than its railway convenience. The development that took place on *Eaton Farm* is likely to have been stimulated by the New Line: Keays' Fairmile was being drawn from the Portsmouth Road towards Oxshott, such that ultimately only the inviolate Heath separated the high class residential development from the west side of the station. The domestic staff that accompanied the large new houses was significant, with the 1901 census showing 15 living-in servants at *Fairmile Court*. The 1901 population numbers for Cobham were boosted greatly by Sandroyd School, which was started in 1890 and named after and located in one of the great Fairmile houses, where there were over 20 staff and over 50 boarders. It is impossible to escape the conclusion that it was the New Line that made possible a boarding school in this location, and no doubt many journeys to and from Oxshott station were made because of it.

The other large land sale in the period was in 1883, while the New Line was under construction, when a large part of the Leigh Hill estate was auctioned. The land was 'fronting the high Portsmouth Road' in Street Cobham and continuing along 'the new Anyards Road to Church Cobham'. It represented the opportunity for

13.17 Clandon station became a popular destination for Newlands Corner; this 1930s view shows the name on the platform sign.

Church Cobham to be physically united with the Tartar Hill area as a prelude to the joining up with Street Cobham: it was an opportunity which the market forces of the time found irresistible. As one would expect, the auctioneer's particulars drew attention to the coming of the railway: while the land was 'admirably' close to the church, post office and the facilities of the town, it was also 'within a short distance the proposed railway station on the new Kingston [*sic*] and Guildford line'. Although there were some commuters from the Leigh Hill area by 1901, it would seem that the development that took place in central Cobham and to the north of it in the late 19th century owed more to the organic growth of a nuclear settlement than it did to the railway station making it an attractive place as a dormitory (except at Fairmile) for those working in London: it is probable that Cobham's growth in this period was stimulated by the impact of the railway on facilitating the movement of goods. It must have been a great period in which to have been a carter in Cobham.

Cricket and soccer

It seems likely that the railway provided a stimulus for the development of activities involving team games and wider horizons for away matches. Cobham's soccer club was founded in 1886 and its cricket club dates from the 1880s and in 1887 the decision to build a pavilion was made. The Revd Phillips had been a patron of cricket in Stoke D'Abernon since at least 1870 and had provided a field for it to be played on his estate. The new artisans of Oxshott naturally took to the game and the founding of Oxshott Cricket Club, with which the headmaster of the Royal Kent School was closely associated, is put at 1896, while in Claygate, its cricket club had started in the year the railway came. One of the benefits of the railway was, presumably, that local sides could travel further for away games: Oxshott is recorded as having played against West Clandon in 1892, an away match involving such an expedition that could scarcely be imagined before the railway came; certainly the railway would often be a convenient substitute for a dependable horse hitched to a farm wagon loaded with its 11 team members and their supporters, together with all the baggage, trundling to a neighbouring village. Although this was extra business for the railway, many were probably nostalgic for 'the old days' with the intimate but somewhat noisy return journeys after dark, probably accompanied by a flagon of cider.

13.18 Cook's Crossing, Oxshott c1909.

Archibald Scott

The theme of this chapter has been how the development patterns of the 20th century were laid out in Claygate, Oxshott and Cobham in the years to 1901, while further down the line not much had happened to offend the 'rustic simplicity' of those outer villages. As far as a railway venture is concerned, there was nowhere near enough traffic, existing or potential, to have justified the building of the line in the first place. Archibald Scott retired from the general managership of the LSWR just before the New Line opened but he served on the board until 1903: it is doubtful that he

was at all surprised at the low numbers in the traffic reports ('A tramway along the Esher road is quite good enough for the Cobham people') but he and others who followed him noticed the huge gains being made by the landowners. The long corporate memory would remember this when, thirty years later, there were calls for new stations on the line to cater for the demand which was to be created, for as the century turned new railway resources in London and social changes at large led to a general acceleration in traffic, from its very low base, and of the further development of our cluster villages.

Chapter 14: Changes in the early 20th century

14.1 *This Class A12 0-4-2 (Adams) locomotive No 556 (built 1889, Nine Elms) stands at Waterloo ready for a Guildford via Cobham service.*

London is the source of demand

The new century saw a relative decline in Britain's competitiveness from the supreme position it had had, and in its share of world trade, but there was as much money to be made – perhaps more – from the mercantile activity than from the factory itself. If Britain at large 'was no longer so much as formerly the world's workshop, she was more than ever its warehouseman, its banker, and its commission agent,'[1] and London prospered and grew as its played to its strengths. As Joseph Chamberlain confirmed in 1904: 'Provided that the City of London remains, as it is at present, the clearing-house of the world, any other nation may be its workshop.'[2] As commerce increased in relative and absolute terms, so London thrived. The British Empire was at its zenith and at its heart lay London, the administrative capital of a quarter of the globe. In culture the London theatre achieved international status. The newspaper industry evolved from being the plaything of individual owners who indulged their whims with their own money to being owned by public companies, which demanded a more economically rigorous approach: the industry grew by bounds, and Fleet Street was its centre. London the powerhouse of the Kingdom and Empire was ever

expanding through trade, culture and as an administrative and diplomatic centre, which in turn brought forth a growth in the professions, all of them led from London. The capital's growth was the driving force for employment and the professional and managerial classes could now look to wider horizons for living while coming up to London by train to earn their daily bread.

This pull of demand was not unique to the area served by the New Line of course; the facilities which it offered were in competition with much of the Home Counties but especially other parts of Surrey – a county known to combine great natural beauty with proximity to the metropolis. The key to being able to exploit the benefits of living in Surrey was not just the journey up to town, but moving to the place of work from the London terminus: in this respect *Waterloo* was at a competitive disadvantage compared with *Cannon Street*, *London Bridge* and *Charing Cross* stations, the first two of which gave direct access to the City, while *Charing Cross* gave

---

[1] *England 1870-1914*: R C K Ensor, 1936, p 507.
[2] *Oxford Dictionary of Quotations*: 5th Edition, Ed Elizabeth Knowles, 1999, p 200.

175

access by the soon to be electrified underground railway. The process of reducing *Waterloo*'s distance in terms of travelling time from the business district of the City and from the West End started in the 1890s but it is no great offence to chronology to discuss it in this chapter because it was not until the new century that the effect of these great developments had any great effect on demand for travel on the New Line.

The reader will recall that the LSWR had been goaded in the evidence given to the May 1881 Select Committee about how inconveniently located was *Waterloo*. In 1893 powers were granted by Parliament for an electric tube railway to connect *Waterloo* to the City and the LSWR quickly decided to support it financially. The *Waterloo and City Line* or *The Drain* as it was later dubbed was opened for traffic in 1898, the official ceremony being conducted by the Duke of Cambridge, the supporter of Onslow's railway. This connection to the City reduced the overall journey times by a measurable amount and it became very popular with many season ticket holders booking through from their home stations. Passenger journeys in 1899 on *The Drain* were 3.5 million growing to 4.5 million the following year. In 1906, in a further enhancement of *Waterloo*'s connection to the existing underground railway infrastructure, the *Bakerloo* tube line from *Baker Street* to *Waterloo* was opened. Not only did this speed up communication

with London's West End but also it connected to the *Central Line* tube railway, which had opened in 1900. In 1905 the first motor omnibuses appeared in London, while in the same year a Royal Commission concluded that the electric tram 'was the most efficient and the cheapest means of street conveyance'. In 1908 the Kingsway tunnel opened and trams now crossed the river. 'Within a few years local travelling in London became, as it never was in the 19th century, really rapid and convenient.'[3] While this was a benefit for London at large, the fact that *Waterloo* was no longer cut off was a key ingredient in the development by the LSWR of its commuter market at large.

The improvements in inner London mass transportation brought about a trend for lower paid workers to be able to live in the suburbs and travel to their jobs. The changes in urban transport had an almost instant effect on housing: 'soon after 1900 a building boom sprang up on the outskirts of towns, and continued until 1910'.[4] It was only the higher paid who could afford to leapfrog the suburbs and they took the opportunity in increasing numbers of living further out and travelling in by train. Practically the whole of Surrey's rail network was now in place, the choice for the would-be commuter was wide open and naturally the New Line was among all the LSWR's lines that benefited from more demand.

Timetable improvements

By summer 1909 the New Line service had improved and a part of the Up timetable is shown below.

Up	am	am	am	am	pm	pm	pm	pm*	pm	pm	pm	pm
Guildford	7.17	7.55	8.36	10.29	12.24	1.34	3.03	4.02	4.37	7.15	7.20	9.13
London Road	7.23	8.00	8.42	10.35	12.30	...	3.08	...	4.43	...	7.26	9.18
Clandon	7.31	8.07	8.50	10.43	12.37	...	3.16	...	4.52	...	7.33	9.25
Horsley	7.39	8.14	8.58	10.51	12.45	...	3.23	...	5.01	...	7.40	9.32
Effingham Junction	7.43	8.18	9.02	10.55	12.49	1.48	3.27	4.16	5.05	7.29	7.44	9.36
Cobham & St. D'Abernon	7.48	8.23	9.07	11.00	12.54	...	3.32	...	5.11	...	7.49	9.42
Oxshott	7.54	8.28	9.14	11.06	1.00	...	3.38	...	5.17	...	7.54	9.47
Claygate	7.59	8.33	9.19	11.11	1.05	...	3.43	...	5.22	...	7.59	9.52
Surbiton	8.07	8.40	9.27	11.19	1.13	...	3.51	...	5.30	...	8.07	10.00
Raynes Park	8.14	8.47	...	11.23	...	...	...	...	...	...	...	...
Wimbledon	8.17	8.51	...	11.27	1.23	...	4.01	...	...	...	...	10.09
Earlsfield	8.20	...	...	...	...	...	...	...	...	...	...	...
Clapham Junction	8.24	8.59	9.41	11.33	1.31	2.12	4.09	4.39	5.43	7.52	8.22	10.16
Vauxhall	8.30	9.05	9.47	11.39	1.38	2.18	4.16	4.45	5.49	7.58	8.29	10.23
Waterloo	8.35	9.10	9.52	11.44	1.43	2.23	4.21	4.50	5.54	8.03	8.34	10.28

* Mondays and Saturdays only

[3] *England 1870-1914*: R C K Ensor, 1936, p 509.
[4] *Ibid.*

14.2 A Class L11 4-4-0 (Drummond) locomotive No 174 (built 1906, Nine Elms) heads a Down Guildford via Cobham train at Earlsfield, c1909.

14.3 The station staff at Claygate pose for the camera as a Down train enters the station, c1907.

The Lens of Sutton collection
14.4 A Down Guildford via Leatherhead pauses at Effingham Junction; date unknown.

In addition to these 12 Up trains there were three others terminating at *Surbiton*, where there was an opportunity to change trains for *Waterloo*. For those passengers joining trains between *Guildford* and *Effingham Junction* there were an additional nine trains per day running to *Waterloo* via *Leatherhead*. The typical times for the whole journey via *Surbiton* were 75 minutes or so, about 10 minutes quicker than the inaugural timetable but still painfully slow by modern standards. For those travellers from *Guildford*, the Portsmouth Direct service gave as it does today the opportunity for fast trains and a journey time of around 55 minutes from the main station: today some commuters from *London Road* start their journey going the wrong way by taking the train to *Guildford* to pick up a fast train to *Waterloo*; the habit has probably always been in existence.

As can be seen from the 1909 timetable there were three fast trains up from *Effingham Junction* running non-stop via Hampton Court Junction until *Clapham Junction*, *Vauxhall* and *Waterloo*; the running of fast trains on the New Line had begun as early as 1897 in which year refuge sidings were built in *Claygate* and *Horsley* (where some trains were turned round) and at *Clandon* and *London Road* in 1898. The reason for *Effingham Junction* station being favoured as the only station having fast trains is unexplained; for the lucky travellers from that station their journey time to *Waterloo* was reduced to 35 minutes from a typical 50 minutes. The 10.29am and 7.15pm trains ex *Guildford* were particularly interesting:

14.5 *Staff on the Down platform at Effingham Junction seem unaware of the approaching train from Leatherhead, c1910; note the absence of tree growth.*

the former was formed of the 9.48am from *Haslemere* while the latter – one of the fast trains – was the 5.45pm from *Portsmouth*. By 1913 five down trains to *Portsmouth* were booked through the New Line and three up. This practice continues to this day, with two up and three down trains booked fast on the New Line. Intermediate stops are no longer made and the refuges have been removed, the faster running time of the electric services allowing sufficient time to clear the road.

The ability to run Portsmouth trains on the New Line was a benefit that came seemingly as a bonus to the LSWR for it was not part of any given reason for building it. Naturally, it was a useful relief line from *Guildford* in exceptional circumstances but the greater benefit lay in the planned use of it to relieve congestion on the main line. The quadrupling between Hampton Court Junction and *Woking* had been completed early in the new century so it was not so much the lack of paths causing congestion on the main line as the pinch-point of the flat junction near *Woking*. When every up movement from *Guildford* joins the main line at *Woking* it requires all the roads to be closed to conflicting movements, but by running some *Portsmouth* services on the New Line the traffic using this junction at *Woking* is relieved.

On the subject of these refuge sidings there is an interesting use of the one at *Horsley*, which appears to

have escaped the security screen covering it at the time. During the Second World War, His Majesty King George VI was making a visit to Portsmouth by train and not for the last time the train was booked through the New Line (probably having come from *Victoria* via *Effingham Junction*). The journey being disrupted by bombing, the royal train was parked for the night in the refuge siding at *Horsley* waiting for darkness to pass.

Congestion at Hampton Court Junction

As the popularity of the New Line increased after the improved tube connections to *Waterloo* – the service interval on the *Waterloo & City Line* was down to four minutes in busy periods – and the number of trains increased so congestion at Hampton Court Junction became a problem. Both the New Line and the Hampton Court branch were first built with a flat junction with the main line and because of the amount of traffic that they were now carrying the conflicting movements at the junctions caused congestion. Powers were obtained in 1906 to solve the problem. This gave rise to the spectacular viaduct and skewed bridging of the main line to carry the down Hampton Court line, completed in 1915. The solution for the New Line was simpler: the up line was deviated northwards 70 chains from the junction and after burrowing under the main line it joined it more or less opposite where the now single down line left it.

14.6 A Guildford via Cobham train waits at the Down platform at Horsley, c1910; the staff are in evidence, but no passengers.

Schools traffic

So far the discussion of the growth in traffic levels on the New Line has been focussed on the growth in population and the tendency of newcomers of the railway to use the line for commuting to London; the exception was the Sandroyd boarding school at Fairmile which brought passengers into the district. Today, the line continues to carry large numbers of schoolchildren usually making intra-station journeys in both directions, but especially to the schools in the London Road area. The United Church Schools Trust, the owners of Guildford High School, was founded in 1883 and the present site hard by *London Road* station seems to have been in use since shortly after the railway opened. Tormead School opened in 1905, attracted no doubt by the accessibility to the station to facilitate travel. The traffic created by the London Road schools, then as now, explains why its station has the highest incidence of use as a destination of any of the other intermediate New Line stations, with nearly twice as many destination journeys as there are origins of journeys.[5] Every generation of these children, it seems, proclaim their tribal mantra by reciting the station-stop announcements.

Leisure traffic

Even before the Edwardian era approached, but increasingly during it, the opportunities for leisure expanded. The railway brought the sporting, cultural and leisure attractions of London within easy reach of the newcomers now populating the line in increasing numbers; horse racing was very fashionable and the LSWR still made considerable profits from carrying enthusiasts to the various race meetings in the district. The boat race was a popular annual outing and boating itself was a favourite pastime, with opportunities at both Surbiton and Guildford easily reached. It was, however, the invention of the Bank Holiday, which did the most for the volume of traffic by rail because it became endemic for large numbers of people to go away for the day by train or as the *Surrey Comet* put it: 'now a general holiday means half of London out of town'; it was the railway: 'the beneficent invention of modern science' which allowed 'the hard working mechanic and the jaded man of business' to escape from town for 'a change of scene; the breath of heather-covered hills, and the pure breeze of the downs'. Some went to the seaside but many came to Surrey.

---

[5] Source: South West Trains.

14.7 The entire Horsley station staff (and a child) have the opportunity to occupy the whole width of the station for this pose, taken from the Down platform; c1910.

14.8 Horsley station from the Up platform looking towards the line summit, with the goods yard on the Down side; the platform staff pose with either a passenger, or the bookstall seller.

The leisure market brought a two-way business for the LSWR. The beauty spots that were within easy reach of the New Line itself brought forth visitors in increasing numbers into districts served by it. The advocates of Onslow's railway had seen from the beginning that the countryside which the line would open up would be appealing to tourists. Matthew Arnold, the Cobham resident observed that:

As I looked at the landscape from the hills above Horsley, the backbone of England, I felt how pleasant a country it was, and how well satisfied I could be to remain all my days in it.

Word got around: 'take the train to *Horsley*' said the ramblers' guides now being published in increasing numbers. *Clandon* station was convenient for Newlands Corner, one of the most delightful spots in Surrey – perhaps even in the south of England – and its platform name signs announced the fact that the station gave access to it. In increasing numbers these early day-trippers, whether as walkers or cyclists, discovered the Silent Pool near Shere and the LSWR put on special ramblers' trains at the weekends and on holidays to feed and create the demand. Guide books spoke of: 'vistas of loveliness, quiet footpaths through green meadows, dense forests, sunny gorse commons, hidden streams, and unspoilt tiny hamlets lying in amazing profusion almost on your door step': romanticized – may be – but before the motor car came there was not one station on the New Line – *London Road* included – that did not allow access to the pleasures spoken of here. 'Within a minute of leaving the station' said a typical walking guide, 'you feel as if you had been magically transplanted into a remote world, for you may walk for the rest of the day and not encounter half a dozen fellow-creatures'; if the rambler kept from the popular beauty spots this would have been literally true. The guidebooks encouraged train travel by identifying rambles that could start at one station, say *Horsley*, and finish at another, at *Gomshall* or even *Cranleigh* for the robust walkers, and ultimately 'go-as-you-please' tickets were developed to facilitate the use of different lines for the return journey. In all these walking guides, the railway stations were the reference points, but in a county that abounded in opportunities for leisure walks, *Clandon*, *Horsley*, *Effingham* and *Bookham* were typically featured as a starting point or somewhere for the faint-hearted to start back for home. *Oxshott* became a destination in itself for a short outing and

tearooms sprang up to cater for the large numbers coming to visit the Heath for a few hours or more. Some day trips were more ambitious and they reflected a growing trend for youngsters as well as adults to escape, some for the first time in their lives, the confines of the village: in 1906 there was a school outing from *Clandon* to *Southsea*; it would be some years before the motor coach became the more favoured conveyance for expeditions of this character among a wide range of social groups.

Guildford was not without its own guidebooks encouraging leisure visits to the fine town. One 1910 guide dwells on the opportunities for both boating and angling on the Wey, but equally the attractions of the Mole at Cobham, which 'can be reached best by train' are given exposure.[6] The guidebook notes how much more attractive is the journey to *Guildford* via the New Line, observing that 'you gain a very much better conception of the beauties of rural Surrey' drawing attention to 'the woods of *Claremont* and the church tower of Stoke D'Abernon' (now obscured by trees): everywhere the countryside is 'beautiful with alternate coppice, pasture and ploughland'. 'In spring the woods which lie thickly along the line are yellow with innumerable primroses.' This description, which is nearly 100 years old, has a validity today that justifies still the description of the New Line as 'a country railway'.

The guidebooks referred to were designed essentially for day visitors from the metropolis but there was another kind of leisure trip by train which became a normal part of life and which was heavily promoted by the LSWR: the annual holiday by train to the West Country or to France. Much of the housing that was built for newcomers was for middle-class families usually with facilities for a live-in maid of which until the Great War there was a good supply. Every year the family would go on holiday by train. The journey would start at the home station and if a boat train were required, *Waterloo* would be the pick-up point. For trains to the West Country there might be as now the possibility of picking up the train at *Woking*; the luggage would be sent on in advance, so the journey would be very comfortable. Dining cars serving

---

[6] *SURREY'S CAPITAL: A handbook for Guildford and its surroundings* (The Homeland Handbooks series – No 11): Joseph E Morris, 1910.

14.9 *A Down Guildford via Cobham train arrives at Guildford, c1909.*

14.10 *A Class A12 0-4-2 (Adams) locomotive No 647 (built 1894, Nine Elms) arrives at Guildford with a Down Guildford via Cobham service.*

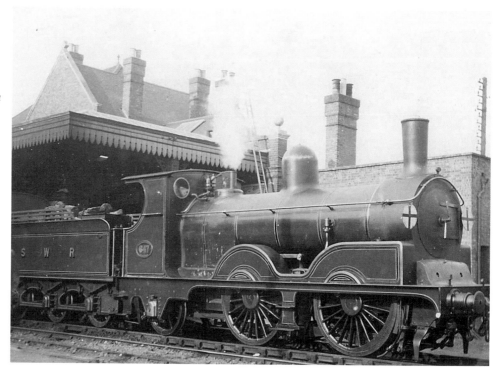

14.11 *A solitary motor car heading for Fairmile on the Portsmouth Road, Street Cobham, c1914.*

breakfast, lunch and dinner had been developed, and the whole atmosphere of the train journey to a holiday destination was one of excitement. *Exeter* had been opened to the railway in 1860; *Bournemouth* in 1870; *Ilfracombe* in 1874, while after the New Line opened, *Camelford* and *Wadebridge* in 1893 and 1895 respectively, followed by *Bude* and *Padstow* in 1898 and 1899. The LSWR (and its successors) was justly proud of its network and promoted it heavily for holidaymaking. Free illustrated guidebooks were published to promote the variety of destinations that were available such as *The Pleasure Grounds of the South West*. For the more adventurous and well off, the LSWR operated their own steamers from Southampton Docks to St Malo and Le Havre, from which connections were made to Paris, while every night in the summer there was a 9.45 train from *Waterloo* that served the Channel Islands. The railway provided the widened horizons for leisure pursuits for the incomers to the New Line cluster of villages.

The arrival of the motor car

In the early years of the new century the motor car was not yet a factor in determining the siting of new housing. They were at first only for the very rich and adventurous, frightening those whom they approached and then covering them in dust as they receded, for at this time few roads had modern surfacing. It is highly probable that the owners of the Oxshott mansions were the first to own them at a time when they 'seemed visible symbols of the selfishness of arrogant wealth'.[7] In 1909 the Road Board took charge of surfacing and the dust nuisance receded. Ultimately the growing use of motor cars would be as an important ingredient in the future development of the New Line cluster of villages – as important as the railway itself – so that in time it would become impossible to separate out their

---

[7] *England 1870-1914*: R C K Ensor, 1936, p 510.

14.12 East Clandon, the estate village of Hatchlands, resisted change through tight holding of land; this view is from c1908.

respective influences. The pervasive and permanent influence of the motor car was famously misjudged: in 1906 the General Manager of the LSWR, allowed his hope to overcome reality when commenting on a sharp decline in race traffic business: he opined that business would improve when the people 'tired of their cars'.

The emergence of golf as a popular leisure pursuit

The new century saw agriculture experience a kind of revival, in the sense that small but progressive rises in prices gave positive returns. However this upturn was insufficient, at least in Surrey, to reverse an established trend. The collapse in farm incomes caused by the agricultural depression of almost a quarter of a century was filled in part by a new leisure use of the land: golf. In the period 1870 to just before the Great War a total of 25,000 acres was taken out of agricultural use in Surrey. Some of this was lost to coppicing, some in Oxshott, while new golf courses took out perhaps over 8,000 acres. In the 10 years to 1895 golf clubs started to spring up with great rapidity, and by 1903 over 40 clubs were chronicled in Surrey. It was the low residual value of land, which coincided with the new fashion for golf, which has in no way receded since, along with the new accessibility permitted by the railways at first and then by the motor car which were the key factors in the

growth of this new activity which became an established part of the social scene. Effingham Golf Club, being founded in 1927, owes more to the motor car than the railway, but the three golf clubs founded 30 years earlier – Guildford in 1886, and Claygate and Surbiton in 1895 – no doubt owe their genesis to the availability of cheap land and proximity to the railway, without which facility they could never have established themselves. The Guildford club, built on Merrow Downs was within easy reach of *London Road* station in a pony and trap. Lord Onslow took to the game, becoming president of the Guildford club, the clubhouse of which was only a couple of miles from the gates of Clandon Park. The Surbiton club, partly in Claygate, partly in Chessington was built on land owned by Lord Lovelace and which would have been bisected by Onslow's railway if his version of the New Line had been built. The Claygate course was built on common land but Surbiton was laid out on pasture that had previously been arable. The early days are well chronicled and reports tell of the course being a delightful carriage drive from *Surbiton* (*Claygate* station was also convenient). To facilitate access by train a regular service of horse drawn transport was introduced to connect with the station. Many of the early members would travel from London, but increasingly as the number of incomers grew, they would come up the New Line.

Increases in population to 1921

The increases in the population of the New Line cluster villages after 1901 and the use of the train were much greater than they had been so far. By 1921 the total population had increased by 6,420 compared with an increase of 2,700 in the first 20 years, an increase over the 40 years of 93 per cent. While the percentage may be impressive, and indeed a sign of things to come, the aggregates were not – at least not if you were trying to run a profitable railway. Even before the Great War the LSWR had realised that their business would be increased by stimulating the trend for the higher paid to live in the country and commute to London; their advertisements for their brochure spoke of 'charming residential districts within easy reach of London' and without doubt had in mind our New Line cluster of villages among the others that were served.

New Line cluster of villages: (ranked by 1921 population)				
	Population			
			Increase 1881 to	
	1881	1921	1921	%
Cobham	2,319	5,103	2,784	120
Claygate	788	2,862	2,074	263
The Bookhams and Effingham	1,867	2,543	676	36
The Clandons and the Horsleys	1,533	1,979	446	29
Stoke D'Abernon (including Oxshott)	408	848	440	108
Total	6,915	13,335	6,420	93

While the population of the New Line cluster of villages rose by 93 per cent in the 40 years to 1921, the overall increase in the population of England and Wales was about a fifth of that, so plainly some important stimulus was at work, which we must take in overall terms to be the effect of London. Increasingly, people wanted to work in London and live outside it and because the motor car was not yet a major influence on the siting of new housing, it was the railway that fuelled the demand for housing in our cluster. The new century had seen a number of important trends, which were hidden within the absolute population numbers. Sanitation and public health had made great strides, which resulted in the 'sensational reduction' in infantile mortality. In opposition to this the birth rate fell – but so too did the death rate. As the overall population rose it was, broadly speaking, contributed to by a smaller drop in the birth rate in the lower paid group than the much faster fall in the birth rate among the rich

families. To the extent, therefore, that the overall population numbers in the above table comprised what we might call the original indigenous population, then the increases are an overstatement of the numbers of newcomers. The extent of this flaw in the measure of incoming numbers is unknown, but it is compensated by the unknown diminution of population by the emigration of young men and some women to the Empire and to the USA, which achieved material proportion, generally, in the period between the South African and Great Wars (1902-1914). One of the great social consequences of the Great War was the massive reduction in the numbers of both men and women who were willing to go back to menial work or domestic service after their emancipating wartime experiences. When one considers the numbers of low-paid men and women who were employed in the great houses of the area – those which preceded the railway, and the addition to their number, specially in Oxshott after it came – and the attrition of their numbers because of the War, the population growth shown crudely by the census numbers are likely to have disguised a decline in the indigenous population and a stronger growth in newcomers than is apparent.

Of the 446 increase in population in the Clandons and the Horsleys between 1881 and 1921, 330 (55%) of it took place in West Horsley; while in the Clandons, East Horsley, the Bookhams and Effingham in the 40 years there was barely any discernible increase in their populations. According to Connell,[8] in East Horsley the only visible effect of the railway by 1897 other than the railway cottages was the construction of the Railway Hotel, and by 1919 nothing had changed. In 1908 West Horsley, with its disused workhouse, was 'a fascinating collection of old cottages, vine bowered and fronted with clipped yews'.[9] Similarly at *Effingham Junction* the only houses in 1919 were the railway cottages while the path from the station to Effingham village had not yet been made up into a road. The growth noted above in West Horsley, which was a greater distance from the station, was largely independent of the railway. The villages of the Clandons and the Horsleys, Effingham and the Bookhams, by their low growth until after 1921, demonstrate that they had resisted in large measure the national and regional changes that were going on

---

[8] *The End of Tradition: Country Life in Central Surrey*: John Connell, 1978, p. 39.
[9] *Highways and Byways in Surrey*: Eric Parker, 1923, p 120.

14.13 *Aston Road, Claygate; part of the railway-induced development that was built before the Great War.*

around them, and serves to emphasise that their 'rustic simplicity' had not been disturbed by the railway.

The population of Stoke D'Abernon (including Oxshott) had doubled but was not of a character to have yet upset the Revd Phillips' 'rustic simplicity', although the seeds of its demise had been sown by the low-density development in Oxshott aimed largely at rich families. All that said, it is plain that both Cobham and Claygate had seen significant expansion; the increases in the populations in the 40 years to 1921 are shown in the table below.

	Population growth		
	1881 to 1901	1901 to 1921	1881 to 1921
Cobham	1,581	1,203	2,784
Claygate	602	1,482	2,084
Total	2,183	2,685	4,868

The growth of Claygate accelerates

From these increases in population it can be seen that the pace of growth in Cobham slackened from 1901 to 1921 compared with the preceding 20 years, whereas the growth of Claygate had accelerated; with a total population in 1921 of 2,862, up from 778, the popularity of Claygate had become marked. There can be little to argue about what was happening in Claygate: its railway station and its proximity to London had induced its expansion by nearly 500 households. Fitzalan Foley's at first faltering development of his estate was probably given a shot in the arm by the development of the transport links to and from *Waterloo* discussed earlier. Claygate was only 15 miles from *Waterloo*; it was the first settlement after Surbiton and even if the writing was on the wall, its own 'rustic simplicity' had not yet been destroyed. On Foley's estate good plots were available on which family homes of between 2,000 and 3,000 sq feet could be built with accommodation for a maid. The buyers of these

homes were not concerned with stabling for horses: space was available for a motor car but this was not necessary for a commuter from Claygate. Although the houses built on the Foley estate could not be dismissed as mass produced, their availability was on that scale. Lesser-priced housing was also developed near the magnet of the new village that sprang up around The Parade. The new centre of Claygate anchored Hare Lane, Aston Road and Norfolk Road to it, while larger family housing was built in The Avenue.

Although Fitzalan Foley started the development of Claygate by his land purchases in the 1880s when more land became available other less notable purchasers took on the role. Between 1908 and 1910 *Titts Farm* was broken up and its 35 to 40 acres sold at auction for development. This land, which lay on the west side of and contiguous with the railway, was bounded by Hare Lane, Hare Lane Green and the Rhythe river (whose valley the railway was following). Station Road had probably been developed on its land as had Rose Cottages off Station Road which pre-dated the railway as brickworkers' homes. The *Titts Farm* land provided the space for the development of Loseberry Road, Raleigh Drive and Rythe Road which when completed along with the development of that part of Hare Lane made a joining up of Claygate and the hamlet of Hare Lane Green.

The demise of Claygate's old village (as it came to be known) as the centre of the retail trade was now certain, but some high value housing was constructed in St Leonards Road and some even larger houses in Church Road on plots large enough to induce the current fashion of demolition in order to unlock the site value – a process which saw, ultimately, the destruction of most of the large houses of Claygate that predated the railway. All this development in the early 20th century, in both the Hare Lane Green area and the old village reinforced Claygate's position as a commuter village, for the station was only a short walk away. For those who wanted to cycle – one must assume that cycling to the station is as old as cycling – a cycle shop opened at 2 Foley Road in 1908,[10] and remained in business for over 90 years.

An improved service encourages theatre-going

Although there was no great improvement in the frequency or timing of the business trains the service overall had improved by 1914; there were more trains during the day and at night the last train from *Waterloo*

---

[10] Reported in the *Surrey Comet*, December 1947.

14.15 The footpath from Claremont Road, Claygate to Arbrook Woods; the railway cutting is in front of Claygate Lodge (demolished 1970s).

The Paul Langton collection

ran at the much later time of 11.45 terminating at *Effingham Junction*. This train gave serious opportunities for theatregoing, being a considerable improvement on the 1909 timetable when the last train was booked at 9.55pm. The greatly expanding population of Claygate was in the best position to exploit the opportunities presented by London, both at work and play, because unlike the residents of Cobham they had no difficulty in getting home from the station. Travellers from Oxshott and the Fairmile would of course be more likely to stay at their London clubs after a night out on the town.

Guildford also staked a claim on theatrical audiences, its earliest support for the arts pre-dating the railways by 50 years.[11] After nearly a century the town's first theatre succumbed to financial difficulties, leaving London as the only alternative for this art form. In 1909 a resident observed that only the very well-off could afford to go to the theatre in the West End (by train) and suggested the resurrection of the local theatre. John Dennis of the engineering works supported the idea and in 1912 a new theatre with a capacity of 1,000

opened in North Street and enjoyed 20 years of success. It closed after licensing difficulties but reopened in 1945 as Guildford Repertory Theatre, but this was forced to close by a fire, to be substituted in due course by the Yvonne Arnaud Theatre. In all the years that the theatre thrived in Guildford before the age of the motor car, its patrons would include those who had travelled there by train, many of them from villages on the New Line.

The availability of land the only limit on development

While it is easy to attribute to Claygate's growth to 1921 to the railway, some caution is required. The whole question of the population expansion within the New Line cluster of villages is as much about the availability of land for development as it is about the pull of London and the countryside making the area a commuter's dream.

---

[11] *Guildford*: E R Chamberlin, 1982, p 169.

188

14.16 A group, c1911, watches an Up Guildford via Cobham train at the recently-built footbridge to supplement the existing Sheath Crossing, which remained until 1967; the extra wide bridge accommodates the brickworks siding.

The uncontrolled expansion that took place until 1939 was driven by the influence of London and the willingness of landowners to dispose of land for development: by the time the protection of the Green Belt came, most landowners who were so minded had succumbed to temptation. In the case of the Lovelace land a dynastic fault-line led to the complete liquidation of the land holding, while for the Crown Estate the coming of the railway and the development of Oxshott was axiomatic. In Claygate Fitzalan Foley had bought land in order to develop it. Before 1939, only the simultaneous occurrence of two key factors prevented a continuous development along the trackside: the unwillingness of landowners to sell and the market being satiated by the supply of land elsewhere.

The concept of rigorous Town and Country Planning with its careful and studied designation of land use through a local plan, which is endlessly consulted over, did not exist. If a landowner wanted to do something, then by and large he did it. There was a presumption in favour of the landowner, which had lain at the heart of English history, and providing certain sanitary and structural minima were observed there was no restraint on development. This approach ought not to have been tolerated in the modern world that the new century brought, but it was. The result, speaking broadly, was that nothing prevented 'the extensions of English towns from being among the meanest, ugliest, and most higgledy-piggledy in Europe'.[12] That there were no particular planning outrages in the districts that we are concerned with owes more to accident than to planning: it certainly owes nothing to the Housing and Town and Country Planning Act of 1909. This Act was a disaster, for although it allowed, nominally, town-planning schemes to come forward there was a raft of deterrent regulations to overcome. The existence of the Act was a barrier to good legislation and grievous damage resulted from it:

> For if, as would otherwise have happened, a real national start had been made with town planning in 1909 or 1910, all the foundation work could have been done before 1914, when building was quiet; and after the war, when the nation needed a flood of new houses, the whole development would have proceeded on planned instead of planless lines.[13]

---

[12] *England 1870-1914*: R C K Ensor, 1936, p 518.
[13] *Ibid.*

14.17 Queen's Drive, Oxshott, part of the Crown lands opened up by the railway.

Planning and development control had to wait until 1947 before it was properly regulated, but in fact because all private building stopped in 1939, there were 30 wasted years, which allowed the unrestrained and notorious excesses of the 1930s.

Oxshott

Oxshott in 1909 had only existed in modern terms for 20 years, and it had grown in the absence of any statutory planning influence but no harm had come to the village, which is what it had now become. There were, however, some very traditional influences on its growth, which worked well, but which were destined in due course to be eroded: a landowner's agent with long vision (Clutton) and the patronage of rich residents: *noblesse oblige*. Let us explore.

In Oxshott the early 20th century development took on a different pattern from the first steps that had been characterised by the development of mansions for the

very rich. The next phase saw the controlled disposal of plots for large houses in the privately planned estates that were laid out by the Crown in such exclusive roads as Queens Drive and various roads in the Birds Hill estate. Development also took place in the east in the Fairoak Lane area. These houses were not what we would have called mansions when they were built and their requirement for live-in staff to run them was on a much-reduced scale; nevertheless the plots were large enough to accommodate tennis courts and croquet lawns.

As the new century progressed Oxshott had become a recognisable settlement with its own character as already noted: very wealthy families on the one hand and a large group of artisans on the other; farming was now a subsidiary affair but at the west end of the settlement the brickworks flourished. There was however no accommodation for traditional Christian worship; the Revd Phillips of St Mary's had died in 1903 but not before he had improved the track from

14.18 St Andrew's Oxshott, the temporary church, built 1904, replaced 1912.

Oxshott to Stoke D'Abernon church which had made easier the Sunday trek to church. It became clear that Oxshott needed its own church and once the realisation was made there was, of course, no shortage of benefactors only too willing to endow it; such was Oxshott's fortune and spirit. At a public meeting in 1904 an offer to donate the land for a site at the corner of Steels Lane and Oakshade Road was made by Sir John Aird's son-in-law, Basil Ellis of *Bevendean*. The meeting decided on a cautious approach of building a temporary church in the first place and Aird himself was one of many benefactors who put up the cash among whose number, notably, was the Crown whose development agenda was supported by the steps being taken to eliminate the one lacuna in Oxshott's facilities. Progress was fast: the decision to build the temporary church, which could accommodate 160, saw it built and consecrated in the same year, with a staff member of Lucas & Aird acting as unpaid clerk-of-works. The fittings of the temporary church were of high quality,

funded of course by benefactors, and by 1905 everything was paid for.

There being no shortage of would-be benefactors in Oxshott, after the temporary church had been established it became a matter of finding a project as an outlet for *noblesse oblige*: the men of the village needed a club and in 1907 the owner of *Danes Hill* donated the present site opposite the church where Oxshott Men's Club was established and continues today under the name Oxshott Club. It was natural that the church should bring together the working men and their masters but not so natural that Oxshott Men's Club should have been patronised over the years by the pillars of Oxshott society, but it has been.

Ellis, who was a founder member of Oxshott Men's Club as well as the donor of the land for the church, died soon after the club had opened. When it was said of him that: all his 'efforts for moral and spiritual and

14.19 A delivery to The Victoria, Oxshott.

material progress of the parish'[14] were felt in every home, it was a reflection of the fact that Ellis – Sir John Aird's son-in-law – was one of the people that had made Oxshott complete in the mere 22 years since the railway came.

The temporary status of the church did not last long for by 1909 a public meeting resolved that 'steps should be taken with a view to [the] early erection of a permanent church' and by 1912 St Andrews Church was consecrated. The speed with which this was accomplished disguised the difficulties that had to be overcome, as well as emphasising the widespread support that existed for the project in the village. Ellis had been the great benefactor of the temporary church, but notwithstanding his death others were ready to fill that breach. It was now time for Oxshott to be its own parish and in 1913 the boundaries were redrawn to include land from the parishes of Stoke D'Abernon,

Cobham and Claygate. Shortly after Ellis's death came news that the *Bevendean* estate was to be broken up, thus starting a new trend, which would provide the sites for more housebuilding in the future.

Cobham's expansion had taken place in spite of large parts of its space being remote from its station in Stoke D'Abernon. This may suggest that other factors were at play: by 1921 wealthy people could afford motor cars and in the golden era of motoring, before nearly everyone owned one, being located at the edge of a village became appealing, just like Fairmile had been before the railway came. As the cars multiplied Cobham's lack of a centrally-located station became less of an issue, at least for those comfortably funded.

---

[14] *Oxshott: the story of a Surrey village:* B S Gidvani, 1996.

192

Earnings estimates: the New Line is still loss making

The New Line probably remained a drain on resources not only for the LSWR but for its successor too until electrification which brought the golden bounty of reduced operating costs and sharply increased traffic. Whether the progress towards viability improved in the early 1910s deserves to be tested but the traffic figures are not available; however we can attempt to interpolate from the broad operating statistics that are available, which unfortunately do not use the preferred measure of collecting costs and revenues per route mile.

We have seen how the analysis of an experienced railway manager showed that Onslow's line would have to be more profitable, if it were to pay its costs, than the average of all the south London railways – an absurd expectation. Conscious as they were of the questionable economics (and being driven by the menace of the District Railway) the LSWR built a cheaper railway, but another witness had asserted in 1881 that the line would only gross between £25 per mile per week 'or at most £30' at a time when the LSWR was grossing £63 per mile per week overall, while the GWR and others were making £67.[15] By 1913 the LSWR's gross earnings per week were down to £55 per mile, which probably reflects the competitive squeeze being applied by buses and trams on the inner urban routes and the effect of motor cars on race and other pleasure traffic.

In 1913 the proportion of the LSWR's total revenue represented by goods traffic was 32 per cent.[16] Applying this proportion to the predicted 'at most £30' per mile means that about £20 per week per mile needed to be generated from passenger traffic if that benchmark were to have been attained. In 1913 the return first class fare from *Cobham* to *Waterloo* was 5/-. To achieve £20 per week per mile for the whole route from *Guildford* to *Waterloo* equates to revenue of £600 per week: it would require 2,400 1st class return journeys per week at an average fare of 5/- to achieve this revenue. When account is taken of the generosity of the assumption of 1st class passengers only (in 1913 they would have been a higher proportion on the New Line than overall) the admittedly crude analysis supports a deep suspicion that the line was making a loss because the assumptions made (which in themselves stretch credulity) are those required to deliver £30 (£20; passenger: £10; goods) per mile per week, whereas in fact on average the LSWR was generating £55 per mile per week from which it earned £20 per week per mile operating profit. The figures are summarised in the table below.

LSWR operating statistics: 1913

	Per mile per week £
Total network*	
Revenue from railway operations: passengers	38
Revenue from railway operations: goods	17
Revenue from railway operations: total	55
Less: costs of running railway	35
Operating profit from railways: passenger and goods	20
New Line	
Revenue per assumptions in text	30
Less costs of running railway, as above	35
Imputed loss per mile per week	-5

* Source: Annual report and statement of accounts of LSWR, year ended 31 December 1913.

If the costs of running the New Line were the same per mile as the system at large (£35 per mile per week) then as can be seen from the above table, on the assumption of revenues of £30 per week per mile a loss of £5 per mile per week would be suffered, and in view of the generous assumptions made it may have been much more. This appears to be the position as the end of the steam era approached and the Great War made any analysis during or after it quite impossible because of the extraordinary (and severe) demands made on the system.

An overview of the way in which development took place into the modern era will be given in Chapter 17. Before that discussion there is a phenomenon to explore: a phenomenon whose impact was seen in all the southern suburbs of London and far out to the coast; a phenomenon whose immediate impact on the New Line cluster of villages in the 15 years from 1925 to 1939 was to make insignificant all the change that had been wrought by the coming of the New Line 40 years earlier; electrification. The impact of this phenomenon was so great, and the economics of steam operation so shaky, that the whole scene took on a shape that hitherto had been unimaginable: we must explore it.

---

[15] Evidence to the Select Committee considering the Guildford, Kingston and London Railway Bill, May 1881.
[16] Annual report and statement of accounts of LSWR for the year ended 31 December 1913.

14.20 *Horsley was the point on the New Line where water could be taken; here an M7 tank engine is being replenished; the Down train looks by its destination board to be booked to terminate at Horsley (1925).*

The H C Casserley collection

14.21 *As the steam era came to its end on the New Line H C Casserley took several photographs; here he has captured two trains at Horsley on 1 June 1925. The Up Guildford via Cobham passes a Down train held at the signal. Note the conductor rails ready for the electric service from 12 July 1925.*

The H C Casserley collection

Chapter 15: Electrification and 'Country Homes at London's Door'

Getty Images

15.1 Schoolchildren line the platform at Guildford on 9 July 1925 to greet the special inaugural electric train which had carried representatives from the government, civic dignitaries and LSWR officials on its journey from Waterloo via Dorking and Effingham junction (the headcode, which would become familiar to users of the Guildford via Cobham service, must have been illustrative).

Competition is the driving force

When the power of the steam engine was first harnessed to provide locomotion the increases in hauling power compared with the horse were so phenomenal that no one noticed or minded that its thermal efficiency was so poor. The energy that was wasted in exhausted steam and hot combustion gases was accepted as unimportant compared with the astonishing step change in the economics of moving great tonnages. In due course the cost benefits of the better thermal efficiency of producing power in the form of electricity from a remote power station, even using the same fuel, would have been given as a reason for change. So too might the fact that electric traction would be popular with the passengers, being cleaner and faster, have been used as a reason for

change; or even the fact that the rolling stock would earn more revenue per route mile because it would work harder; or that labour costs would go down because no fireman was needed in the cab of an electric train; or even that the cost of shunting would be eliminated because the multiple train units were reversible; or electric trains dispensed with the costs involved in engine cleaning, removal of ashes, cleaning out fireboxes, topping up coal and water and lighting a fresh fire before steam locos could return to traffic after a day's work. For none of these reasons was electrification suggested for the above-ground railways in the early 20th century: it was the market that forced the suburban railway operators to embrace electric traction, and when they did they found that not only did the passengers come in their droves but they got cost benefits as well.

South of the Thames the motor omnibus and the tram were winning the competition for passengers in the inner urban areas and the revenues of all the railway companies that had been carrying large numbers of people to their work in inner London were being badly affected. Although the motor car was coming, it was never to make a really significant impression on the level of commuter traffic into London. The railway companies had no grounds to complain about the market: they lived by it and had, by their forces, excoriated the canals. The LB&SCR had carried eight million passengers on their South London line in 1902 but were carrying less than half this number in 1909. They were the first main line company south of the Thames to respond to the competitive threat, and taking powers in 1903 to electrify the whole of their system, their first electric railway opened in 1909 using overhead wires to supply alternating current at high voltage, a system that we are familiar with today on inter-city railways.

The new century found the LSWR's inner suburban traffic suffering along with the other south London companies, and not without some irony the first electric trains to run on LSWR metals were those of the District Railway. Instead of building the line from Fulham to Surbiton via Kingston, which had been the object of the Kingston and London Railway Bill, the LSWR had made a junction with the District at *Putney Bridge & Fulham* and a new line thence to Wimbledon over which the District was allowed to run from its opening in 1889. This had been electrified for the District services to Wimbledon in 1905 but the LSWR hesitated.

The process of electrifying the LSWR suburban lines using the same system as the LB&SCR would cost much capital and the directors were slow to grasp the nettle. Publicly expressed dissatisfaction with the steam services provided in the Thames Valley in 1912 and a threat that the new tube railways might be extended into their territory crystallised the need for a decision which could be deferred no longer: in 1913 the LSWR announced its intention to undertake a comprehensive plan to electrify its suburban network, not it should be noted, so that a new dawn would open up a tremendous new market but with no greater ambition than to recover its lost market share. It was a far-reaching decision in terms of the method chosen: the LSWR opted for a system that was much cheaper in capital cost and already in use by the District on their Wimbledon service: direct current fed by conductor

rails. The decision made, no time was lost in starting to order and install the new hardware but unhappily the immediate good progress that was made was inevitably deranged by the monumental demands made on the LSWR by the Great War. It was not until late 1915 that the first electric trains ran – a regular 20-minute service from *Waterloo* to *Wimbledon* via *East Putney* – to be followed the next year by services on the *Shepperton, Kingston, Hounslow* and *Hampton Court* lines. Additionally, to avoid the inconvenience of terminating electric services in *Surbiton* station, from 20 November 1916, an extension of the electrification was made to *Claygate.* Passengers on the New Line would take a steam push-pull service up to Claygate then detrain onto the half-hourly electric service for the rest of the journey. Very little has been written about the impact of this tentative partial electrification of the New Line. To suggest that it was neither one thing nor the other would be to miss an essential feature: a half-hourly service from Claygate was a considerable improvement and, bringing as it did a commuter railway into the modern world, it would be very popular when conditions returned to normal.

Through this awful wartime period the *Claygate* electrics carried on but in 1919 the service was withdrawn in order to concentrate the scarce resources (the *Claygate* service being anomalous) on those lines that could better exploit them. This was only a pause in the story, however, for when the electric service on the New Line resumed, not only was it complete but it offered a stunning service which brought forth a new secular trend of increasing passenger numbers and brought profitability to the line for the first time.

Railway company grouping and the choice of electrification standards

The railways had come under government control during the war and after it had ended it was minded to make permanent its control by nationalisation, partly as a way of speeding up the electrification process. The fact that grouping (as it became known) eliminated any pretence of inter-company competition, at least among London's suburban railways, and gave way to a tacit acceptance that the essential choice that consumers had was between road and rail. When the post-war boom turned to a bust in 1921, the Railways Act of that year obliged the companies to amalgamate into four regional groups.[1] The LSWR formed the largest part of a merger with the LB&SCR and the SE&CR to form the

15.2 Later on 9 July 1925 after a ceremonial lunch, the inaugural train seen here at London Road, returns to Waterloo.

The Patrick collection

Southern Railway (SR), which commenced business on 1 January 1923. One of the main problems that the management had to confront was the operation of the heavy suburban traffic, the volume of which had recovered substantially after the first electrifications. The rush hour became shorter because of changed working patterns and at peak hours steam working (with its engines running light into and out of the termini) caused congestion. Although the solution lay in continuing the electrification programme, the new company had inherited three different traction systems but led by the forceful former LSWR General Manager, Sir Herbert Walker, the new company decided to adopt the direct current conductor rail system for all new schemes, two of the attractions of which were the much cheaper costs of initial installation and annual maintenance.

The New Line is electrified

The SR put in place an electrification programme, which by 1939 saw not only almost all the whole of the suburban network converted but also many of the main routes to the coast, including Portsmouth.[2] The big day

for the New Line was Sunday, 12 July 1925: 'After two and a half years of reconstruction and reorganisation' ran the advertising campaign:

> two more sections of the Southern Railway's suburban system are ready for the new electric trains. To Guildford and Dorking, in rural Surrey, on the one hand, and to Orpington, in the countryside of Kent, the clean green trains will start to run on July 12, replacing to a large extent the older steam trains now maintaining the service.

Unemployment was non-existent during the war but between December 1920 and March 1921 it more than doubled and in June 1920 it passed two million. Heavy

---

[1] If grouping had not taken place in 1923 at government instigation it is certain that the electric railways of the constituent companies of the Southern Railway would ultimately have been nationalised in 1947 with three incompatible methods of electric traction.

[2] The main part of Southern Railway's history is concerned with electrification, a process which only reached its final stages in 1967 when the Bournemouth line was electrified and, ultimately, Weymouth in 1988.

197

Getty Images

15.3 The official party poses outside the Guildhall in Guildford High Street prior to the luncheon to celebrate the inaugural run of the electric trains on the New Line on 9 July 1925; the Town Crier, Mr Albany Peters is on the left; Alderman William Patrick (who also travelled on the first steam service on the New Line) is sixth from the left, while the Mayor of Guildford, Cllr John Rapkins is ninth from the left.

industry was in trouble. Although the SR's business was largely immune to this distress the electrification project had 'given employment, directly and indirectly, to thousands of workers all over Britain'. There was, therefore, something for the national interest in the electrification project and the SR claimed credit publicly. 'It was no small task to carry the "third rail" over 182 miles of track, while the steam services were still running', said the SR; 27 sub-stations were required along the routes to regulate the current, and of course considerable staff retraining was necessary. At *Guildford* a new bay platform was built for the terminating trains and to accommodate them after duty a seven-road shed was constructed on the Down side at the country end of *Effingham Junction* station.[3] The total cost of the project in 1920s £s was £2,500,000 or nearly £28,000 per route mile, which in relation to the original cost of the New Line was considerable, but the benefits were to be phenomenal.

There had been a formal opening of the electrified routes on 9 July 1925 when a special train, threading its

way through the steam services, conveyed the Minister of Transport, Col Ashley MP, the Chairman of SR, Brigadier-General the Hon Everard Baring, the General Manager, Sir Herbert Walker and many civic dignitaries from Guildford, Dorking, Kingston and Epsom and other towns from *Waterloo* to *Dorking North*, from where it ran to *Guildford* via *Leatherhead* and *Effingham Junction* on the New Line, to be greeted by a host of schoolchildren and others on its bunting bedecked platform. The 5th Earl of Onslow, Richard

---

[3] This facility is no longer in use for its original purpose; most of the Guildford via Cobham trains being stored in sidings in Guildford overnight. The sheds closed in the early 1990s, the track being lifted on all but one line, and were used to store equipment for the Surbiton and Guildford resignalling schemes. More recently, however, the track has been re-laid, the depot refurbished and it is now used as a base for Network Rail's engineering vehicles, including de-leafing and de-icing trains. The existence of this facility explains why so many engineering-train movements can be observed on the New Line.

198

15.4 On 9 July 1925, the inaugural electric train rounds the sharp curve into London Road station.

The Patrick collection

William Alan Onslow, the son of the man who had done so much to inspire the building of the New Line in the first place, and now High Sheriff of Guildford, had been invited but was not present.[4] After the civic luncheon the train returned to *Waterloo* via *Cobham*: an exciting new era was at hand.[5] Everyone who was on board who was familiar with the New Line would have observed how the new trains powered up the gradients over which the steam locos had laboured. Equally, the housewives who lived in houses near the line facing the prevailing wind would marvel at being able to desist from timing the hanging-out of washing according to the timetable in order to avoid the smoke and cinders, except when a freight train passed.

The improvement in service was astonishing; 97 electric trains operating under a headcode of $\overline{H}$[6] replaced 39 steam trains a day. Sir Herbert Walker, ensured that all trains on every service were timetabled in a metronomic fashion: three trains every hour at the same minutes past the hour through the day; the 'clockface' principle was applied across the network. After some early operating problems were eliminated, the passengers loved the new service, which had cut the journey time to Guildford down to 52 minutes. One of the problems was a very unpopular disruption to the service between Wimbledon, Kingston and Surbiton, which involved trains not stopping at *Raynes Park*. Complaints were voiced vociferously[7] and some months later the problem was designed out by a change which was to bring a huge benefit to all those who travelled on the New Line: from 1 December 1925 all trains were booked fast on the through lines between *Surbiton* and *Waterloo*. This practice was still continued into the 1960s when the rush hour trains all

---

[4] *Surrey Comet*: 11 July 1925.

[5] The grandfather of Clandon resident, Terence Patrick, scored a rare steam/electric double on 9 July 1925: William Patrick had travelled as a child on the very first train out of *Guildford* to *London Road* on 2 February 1885, and then as an Alderman of the Borough of Guildford, he was a guest on the inaugural electric service 40 years later.

[6] A correspondent in the *Surrey Comet* of 18 July 1925 noted that about 20 passengers had arrived at Claygate having expected to go to Hampton Court, confused evidently by the headcode '$\overline{H}$' for the New Line and 'H' for Hampton Court. This appears to be an isolated example of the confusion. The numeric code '42' did not come into use until the introduction of metal-bodied rolling stock after the Second World War.

[7] *Surrey Comet*: 18 July 1925.

15.5 The change of an era: a Class A12 (Adams) 0-4-2 locomotive No 527 (built 1887, Nine Elms) pauses with an Up Guildford via Cobham train at Guildford station in July 1925; on the adjacent platform an electric train set also pauses, among the bunting celebrating the start of the new electric service; this may have been the inaugural service of 9 July 1925.

ran fast, with the other trains making a stop at the important interchange of *Wimbledon*, but never at *Clapham Junction* or *Vauxhall*, which had no interchange status until 1971 when the *Victoria* to *Brixton* section of the *Victoria Line* tube began service. With the *Guildford via Cobham* service running fast from *Surbiton*, the alternative service via *Bookham* was a slow method of getting to London, requiring a change at *Effingham Junction* where the Leatherhead trains terminated.

The overall impact of the SR's electrification was impressive. The suburban lines that had been electrified by the LSWR in 1915-16 were carrying 111 per cent more passengers in 1929 than they had in the last steam year, 1914. Overall, in 1923 the total number of passengers carried on SR's electrified lines was 236 million, a number that had already been enhanced substantially by the pre-grouping electrifications. Two years later, in 1925, 301 million passengers were carried, an increase of 28 per cent. By 1938, a year which may have seen traffic levels reduced by the international crisis, the number was

371 million, an increase of 57 per cent over the 1923 level. On those lines that remained being worked by steam the traffic was static. Figures for the New Line are harder to come by: in 1929 it was said that traffic on the 'Guildford and Dorking lines …[had increased] by 25%'.[8] Although it seems that the increment in traffic levels on the New Line was less than overall, there is an important point to make: we can say that practically none of the increment was due to substitution of one form of travel by another; it was real growth whereas in the wider case the SR's business had recovered passengers which had been lost to buses and trams. A possible exception here is that some passengers from Guildford may have travelled on the electric service in preference to the steam service on the main line. The important increase in passenger numbers on the New Line came

---

[8] *Southern Electric 1909-1979*: G T Moody, 5th (revised) edition, 1979, p 74.

15.6 At Guildford station, probably in July 1925, staff pose with one of their new electric train sets.

The Lens of Sutton collection

about through growing numbers of the middle classes who worked in London choosing to live in and commute from our cluster of villages, which were now served by an excellent service of fast, frequent clean trains.[9]

The New Line was in a special position in this respect, for it would be 12 years before Guildford's main line to Portsmouth along with Farnham and Alton would be electrified.[10] In 1925 it was the New Line which allowed the Chairman of LSWR to claim that Guildford had 'a better service than any other town 30 miles from London'.[11] For those would-be commuters who were working in London but who could cast around Surrey beyond the suburbs for their place in the country served by the modern train service, they would find only the Dorking route, which had opened up Leatherhead, Epsom and their intermediate stations including Ewell and Ashtead, and the New Line. With this limited choice, the combination of the modern train service and the intrinsic attractions of our cluster of villages, the increasing numbers of commuters transformed the economics of the line.

In 1938 the total mileage worked electrically on the SR was 37 million, but because everything west of Woking, the Kent coast and all freight was still worked by steam, that traction accounted for 47 million miles: the annual report of the SR for 1938 gave a breakdown of the costs of each. When the costs are reduced to a common base they show that the cost of working the equivalent distance by electric traction was only a little over two thirds that of steam.[12] To this cost saving, which was not part of the rationale for electrification in the first place, must be added the extra revenue which came from the sharply increased traffic. Of course, within these effects the cost of the extra trains had to be found, but overall, electrification was a money-spinner for the SR.

---

[9] For an account of the rolling stock used for the suburban routes to 1939, see *Southern Electric 1909-1979*: G T Moody, 5th (revised) edition, 1979, pp 77-83.

[10] It was because the Guildford via Cobham service operated fast on the main line between *Waterloo* and *Surbiton* that it was used in 1933 to run trials of the newly-electrified Brighton line train sets prior to their being brought into service.

[11] *Surrey Comet*: 11 July 1925. The claim was also made that there was no other town in the world at Guildford's distance from its metropolis that was as well served.

[12] Southern Electric 1909-1979: G T Moody, 5th (revised) edition, 1979, pp 75-6. Calculation is based on Moody's table of costs abstracted from the 1938 report and accounts of SR.

15.7 A wooden-bodied first generation electric train set arrives at Clandon station with a Down service.

The Patrick collection

The changing profile of the population

The building of private housing virtually stopped in 1914 and an acute housing shortage ensued, which was exacerbated by an increase in household formation after the war. The post war housing shortage was addressed by the Housing, Town Planning, etc, Act of 1919, by which the role of local authorities in providing low cost housing was embedded by a somewhat wasteful method of government subsidy. As a result Guildford Rural District Council erected about 50 Council houses in the Clandons and the Horsleys, which while adding to the housing diversity did little for traffic on the New Line.

When the Great War broke out the population of the New Line cluster of villages included a very large but unknown number of domestic servants, but after the war domestic servants became hard to come by. Generally:

> their number had been halved during the war and did not recover even during times of economic depression. Households which had kept five servants dropped to two; those formally with two to one; and the rest of the middle class made do with a daily woman.[13]

The population statistics disguise within their aggregates the change in mix of the population: as the population increased, and the number of domestic servants declined, so the remaining components of the population were more likely to be users of the New Line, whether as commuters to London, leisure users or school children. Additionally, as the old indigenous 'rustic' population died out, or emigrated, they were replaced by incomers – the very people attracted to the district by the convenience of its railway, and increasingly it has to be said, of its road access to London and elsewhere.

Population growth after electrification

To measure population growth we have to make do with official figures and as the present day approaches the greater is the corruption of individual village figures because of boundary changes which are made with increasing frequency: while democracy may be served by these changes, historiography is not. It would have been interesting to isolate the impact of

---

[13] *English History 1914-1945*: A J P Taylor, 1965, p 177.

electrification on population change, but this can only be done by reference to the base of the 1921 census. By 1931, the impact had had only five years to impress itself. The 1941 census was not conducted, but knowing that war was coming the government made emergency arrangements for a quick count in the month war broke out: unhappily there is no disaggregation of these figures below district council level, so the figures are of no use for our purposes. This means there is a twenty-year gap – 1931-1951 – in the availability of population figures at the village level. The situation is not quite as bad as may be feared. When war came all new private building came to a halt, and in the early post war years it was severely rationed by licence, with priority being given to public housing especially in the bombed cities. As it happens, therefore, the housing stock in the New Line cluster of villages would not have been materially higher in 1951 than it was when building stopped. On this basis, although it is crude, the official population figures of 1951 can be used as a surrogate for 1939 and used as a measure, admittedly makeshift, of growth during the period following electrification and the 1930s housing boom. The table below shows the rate of change in the populations of the New Line cluster of villages, with the figure for each census being compared to the previous one.

New Line cluster of villages
Increase in population compared with previous census (excluding Hinchley Wood)

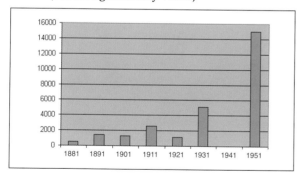

As can be plainly seen from the above table, the increases in the populations of the 19th century were but nothing compared with what was to come. The 1951 figures for Hinchley Wood have been omitted in order to give emphasis to the effect of the post-electrification boom on the original New Line cluster of villages; Hinchley Wood will be discussed separately. The growth in population to 1911 shows acceleration

but this is not repeated in the ten years to 1921, presumably because of the impact of the Great War. If the increase in the population to 1931 was great, the increase to 1951 (effectively 1939) was startling.

East Horsley is developed

The overall increase in the populations between 1921 and 1939 of the original New Line cluster was of the order of 20,000 of which just over 5,000 appeared by 1931 and a further 15,000 by 1939. Of this increase 3,700 was contributed by East and West Horsley (East Clandon remained static as usual while West Clandon grew by 350 only) with much the greater part being attributable to East Horsley. The endemic social changes which were wrought by the Great War were bound to be felt in the Horsleys and the Clandons, where little had changed since the railway came, but in spite of their vulnerability to external events they remained in the early 1920s excellent examples of untouched country villages. Observations such as 'singularly primitive and pleasing'; 'deserted tract'; 'ideal rustic life'; 'typical and old fashioned' retained their validity for the influence of London had not yet given rein to the housebuilder. Of Ockham, a little north of the railway station it had been said, and it remained the case: 'our little village ... only 21 miles from Hyde Park Corner; it still remains what it was nearly 1,000 years ago, a hamlet of oaks'[14] At the end of the Great War the whole area to the west of Cobham until Merrow was reached remained physically much as it had been before the railway came, and the significant features of the villages on that part of the line was that their 'rustic simplicity' was still preserved from the alien influences of the capital. In 1921 mains electricity arrived, which for outsiders was the equivalent of being mentioned on a map, but it also meant that wireless could arrive too and lessen the sense of isolation from the metropolis.[15]

From the 1920s the history of the Horsleys became set on a new course. A wave of new migrants reached the parishes and their orientation towards London became an increasingly important fact of life. The range of

---

[14] *The Oak Hamlet: Being an Account of the History and Associations of the Village of Ockham*: H St J H Bashall, 1900, p 1.
[15] For a fuller discussion of these changes see *The End of Tradition: Country Life in central Surrey*, John Connell, 1978, pp 37–46.

15.8 The Southern Electric carriage sidings at Effingham Junction, 1925, before the erection of the sheds; this facility is now occupied by Network Rail.

The Lens of Sutton collection

occupations available for the indigenous population continued to dwindle, and mechanisation reduced the demand for farm labourers. The decline in the relative importance of agriculture was much more marked than in, say, Cobham with its diversified economy: in the Clandons and the Horsleys the impact of the New Line was retarded by 30 years or more. There had not previously been any similarity with Oxshott, the character of which was established from about 1890, while Claygate's position as a commuter village was well established before the Great War.

The break up of the East Horsley Lovelace Estate commenced when its then owner, T O M Sopwith (of aircraft fame), disposed of 2,085 acres in 45 lots in 1920, following which land came on to the open market at intervals. By 1925, the year of electrification, the land had been broken down even further: that from *Manor* and *Place Farms* was sold in lots of between 0.7 to 3 acres and marketed as 'excellent sites for the erection of good class houses'.[16] Where in Oxshott the developed character had been set by John Clutton, that of East Horsley was set also by a single individual – Frank Chown. Where Clutton had noted the attractions of Oxshott to rich London families, who by means of the New Line could combine living in their country mansions with maintaining their London facilities,

Chown (who was also a surveyor, and an architect), noted that electrification would do the same for East Horsley as the steam railway had done for the second phase of Oxshott's development, which was characterized by the rich commuter living in a house on a large plot with his tennis court in the garden. Electrification had shaved about 17 minutes off the journey time from *Horsley* to *Waterloo*, and trains, now both clean and frequent, did the journey in 37 minutes.

Where Clutton had kept control over the character of Oxshott by selling only on leasehold terms, Chown retained control over the land that he sold for development, whether by himself or by like-minded associates with whom he cooperated, by means of restrictive covenants covering site layout and style. Chown bought almost all the land between the station and the Guildford Road some two miles to the south. Where Chown 'did not own all the land the old field boundaries are maintained in the housing layout; no roads cross the field and lot boundaries of the Lovelace Estate'.[17] Chown and those working closely with him were responsible for The Warren, Pine Walk, Farm

[16] *The End of Tradition: Country Life in central Surrey*, John Connell, 1978, p 70.
[17] *Ibid*, p 71.

Head Codes
denote routes
as under

H HAMPTON COURT
ō HOUNSLOW
V TEDDINGTON & KINGSTON
I CLAYGATE
S SHEPPERTON

HOVIS

The route to health

15.9 The Hovis brand soon recognised the capacity for mutual exploitation of the mnemonic available from the set of the headcodes which LSWR used for their new electric trains; advertisements such as these became commonplace, and this one refers to the Claygate service which was suspended in 1919.

Lane, Woodland Drive, Nightingale Road, Hooke Road (part) and Cobham Way, Penneymead Drive, Lynx Hill, Glendene Avenue and The Highlands.[18] Many of the roads built or inspired by Chown are private roads and cul-de-sacs and have the exclusiveness that comes with individual houses built on their own large plots. Although Chown's vision was coherently and consistently applied, because it was subjected to neither town planning nor the diversity which usually comes with a more pluralistic approach, the result is a more homogenous settlement than Claygate, with consistently high quality houses. Because Chown wanted to build a commuter dormitory he resisted building shops at first:[19] although this was reversed later, it was in contrast to Oxshott where, as already noted, the market was given freer rein and when shops were needed they emerged. Moreover the diversity in Oxshott never gave way to homogeneity: *noblesse oblige* and artisanal life lived side by side. As Connell put it, development in East Horsley was extremely unbalanced because it favoured 'high-quality, low density residential development at the expense of everything else'.[20]

The growth of East Horsley from 1925 to 1939 illustrates another theme, which has been remarked on before: for development to take place, there was needed the conjunction of the right market conditions – railway electrification was a good example – and the availability of land. The new Lord Onslow (the 4th Earl had died in 1911) was not interested in profiting from the sale of land in West Clandon for residential

development, or perhaps Chown in East Horsley had preempted him. Land in East Clandon remained in the control of the owner of Hatchlands, and therefore also unavailable to the builder. 'West Horsley north of the railway was virtually a part of East Horsley' but although the same players developed it, they did not do so in the exclusive mould which Chown had set for East Horsley: 'the standard of construction fell as distance from East Horsley increased'.[21] Although all the land developed was reasonably near the station its availability, unlike the Lovelace land, was unpredictable and the offering was therefore less homogenous as well as being lower value.

'Country Homes at London's Door'

Adopting the brand name *Southern Electric* the SR continued the theme commenced before the Great War, pushing hard to attract commuters by promoting its residential areas served by more than 150 stations in Middlesex, Kent and Surrey as places from which to commute. 1929 saw a third edition of their *Country Homes at London's Door*, a version of which first appeared in 1926, which spoke of how the new electric train service had 'opened up virgin country for the busy city worker' by bringing within easy daily reach of London 'many places in and surrounded by the real,

18 *Ibid*, p 71.
19 *Ibid*, p 72.
20 *Ibid*, p 73.
21 *Ibid*, p 74.

15.10 The ubiquitous slogan of Southern Electric 'To your home in the country' from their 1929 Residential Guide.

beautiful country, to be found everywhere south of the metropolis' and continued:

> London's daily workers can spend their leisure and sleep in pure air and in a beautiful country which before was more or less inaccessible because of the time taken, the infrequency of trains and the greater comparative cost.[22]

The handbook gave details of each of the places promoted with helpful information on housing market conditions and costs and particulars as to the surrounding country; population; subsoil; altitude; provision for sports and recreation; utilities; the character of shops and schools; as well, of course, as rail fares.

Horsley

Horsley station, announced the guide, 'was originally opened to serve the four adjacent villages, East and West Horsley, Ockham and Ripley. Taking its cue from a tourist guidebook, and finding irresistible a mention of *Horsley Towers* and the Earls of Lovelace, in spite of their severed connection, the reader was assured that from the park walls:

> … wonderful beech woods stretch southward for two miles to the crest of the North Downs above Gomshall and Shere. Various tracks … lead … to Hackhurst Downs and Netley Heath, which secluded as they are, rank among the most exquisite of Surrey's upland beauties, 700 feet above sea level. All residents hereabout, then, are favoured in living near to some of the most beautiful of the unspoiled commons and highways of Surrey, and yet within easy reach of Town. Woodland glade, hill and dale abound in charming variety, carpeted in spring with wild violets, primroses and bluebells, and in summer with wild rhododendrons.[23]

Could Chown's own copywriter have done better? Chown himself had probably been consulted, for the guide went on:

> Various parts of the Lovelace Estate are now available for the lover of the country who must live within easy reach of town. Land can at the moment be bought at from £2 per foot frontage in the vicinity of the station … and at a mile or so from the station at about £150 per acre.[24]

Almost apologetically, was added that 'In some situations there are restrictions as to the size and character of the houses to be built' – the very attribute Chown had taken such care to impose. It is difficult to imagine the commercial interests of two parties being better aligned than were Chown's and *Southern Electric's* at Horsley, and would-be buyers, who would benefit from the 'healthy and bracing air' owing to the elevation of '250 to 400 feet upwards', were directed to Chown's advertisement in the guide. Whenever elevation above sea level was a feature of a location it was strongly promoted for its healthy and wholesome image.

Those members of the minority who opposed change in Horsley were soon overwhelmed: in 1933 a village meeting discussing a drainage scheme was addressed by Chown whose agenda was plain: in an echo of the taunt of the Revd Phillips the developer said that the Parish Council 'wanted Horsley to remain a rural district, but it was not possible. They had to move with the times' and because 'they were not far from London' (and because he had land for sale) it was inevitable that Horsley should come within its influence. He was right, of course, and about the sewerage too: operations began on a new scheme in 1937.[25]

Before *Southern Electric* and before Frank Chown the 20th century had hardly touched East Horsley. The people subsisted largely on what their own industry could extract from the soil and be gathered from the countryside. There may have been some minor trade with other villages, but generally their form of 'rustic simplicity' was much the same as described in Chapter 12. A contentment came with the certainty that year would follow year unchanged: they did not know how to be discontent. All this, which was observed elsewhere in Surrey and written about by George Bourne,[26] but change came very fast. In 1930 there were complaints to the Parish Council about 'itinerant vendors' of ice cream and as a result Walls, the manufacturer and owner of the distribution vans, gave instructions to their salesmen to cease bell-ringing on East Horsley rounds.[27] It was as if the traditional rural

---

[22] *Country Homes at London's Door*, 3rd edition, 1929: Southern Railway.

[23] *Ibid.*

[24] *Ibid.*

[25] *The End of Tradition: Country Life in Central Surrey*, John Connell, 1978, p 47.

[26] *Change in the Village*: George Bourne, 1956, pp 77-8 and generally.

[27] *The End of Tradition: Country Life in Central Surrey*, John Connell, 1978, p 51.

15.11 Newlands Corner c1910; even before the motor car this beauty spot was popularised by train travel to Clandon.

population was to be given notice to quit: even those who stayed were destined to be submerged by the modern world of the newcomers with their different habits and customs and their tennis parties. As George Bourne said of these changes:

> They betoken to all the labouring people that their old home is no longer at their disposal, but is at the mercy of a new class who would willingly see their departure.[28]

Writing in 1912 Bourne observed that: 'in another 10 years time there will be not much left of the traditional life whose crumbling away I have been witnessing during the 20 years that are gone'. In East Horsley it all happened later but much faster – less than 10 years, it seems, is all that it took for the indigenous population to be overwhelmed by the new. The village was passing out of the hands of its former inhabitants who were

> becoming as aliens in their own home; they are receding before newcomers with new ideas, and greatest change of all, they are yielding to the dominion of new ideas themselves. [29]

Although East Horsley's status as a nuclear village was long established, from 1925 it changed in character: the electrification of the New Line was the single most important reason, but the growing popularity of the motor car among the better off became an important

force. Ultimately, the demand for local shops, at first denied by Chown, could be resisted no longer: by 1938 there were distributed at both ends of the village, some near the station, 31 shops in East Horsley, a number which expanded further after the Second World War, but not before there had been solid objections from 'a large number of influential residents' who were presumably car owners. As Connell notes, from the late 1920s onwards, the minutes of the Parish Council continually record the grievances of 'influential residents with little indication that it ever took time to consider the needs of the underprivileged'[30] and original parts of the population. This is exactly what George Bourne observed and wrote about in *Change in the Village*.

Clandon

Clandon was given equal praise in the SR residential publicity, which talked of the two villages, which 'stand on the north-facing slopes of the North Downs', and 'everyone who knows Surrey knows that the most delectable country and the most beautiful views are at hand'. Disguising the fact that development land in

---

[28] *Change in the Village*: George Bourne, 1956, p 121.
[29] *Ibid*, p 11.
[30] *The End of Tradition: Country Life in central Surrey*, John Connell, 1978, p 51.

208

15.12 *A delivery at Effingham Stores, c1910.*

Clandon was scarce, there were in 1929, on the road north from the station, 'some charming and delightful houses of various types, with good gardens and open surroundings'. Would-be commuters would soon discover that these houses were already occupied, but 'Land here – at varying distances up to a mile from the station – is to be had at from £200 to £400 per acre [a very high price], and houses, to plans which must be approved by the estate owners may be built at from £1,000 upwards'. It is interesting to note that Horsley was strongly promoted to the London commuter, on account of the large availability of land there, while Clandon with little supply, was engagingly promoted as only eight minutes by train from Guildford which was convenient when any 'extra shopping is required' or when a visit 'to the theatre, cinema or other entertainment may appeal'.

Guildford

The virtues of Guildford itself as a commuter town were, of course, also promoted. Some of the new

housing development which was described was relevant to commuting from *London Road* station: at the Edgeborough Estate 'adjoining Merrow Downs and the golf course', houses of about £1,500 to £3,000 could be purchased, while on Pewley Hill, above the town, 'there are sites for good class houses, and at various points on the outskirts of town plots of land are available'.

The Bookhams and Effingham

There had been in 1905-6 some railway-stimulated new housing at Bookham, south of the line just west of the station, but in the 10 years to 1921 the population of the Bookhams and Effingham was static, with Little Bookham and Effingham actually showing small declines. Since the railway came the populations of the three villages had only risen by 700 to 2,500; their 'rustic simplicity' had been, it would appear, very durable, but great change lay immediately ahead. By 1931 the population of Great Bookham doubled in size, with Effingham not far behind while by the time the war

209

15.13 Part of Bacon's Atlas of London and Suburbs, early 1900s, showing a very sparsely developed Claygate, but with the road network of Fitzalan Foley's estate laid out: Beaconsfield Road, Claremont Road, Foley Road and Gordon Road (unnamed near the railway).

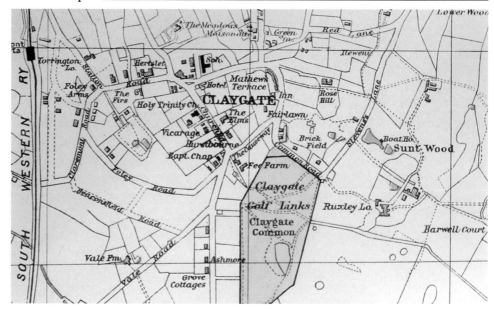

came the population of all three villages was 2.3 times what it had been in 1921; leaving aside East Horsley, whose expansion had been phenomenal, this was a rate of expansion which was quite the greatest of any of the villages in the cluster. In the 1929 edition of *Country Homes at London's Door* the SR said of Great and Little Bookham:

> ... no place in Surrey has so completely changed its aspect in recent years. Walkers of 25 years ago knew the Bookhams as villages which had survived almost unaltered from medieval times. You approached them from Dorking or Leatherhead and came right from open fields on an ancient park, the village with its sturdy church, farms, generous barns, old inns and beautiful cottages. No hint was there of any development on the outskirts.[31]

This is a description that Sir Walter Farquhar of Polesden Lacey would have recognised from when he wanted the railway built. 'The character of the district now [1929] is that of a charming modern settlement with the two villages forming its core.' The guide continued:

> The outer charm of Bookham is that it is entirely rural in its setting. Like many Surrey villages it has an immense common ... now vested in the National Trust. Its altitude ranges from 200 to 300 feet, and the air is inspiring.[32]

Naturally, the proximity to the North Downs was emphasized, it being 'the wildest, most secluded country near London'. Reading these descriptions of the attributes of the Downs over 75 years later gives one no feeling of undue licence being taken: the trouble was, and this applies to practically everywhere that the SR promoted as a fine place in the country, the very success of their campaign resulted in unbridled development of it until the last vestiges of 'rustic simplicity' were inevitably extinguished, except where protected by the Green Belt (and not always then). This was the period of the great joining up of villages; a process which was slowed only by landowners being unwilling to allow it, then by the war and then the Green Belt. Today, a glance at the map shows a continuous development of the Bookhams and their joining with Fetcham, with Effingham only just being spared a complete connection. In 1929 *Country Homes at London's Door* announced where the building was going to happen.

> Eastwick Park has now been given up to residential development, nearly 1,000 acres being available. In the park proper are many delightful ... sites ranging from the neighbourhood of the station and common to that

---

[31] *Country Homes at London's Door*, 3rd edition, 1929: Southern Railway.
[32] *Ibid.*

15.14 Looking east along the north side of The Parade, Claygate, from a postcard sent in 1908; note the construction of further shops at the Hare Lane end.

The Paul Langton collection

of the church and village street of Great Bookham, available only for residential purposes, and for homes of not less than about £1,000 prime cost.[33]

On that part of the Eastwick Park estate which lay near the main Leatherhead-Guildford road at up to a mile and a half from the station:

> A revolution has been effected, and what is known as Bungalow Town has sprung into being. Land here is cheaper. It may be bought for about £150 per acre. Small bungalows may be put up here at from £500-£600 upwards.[34]

Whether rail commuters were attracted to this development is not recorded but as it turned out it acquired a sullied reputation as 'a rash of unsightly low-cost bungalows set along rutted, unsurfaced roads over the lower slopes of the North Downs'[35] and eventually it was replaced by conventional housing.

Meanwhile it would appear that *Effingham Junction* station was still located in a field, for

> the passenger who quits the train [there] may be forgiven for wondering at its inclusion in a book dealing with residential possibilities, for he finds himself on a wide expanse of open, characteristic Surrey common, backed by woodlands, interesting as country, but little suggestive of houses for London workers.[36]

This was in spite of the fact that in 1927 'houses "overlooking Effingham Common"' were advertised with much stress on the 50 or so new electric trains each way to and from *Waterloo* daily.[37] The station was, of course, a mile and a half from the village, which was 'all the better from the point of view of househunting Londoners' for those who came to Effingham would 'want their houses set in rural surroundings'.

> The very appearance of the landscape outside the station will assure such people that if they are fortunate enough to find or build what they want, the permanent preservation of such an atmosphere all round the station is certain.[38]

Southern Electric used this language to say that there was not much development possibility. They did predict, however, that Effingham 'will never be a place thickly clustered round the railway' unlike most of the other villages on the New Line 'that were not in existence

---

[33] *Ibid.*

[34] *Ibid.*

[35] *The Railway in Surrey*: Alan A Jackson, 1999, p 126.

[36] *Country Homes at London's Door*, 3rd edition, 1929: Southern Railway.

[37] *The Railway in Surrey*: Alan A Jackson, 1999, p 126.

[38] *Country Homes at London's Door*, 3rd edition, 1929: Southern Railway.

when their station was built';[39] this prediction proved to be correct because the area to the south of the station was common land, but further south 'a scattering of new houses appeared along the road from the station to the village' between the late 1920s and 1940.[40]

Effingham Golf Club had opened in 1927 (to the great appeal of those new members of local society who were car owners) and part of the course was built on the Beechwood Estate. The SR's guide proclaimed that the Beech Avenue Estate 'which overlooks the golf course' and the Northern Estate 'are both in course of development, several houses being ready for immediate occupation'. Further land 'will be available' on either side of the Leatherhead Road, 'part of it in the neighbourhood of the village' but some of this was as much as two miles from the station. The SR was bound to include Effingham in its guide but because much of the new development would continue to be some distance from the station, the appeal of the *Southern Electric* train service would be more attractive in other locations. The delights of the Downs, which were easily reached from Effingham along Beech Avenue, were mentioned but as a location for living this was an area much more appealing to the car owner; indeed Dr Barnes Wallis, the famous technical and aero designer, was an early resident who drove daily to his office at the Brooklands site of Vickers in Weybridge. Here is an interesting example of the different influences of the motor car and *Southern Electric*, both of which were by now having an impact on the location of high-class housing development. The SR guide gave early notice of expected development in the area 'equidistant (ie about half a mile) from both *Effingham Junction* and *Horsley* Stations [which] will shortly be available'. South of the railway, the two locations were soon to coalesce.

Journey times and fares

So far in this chapter we have considered only the impact of electrification from Effingham Junction south to Guildford, and Bookham. Naturally, the SR did not attempt to be judgmental about particular locations: that was a matter of would-be train user's choice, and all the locations had attractions. If any reader of *Country Homes at London's Door* were making comparative assessments of where to commute from, his choice would be made according to housing cost and availability, accessibility and availability of schools, fares and journey times: with the frequency of services set at three trains an hour (with additional services

via Leatherhead) *Southern Electric* had established a fabulous train service. Full details of conditions at and around every station were given and the following table, abstracted from the residential guide, shows the journey times to *Waterloo* and 3rd class ticket fares (today's standard class equivalent) are set out in table form. Generally, the first class fares were about 50 per cent higher than for 3rd class.

New Line: advertised journey times and fares by *Southern Electric* to *Waterloo*, 1929

	Journey time (minutes)	3rd class fare		
		3 month season ticket	Return fare	Cheap off-peak Fare *
Claygate	22	£4 11s 6d	3s 6d	1s 9d
Oxshott	26	£4 17s 9d	4s 6d	2s 3d
Cobham	30	£5 4s 0d	4s 10d	2s 5d
Effingham Junction	36	£5 13s 6d	5s 6d	2s 9d
Horsley	37	£5 16s 6d	5s 8d	2s 10d
Clandon	42	£6 8s 6d	6s 6d	3s 3d
Guildford, London Rd	49	£7 0s 6d	7s 6d	3s 9d
Guildford, main	52	£7 0s 6d	7s 6d	3s 9d
Bookham	43	£5 10s 6d**	4s 10d	2s 5d

* Available every day from Claygate but on Wednesdays and weekends only from all other stations.
** Available to *Waterloo*, *London Bridge* and *Victoria*.
Source: *Country Homes at London's Door*, 3rd edition, 1929: Southern Railway.

It has not been possible to establish why travellers from Claygate should have been able to have cheap off-peak fares every day while from all other stations on the line they were available only at weekends and on Wednesdays. The journey time from Claygate was very appealing at 22 minutes, but Oxshott (26 minutes) and Cobham (30 minutes) also gave the opportunity for door-to-door travel times to the City of an hour or less.

Increases in population: Claygate compared with Oxshott, Cobham and Stoke D'Abernon

Although it was not of the order seen in Horsley or Bookham, all of Claygate, Oxshott, Cobham and Stoke D'Abernon showed large increases in population after electrification. Because of boundary changes and the

---

[39] *Ibid.*
[40] *The Railway in Surrey*: Alan A Jackson, 1999, p 126.

15.15 Cobham High Street, c1914 has taken a townscape feel; this view is looking towards Street Cobham and in the background is the site of the 1860–1881 proposed railway stations.

process of joining up it is convenient to look at population trends for the combination of Oxshott, Cobham and Stoke D'Abernon. The growth of these three villages combined, and Claygate separately over the census periods from 1911 to 1951 is shown in the chart below.

Claygate compared with Oxshott, Cobham and Stoke D'Abernon
Increases in population compared with previous census

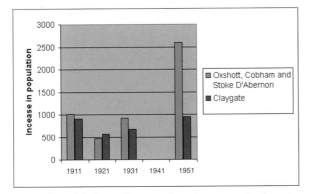

From this table it can be seen that there was, in the rate of growth in the early years of the century to 1921, a certain parity between Claygate and the other settlements, with each showing the familiar reduced rate of growth in the period covering the Great War. The

stronger growth in the 10 years to 1931, which covers the start of electrification beyond Claygate, is a measure of its impact, but the really remarkable feature of the chart is the strong acceleration in Oxshott, Cobham and Stoke D'Abernon in the period to 1951, which we are taking as a surrogate for 1939. Between 1921 and 1939 the population of these three settlements grew by nearly 4,000, while Claygate's grew only by about 1,500.

Cobham and Stoke D'Abernon

The SR had given up on making a distinction between Cobham and Stoke D'Abernon: only Cobham is referred to in *Country Homes at London's Door*. 'A town or village which actually stands upon a river' was a fact which would-be commuters were reminded of, for 'there are not many riverside places in Surrey … [except on the Thames] which offer residential facilities for London workers'.

> Cobham has the River Mole meandering through its area, affording many delightful sylvan scenes as it winds along its way, now through the verdant pasture-lands adjoining its course, and again as it borders some of the local thoroughfares. Originally it was but a riverside village.[41]

---

[41] *Country Homes at London's Door*, 3rd edition, 1929: Southern Railway.

213

I've arrived, think I'll stop.

15.16 Old habits die hard; from a postcard of 1913.

Even the Revd Phillips would have recognized the 'rustic simplicity' described here in somewhat loquacious terms. The process of joining up Street Cobham with Church Cobham and the latter with Stoke D'Abernon; and the Fairmile district with Oxshott had started – a process which was the result in part of electrification – but no developer was ever able to build down to the river. Whether this was due to the local authority grasping the planning initiative and creating what was later termed green belt planning, which is what was claimed in *Country Homes at London's Door*, or much more likely, the builders avoided the flood plain when there was plenty of usable land elsewhere, is not a question that needs decision: the attractions of Cobham's river have never been violated.

Having established Cobham's riparian attributes, the *Southern Electric*'s guide changes tack by explaining that:

> Being in an extremely pleasant and entirely rural part of Surrey, Cobham was bound to grow, and it has. Street Cobham and Church Cobham are now united. Semi-urban conditions are established with streets, shops, electric light, gas, a good water supply, and other town conveniences; yet a few minutes in any direction is enough to take one out of anything savouring of town life right into the real and ancient country.[42]

Housing development was going to take place 'within half-a-mile of the station in the neighbourhood of *Brook Farm* and *Knowle Hill* where there was 'a great deal of land with good road frontages' available for 'good-class houses to cost about £1,000 upwards'. Cook (of Oxshott brickworks) was the previous owner of the *Knowle Hill* Estate; soon after he died in 1904 the land was sold at auction but it seems that parts of it were still available for building in 1929. Frederick Keays of *Fairmile Court*, was the staunch advocate of Lord Onslow's railway (favouring Oxshott as his local station): now that the railway had come (and perhaps the motor car too) and electrification had given such a good service to London, the Fairmile district was even more popular and land was available in 1929 'for good-sized country houses [of] say, £4,000 to £15,000 in value'.[43]

Oxshott

In Oxshott, about which 'little or nothing has been written' the commons and pine-woods 'are among the most beautiful in Surrey', announced *Southern Electric*'s guide. The language used to describe Oxshott's charms was unduly excessive:

> In their season, foxgloves, willowherb and ragwort light the glades, and deep amid the pines is hidden Black Pond [which is] a piece of water which recalls the perfection of Japanese art in the simplicity of its dark beauty and its cincture of pines with the splash of colour made by, perhaps a single patch of bright yellow or rose-pink upon its banks.[44]

'Sounds good' the reader may have thought, 'but what about the housing situation?' 'It must be admitted' concedes the guide 'that there is not a great deal of land

---

[42] *Ibid.*
[43] *Ibid.*
[44] *Ibid.*

214

15.17 A delivery, probably from the goods yard, to The Hare and Hounds 'Hotel', Claygate, c1910.

The Paul Langton collection

available for building, and most of it is expensive'. For those lucky enough to find accommodation, the guide gives its version of 'rustic simplicity,' which had not yet been spoiled by the motor car:

> Those who would pierce back from the present to the original hamlet of Oxshott must walk for five minutes … Here at a curve in the road, the road to Cobham goes off south. At the opposite corner is an old farmhouse of brick … and tall gables, and its generous outbuildings border the road. At the opposite corner is an ancient timber-framed cottage. On yet another corner is the inn. This … is old Oxshott, set in a little hollow beneath a great pine-crested sandy knoll, and, though a few modern shops and the post office have been built, the road junction can still look very primitive when, as often happens, great farm wagons, drawn by horses … roll slowly in and out of the farmyard [of *Birds Hill Farm*] at the corner.[45]

Apart from the Crown Estate where land was only available on leasehold terms, there were, 'here and there' plots that could be bought outright 'on which smaller and less expensive houses can be built'. The Sandy Lodge Estate, 'between Oxshott and Fairmile, a very rural situation in woodlands bordering the heath, at 10 minutes from the station, is available' with 'a few

houses from about £900 to £3,000'. In the Little Heath neighbourhood on the Cobham road houses were available for 'a little under £1,500, while on the Leatherhead road there were a few freehold sites available 'but suitable only for houses of a good class'.

Claygate

The position of Claygate became special because it was 'the first of the country settlements which border the … [New Line] at intervals along its whole length'. Emerging from the station in 1929 'Claygate appears to be an entirely modern settlement'. Clinging to the vestiges of 'rustic simplicity', *Country Homes at London's Door* announces that although 'the modern part certainly accounts for the greater part of its population', the reader is assured that 'there is an old hamlet – about half-a-mile east of the station – where old houses cluster on the edge of Claygate Common'. By 1929 the 'old village' had been relegated by the station, where

---

[45] *Ibid.*

215

15.18 The Southern Electric residential guide of 1929 announced that there were available 'a number of commodious houses which command fine views' in Beaconsfield Road, Claygate; this view is from earlier in the century.

15.19 St Leonards Road, Claygate, c1910.

15.20 A delivery probably from the goods yard, to the Bear Inn, Oxshott, c1905.

The Paul Langton collection

the 'new village' had sprung up. Nevertheless, and in spite of the development which had taken place, 'even if there were not a considerable belt of country between Claygate and Surbiton' (on which was about to be built Hinchley Wood) 'Telegraph Hill would effectively cut off every sight and sound of the outermost extension of' London. 'Claygate' proclaimed the guide 'is set in an entirely rural environment'.

Country Homes at London's Door was a well-researched publication. It was only the year before in 1928 that it had been announced that Esher Council, as it then was, had decided to buy Telegraph Hill in order to prevent development on it: there is no doubt at all that that decision was instrumental in preserving the rural environment which was part of Claygate's appeal in 1929. (Telegraph Hill also marks the limit of Hinchley Wood where on its southern side the Metropolitan Green Belt reinforces the Council's 1928 wisdom.) Claygate is still substantially surrounded by farmland (often the first cattle to be seen when journeying from *Waterloo* can be seen from *Claygate* station) and in 1929:

all situations in Claygate are pleasant but perhaps the most enjoyable is that along the crest of the little bluff at its southern end, east of the railway, along which are built [on the Foley Estate] a number of commodious houses [in Beaconsfield Road] which command fine views over … [*Horringdon Farm*]

Electrification had brought all this charm within 22 minutes of *Waterloo*, and the guide noted the disparate nature of the housing stock – a feature which remains endemic in Claygate today:

Houses in Claygate may be reckoned as of all values, from about £700 to £900 up to £3,000, and there is ample provision for the building of new ones at almost any figure between these limits. Estates in course of development are; Claremont Park Estate [in Esher] within about five minutes [by car?] of the station, [where there are] plots of land at £3 a foot frontage for houses … from not less than £600 upwards; Rythe Road (close to the station) …[where there are] houses at about £950; *Fee Farm* (in the neighbourhood of the [old] village, for detached houses at prices varying from about £1,250 to about £2,000; [and] Dalmore Avenue (3 [?] minutes from the station) for houses about £1,000.

15.21 Scovell's Tea Rooms, High Street, Oxshott, with Bird's Hill Farm buildings in the background.

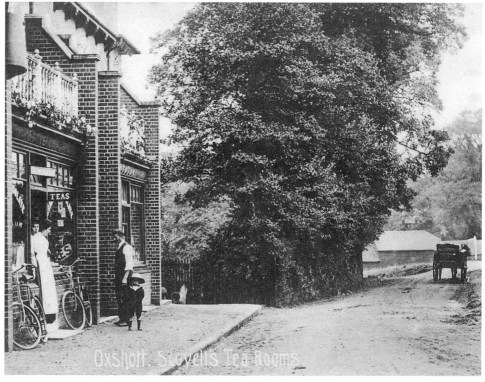

Oxshott. Scovells Tea Rooms

The Paul Langton collection

The most interesting offering was the development of what had been part of Lord Foley's estate on the northern slopes of his seat at *Ruxley Lodge* by now renamed *Ruxley Towers*. It is possible that this land may have come forward for development much earlier if Onslow's route for the railway, which would have taken it close by, had prevailed in the tussle with the LSWR. Its proximity to a station somewhere in the vicinity of Church Road could have prompted the development of a high-class estate along the lines of Chown's in East Horsley and Clutton's in Oxshott. As it was the development was more likely to appeal to car owners because, being at the edge of the village, it was inconvenient to commuters. Nevertheless, in 1929 'the first houses are already up, and they are very pleasing old world designs' at prices ranging from 'about £1,000 to £3,000'. Who brought this land forward for development is obscure, for when *Ruxley Lodge* together with its 143 acres was put up for sale by auction in October 1919, not a single bid had been forthcoming and the lot was withdrawn.[46]

Southern Electric goes with the grain

The 1925 electrification of the New Line (together with the Dorking line) has been described as 'a bold measure, for the areas served were still largely rural'.[47] This observation fits well with the view that the New Line never made a profit in all its steam days, for a doubter might suggest that the cost of electrification was throwing good money after bad; but the impact of electrification on the suburban routes was well known to the management – where 25 million passengers had been carried in 1913 on suburban steam services the equivalent figure in 1920 on electric was nearly 53 million[48] – so the boldness lay in the belief, which turned into the reality, that traffic could be created by offering a fast, frequent and clean train service to the

[46] *Surrey Comet*: 18 October 1919.
[47] *A Regional History of the Railways of Great Britain, Vol 2 – Southern England*: H P White, 1961, p 182.
[48] *Ibid*, p 181.

The Julian Morgan collection

15.22 One of the first electric services is captured crossing Stoke Road, Guildford on its descent from London Road station (1925).

capital. London had lost none of its ability to grow and prosper, so it was probably very easy for the management to sanction in 1926 the marketing of commuting in *The Country at London's Door*. When the name of the publication was soon changed to *Country Homes at London's* Door', *Southern Electric*'s mission was explicit – to help London workers find somewhere to live in the country and so become a customer for the rest of their working life – and they were going with the grain of the trend of leaving the noise and dirt of London for better and less dense housing further out. Moreover, *Southern Electric* had a golden business paradigm – an expanding market served at less cost. On the New Line in particular the SR may have had in mind the additional margins from First Class travel.

In October 1929, even as buyers were committing to their new houses, the world changed. In New York the stock market, which had been driven up by a speculative frenzy, reached an unsustainable peak; when all investors rushed to sell at once, and there were no new ones left to buy, Wall Street crashed. Fortunes were lost and soon the economic blizzard crossed the

Atlantic and the whole world was engulfed in the great Depression. Although the 1925 electrifications had been immediately popular, the SR had nowhere near recovered its large investment. In the new anxious climate no one knew what was going to happen; most were fearful.

15.23 The gradient board at Oxshott station; the new electric trains had no difficulty with the gradients on the New Line

219

15.24 *In the 1930s, Claygate's 19th century Old Village retail centre continued to thrive on account of its nearby resident population in spite of the pull exerted by the station and its associated and bigger shopping facilities; this view is from the 1920s.*

The Paul Langton collection

15.25 *After the New Line was electrified in 1925 all other workings in Guildford were steam operated until the Portsmouth service was electrified in the late 1930s. This view of Guildford shed c1950 shows how important steam remained in the post-war years.*

Chapter 16: The 1930s housing boom

16.1 A 4LAV unit being tested on the New Line prior to it being brought into service on the Brighton line in 1932; this Down Guildford via Cobham train has been photographed between Effingham Junction and Horsley.

Motor traffic threatens the railways

Before developing the theme on which the last chapter closed – the great Depression – we must consider some trends that started earlier. For reasons that were not wholly understood at the time, the national birth rate started to fall in the 1920s; reflecting one of the contemporary explanations that the cause was economic, the celebrated Oxford historian, A J P Taylor, observed with some exaggeration: 'The baby Austin ousted the baby. The nursery gave way to the garage', adding:

> The motor car was undoubtedly the great formative influence … transforming social life even more fundamentally than the railways had done before it. In 1920 the number of private cars registered was under 200,000. Ten years later it exceeded a million and reached nearly two million before the outbreak of the Second World War.[1]

The concentration of this growth in motor car ownership was, of course, in the more prosperous South East of the country. In the districts that we are concerned with it would be reasonable to assume that cars were more likely to be found in Oxshott, Cobham and East Horsley, among those richer households who lived, in many cases, at a fair distance from their station, shops and church. In fact, the garage trade started in Claygate in 1919 and in 1929 the Station Garage opened. At first the motor car was an instrument of pleasure; a prestige symbol, at first largely confined to the rich and then characteristically a middle class possession. Increasingly, the wealthier owners began to use it for day-to-day transport but commuting to work in his own car was still far from being the breadwinner's normal pattern between the wars.

The strategic importance of the railways had been proved by the workload into which they had been pressed in the Great War, but in peacetime conditions the competitive threat from road transport challenged the effective monopoly which the railways still enjoyed outside the towns. It was in the period up to about 1930 that the 'close network of coach and rural bus services

---

[1] *English History 1914-1945*, A J P Taylor, 1965, p 302.

16.2 *An unregulated rush into road haulage in the 1920s led to a competitive threat to the railways, but the letterhead of this Claygate carter (from 1926) shows the importance still of railway haulage, and judging by the item billed, horses too.*

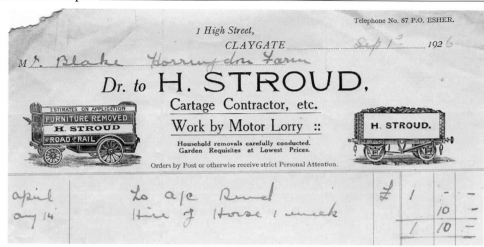

The Jo Richards collection

emerged'[2] penetrating where the railways had not so much failed to do as had done incompletely. Claygate's first bus service did not arrive until 1936. More competition appeared for freight business: demobilised servicemen 'sank their gratuities in army-surplus lorries and joined in the almost unregulated free-for-all then obtaining in road haulage'.[3] The loss of railway freight business was accelerated by railway strikes in 1919 and 1924, and the General Strike of 1926. In order to accommodate the increasing volumes of lorries, coaches and motor cars the existing roads had to be widened, which encouraged more cars, which caused congestion in towns, notably Leatherhead, Guildford and Dorking as well as Kingston, all of which had to be by-passed before the Second World War. Congestion in Kingston had been noted even before 1914. It was not the sheer volume of motor traffic but rather the mix with cycles, horse-drawn transport and trams that was the problem; it was to be the first town in Surrey to which a radical solution was applied.

The Kingston By-pass

In 1927 'a new road bridged a railway line at a place which had no name. It is here, where two arteries of London met, the Kingston By-pass and the New Line',[4] that the story of Hinchley Wood begins. Although the By-pass alone would have been sufficient to ensure some development (as happened around it further east) the rapid emergence of the new settlement was much assisted by the almost simultaneous opening of a new railway station with an excellent train service.

Just as the New Line had done 40 years earlier, the Kingston By-pass opened up huge tracts of land for development but by-passes liberated traffic and the rise of the motor car and the bus marked the point where the railway lost much of its primacy as an influence on the siting of new housing development. It is also at this point where the impact on the development of the New Line cluster of villages, which was caused by the railway, becomes blurred. As Taylor put it:

> Englishmen were emancipated from the iron frame of railways and tram lines which had previously dictated their lives. The map of any town shows the change. The towns of the early 20th century centred on the railway station and radiated outwards from it ...[5]

Taylor was thinking of towns like Kingston, Surbiton, Leatherhead and Guildford, but in our cluster of villages, the growth of car ownership added an extra ingredient to the delights of *A Country Home at London's Door* as promulgated by *Southern Electric*. Local traffic levels were growing fast: on the Portsmouth Road the increase, compared with pre-war levels, was 70 per cent by 1922 and 163 per cent by 1925. The decision to build

---

[2] *A Regional History of the Railways of Great Britain, Vol 2 – Southern England*: H P White, 1961, p 180.
[3] *Ibid.*
[4] *Hinchley Wood: the Origins of a 1930s Settlement*: Howard Mallinson, 2002, p 1.
[5] *English History 1914-1945*: A J P Taylor, 1965, p 304.

16.3 An official Surrey County Council photo (1927) showing the newly-built bridge carrying the Kingston By-pass over the New Line at the point of the bifurcation of the tracks where Hinchley Wood station was built three years later.

the Kingston By-pass was made as early as 1923 when the *Guildford via Cobham* trains were still steam-hauled. Even before the first sod for the new road was cut, the speculative possibilities that it might throw up were being considered in the offices of Surrey County and the District Councils along its route, as well as at the SR headquarters at *Waterloo*. Even as the new motor road was being built, Drivers Jonas & Co (a surveying partnership which survives to this day in independent ownership in Mayfair), was active on their client's acres. In the mindset of John Clutton in Oxshott before them, they astutely put forward a proposal in 1926 to have a sewer laid under the By-pass, then being built, at Manor Road (then part of Thames Ditton) to enable the development of housing.

As Moody observed:

> From 1925 to 1939 there was intensive housing development in the electrified area, and while some of it would have taken place if the lines continued to be steam-worked, there is no doubt that it was greatly increased by the advantages of the electric services. The speed and frequency of the latter was a point which estate agents did not fail to mention when advertising their properties.[6]

But, although there was a railway – a newly electrified railway – in the place where Hinchley Wood was to be built, there was no station. The manner in which it came to be built is fascinating.

Hinchley Wood station

G T Crouch was a property developer of some vision whose business, which pre-dated the 1930s housing boom, survived well into the post-war era. He was one of the first to recognise the development opportunities that would be opened up by the Kingston By-pass, and to exploit them he brought under his control in the mid-1920s much of the land on which Hinchley Wood was to be built, the major exception to this being some land which had been part of the Lovelace Estate, but soon to be in another speculator's hands. When Crouch[7] conceived the development plan he had in mind the good road communications offered by the By-pass and he could see how readily the railway's potential could be exploited simply by building a station. For Crouch the railway and the By-pass were to be for Hinchley Wood what the New Line alone was to Chown in East Horsley and had been to Clutton in Oxshott 40 years earlier. Indeed, it may even have been what Chown was doing in East Horsley, even as work on the By-pass started, that inspired Crouch in Hinchley Wood. He

---

[6] *Southern Electric 1909-1979*: G T Moody, 5th (revised) edition, 1979, p 76.

[7] Couch had an obscure business relationship with a Percy Fisher, about whom little is known, but he was almost certainly the financier for whom Crouch was fronting the land deals. In the shaping of Hinchley Wood, Crouch is the important character.

presented his plan to Esher Council who had zoned the whole area for a 'superior' new settlement; the adjectival qualification was relative: the intended superiority was achieved in relation to much of the heartless and unregulated development that took place in the 1930s,[8] but in relation to the other settlements on the New Line, that which was erected in Hinchley Wood, while soundly built and presented, provided a generally lower standard than the best housing further down the line.

In September 1929 Couch's plan to build 1,017 houses on 147 acres at 6.9 houses per acre to be called 'Hinchley Wood' was approved. Looked at in the context of the housing stock that was available along the New Line, a helpful price diversification was provided with the best houses in Hinchley Wood being more affordable for the majority of the middle class market than the mostly more spacious properties erected on larger plots in Oxshott, Cobham and East Horsley. Having been given planning permission to build Hinchley Wood, the station was an essential component of his development plan, and in the following month a deal was struck with the SR for the construction of it.

When the New Line was laid down there had been no purpose in considering any stop between Surbiton and Claygate, but in the early 1920s, by which time development had taken place in Long Ditton, Esher Council promulgated the notion of a halt somewhere in the Angel Road area, but the SR was not interested in a proposition that would bring no incremental traffic. In 1925, Esher Council considered a petition from the small number of residents of Manor Road, in which ribbon development from Thames Ditton[9] was taking place, for the provision of a station. The SR, however, baulked at using their shareholders' money to put value into landowners' pockets again and they could afford to wait and see what happened.

Like the landowners who had profited from the building of the New Line in the first place, residential developers were quick to spot how a station would create demand for houses. Although the SR knew well enough that a new settlement would bring incremental business, it knew the impact on land values. At its annual general meeting in 1927, the Chairman called attention to the 'great increment in the value of the land, which goes into the pockets of vigilant people at our expense'. As we have seen before, the corporate

memory of a railway company was elephantine: these were the days when many a railwayman in senior positions had seen 50 years' service. Some of them may have seen for themselves that the New Line had brought great wealth to the landowners at the same time as operating losses to the LSWR. When Crouch approached the SR for a new station, they agreed provided the developer contributed one-third of its cost.

Crouch's contribution was £2,500 plus a small amount of land by which access to it could be achieved. The site for the station chose itself: where the Kingston By-pass bridged the railway was at the point of the 1908 bifurcation of the tracks to take the Up line under the main line, and by placing the station buildings between the tracks no development land was used, but the site also made the buildings more economically built, and then manned. The SR bought some more land from Crouch at £420 per acre for a goods yard, which in the event was never built because competition from road haulage became too great, but the land was retained, ultimately to allow a car park to be provided. Reflecting the SR's interest in the new station, namely incremental traffic, a guarantee was introduced into the deal: Crouch deposited £500, which would be forfeited if 150 houses were not built within three years. This threshold was safely met a year after the station opened, such was the speed at which building took place. The new railway station of *Hinchley Wood*, opened on Monday 20 October 1930 with no ceremony and, almost certainly, with hardly any passengers either; they were to come a little later, at first just a few; then dozens; then scores and finally, by the hundreds.

The 1930s: an extraordinary decade

We must revert to where the previous chapter left off: just as the *Hinchley Wood* station deal was being done, the 1929 Wall Street Crash occurred and the great Depression began. Crouch and his backers had bought over 147 acres of land and they were exposed to both

---

[8] For a highly regarded account of the suburban spread of London see Alan A Jackson's *Semi-detached London: Suburban Life, Development and Transport, 1900-1939*, 2nd edition, Wild Swan, 1991.

[9] The land on which Hinchley Wood was built was at first, for both ecclesiastical and civil purposes, part of Thames Ditton, a village which was itself featured in *Southern Electric*'s *Country Homes at London's Door*.

their bankers and to the SR. It was not an option to see how the wind was blowing from the USA before committing to building houses; they were on the hook to build, not sell be it noted, 150 houses in three years. It must have been very uncomfortable as the gloomy events in the USA unfolded. Surprisingly, in a way which not even the ultra-prescient could have seen in 1930, the decade which was opening up with a deep sense of economic foreboding gave way to the most astonishing housing boom in history. Even from its very beginning Hinchley Wood worked because of its own essential topography: the station, the By-pass and its contiguous countryside, the credit for which lies wholly with Esher Council. It was the Council that had bought Telegraph Hill to preserve it from development, and had zoned Surbiton Golf Course (on land owned by the Lovelace Estate) as private open space as part of its greater plan of zoning Hinchley Wood as a housing area. Even without the extraordinary events, which unfolded after work on the station started in March 1930, Hinchley Wood would have worked.

The 1930s was an extraordinary decade of contradiction and paradox. For example, there was the paradox of a boom in housing and consumer goods coinciding with desperate levels of unemployment in the north of England leading to the famous hunger marches. Policy contradictions at home polarised on whether government should spend its way out of the economic depression and run a budget deficit, or economise and keep the budget balanced. Abroad, there was trouble for Britain in Palestine, India, Egypt and Ireland. Communism was the great bogey: fascism was emerging to oppose it; Italy was in the grip of a dictatorship; Spain had a civil war, followed by a dictatorship. The King died and his son abdicated. The Nazi tyrant, having been barely noticed when he first came to power in January 1933, induced the greatest contradiction: appeasement or rearmament?

When the bubble had burst in 1929 Britain was at a high tide of prosperity even though over one million were already unemployed. Following the Depression British exporters saw their markets disappear. By the end of 1930 unemployment had reached two and a half million: such was the paradoxical economic background to the building boom. In September 1931, when houses were being produced in Hinchley Wood at an increasing rate, a new crisis rocked the government with confounding speed: Britain was forced to break the link between the value of sterling

and gold. There had never been anything quite like this, but the anti-climax after the break with gold took everyone by surprise, as indeed had the crisis in the first place. In October 1931, the government proposed a programme of severe austerity and sacrifice: the unemployed could get no succour from such parsimony. But the devaluation of the pound by about a quarter did not stop those people still in work from spending the pounds in their pocket, which because of the collapse in world prices could now buy more goods than before. More due to cyclical influences than government action, the economy began its upturn in 1933, and it was probably from this point that building activity was stimulated further down the New Line from Hinchley Wood.

London continues to prosper

One of the 1930s paradoxes was the unbalanced way in which the Depression impacted on different parts of the country: despair and sufficiency side by side in one nation. The staple industries of the north contracted, but these were remote from London whose light industries actually started to prosper as the economy recovered. London's role as the administrative centre was undiminished: as Taylor noted, 'Until August 1914 a sensible, law abiding Englishman could pass through life and hardly notice the existence of the state, beyond the post office and the policeman.'[10] The Great War had started the trend of an increasing scale of state activity and the number of civil servants grew rapidly. Alongside this, there was a shift in the pattern of new jobs towards clerical and administration work in local government, in insurance and the like in other parts of the private sector; just the sort of activity that London was good at supporting. Those people who were in work discovered that the economic imbalances meant they had never been better off. Naturally the civil servants were located in London, as well as were many of the other salaried jobs, and their increasing numbers in the 1930s created new demand for radial commuting all around the metropolis, including from the New Line; Hinchley Wood, the closest of its stations to Waterloo, was bound to benefit from these trends.

The boom conditions of the 1930s were in evidence all over suburban London. Broadly, it was the new middle class that was in work; aspiring, creatures of the 20th century, attracted by home ownership, moving away

[10] *English History 1914-1945*: A J P Taylor, 1965, p 1.

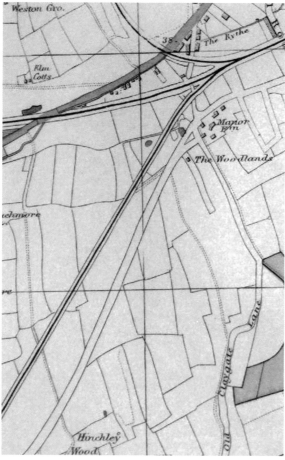

16.4 Part of Bacon's Atlas of London and Suburbs, *early 1900s, showing where Hinchley Wood was built in the 1930s; it shows the New Line before the bifurcation and the original flat junction for the Hampton Court line. The River Rythe is also shown, just above the junction; it was the valley of this minor river that gave the best route of the New Line from the main line to Oxshott. Old Claygate Lane marks the future eastern limit of the 1930s settlement of Hinchley Wood.*

from the centres of towns; attracted to the suburbs. Through a fluke in international markets, this group found they had stable incomes, falling prices, and cheap money and after about 1933, eager lenders, all at a time when the suburbs and the country villages beckoned. This is the extraordinary paradox of the 1930s: mass unemployment on the one hand, while large parts of the population were enjoying a richer life than they had ever known.

Hinchley Wood and the housing boom

The boom in housebuilding was a major contributor to the economic recovery of the early 1930s. The private sector built nearly three million houses during the decade, which was nearly twice as many as the public sector in the 1920s. When recovery came, activity in the building industry increased at about twice the general rate. Commenting on the phenomenon of the 1930s housing boom Taylor wrote:

> Men with new houses bought radio sets, electrical equipment, and new furniture. They raised their general standard of living. Many of the houses had their own garages, and this went along with the sales of motor cars. Most of the unsubsidised houses were built in new districts … The south of England, like the new houses and the new industries, was more high class. Hence there was a demand for new roads, new schools, new public buildings and cinemas; and these had to be of a higher standard.[11]

All these forces are recognisable in the expansion of our New Line cluster villages but of all these settlements Hinchley Wood stands as the best monument to the 1930s (even though its cinema was never built):

> The boom did not create Hinchley Wood; but when it came it contributed to the speed with which everything happened: from a standing start in 1930, Hinchley Wood had its first shops and its residents' association by 1931; its first councillor by 1933; its recognition as a separate ward with its own polling station in 1935. It celebrated its first Christian service in 1933 and by 1935 it had built its Hall Church (which was to serve until the proper church was built in 1953); and by 1939 there were over 2,000 new adult residents. The station was the magnet drawing London's workers to 'a place in the country' which the Southern Railway had been promoting. Crouch new this, and even before the boom had any impact, development was fast.[12]

Southern Electric caught the mood of the times and prospered from the increased traffic. In the light of the conditions and impulses of the 1930s described above, with affordability reaching out to the middle classes, the suburban expansion was assured. Once the station was open the housing development went ahead, its success secured despite the economic circumstances at the beginning. In early 1930 the station catchment area

---

[11] *Ibid*, p 344.
[12] *Hinchley Wood: the Origins of a 1930s Settlement.* Howard Mallinson, 2002, p 21.

16.5 The shopping parade in Manor Road North, Hinchley Wood, developed in the early 1930s and integrated with Station Approach.

The Tony Goodbody collection

contained barely 100 residents but by the outbreak of war in 1939 there existed a thriving settlement which only needed some smaller scale development (some of it newly conceived on Lovelace land) to complete it. The speed at which the development filled up was astonishing: apart from the economic conditions, which became most favourable, and the fast, frequent and clean electric train service which the passengers loved, the speed of development was helped by Crouch's decision to bring in other developers, notably Berg, Stokes and Montgomery, who all had a slightly different offering available to the eager public at more or less the same time. Crouch's commitment to the SR to build 150 houses in three years must have given cause for concern at first, but as the economic gloom gave way to boom, there was never in any danger of the guarantee being called.

Hinchley Wood works well in terms of how the street scenes and road layouts look and feel; much of the credit for this belongs to Esher Council by their proactive approach, including influencing the density of development, and their requirement that developers build to a quality that would set the tone of the district. The Council also influenced the road layouts and widths and the absence of clinical, street grid layouts, which is a feature of Hinchley Wood, was the result. Unlike any other on the New Line the station has always been at the heart of the settlement, where its shops were built, and the new houses radiated out from

this nucleus on both sides of the railway to give the largest concentration of houses within 10 minutes walk of the station anywhere on the New Line. Development took place on both sides of the Kingston By-pass too, with the northwest quadrant being completed in the 1950s and 60s. In 1940 the secondary school opened and this led to a yet further expansion of railway traffic in the form of schoolchildren.

The opening of the station meant that the journey time to *Waterloo* for all those commuters further down the line was increased but there was another important impact: before 1930 once Hampton Court Junction was passed on the homebound journey, there was no urbanisation visible from the train, until Claygate was reached. Because Hinchley Wood was deliberately built round the railway, both sides of the tracks are developed. This is not typical of the New Line: apart from small parts of Claygate and parts of Oxshott the development which exists today is generally only on one side of the railway until Merrow is reached. The post-war completion of Hinchley Wood extended its contiguity with the railway.

Because Hinchley Wood has now arrived on the scene we must redefine our *New Line* cluster of villages to include it. By 1951 the combined populations had grown to 32,000 of which Hinchley Wood accounted for 4,000. With the exception of Claygate, which in this period grew by less than 1,000 to 4,500, all the other

16.6 Hinchley Drive was one of the first roads in Hinchley Wood to pre-date the opening of the station; it was developed by E & L Berg.

The Tony Goodbody collection

combinations in the cluster grew by between 2,500 and 3,800. A chart showing the respective growth in population between 1931 and 1951 is given below.

**New Line cluster of villages
Population growth, 1951 over 1931**

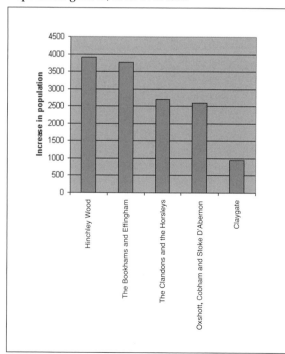

Further down the line

The low level of increment to Claygate's population which can be attributed to the 1930s housing boom in absolute and relative terms is probably a reflection of how much development had taken place there earlier in the century and the greater availability of land in the other villages in the cluster. Apart from infilling – it was during this period that Claygate finally joined up with Esher and almost with Hinchley Wood – most of the development in Claygate was in the Oaken Estate, on an area of land lying to the east of Oaken Lane which was probably part of *Slough Farm*. In their sales pitch, the developer noted that the electrification of the New Line had given 'an excellent service of trains' adding that 'the chief result of this has been the influx of numerous residents whose livelihood rests in the City'. This was undoubtedly so, but it was increasingly difficult to build a new house in Claygate that was near the station. The development of Lord Foley's former land on the Ruxley Estate, over a mile from the station, had started in the 1920s, but the development of Mountview Road, Ruxley Crescent and Hill View Road continued in the 1930s

Social conditions were changing: gone were the domestic servants and the middle-class villa life that had been an important part of the Claygate scene before the Great War. There was no demand any more for new three-storey houses, which had characterised

16.7 A Down Guildford via Cobham service passes a signal box at Clapham Junction.

The J N Faulkner Collection

building in Claygate in the period just before and after the turn of the 20th century: by the 1930s ceiling heights had dropped and new houses that were built on the Oaken estate were for the new middle class, with no live-in domestic servants.

To extend its land holdings in Oxshott the Crown Estate had bought, after the New Line had opened, two Claygate farms, *Loseberry* and *Horringdon,* both of which were contiguous with the New Line but on opposite sides of it. In the 1930s large advertising boards were erected on *Horringdon Farm* to promote to passing passengers the availability of land for sale through Cluttons on the Crown's Oxshott estate.[13] Whether the Crown had any ambitions to develop land on the Claygate farms in the 1930s is not properly evidenced, but the internal rationale for restricting their development activity to Oxshott only would be a bit thin. Happily, Oxshott was never joined to Claygate and they are separated still by undulating meadows, which support animal husbandry. In springtime lambing takes place in fields by the railway, protected

from foxes by a llama known locally as 'Lucy'. We have already entered the point where the *Guildford via Cobham* can truly claim to be 'a country railway'. Since before the 1939-45 war, when the cows of *Manor Farm* in Hinchley Wood gave way to the developer, herds cannot now be seen until Claygate is reached: is there any other station as near as 15 miles from *Waterloo* where cows graze alongside the waiting room? It is only the Green Belt that made this secure: is there anyone living in Claygate today who does not rejoice in what they consider to be *their* cows grazing on *Loseberry Farm?*

In addition to the further development of their land in Oxshott, in 1935 the Crown Estate bought at auction the 44 acres of land previously belonging to *Bevendean,* the mansion which Sir John Aird had built for his

---

13 The author is indebted to Mrs Jo Richards who has photographs of these boards but unfortunately they are not suitable for reproduction.

16.8 In the early 1930s a Cobham estate agent used this aerial photo to promote the development which was going to take place; the chimney of Oxshott brickworks can be discerned in the background, below which is the already-developed Fairmile area; the new residential roads have been named and are marked among the fields in which a high-class residential area is to be built.

16.9 Leigh Hill, Cobham, c1930s.

230

daughter and son-in-law, and whose entrance was in Warren Lane. On this parcel of land, with frontages on Goldrings and Holtwood Roads, the Crown developed a further series of fine houses on good plots. This was also the theme on the development of land that brought about the joining up of the Fairmile district of Cobham with Stoke D'Abernon and practically Oxshott. As the wealthy families with their mansions either died out or were impoverished by the rising burden of taxation, the land that they occupied provided sites for a new type of wealthy resident – the City commuter, who unlike Keays in Fairmile Court before, had no material private means. In addition to the higher value housing that was built in the 1930s in the New Line cluster of villages, measurable numbers of Council houses were built to add to the population numbers and use up the available land.

Improvements to *Waterloo* station

In the 1920s and 30s there was a series of improvements at *Waterloo* station which improved the travelling conditions for commuters, and long-distance travellers alike. The LSWR's London terminus had grown piecemeal with four separate stages of construction since it had opened in 1848. Under its General Manager, Sir Herbert Walker, newly appointed to the LSWR in 1912, a fundamental rebuilding of *Waterloo* was ordered. The bridge over what is now the concourse, which gave the connection to *Cannon Street* (and which had received adverse criticism for the awkwardness of the interchange at the Guildford, Kingston and London Railway Bill hearing) had been removed in 1911, the *Waterloo & City Line* having made it superfluous. This eliminated a serious barrier to the reconfiguration of the terminus, the muddle of which had been the butt of Jerome K Jerome's humour. The rebuilt station, which was completed in 1922, included a subway under the platforms, which facilitated easier interchanges with the tube network and the *Waterloo & City Line*, as well as spreading the load on the platform barriers.

Walker had driven through the third-rail electrification project for the newly created SR and the station became the first terminus to be designed specially for electric train operation. The new concourse abutted all the platform heads, making it feel like a coherent new design, whereas in fact the former North (Windsor Lines) station was incorporated into the new structure. The year 1926 saw the completion of the Northern Line tube extension from *Charing Cross* to *Kennington*. This

meant that commuters and long distance travellers could now get to *Euston* (and intermediate stops) directly from *Waterloo* underground station for the first time. As the electrification project expanded further in the 1930s, congestion increased in the approaches to *Waterloo*. The problem was that somehow the increasing numbers of suburban trains had to be kept from fouling the main lines, which they were bound to do somewhere when their direction was reversed: the solution was to build the Wimbledon flyover,[14] which opened in 1936 to carry slow Up services over the Up and Down main lines. As already noted, the *Guildford via Cobham* trains were routed on the main line from Surbiton, and as a result of the flyover were less vulnerable to delays through conflicting movements; unhappily, such priority is no longer given, and they now use the flyover.

The period from the opening of the Wimbledon flyover in 1936 until war conditions applied must have been the high peak of the *Guildford via Cobham* service: three trains per hour through the day, 1st and 3rd class accommodation, porterage at the stations and, with the main line now decongested, fewer delays on the booked non-stop run between *Surbiton* and *Waterloo*. Although all these features were restored after the war, none has survived to the present day.

Population shifts

All the development along the New Line that has been considered in this chapter took place in the context of a social trend that was endemic in the period: the desire to move out from inner London as far as incomes and travel-to-work-times would allow. Between the census of 1921 and that of 1951, the inner area of London 'was the only county in the country which showed an actual decline in population'.[15] At the same time the population of many of the Home Counties, including Surrey, more or less doubled. Much the greater part of a this shift in the population took place in the 1930s, and as a localisation of this trend, in the years 1931 to 1939 the population of Wimbledon fell by 19 per cent; Richmond's by 13 per cent and Kingston's by 5 per cent. In the same eight years the population of the New Line cluster of villages rose by a dramatically higher

[14] As a testament to the ability of electric trains to tackle gradients, the climb up the flyover is at 1:60.
[15] *English History 1914-1945*: A J P Taylor, 1965, p 167.

16.10 *Waterloo station, c1925, showing the main line and boat train platforms at a slack time; note the cab approach road, removed c1970.*

16.11 *Waterloo station, c1938; most of the space is dedicated to railway business, for it was not until the 1970s that the value of retail lettings was realised.*

16.12 *Claygate Brickfields Ltd, makers of the famous fireplaces, Common Road Head Office, c1934; the building survives as offices. A top-of-the-range fireplace product would sell in the 1930s at £25, free-on-board Claygate goods yard for onward freight to a customer's nearest yard.*

figure. 'The middle classes set the standards of the community' wrote Taylor and 'they were its conscience and did its routine work'. Their number, employed in both the private and public sectors, increased dramatically and in the 1930s many came to live in one of the New Line cluster of villages commuting to London in such numbers that the character of the villages took on a recognisably modern feel, with the one qualification that the incubus of the motor car had not yet blighted their roads and space.

The growth of the use of the motor car for travel-to-work, in the proportion that is now endemic, has diluted the rail commuter as a proportion of the whole. Surrey County Council estimates in 1938 suggested that about 700 people travelled to London by the *Guildford via Cobham* line daily from Claygate; this would have been a very significant proportion of the men of working age, and a smaller number of single women (wives generally remained at home in this period). It may also have been a reflection of different demo-

graphics: people were less likely to retire into one of the New Line cluster of villages, but many will have stayed in them after the end of their working life, reducing the proportion of working people within the whole.

When War came, the furthest extent of the building activity marked the point where the expansion of the metropolis ceased; the builders were never to be given free rein again. As it happened, the end of the 1930s more or less defined the boundaries of the New Line cluster of villages for good, the only exceptions being where proper control was to be exercised over the market forces, which until 1939 had been unbridled. Evelyn Waugh noted this in *Brideshead Revisited*: 'Another year of peace would have made the place part of the neighbouring suburb': Claygate had joined with Esher; and Cobham with Stoke D'Abernon and Oxshott but as we shall see, even though there was a war on, something had to be done to keep separate that which was still unjoined by designing the 'proper control' over development.

233

16.13 Effingham Junction looking Up the line (2004).

16.14 The Cross Lanes viaduct on the Up side of London Road station (2004).

Chapter 17: The post-war years

17.1 *The local goods train was a feature of the New Line from its inception; a train came every day until the 1960s; here, a '700-class' mounts the summit at Horsley with a local pick-up goods train on 29 April 1961.*

The Peter Tatlow collection

The Metropolitan Green Belt

The coinage of the term *Green Belt*, and its place in the lexicon both belong in the 1920s, shortly before *Southern Electric*'s promotion of *A Country Home at London's Door*. The first bureaucratic use was when the London County Council floated the notion of the desirability and practicability of retaining an undeveloped ring around London, the great capital city whose generative influence on development in the Home Counties, if protracted, had sinister implications: it seemed wrong to County Hall to allow the unrestrained growth of London on the one hand and equally the need was recognised for pleasant open spaces for the recreation of those that lived in towns: a part of the rationale of the Guildford, Kingston and London Railway Bill in the Select Committee had been to open up the commons to the poorer sections of London's population. The planning regime of the time, even though it was evolving slowly, was not conducive to the establishment of an effective, local, regional, let alone national approach and the only certain method

of development control was by ownership: the decision by Esher Council to buy Telegraph Hill is an excellent example of this. The Green Belt (London and Home Counties) Act 1938 reflected the growing concern, and facilitated public ownership of 'green' land but when war came the presumption of a landowner's right to develop had not been overturned except by the emergency. Even as war was declared a Royal Commission, acknowledging that the horse had bolted, was investigating how to get it back in the stable.

One of the problems of planning legislation to date was that planning schemes could not be refused on the ground of better locations elsewhere: in other words the availability of land controlled development rather than the desirability of development. We have already seen how East Clandon remained undeveloped because the landowner who owned most of it chose the *status quo*, and in contrast how Claygate was joined to Esher, and Cobham with Stoke D'Abernon and Oxshott because the market had made the land that separated

235

17.2 The goods yards, although isolated at first, quickly became a centre of activity; this view of Claygate's from Station Approach, is from the 1920s; it remained active principally for coal until the 1960s.

The Paul Langton collection

them available for development with no reference to higher-level appraisal. In a planned environment undeveloped 'lungs' would have been left between settlements as an act of deliberate policy.

When the Barlow report (as it was called) was published in 1940, there was considerable material in it for a post-war revision of the planning regime. It became common ground among administrators that preservation of land from development by ownership had to be substituted for control over it based on some long-term higher-level plan. It was absurd that schemes could not be refused on the ground of there being a better location elsewhere, and equally if a local authority refused planning permission, where no planning scheme under the existing legislation had been adopted, it had to pay compensation to the landowner. Barlow recited the economic consequences of congestion and proposed that all land should come under planning control.

The destruction of large parts of London and many other cities by bombing went hand in hand with the new intellectual approach to planning the reconstructions that would follow the victory, which no one seemed in the mood to doubt. Although our cluster of villages was not affected by bombing, save for a few

isolated incidents and random hits by V1 flying bombs and V2 rockets (one of which fell in November 1944 near the Hampton Court Junction viaduct), naturally the new thinking on post-war development was applied to it even though reconstruction was not an issue. The Town and Country Planning Act of 1947 gave legislative backing to the new professional approach. By this Act the presumption of the right of a landowner to develop was overridden by development control based on a forward-looking development plan: the bogie of paying compensation for refusal of planning permission was slain.

It was by the 1947 Act and later amendments that local authorities were given the power to create what became known as the Metropolitan Green Belt. Surrounding Greater London, this emerged in the 1950s and included most of the area around the New Line south of Hinchley Wood as far as the outskirts of Guildford. In practice by early 1940 all development by private enterprise on open land had ceased and post-war shortages of building materials and labour along with rationing of new construction had virtually stopped uncontrolled private building until the 1947 Act was in force. It is therefore practically correct to suggest that the building lines of 1939 marked the limit of London's centrifugal expansion.

17.3 The goods yards created a busy atmosphere at the stations; in this scene at Horsley on 4 April 1925 an Up passenger train via Leatherhead waits in the platform hauled by a Class M7 (Drummond) 0-4-4T No 674 (built 1897, Nine Elms) in Southern livery; while the goods train passes on the Down line; empty wagons wait in the yard.

The H C Casserley collection

The new world of post-war planning as it affected Greater London was owed to an astonishing initiative: even as the bombs fell on London post-war planning was put in hand. With the Barlow report fresh on the desk and a universal acknowledgement of the folly that had characterised much of the development of the previous 20 years, at the request of the Minister of Town & Country Planning and on behalf of the Steering Conference on London Regional Planning, Professor (later Sir) Patrick Abercrombie prepared *The Greater London Plan 1944*. Published in 1945 by HM Stationery Office, its significance cannot be overstated. Abercrombie, then the recognised head of the planning profession, has been credited with much of the Barlow report conclusions. His philosophic and sociological input to his work gave it huge authority; his life's work at the heart of planning and architecture was harnessed to his task.

Abercrombie's plan was bold, it being the first attempt ever to get to grips with London's inordinate problems and to offer a solution covering all aspects of society by bringing a strategy for housing, transport and industry into a coherent whole. If there had been some forebear of Abercrombie around in the 1880s, it would have been to him and not to Parliament, that the advice on the desirability of building the Guildford, Kingston and

London Railway would have been passed: he would have considered the strategic benefit of a new route to London (and probably approved it) and as a corollary he would have suggested how commuter developments should be planned around it. He might have specified the retention of belts of undeveloped land separating each of the settlements. But Britain grew great from free trade and private enterprise and it took practically the whole of Abercrombie's working life (he was born in 1875) to substitute planning for naked market forces. We saw in Part I that the New Line's *raison d'etre* was London: although the influence of Lord Onslow and the District Railway was seminal, everything comes back to London; in the 60 years of progress between the first proposal to build the New Line and the publication of the Barlow Report, London continued to build its status as a world city. As Barlow recites: 'So the process of growth continues – market and population acting and reacting upon one another to build up an ever greater collection of people and industries. Nothing succeeds like success.'[1]

Although Abercrombie's work was a monument to planning all aspects of land use and transport (and the

---

[1] Quoted in *Greater London Plan 1944*: Patrick Abercrombie, HMSO 1945, p 4.

17.4 *Clandon station (with the signal box on the platform) and goods yard after it had closed; (1966).*

The Patrick collection

New Town movement) we are concerned only with one aspect of his contribution: the essential need for statutory force for a Green Belt round London and his identification of the limits to the 'rounding off' of the existing settlements comprising our New Line cluster of villages. Abercrombie conceived of four concentric rings around London for zoning purposes. Next to the inner ring was the second ring of 'suburban London', where each settlement 'tends to coalesce with its neighbour', which had an outer boundary broadly 12 miles from Charing Cross. The third ring is the one that concerns us: described as a 'Green Belt Ring' it included most of the public land that had been preserved already, but Abercrombie proposed the inclusion of private land to be 'permanently safeguarded against building' by legal powers. He observed that:

> it has often been pointed out that if action had been taken 25 years ago a real belt of open country round London could have been secured, not only more completely rural than the present proposal, but nearer in.

It is unclear whether Abercrombie was alluding to the desirability of Hinchley Wood having been left unbuilt and the land retained as the start of the Green Belt Ring and that the housebuilding activities of the likes of Crouch should have been redirected to the new and expanded towns to be built much further out from

London to absorb the displaced demand. As it was, Hinchley Wood *was* built and there were failed attempts just before the war to join it, along with Claygate, to Hook and Chessington by the development of land formerly in the Lovelace estate through which the Guildford, Kingston and London Railway might have been built: such a joining up would have been a planning catastrophe to make even worse the given position from which Abercrombie was obliged to start.[2] Saved as it was by the war from being joined indissolubly from Abercrombie's suburban London, Hinchley Wood was to be protected on its eastern, south western and southern boundaries by the Metropolitan Green Belt when it came in the 1950s.

The Green Belt Ring 'is of paramount importance to London' because it would provide 'the first stretches of open country and within it would be made up 'the public open space deficiency' of London – and through this ring ran the *Guildford via Cobham* railway like the spoke of a wheel. Abercrombie observed generally that in the Green Belt Ring that he proposed were to be found a 'larger number of communities than one would have liked, some old some new': it was necessary to

---

[2] For an account of this saga see *Hinchley Wood: the Origins of a 1930s Settlement*: Howard Mallinson, 2002.

238

17.5 A Down
Guildford via
Cobham train enters
Horsley station on
4 April 1925, while
passing another
train in the refuge
siding. The goods
wagons only just
avoid fouling the
entrance to the yard.

The H C Casserley collection

limit within this zone 'very strictly' any expansion of existing communities. One of the exceptions to this that Abercrombie acknowledged was to allow for the building of 'certain immediate post-war housing' needs, of which as we shall see there was a considerable amount.

Abercrombie had no criticism of Hinchley Wood, which he noted as 'a modern suburban development based on the railway with a sensibly planned little shopping area round a green off the Kingston By-pass'. He was unequivocal that 'The un-built on areas along the By-pass should be kept open' and 'on no account should any part of it be used for industry'. He made a particular point of observing that the war-time use of government buildings on the By-pass (which were supplemented by yet more in a different part of Hinchley Wood after the war, to the great benefit of local employment and railway traffic) 'should not prove harmful to the neighbourhood' if continued after the war. Abercrombie found in these offices, as well as the Milk Marketing Board in Thames Ditton considerable benefits: by decentralisation 'daily travel to London would be avoided'. This was a dramatic observation: a mere five years after *Southern Electric* had been obliged by the war to cease its famously successful campaign to sell the idea of commuting from

A Country Home at London's Door, here was the doyen of the planning world holding up the benefits of local employment in order to avoid commuting.

Abercrombie observed that the large suburban growth that had characterised the 20th century to 1939 had found a system of railways ready to hand and that because development had followed them the gaps between routes had been undeveloped giving an open opportunity of preservation in a Green Belt. Moreover, because the settlements outside the Suburban Ring showed a greater tendency to a separation from its neighbour, such separation should be made permanent: 'no further development should be permitted between Stoke D'Abernon, Oxshott and Claygate' was his injunction and by it the claims of the *Guildford via Cobham* line to have been preserved as 'a country railway' are established. For Abercrombie it was not just London that needed its Green Belt: 'lesser girdles for the separate communities' should be retained. The Green Belt when it came gave sanctity from a line drawn at the undeveloped fringes of the villages, allowing what Abercrombie referred to as 'rounding off', but preserving the separation that existed between them. At the country end of the *Guildford via Cobham* line this presented fewer problems, but nearer London, by placing the farms of Loseberry, Arbrook and

17.6 Claygate station from the Up platform, with the goods yard on the Down side; date unknown.

Horringdon, as well as land near Littleworth Common in the Green Belt, all the countryside that remained undeveloped in 1939 that was contiguous with the railway was preserved, to the extent that Hinchley Wood is only tenuously separated from Claygate but the space between it and Oxshott has remained inviolate as Abercrombie said it should.

Observing that development of low-density expensive housing had taken place, Abercrombie thought that the considerable areas of partly developed lands in Cobham and Oxshott should be 'filled in and rounded off', which in due course they have been. He had little to say about Claygate: 'once a quiet rather ordinary small Victorian village half a mile from the railway, which has developed with some scattered modern housing and a small but good central shopping area adjoining the station'. It was almost as if, with Claygate being on the way to nowhere, and its protection by a Green Belt easily prescribed because of agricultural use of its outer land, he had moved on quickly down the roads and railways radiating from London. While

overlooking the brick industry of Claygate in particular, Abercrombie favoured the separation of brickworks from towns 'owing to the pungent sulphurous odour which they give off'.

On the subject of agriculture, Abercrombie introduced a planning criterion that had hitherto been neglected along with all the others. He observed that if land had been available for building no attention was given to its agricultural quality: the difference between the best farming land and the worst was not a factor in determining its development value, and this could not be right; 'even market garden land with its often irreplaceable value as providing fresh food for London, had been violated by the 'insistent claims of building as a better profit maker'. Abercrombie noted the poor soil of Oxshott, without observing that its development had not been because of that fact: it had been developed because it was there and the Crown's land was available. The area between the two Clandons has been described as containing the finest ploughland in Surrey; it remains undeveloped.

The Alan Jackson collection

17.7 *This view of Hillcrest Gardens, Hinchley Wood, taken from Telegraph Hill, is from the early 1930s. Development followed the previous field patterns, but this point was later to mark a boundary of the Metropolitan Green Belt.*

The Metropolitan Green Belt features strongly in the spatial planning of the South East Region of England as part of the need to sustain London as a world city: the District Railway had 'cast eyes upon the fair and rich traffic district of the South Western suburban system' as a method of doing just that. Surrey County Council, in its policy today on the Green Belt, uses language drawn directly from Abercrombie's report of 60 years ago when it speaks of preventing urban sprawl; preventing the coalescence of settlements and in protecting the countryside. The survival of *Guildford via Cobham* as a country railway running through the Metropolitan Green Belt can be traced to work that was done as the bombs were falling on London.

Population change

Professor Abercrombie's Greater London Plan of 1944 was accepted as the blueprint for post-war planning: no new settlements, no new Hinchley Woods, were to be allowed along the *Guildford via Cobham* railway and limits were placed on the spatial expansion of our New Line cluster of villages. Once these were set, the Metropolitan Green Belt was imposed on the map to fix whatever separation between the settlements that had remained from 1939 and mark the boundary beyond which no expansion would be allowed – the so-called 'rounding off'. London's status as a world city continued to grow unabated and its gravitational pull was diminished only by a degree of decentralisation of offices into the district – a process that had started during or in anticipation of the war: Foley's *Ruxley Towers* was occupied by the NAAFI; Charles Combe's *Cobham Park* became the headquarters of the Eagle Star Insurance Company: Queen Victoria's *Claremont* became the design office of Hawkers, while after the war the Inland Revenue set up an office in Hinchley Wood on the site of a former prisoner-of-war camp; the Central Electricity Generating Board established a training centre in Lovelace's *Horsley Towers*; and Brown & Polson decentralised to a large new office block between Claygate and Esher, with Cobham also attracting office users. All these new office developments, including the further expansion of

241

Ruxley Towers were excellent examples of Abercrombie's vision of taking the pressure off the railway infrastructure caused by the volume of demand from commuters to get into London.

Gradually the pattern of commuting changed, not least because in the electronic age and in the post Big-Bang revolution the working habits and hours of London commuters are barely recognisable from the past, but in the 20 years to 1971 it was not only the decentralisation that changed the work pattern of residents of the New Line cluster of villages: car use for travel-to-work expanded and some counter-flow movements on the *Guildford via Cobham* line by office workers were observable: the Inland Revenue office in Hinchley Wood had its own dedicated access and egress to the station platforms, with their own ticket-collectors' booths.

In the 20 years to 1971 the population of Surrey grew by a quarter of a million, or by one third, to one million people; in the same period the total population of the New Line cluster of villages grew by more than 50 per cent to 48,000: the figures are set out in the table below.

Population: New Line cluster of villages

	1951	1971	Growth 1951-1971 Number	%
Hinchley Wood	4,263	5,209	946	22
Claygate	4,488	6,921	2,433	54
Oxshott, Stoke D'Abernon and Cobham	10,177	14,724	4,547	45
The Clandons and the Horsleys	5,980	8,323	2,343	39
The Bookhams and Effingham	6,527	12,811	6,284	96
Total	31,435	47,988	16,553	53
Surrey (in thousands)	746	1,002	256	34

Hinchley Wood

Hinchley Wood shows the smallest growth. When building stopped in 1939-40, its south-west corner (Medina Avenue, Heathside and Harefield) was left unfinished. Following a long pause after the war, during which a post-Abercrombie appraisal of much wider issues was conducted, the development was completed in the 1950s and 1960s. This 'rounding off' was wholly compatible with Abercrombie but it meant that the 'country railway' status of the *Guildford via Cobham* line was diminished because the contiguous land on both sides of the track south of the station was now built up.

This development accounts for the greater part but not all the post-war growth of Hinchley Wood. In what was one of the first incursions into the Green Belt for residential development a public enquiry was held in 1953 over the Council's decision to refuse planning permission for a parcel of land which was formerly in the Lovelace estate holding and which was contiguous with the Kingston By-pass: the land had come in for particular attention by Abercrombie who had said 'The un-built on areas along the By-pass should be kept open'. In spite of this, the Inspector at the Inquiry was persuaded that the original inclusion of the land in the Green Belt was anomalous because it was a penetration through the natural eastern boundary of Hinchley Wood: in consequence Severn Drive and Hill Rise were developed but no effective precedent was established for Green Belt incursion because of the accepted anomaly.

After this development had taken place Hinchley Wood had been 'rounded off' and the only place for further development was by back-land development, which has become endemic generally because it is the direct consequence of continuing unsatisfied housing demand and the restriction of land supply by Green Belt dogma. In recent years all the decentralisation of offices into Hinchley Wood has been undone by the demolition of offices, actual and proposed, and their replacement with houses – a perverse reversal of Abercrombie.

Claygate

Claygate's population expansion in the period 1951 to 1971 was at the same rate as the average over the whole New Line cluster: the population rose just over a half to nearly 7,000. The space for this expansion was provided by marking the eastern boundary at Richard Jefferies' beloved Claygate Lane and protracting the sweep of Foley's Ruxley land (which had been developed pre-war) round to Woodstock Lane to more or less meet it. The lower-value housing that was built in the areas made available was among the furthest from the station of any in the village: with the age of travel-to-work by car approaching, this had less importance than in former days; the railway was losing its centrality. The

The Jo Richards collection

17.8 The farms had from the inception of the New Line been an important source of traffic; this Southern Railway invoice from 1925 is for the freight of nearly 13½ tons of manure to Horringdon Farm, Claygate from Nine Elms. As the population of horses in London declined with the rise of the motor lorry, the traffic in manure declined, ultimately to zero.

former brickworks were a source of land as well from agriculture but the development in the Cavendish Drive area on a former brickfield extended the trackside housing development to the point where only a tenuous avoidance of the coalescence of Claygate with Hinchley Wood has been established. The garden centre that was on the Oaken Lane site was a permitted use of land in the Green Belt; the future development of the site is an open question.

Oxshott, Stoke D'Abernon and Cobham

Boundary changes and 'coalescence' make it virtually impossible to consider Oxshott, Stoke D'Abernon and Cobham separately for comparative purposes. The combined population growth in the 20-year period was slightly less than average at 45 per cent. The area had been 'filled in and rounded off' as suggested by Abercrombie. Trackside development has been controlled in the post-Abercrombie desire to avoid (successfully) the coalescence of Oxshott and Stoke D'Abernon in Blundel Lane. Nevertheless, when the bucolic separation of Claygate and Oxshott comes to an

end at the Crown Estate development only Oxshott Heath intervenes before the country area is rejoined down from the former brickworks. Once Cobham station is left behind the rural scenes across the Mole flood plain have differed little from the Revd Phillips' 'rustic simplicity' of Stoke D'Abernon.

The Horsleys and the Clandons

The population of the Horsleys and the Clandons combined grew less than average in the 20 years to 1971 but this disguises some wider variations between the four parishes. The figures are set out below:

Population: The Horsleys and the Clandons

	1951	1971	Growth 1951-1971 Number	%
East Horsley	2,642	3,972	1,330	50
West Horsley	2,222	3,045	823	37
East Clandon	345	278	-67	-19
West Clandon	771	1,028	257	33
Total	5,980	8,323	2,343	39

243

Abercrombie had observed that East and West Horsley 'are extensions of the suburban influence of London developing from the railway' and in echo of the continuous theme of this book he noted that 'to the south lies some of the finest scenery in Surrey'. Abercrombie thought that both villages needed 'rounding off rather than expansion and improvement in their shopping facilities' – facilities which Chown had not wanted to provide in East Horsley in the first place. Rather more of this rounding off seems to have occurred in East Horsley, where growth in the 20 years to 1971 was 50 per cent taking the population to nearly 4,000. Development took place on either side of Forest Road including that part which approaches *Effingham Junction* station in a sort of ribbon development. This together with the carriage sheds presents an urban scene for practically the whole of the one mile which separates that station from Horsley, where development has been allowed on both sides of the tracks.

Abercrombie had observed that the 'unspoilt villages of the region are an asset of the first importance to London' and that East Clandon was 'a good example of an old self-contained village situated near to yet quite divorced from the main traffic route'.

> Everything in East Clandon is what it ought to be, and everybody does what he ought to do. The timbered cottages are old and quiet; the barn roofs by the churchyard are long and lichened; the churchyard is bordered by a thick holly hedge, and about its graves, little clipped yew trees stand like chessmen ...; the cottage gardens are full of simple flowers and fruit-trees, and the cottagers work in them as if it were the best work to do, which it doubtless is. There could be no happier looking village.

This could have been written yesterday; it could have been written two hundred years ago, but in fact the piece comes from *Highways and Byways in Surrey* by Eric Parker, written in 1908. In the 200 years from 1801 to 2001 the population of East Clandon has remained within the limits of 228 (1811) and 366 (1931). In every census from 1951 the population has shown a reduction from the previous one: we can conclude that the *Guildford via Cobham* railway has had no impact, if anything else has, on East Clandon, and a visit to it will easily transport the beholder to scenes which were typical in the New Line cluster of villages in the 1880s when the railway came, except for the absence of horse traffic, and the noise of aircraft and the roar of the A246.

The post-war population growth of West Clandon to 1971 was at the same rate as the Surrey average and was not of a character to have materially changed the village. Even at a population in 2001 of less than 1,300 West Clandon has a smaller population than had Claygate 100 years before. One of the things which characterises the small expansion of West Clandon, which has a north/south orientation along Clandon Road and The Street, is how little of it took place on land contiguous with the railway, and on one side of it only. On leaving Clandon station we must take in the last of our country railway scenes.

Merrow and Burpham

The post-war expansion of Merrow and Burpham has been dramatic, such that as soon as we reach the industrial scene on the former Merrow sidings the trackside urbanisation is complete on both sides, save for the odd copse on New Inn Lane, until Guildford main line station is reached some three miles further on. Abercrombie noted that Guildford was one of those many towns in the Home Counties, about the same distance from London, which have 'old communities that still, in spite of accretions, retain their focal points'. He highlighted Guildford's suitability as a reception centre for the decentralisation of some London businesses (he mentioned insurance) to give local employment to 'black-coat workers now travelling daily to London'. We have noted already that the prediction was made well before the age of the motor car that 'Merrow will soon be joined to Guildford' and that *London Road* station itself had reinforced the existing trend to shifting Guildford to the east. In the post-war years the coalescence of Burpham, Merrow and Guildford proper became absolute, with an eastern boundary at Merrow Common and Park Lane, as Abercrombie had suggested. The huge expansion of Guildford since the war was induced by 101 factors, not wholly anticipated by Abercrombie who saw a redistribution of population, not an increase – the expansion of Surrey's population by one third would have come as something of a shock to him. If the *Guildford via Cobham* railway was one of the factors inducing the growth of Guildford it must have ranked very low among all the others.

Population growth: 1881-1971

The reader will be aware that after the immediate post-war years the influence on population growth in the

New Line cluster of villages that could be attributed to the railway became somewhat tenuous: the motor car became endemic, perfidious even in its primacy and no claim for any discernible influence on population change or siting of new residential development can be made after the 1970s which was motivated by the railway. It is appropriate, however, to review now the total changes in population that have occurred in the villages that concern us in the period 1881 to1971. The figures are set out below.

New line cluster of villages: Population growth: 1881 to 1971

	1881	1971	Growth factor 1881-1971
Hinchley Wood	-	5,209	-
Claygate	788	6,921	8.8
Oxshott, Stoke D'Abernon and Cobham	2,727	14,724	5.4
East Horsley	275	3,972	14.4
West Horsley	371	3,045	8.2
East Clandon	291	278	1.0
West Clandon	597	1,028	1.7
The Bookhams and Effingham	1,867	12,811	6.9
Total	6,916	47,988	6.9
Surrey (in thousands)	250[3]	1,002	4.0

The population of Surrey (adjusted for boundary changes) grew four times in 90 years, while taken as a whole, the growth of the New Line cluster of villages has been 6.9 times the 1881 figure: there can be no doubting the influence of the New Line on this result. The absence of any influence on East Clandon has already been noted, but West Clandon has seen its population grow by less than double in the period. The prize, if that is what it is, goes to East Horsley for all those villages for which the collection of official statistics allows this kind of comparison: at 14.4 times, the growth of the village between 1881 and 1971 was phenomenal, and with the station being less convenient for West Horsley the lesser growth (8.2 times) of that village is perhaps explained.

The discussion of the figures for Oxshott, Stoke D'Abernon and Cobham is made more difficult by the muddling of statistics caused by boundary changes and the fact that although Oxshott became an identifiable place, its numbers continued to be collected with Stoke D'Abernon. The population of Stoke D'Abernon in 1871 (which included the few who lived in Oxshott at the time) was 408: the population of Stoke D'Abernon

and Oxshott in 1971 was 5,555. This population explosion is great but impossible to break down in a scientific way - suffice it to say that in 2001, when separate numbers became available, the population of Oxshott as defined was 3,419 whereas in 1871 the population in the same land area might not have amounted to 100. It is, therefore, the areas comprising Oxshott and Hinchley Wood that have shown the greatest change of all the New Line cluster of villages.

The limits of development proposed by Abercrombie have held, but the density of development within those limits by infilling and construction of apartment blocks grows year by year, as does the volume of local traffic: it can only get worse because of the continuing success of London and the Green Belt dogma. Until road pricing arrives to regain some fairness in the competition between car and public transport, congestion will continue to be pervasive.

The goods yards close

Naturally, as the use of motor vehicles increased especially for the carriage of goods and passengers, so the vast population of horses needed in the capital reduced; a few readers may recall milk floats and rag and bone men with their horse drawn carts but by the late 1950s these had practically disappeared. With this equine decline, which took place over a considerable period, went the inexorable reduction in railway freight business in the carriage of hay from the farms to London and the return of manure from it. The farms continued to use rail freight for the import of animal feedstuffs and manufactured fertiliser, but road transport became more economic because it was quicker over short distances, not least because the goods would go direct from factory to farm with no intermediate hanging around and extra handling in the goods yard. While the use of the railway goods yard for farm produce and imports was still commonplace in the 1920s, by the 1950s the end was in sight.

Oxshott's brickworks had had its private siding since the opening of the line. London refuse was amongst its inward traffic as well as coal; the refuse was burnt on the site to produce ash used to make a cheap brick. The siding and works closed in 1959; Claygate's brickworks

---

[3] No figure is available from Surrey County Council for 1881 The number given is interpolated from the official figure for 1891 of 266,000.

lasted only into the following year. Some remember the noisy nocturnal shunting in the yards,[4] but their closure was not lamented apart from the minority who feel a certain nostalgia for the early 20th century railway sights and sounds. The major business of the yards, especially in their later years, was coal and coke, this mostly for domestic use. Bagged in the yard by the fuel merchants, it was delivered by horse-drawn carts and later, by motor lorries.

In a remarkable record of historical observation, a log exists of the whole shunting operation at Claygate station on the morning of 18 August 1955.[5] The 0-6-0 steam engine arrived at 5.30 am and entered the yard with 22 open wagons and two brake vans; 18 carrying coal and four stone chippings. After 27 shunting movements, the loco was ready to leave with its train comprising a total of 18 open wagons and two brake vans; the operation had involved a net deposit of four wagons, and those that were taken away were, evidently empty. On that August day in 1955 there were no movements of agricultural items: the quantity of coal being moved must have been related to the summer price discounting that the merchants offered.

As the trend to domestic central heating gathered pace in the 1960s, when gas, oil and electricity (mostly the former) replaced solid fuel for heating water and fireplaces, the traffic in the yards declined sharply. In March 1963 the Beeching report hastened what the market would make inevitable. Interestingly Abercrombie had observed 20 years earlier that there was no need for so many yards all located near to each other, when motor transport could fill the gaps. While the closure of the yards at *Oxshott* and *Clandon* pre-dated Beeching, all bar *London Road* followed soon after, the facility at *Merrow* having closed in 1961. The dates are given below.

Guildford via Cobham:
Goods yard closure dates

Claygate	May 1963
Oxshott	September 1959
Cobham	May 1965
Horsley	May 1964
Clandon	February 1963
London Road	January 1969

Source: *The Railway in Surrey*: Alan A Jackson, 1999.

Bookham's goods yard closed in May 1965, shortly before *Leatherhead*. The yard at *Surbiton* closed in

November 1971, while that at Guildford survived until October 1985. The rise of the motor vehicle having usurped the role of the goods yard, the space they had occupied was heaven-sent for the car parks, to which use they were quickly converted. The extent to which these were used depended, as it does today, on whether there is an on-street alternative, or how far away from the station is the nearest unregulated kerbside: even in 2006 the railway has a changing impact on some of the villages in our cluster; commuters' cars litter the streets where parking is free, and the former goods yard car parks are under-used.[6]

The closure of the goods yards prompted or was anticipated by the closure of several signal boxes, many of which were sited on station platforms to allow staff to perform multiple tasks. *Claygate, Oxshott, Cobham, Horsley, Clandon* and *London Road* boxes all closed around the early to mid 1960s, leaving only those at Cooks Crossing and *Effingham Junction* as the only signal boxes, for a time, between Hampton Court Junction and Guildford.

Service degradation and timetables

The fabulous service that had existed on the New Line in the 1930s, although severely diminished during the war, was for a time restored after it, but in the new post-war conditions, the service suffered a number of irreversible degradations. In January 1951, the railways were required to contribute to government plans for reducing the consumption of coal by reducing train services. The 20-minute service interval was restored in the 1950s only to be lost in 1958 when economies were needed to fund the cost of pay increases for railway staff; this resulted in the half-hour interval which operates today. Sunday services became hourly compared with the half-hourly service which had been the norm. First-class accommodation was reintroduced for about 10 years to 1984 when the Class 455 sliding door stock was introduced. The corridor stock that had

---

[4] Mrs Jo Richards has related her memory of being kept awake when she lived near the Claygate yard.

[5] Mr John Field of Hinchley Wood has kindly supplied this authentic contemporary record.

[6] A current proposal is extant to combine the station car park site at Claygate with the contiguous site of the former Station Garage, for redevelopment for residential development and parking, including a reconfiguration of traffic flow around the station area.

been used to provide first-class accommodation was not popular with second-class passengers on account of the reduced seating capacity, which made worse the existing overcrowding problem.

Memories of travelling on the *Guildford via Cobham* line in the 1960s include those of severe overcrowding: the 08.13 from Hinchley Wood – a train which would get a commuter to his office in the City by 9am – already had standing passengers when it arrived from Claygate. Also, severe disruption from sulphurous winter fogs was endemic into the 1960s, but the service was fast: rush-hour trains were still running non-stop to and from *Surbiton*, as they had since 1925. The journey time from *Hinchley Wood*, with *Waterloo* the second stop, was a mere 19 minutes, on the popular trains all of it spent standing. Taking *Cobham* as the benchmark, a commuter had a choice of eight trains between 07.11 and 09.13, while today there are only six trains between 07.24 and 09.25.

Once the morning peak had finished, the Down service reverted to half-hourly starting with the 10.22 until the 15.52 from which time a 20-minute service ran for three-and-a-half hours until 19.22, when the interval fell back to half-hourly. All Down trains between 17.12 hours until the 18.12 ran fast to *Surbiton* after which time the normal off-peak pattern of a single stop at *Wimbledon* was resumed. The journey times for a typical rush hour Down train were rapid, considerably better than the present day: a table showing the journey time for the 18.12 in 1961 compared with the times for the 18.02 of 2005 are set out below.

Guildford via Cobham:
Typical journey times from *Waterloo*, evening rush hour (in minutes)

	1961	2005	Increase
Surbiton	16	25	9
Hinchley Wood	19	33	14
Claygate	22	35	13
Oxshott	26	39	13
Cobham	29	42	13
Effingham Junction	35	47	12
Horsley	38	49	11
Clandon	43	54	11
London Road	48	59	11
Guildford	52	65	13

Source: British Rail Southern Region Summer Timetable, 1961; South West Trains June to December timetable, 2005.

In the 1960s there were seven trains in the two hours from 16.52 to 18.52 hours, four of which ran fast to *Surbiton*, whereas in 2005 there are six in the two hours from 17.02 to 19.02 hours, only one of which (18.48) is fast to *Surbiton*. In spite of this reduction there is, to make a subjective assessment, probably less overcrowding in the evening peak, which was normal on the 17.52 in the 1960s until *Surbiton* was reached. Nevertheless, a commuter leaving his office in the City at 5.30pm might expect to catch the 17.52 from Waterloo, from which he might alight at *Hinchley Wood* or *Claygate*, and after a five or 10-minute walk, be indoors less than an hour after leaving his office.

A large part of the increase in journey times is explained by the present-day policy of stopping all suburban trains (with the odd exception) at the interchange stations of *Wimbledon*, *Clapham Junction* and *Vauxhall*, and overall the standard of service is better as a result. Another lesser factor is that increased dwell times have been introduced at several stops because the present-day sliding-door trains take longer to load and unload than the slam-door trains that they replaced. Somewhat perversely, the off-peak trains are a touch faster, in spite of the fact that they all stop at *Earlsfield*, which is an innovation designed to improve the service from that station, but one which diminishes the service on the *Guildford via Cobham* line as well as on other routes.

Travel to work

The censuses of the last 40 years reveal some interesting changes in the pattern of where people work and by what means of transport they use to get there, and of course, increasing levels of car ownership. These data are not available down to the level of our village cluster but Surrey County Council provide the figures by district, and by looking at the statistics for Elmbridge and Guildford a reasonable surrogate is achieved.[7] Most of the growth of car ownership had already taken place by 1971 when 71 per cent of all Surrey households had a car, with 72 per cent in Elmbridge and 64 per cent in Guildford. We can assume that most of this growth took place post-war, in the late 1950s and through the 1960s after which proximity to a railway station became less important as a criterion for choosing where to live, especially after the closures of the goods yards allowed

---

[7] The author is grateful to Kathy Trott of Surrey County Council for her collation of data from the censuses.

car parking at the stations. Whereas earlier generations of commuters walked to the station (or went by bicycle) now there was an indifference to a short car journey as well as a commute by rail. By 2001 car ownership by households had reached the probable saturation levels of 86 per cent across Surrey but much more significantly from the point of view of traffic movements and competition with public transport, the number of cars available to each household rose by about 50 per cent in 30 years. In 1971 each car in Surrey was available to 3.14 people but in 2001 the availability had improved to one car for 1.63 people, with the availability to Guildford residents showing the greater increase. With approximately 75,000 cars kept in each of Guildford and Elmbridge Boroughs, it is perhaps surprising that traffic levels on the *Guildford via Cobham* line have remained robust, or perhaps it is a measure of the continuing importance of London among the ever growing diversity of job opportunities, and the problems and costs of driving to central London.

In the 30 years to 1991 there was a consistent trend of greater diversity of work destinations with the numbers working within their own district falling to about parity in 1991 from about 60 per cent or more in 1961; in the 10 years to 2001 there was a small reversal of this trend. The propensity to work further from home has seen a strong bias to other parts of Surrey and outer London (which would cover Heathrow airport) and further afield and naturally the greater part of these journeys is made by car; the orbital opportunities for these journeys has been radically improved by the M25 motorway, which of course now straddles the New Line just south of Cobham, and radially by the improvement of the A3 to near motorway standards especially where that road is on a more or less parallel route to the New Line.

In spite of the scope for working elsewhere, the numbers of journeys to work in inner London from Elmbridge and Guildford remain robust with nearly 11,000 Elmbridge and 5,000 Guildford residents travelling to work in inner London in 2001; three-quarters of these travelled by train, a proportion which increased by five percentage points in 10 years. Although the majority making up these statistics would not be travellers on the New Line, it seems that there is an established trend of people giving up on driving to inner London to go to work and going by train instead, which is a trend reinforced by the London Congestion Charge, introduced in 2003. It is not just the proportion

of people travelling to London by train that is increasing: the total number of people who travelled to work in inner London from Elmbridge increased by 14 per cent to nearly 11,000 in the 10 years to 2001, but the numbers who travelled by train increased by 24 per cent to nearly 8,000, with the numbers travelling from Guildford showing a rise of less than 10 per cent.

The astonishing growth in train use by inner London workers in the 10 years to 2001 is not, however, a phenomenon without explanation: 1991 was a year which saw the greatest recession to affect London in the lifetime of any working there at the time – perhaps even greater than the Depression years of the 1930s – and the recovery of rail travel in the 10 years is the measure of the sensitivity of ridership numbers to the economy, and especially London's position in the global economy. In addition to the recovery in London, the total working population in our districts has increased by about 10 per cent in the 10 years to 125,000, but with a significant increase in people working from home, which in 2001 amounted to nearly 14,000 in Elmbridge and Guildford.

In spite of modern electronic communication, all this translates to a robust market for rail travel on the *Guildford via Cobham* line, with some stations showing car parking capacity problems. The ridership numbers are improving because of another discernible trend: increasing numbers of people at the western end are using the line to travel to Guildford for evening leisure journeys. The frequency of service from stations between *Effingham Junction* and *Guildford*, combined possibly with car parking in the town becoming tiresome, is attracting greater use of the train, or is it possible that on a summer evening a journey on a country railway has an attraction of it own? – or perhaps attitudes towards alcohol come into play.

South West Trains

During its 120-year life the New Line has been operated by successively the LSWR until 31 December 1922; its successor grouping company, the SR, until 31 December 1947, when it was nationalised under British Railways, which continued the succession of owner/operators until privatisation, when South West Trains was awarded a seven-year franchise from 4 February 1996. A one-year extension was given in 2003 followed by a renewal for a further three years, leaving the franchise to expire, as things stand, in 2007.

The total number of journeys which either started or terminated on the *Guildford via Cobham* line in the year to 31 March 2003[8] was over 2.4 million or an average of nearly 47,000 per week. To put this seemingly large number into perspective the average number of journeys for which *Guildford* main line station was the origin or destination was 117,000 per week; thus nearly two-and-a-half times more passengers used the *Guildford via Cobham* line station terminus than the aggregate for the intermediate stations. There can be no more graphic illustration of Guildford's status as railway hub and the relative unimportance of the New Line in terms of any aggregates that may serve to direct the business decisions of South West Trains.

The busiest stations on the *Guildford via Cobham* line in terms of the volume of passengers using them are currently *Claygate*, *Oxshott* and *Cobham*, as can be seen from the chart below. Although *Hinchley Wood* is less busy, it is probably as great per head of population. The low volume of passenger numbers using *Clandon* station is a reflection of the absence of significant development in its catchment area (some commuters drive over the Downs to use *Clandon* station, it being a convenient way of avoiding road congestion in Guildford) but it enjoys more patronage than *Bookham*, probably because the latter's rail users drive to *Leatherhead* or *Ashstead* where the service is more frequent and trains also run to *London Victoria*.

Annual journeys - station as origin and destination: year to 31 March 2003

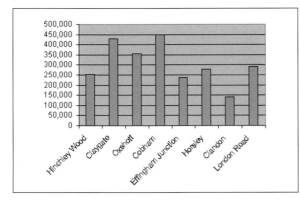

Source: South West Trains

The status of the *Guildford via Cobham* line as a commuter railway is evidenced by the proportion of passengers that use stations on it as a point of origin as

distinct from a destination. As a benchmark, and demonstrating its wide use by passengers for a large variety of purposes, *Guildford* main line station is used more or less equally as a destination as it is as a point of departure, the attractions of the town as a destination for work, shopping or leisure being significant reasons for travelling to it. Leaving aside *London Road* station, about which special mention will be made below, all the other stations are characterised by the balance being heavily biased in favour of use as a starting point for a journey. A little care is required here because the data is for South West Trains services only; a few services operated by Southern[9] on the Leatherhead branch are excluded from the data.[10]

On average on the whole line, except *London Road*, only around 15 per cent of total use of the stations is as a destination: in other words about 85 per cent of the passengers using the stations are starting there and going somewhere else, usually London. This bias to use as a point of origin rather than destination is the greatest at *Claygate* with nearly seven times as many uses as an origin as for a destination; the bias is weakest at *Cobham*, which has the highest proportional use as a destination, where the ratio is less than five. *Effingham Junction* also has a relatively high bias to use as a destination station, but this is probably explained by its low absolute use and a large number of schoolchildren travelling to it. That is certainly the explanation at

---

[8] The source of all passenger statistics is South West Trains; the data for Southern (another Train Operating Company) are excluded.

[9] For many years there have been peak hour through trains between *London Bridge* and *Guildford* via *West Croydon*, *Epsom* and *Effingham Junction*. There are currently two return workings in the morning peak and three in the evening peak, all worked by Southern.

[10] From the late 1980s to the mid 1990s, *Bookham*, *Effingham Junction*, *London Road* and *Guildford* were served by Thameslink trains half hourly in the off peak and all day Saturdays, establishing new through services from the southern New Line stations to *Sutton*, *Croydon*, *Blackfriars*, *Kings Cross* and *Luton*. When these were withdrawn in the mid 1990s, they were replaced by a half-hourly through service off peak between *West Croydon*, *Sutton*, *Epsom* and *Guildford*, which stopped at all New Line stations. This was in turn replaced from September 2004 by half-hourly *Waterloo–Guildford* via *Epsom* trains. So far from there being a decline in service, stations south of *Effingham Junction* now have a best-ever four trains an hour to *Waterloo*, Mondays to Saturdays. In contrast, the line via *Bookham* is now completely closed on Sundays.

London Road, where the station use has the opposite profile to all the other stations: a large number of present day schoolchildren emulate their predecessors, who used the station more or less as soon as it opened to travel to the large number of schools served by it. Of the total use of *London Road* station, two thirds of the passengers are ending the journeys there, and this contributes to it being the fourth busiest station on the line. This fact should be tempered by the large concentration of traffic at school-times and a paucity at other times in the day and in the holidays. A chart showing the use of the stations as a destination is given below.

Annual journeys - station as destination: year to 31 March 2003

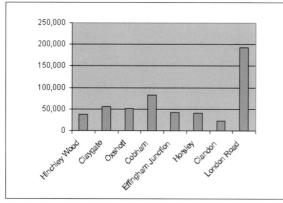

Source: South West Trains

The best reflection of the use of each station on the New Line by London-bound commuters is given by the statistics for use as a station of origin for a journey; a chart showing these statistics is given below.

Annual journeys - station as origin: year to 31 March 2003

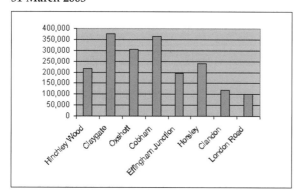

This shows again the importance to the traffic aggregates of *Cobham*, *Oxshott* and *Claygate*: two thirds of all journeys which originate on the *Guildford via Cobham* line start at *Cobham* or at the three other stations nearer to *Waterloo*.

In December 2004, South West Trains made a wholesale revision to its network timetable, which had not previously been recast from the bottom up since 1967 when BR phased out the last steam services. One of the most significant principles on which the new timetable was based was a cast back to Sir Herbert Walker's doctrine of running trains at the same minutes past each hour, a principle which is now broadly observed. In addition, the recasting of the timetable was a major undertaking aimed at giving a service which reflected better the changing patterns of passenger demand; and simplifying train movements, making the timetable more easily recoverable after an incident. The revision has achieved one of its objectives – better timekeeping – albeit at the expense of longer journey times.

Leaves on the line

We have seen how *Punch* was merciless in its lampooning of LSWR in the 1880s with its *Wags of Waterloo* allegories on the inadequacies of the train service and their view of the overarching reason for it: 'the placing of shareholders' interests over customers'. It seems endemic that the railways should be blamed, over the generations, whenever something does not work quite correctly, although when we consider what is achieved on most days, with an astonishing number of train movements in and out of *Waterloo*, it is perhaps the more remarkable that the service operates so smoothly: many of the railways' critics would not be comfortable if their own peccadilloes were so exposed to public view. To mock, however, is the public's right and 'the wrong kind of snow' will always haunt the explanation of a legitimate problem caused by fine snow to some trains.

Groans are also offered when 'leaves on the line' is given as a reason for late running. This returns in late autumn every year and timetables are even rearranged to accommodate it. It will be remarked that 'it never used to happen', which is broadly true because the weight of locomotives is more concentrated than the almost equally distributed load of multiple unit trains. Steam and diesel hauled trains thus enjoy better adhesion between wheel and rail than electric and

17.9 Several units of the 1950s suburban electric stock, including one on route 42, Guildford via Cobham, wait at Waterloo.

diesel multiple units. Another factor is that disc brakes have replaced brake shoes acting directly on wheel flanges which helped to keep them free of the goo from squashed leaves. Lineside trees have been allowed to grow much more freely than in the past when vegetation close to the railway was regularly trimmed to reduce the risk of fire caused by the exhaust of steam locos in dry weather. The evidence of Mr Michael Baldock is interesting on the problem of loss of adhesion due to leaves; although now a train guard with South West Trains (and sometimes operating on the New Line) Mr Baldock was with BR in the 1980s and worked at every station on the New Line bar Hinchley Wood. He recalls the Up line at Claygate, where the approach to the platform is on a falling gradient of 1:110, as being a particular problem with trains often 'losing their feet' as the driver applied the brakes, and over running the platform as a result. Special trains are run for de-icing and de-leafing to avoid skidding or stalling from loss of adhesion. Cutting back the tree canopies has been tried to tackle the problem at source, but this brings a new bout of criticism from sections of the public for whom either trees seem to be sacred, or the screen and baffle which they offer is welcome. On this point there is no salvation for the railways because others will pay to have trees removed in order to restore an open view of the Green Belt of which they had been robbed, over the

years since the 1960s, by the inexorable arboreal growth. The fact is that over the years the views enjoyed by all railway travellers of the countryside through which they pass has been diminished by tree growth: some would rather have the view.

Opportunities

Both Surrey County Council and Guildford Borough Council have had a long-standing ambition to see the building of a new station on the New Line at Merrow on the County Council depot site (the original LSWR public goods sidings). The merits of such a station would be as a useful facility for local residents to reach Guildford, and thus reduce road traffic on congested roads, and also provide a convenient station for London commuters. The present most convenient station for Merrow residents travelling to London is *Clandon*. The County Council has over the years commissioned a number of studies of the proposed station, which have found a positive case for a station and South West Trains is supportive of the idea in principle. The train operator takes a cautious view as far as the funding of the station is concerned and explicitly links its own willingness to invest on the length of the franchise it is awarded: the concept of a 20-year franchise is unwelcome by the government and a three-year franchise, which is what South West Trains has, is hardly a basis for long term planning. On this basis the opportunity for rail users funding a new station, at least in part, is lost. In the meanwhile estimates of the cost of providing a station have risen from £1million in 1993 to nearly £5million in 2004. *Hinchley Wood* station, which was a much simpler affair, cost £8,000 in 1930s £s, of which one third was paid by the party most benefitting from it – the developers of the new settlement: this arrangement made everyone happy – the SR got more traffic revenue and the housebuilders sold their houses.

The Merrow station project is presently on hold for want of viability, and its seems unlikely that this will change unless some large new ingredient comes into the mix, such as a massive new release of nearby land for housing. How it came to pass that Merrow was joined to Guildford by the building of thousands of houses, presumably at great increments in land values, without the beneficiaries of that windfall funding a new station is well beyond the scope of this book. In 1885 Lord Onslow had the benefit of the New Line and *Clandon* station for his convenience at no cost to himself and to the great advantage of himself and others in terms of land sales; in 1930 the successors to the LSWR, two generations of whose shareholders had been funding losses while landowners pocketed their gains, got smart and extracted a contribution from the landowner to subvent part of the cost of *Hinchley Wood* station. The large-scale post-war expansion of Merrow (and Burpham too), with no contribution by the private sector to infrastructure investment on the railways was, to put it at its most gentle, a lost opportunity.

... and threats

There is no threat in a Beeching sense to the New Line, for its role as the transport method of choice for thousands of commuters is embedded. Gareth Leslie, the Group Station Manager for the Guildford area for South West Trains, with responsibility for the New Line, has said 'We are very glad we have the New Line'. This was not a reference to its profitability under the privatised regime but to the operational flexibility that it offers. The conjecture made in the Preface of this book regarding the original rationale for building the line did not embrace this; the benefit as a relief line came fortuitously. The existence of the New Line today, representing a tiny fraction of South West Trains services, is vital to the smooth running of a large part of their network, and the reason is the flat junction of the Guildford branch at Woking. At the busiest periods the junction operates at practical capacity, and is thus the limiting factor on how many trains can be run west of Woking at peak times. Just as in the LSWR days, relief of pressure on it is achieved by booking several Portsmouth trains fast through the New Line, giving their passengers the extra bonus of running on 'a country railway'. This gives Portsmouth-based drivers the ability to maintain their route knowledge but the operational benefit goes much wider than a handful of Portsmouth trains booked fast via Cobham. When something goes wrong unexpectedly, the New Line can be, and is, brought into use for unscheduled diversions, which give relief to the main line. It is not just at times of some emergency that the benefit comes into play: whenever there is a planned maintenance or renewal of track involving closure of part of the main line, or the section between Guildford and Woking, the New Line can be pressed into service. An excellent example of this occurred at the Christmas and New Year period in 2005 when the junction at Woking was closed for an eight-day period. Buses provided the link for some of the main line routes, but all the Portsmouth services were routed on the New Line as well as the hourly Weymouth service, which found its way to Southampton via Cobham, Guildford, Havant and Fareham. All these extra services were timetabled to fit in with the normal scheduled trains, both *Guildford via Cobham* and on the Leatherhead branch, with the result that 14 train movements per hour were observed on the *Effingham Junction* to *Guildford* section of the route.

Tangentially, there have been a number of specials which have made use of the New Line and one of the most notable was the royal train carrying Her Majesty Queen Elizabeth, which was booked on 18 April 1956 through from *Portsmouth Harbour* to *London Victoria*. The West Country class loco No 34092, *City of Wells*, hauled the Pullman train, which went up the New Line between *Guildford* and *Effingham Junction* and then took the Leatherhead branch. This use of the New Line was more a question of the access it gives to *Victoria* and its convenience for Buckingham Palace, rather than as a relief for the main line.

The role as a relief line may explain why it sees continuing investment. The discerning rider may appreciate that the metals of both the up and down lines are a mixture of the old section-jointed rails and the modern continuous welded type. The next few

17.10 *The practice of using the New Line as a relief line, usually for fast services to Portsmouth, is long established; this refuge siding was built at Claygate in the early 20th century and removed in the early 1960s.*

17.11 *This scene shows the same track in 2004 with a fast service; note the amount of tree growth in the 40 years since the refuge line was removed.*

17.12 A Guildford via Cobham service runs down to Hinchley Wood station; until 1908 this was a double track (c1965).

The J N Faulkner collection

years may see the completion of this investment programme, the economics of which are supported by reduced inspection and maintenance costs. The benefits to the passengers are a smoother and quieter ride where the more perceptible noise is that of the motors which can now be heard above the gliding of wheels over the rails. Mrs Brenda Golden, who arrived with her bicycle at *Clandon* station in 1942 to work as a Land Girl on *Cuckoo Farm*, and stayed ever since, relates an interesting anecdote. Evidently, in the blackout there was never a risk of missing *Clandon* station when returning from visits to her family in Wimbledon: the track on the Down line consisted of such short lengths of rail that there was a noticeable increase in the beat of the *clackety clack* as the station was approached. Could this have been an example of the original rails, which at the time would have been nearly 60 years old?

This chapter started on the role of the Metropolitan Green Belt in saving 'a country railway', and it now ends on the threats to that role. The threats to the New Line status as a country railway takes the form of the threat to the Metropolitan Green Belt itself and with the possibility of considerable overcrowding on the line if land within it near our village cluster were to be released for housebuilding. Most people may have the impression that the green belt is forever; a perception that was probably encouraged when to everyone's

great relief it was created, but according to a report by Surrey County Council:[11] 'There has been a lack of a clear policy about the permanence of green belts'. A House of Commons Select Committee of 1984 concluded 'that green belts should not be seen as literally permanent or immutable', but nevertheless talked in terms of creating a presumption against development for an indefinite period. The present government, however, has said it is strongly in favour of maintaining the Metropolitan Green Belt, but exceptionally, a review of boundaries might be justified where planned development would be the most sustainable of the available options, or where the boundaries 'have been tightly drawn': to most people this is a rationalisation of why green belts are no longer sacrosanct. Quite what Professor Abercrombie would have made of it, we can only speculate but the fact is that while there are too many people in the South East of England, there are ever more thousands who want to join them. The debate about the supply of housing land in the South East has reopened discussion about the implications for green belt policy for sustainable patterns of development.

[11] Technical Paper 5: *The Green belt in Surrey*, Surrey County Council, Planning & Development, November 2002

The Michael Baldock collection

17.13 This de-icing train seen passing Claygate on the Up line in the early 1980s was made from former suburban electric stock probably from the 1940s.

A theme of regional thinking and wider policy is to encourage a revival of urban living, a reversal of *Southern Electric*'s efforts, and to concentrate development in existing built-up areas. In the last 20 years Surrey has been successful in its policy, in defence of the green belt, of providing land for housing by the more intensive re-use of previously developed land. In every village in our cluster, except perhaps East Clandon, the evidence of this is rife: as we complain about the effect of all the rampant infilling – the demolition of a few houses with big gardens to make way for a couple of dozen flats; the demolition of a house or two to open up the backland for another dozen – the effect on local traffic levels, where residents have to queue to leave their village or to get back in, is to make worse what is already bad. This misery, it is said, is the price we pay for the Metropolitan Green Belt.

It is also said that there is a need for closer integration between land use and transport policies, which has led to a number of calls to reappraise green belt policy. The concern is that by limiting the outward expansion of existing settlements, green belts have contributed to increased distances of car commuting, leading to greater consumption of resources and generation of pollution. This has led to calls for both the release of land from inner Metropolitan Green Belt areas to allow urban expansion and for development along existing transport corridors within the Metropolitan Green Belt:

such as along the New Line? This style of thinking is a throw back to the 1920s and 1930s when *Southern Electric* actively promoted such corridor development. Presently, the main radial routes from Surrey into London, whether road or rail, are heavily used and unlikely to provide significant capacity without considerable investment; but the problems remain.

Strong market pressures, not least those emanating from London's place in global financial markets, have led to a buoyant housing market in Surrey, with prices higher than elsewhere in the South East outside London; the evidence of this is in every village in our cluster. These high prices bring difficulties of access to housing by the lower paid and the young, and are used by some to argue for the release of land from the Metropolitan Green Belt to increase the supply and make it cheaper. Surrey County Council roundly rejects such a proposition[12] for the overarching reason that to have any effect, the release of land would have to be on such a scale that the very existence of a green belt in Surrey would be threatened.

The Surrey view is that it is important not to overlook the purposes of green belts: their role in promoting urban regeneration is one thing but the 'containment of urban sprawl and preventing the coalescence' of adjacent settlements are equally relevant to the green belt. It is fascinating that the language of Abercrombie lives on and so does the view in County Hall that a firm rigidity in definition of green belt boundaries is necessary for the policy to be effective. Says the Council:

> The density of the settlement pattern in Surrey is such that these purposes [containment of sprawl and avoidance of coalescence] must be given serious consideration in any decision on the future scale of development in the county. In areas of Surrey inside the M25, the settlement structure is such that maintaining the detailed boundaries of the Metropolitan Green Belt is essential to the achievement of the purposes of the green belt … Outside the M25, the settlement pattern is less dense but the spread of suburban development, radially along transport corridors, *does mean that the function of the green belt in preventing coalescence and maintaining the separate identity of towns and villages is often significant* [author's italics].[13]

12 *Ibid.*
13 *Ibid.*

17.14 Kennel Cottage, East Clandon c1913; of all the villages in the New Line cluster East Clandon has been the most resistant to change.

The Metropolitan Green Belt in Surrey is a complex area in which there are numerous separate towns and villages rather than open countryside on a vast scale. The outward spread of development pressures from London along the radial roads and railways has produced a particularly dense pattern of development the nearer one gets to the Greater London boundary. The avoidance of the coalescence of towns is vital because where there is no empty area of countryside even relatively small gaps, such as that between Hinchley Wood and Claygate, and Oxshott and Stoke D'Abernon, are significant and give some help to conserve the identity of separate communities.

In the judgment of Surrey County Council 'there is no regional case for review of the Metropolitan Green Belt' and the government's requirements for new housing in the county to 2016 'should be set at a level which does not prejudice the Metropolitan Green Belt as presently defined'. Somewhat ominously they observe that the ultimate control lies with the government. On this footing, they have to accept that 'a limited release of land from the Green Belt' should not be rejected out of hand, and if the pressure to build, from the government and the industry, was to be irresistible, then 'any releases should be sought around towns outside the M25' and that new building should relate to 'established public transport corridors'.

It was, perhaps, for these reasons Surrey County Council was compelled to consider releasing land for 6,000 houses on green belt land adjacent to Guildford and Woking. If the pressure from the government to release land to meet its targets to 2016 were to engulf Surrey County Council then it seems probable that this is a site that might be released. One third of the total houses on this release might be on *Gosden Hill Farm*, an area of the green belt which marks the eastern limit of Burpham's (and therefore Guildford's) urban encroachment. Merrow Lane marks this boundary, but if it were to be developed, there would be a serious risk of coalescence towards West Clandon.

The Clandons have shown the least impact from either the building of the New Line or the improvement of the A3 trunk road: in the words of Abercrombie the 'unspoilt villages of the region are an asset of the first importance to London'. The whole area along the New Line – 'an existing transport corridor' – would be vulnerable if the first step at a new coalescence were allowed, but even as the story of the origins of the New Line was beginning, the merging of Merrow and Guildford was accurately predicted. In 1885 it was the competition policy of the day – the market will decide – that brought us the railway; from 2006 the market, no less insistent, is the only force that can stop *Guildford via Cobham* remaining a country railway.

APPENDIX A

DRAMATIS PERSONAE – BIOGRAPHICAL NOTES

The dramatis personae are those who had a significant part in the story of the origins of the New Line to Guildford

Her Majesty Queen Victoria (1819-1901)

Queen Victoria was no stranger to railways: her reign saw the start of passenger travel and by the time of her death the golden age of railways had not yet been eclipsed. Although trains allowed her to travel extensively through her kingdom, and facilitated her trips to *Osborne* and *Balmoral*, she was very much opposed to the prospect of a railway running close to her other favourite home, *Claremont*. When it was proposed that a railway should be built within a few hundred yards of *Claremont Park* and within sight of her when she went out riding, she made her objections plain to her private secretary, who with customary skill, contrived to assist other objectors to kill the scheme for their own separate but convenient reasons. This assistance included financial support given by the Queen from her own resources to the objectors' fighting fund.

When some years later the New Line was aligned, it was sufficiently remote from *Claremont* not to be a nuisance, albeit not entirely out of sight and sound. The Queen's general objection to a railway near *Claremont* gave her Crown Receiver of Woods, John Clutton, a particular problem that he handled with great skill. Her Majesty's objection on account of disturbance to her quiet enjoyment of her property was one thing to be respected, but to drive the railway away completely would be to lose the favourable economic impact of it on the Crown lands at Oxshott. It was John Clutton who reconciled the Queen's private wishes with the longer run interests of the monarchy, and saw to it that the route taken would give *Claremont* the widest berth consistently with taking the line through the Crown land, on which a station would be built, to allow residential development to take advantage of it.

Sources:
The Royal Archives, Windsor Castle.
Various testimonies to Select Committees considering local railways.

His Royal Highness, the Duke of Cambridge (1819-1904), soldier

HRH, the Duke of Cambridge, a cousin of Queen Victoria, was a soldier rising to the rank of Field Marshal and being appointed Commander-in-Chief of the British Army. He served with distinction in the Crimean War, being twice mentioned in dispatches and thanked by Parliament. He took a keen interest in military music and founded the School of Military Music at Kneller Hall in 1857. He was President of the National Rifle Association, whose shooting ranges were located on Wimbledon Common in close proximity to the proposed Guildford, Kingston and London Railway. The Duke was an enthusiastic supporter of the proposed railway because it would run through his estate at Coombe for several miles, and with the proposal to build several stations it would open up thousands of acres for development to the east of Kingston through to Putney, bringing significant increments to the value of his estate. He took no part in the promotion of the railway, being careful not to be seen to be advancing his private interests, especially because the route chosen brought objections in high places from the Conservators of Wimbledon Common. Lord Onslow, the leading figure among the Promoters, had been first introduced to the Duke while on a visit to Paris 11 years before Onslow familiarised him with the proposed railway project.

Source:
The Oxford Dictionary of National Biography.

James Bell, Solicitor

Whether James Bell was motivated by some other interest, beyond earning professional fees, in bringing the railway to Cobham has not emerged. He practiced in Kingston and brought forward a succession of failed schemes in his attempts to put Cobham on the railway map, usually in league with Charles Combe, and always to the great irritation of the LSWR, which killed his schemes through obfuscation and by methods that did no credit to the monopoly railway company of the district. Archibald Scott dealt with him so brusquely that the succession of schemes that he was offered for LSWR support may have become an irritation. There is some suggestion of naivety on Ball's part, for he was very slow to divine the objection of Queen Victoria to his somewhat flimsy proposal to route a narrow gauge railway near *Claremont*, even when it had been made plain by John Clutton that the scheme could never be acceptable. Ultimately, and in despair after the final dispatch of a Cobham railway scheme by the LSWR, he joined forces with Lord Onslow who, with his Guildford, Kingston and London Railway Bill, was to make an enterprising and ultimately partially successful challenge to the LSWR, which ended in the New Line to Guildford being built. Perversely the New Line was routed through Stoke D'Abernon and Bell, the greatest friend of Cobham's quest for its own railway, achieved only a pyrrhic victory over his adversary, the LSWR. However, the New Line made its connection with the main line at Hampton Court Junction – the route from Surbiton to Oxshott offering the cheapest construction cost. Bell's thwarted scheme of 1880 was the first to follow this route, which was copied by the LSWR.

Sources:
Various testimonies to Select Committees considering local railways.

John Clutton (1809-1896), first President of the Royal Institution of Chartered Surveyors

John Clutton, the grandson of the founder of the famous surveying firm of the same name, was a doyen of his profession. In 1837 he set up business in London where the sudden growth of a large volume of surveying business negotiating land purchases for railway construction had necessitated being close to Parliament. His introduction to land purchasing came from the SER who gave him the task of acquiring all the land and house property for 120 miles of railway. His reputation as a skilful valuer, negotiator, and arbitrator in railway business grew and in 1845 he was a key expert witness before the Select Committee of the House of Lords on compensation for lands taken by railways.

Clutton's thriving practice was diversified and enlarged by work for the Church: in 1845, he was commissioned to conduct a survey, valuation, and report on all the lands and properties of the Ecclesiastical Commissioners in the southern half of England and Wales. When completed over the next decade this survey formed a definitive account of lands, and made Clutton the obvious choice as regular agent for this vast estate.

Success continued with the addition of the Crown Estate business. He was commissioned to report on the condition of the New Forest and the Forest of Dean, and gave evidence to a Select Committee. His impressive grasp of the intricacies of the business of woodland management was noticed and in 1850 he was appointed Crown Receiver for Woods and Forests for Surrey, extended in the following year to all the midland and southern English counties. Clutton thus became the established woodland expert of the day, with the agency for 47,000 acres of Crown lands. On his advice the policy of disafforestation was carried out which, although right at the time, led to the creation at great expense of unwanted extra agricultural acreage, which predated and added to the problems of the great agricultural depression described in Chapter 4, a depression unprecedented in its cause, severity and length.

In March 1868 he took the lead in arranging a meeting of influential surveyors at the *Westminster Palace Hotel*, a favourite rendezvous of railway valuers and arbitrators, which stimulated the foundation of what became the Royal Institution of Chartered Surveyors, to which 'as a matter of course', he was selected as first President.

Clutton was an unassuming, unpretentious, but firm-willed man. To his practical facility for business can be added calm temperament, careful judgment and natural caution. Lacking in eloquence himself, and neither speaking nor writing with fluency, he paid scant attention to the rhetoric of expert witnesses or Counsel when acting in arbitration cases. In the course of a long and distinguished career he built up a formidable experience of appearances before Select Committees in Parliament, where his expository powers were inferior to his sharp and ready absorption of the essence of matters under consideration. Although chary of speech, his habitual reticence sat well with the Select Committees by which he was heard because he never gave the notion of suppression or concealment: no one knew better than he the danger of ill-considered remarks; 'he was the sworn enemy of adjectives', aiming always at precise meanings. Such a man was bound to disdain the anarchy of the adversarial system: being subjected to the fire of questions from half-instructed men; and being pulled and pushed between various aspects of an issue with more respect to theatre than to reason, was a torture which only 'his quiet strength and half-conscious humour' could overcome.

Through all his business dealings, over a long, varied and hugely successful life, Clutton maintained the most cordial relations with his peers and enjoyed universal respect. His great legacy in relation to the New Line is the fact that by his quiet skill – perhaps by his ability to appear to be following, not leading – he induced both the LSWR and the Guildford, Kingston and London Railway to lay out their railways through the Crown land at Oxshott, and so lock in the development value which the railway would bring whoever built it. Of the two competing schemes for a new railway, their respective routes had only three points of congruity – their start and finish points, and their alignment through Oxshott. That this was achieved at the same time as assuaging Queen Victoria, who feared for the intrusion of her privacy at *Claremont*, is a testament to the skill and the business acumen of John Clutton – the great surveyor of his day.

Sources:
The Oxford Dictionary of National Biography.
Memoir of John Clutton: by JCR [*sic*], 1896, from the *Transactions of the Surveyors' Institution.*

Charles Combe (1836-1920), landowner

Charles Combe was the philanthropic owner of *Cobham Park*, an estate which during the second half of the 19th century was central to Cobham affairs. In his early life he served with the Indian Army in the 3rd Bombay Cavalry in Persia and in the 1857 Indian Mutiny. The Combe family were brewers and a great uncle of Charles Combe bought the estate in 1806. When Combe was in India he inherited *Cobham Park* from his uncle, the son of the first owner. A new mansion, built at a cost of £26,000, was completed in 1873. It was designed by Edward Middleton Barry RA, third son of Sir Charles Barry, architect of the *Palace of Westminster* and the *Charing Cross Hotel*, and an elder brother of John Wolfe Barry, the engineer of the Guildford, Kingston and London Railway.

Charles Combe is most notably remembered for his encouragement, sponsorship and in some cases, the funding of the development of Cobham's infrastructure. Having purchased Downside Mill in 1865, he installed a generator there (*Cobham Park* was one of the earliest users of electricity in the country). Combe had also been instrumental in organising a public meeting in 1866 to ascertain the desirability of bringing mains water into Cobham and, two years later, he chaired a public meeting to consider bringing in gas.

The Cobham Gas Light and Coke Company was formed two years later. Street lighting was introduced in 1899 and mains drainage followed a few years after that. Combe provided the village with a Merryweather fire engine, which was handed over in a grand ceremony in *Cobham Park* in 1899. The engine remained stationed on the Stoke Road near the Tilt until the 1960s. Charles Combe gave £500 towards the building of the village hall, which was opened in 1888, while in 1885 he presented some land on the Tilt for the site of the present cemetery. His name is recorded as a benefactor of St Mary's, Stoke D'Abernon, in an appeal by the rector for funds for the restoration of the church.

Of all Combe's involvement with improvement of facilities in Cobham, none is more important than his attempts over many years to get a railway into Cobham, and few worked harder than he in the attempt. His estate would benefit from the reduction in freight charges for the various imports and exports from the farms, including the stud, which occupied 200 acres of the Park, and of course coal for the house. Combe worked with the several schemes that James Bell espoused for bringing a railway to Cobham, including the ill-fated narrow gauge project, and with Lords Onslow and Lovelace on the West Surrey Railway scheme, which proposed a line to Cobham from Leatherhead. All the initiatives on which Combe toiled collapsed under the crushing dead hand of the LSWR monopoly. It was in despair of ever persuading the LSWR to relent that Charles Combe abandoned his attempts to bring a railway to Cobham and threw in his lot with Lord Onslow's scheme to take a railway through Stoke D'Abernon. He became a Promoter of the Guildford, Kingston and London Railway Bill. By this change of favours, and with ironic perversity, Combe found himself having to defend a railway through Stoke D'Abernon and to oppose the LSWR's late change of mind to run a line through Cobham, which would have suited his own interest better.

The Combe family gave up *Cobham Park* as a family residence in the 1930s, Charles Combe having moved to *Pains Hill* in 1904.

Sources:
Cobham – a History: David Taylor, 2003.
Various testimonies to Select Committees considering local railways.
William, Earl of Lovelace, 1805-1893: Stephen Turner, *Surrey Archaeological Collections*, vol 70 1975 (for 1974), The Surrey Archaeological Society

Henry Thomas Foley, 5th Baron Foley (1850-1905), landowner

Henry Thomas Foley inherited the Barony from his father, Thomas Henry in 1869, becoming the 5th Baron, and in the following year purchased *Ruxley Lodge* in Claygate together with over 100 acres of land, which included *Barwell Court Farm*, and *Chessington Lodge*. The family wealth had been derived in the early 17th century from the iron industry in Worcestershire. The attractions of Claygate to the young Lord Foley (he was but 20 when he arrived) can only be surmised: its proximity to London with the LSWR station at Esher would have been an attraction. In addition to the general location it is possible that the close proximity of *Claremont* was appealing but *Ruxley Lodge* was certainly not. Lady Foley took such a dislike to it that no sooner had Foley bought it, he had it substantially reconfigured and enlarged. Before the young couple settled into their new home, its character had been extensively changed, not least by the addition of the present tower, giving rise to its modern name, *Ruxley Towers*. The tower gave commanding views over the surrounding countryside and became a local landmark. Lord Foley remained in *Ruxley Lodge* for the rest of his life.

It is not recorded whether Lord Foley took any interest in Westminster affairs, but in 1880 he was invited to be a member the Provisional Committee of the Guildford, Kingston and London Railway, the company which proposed a railway through Claygate on an alignment which took it much closer to the Foley landholding than the line ultimately built by the LSWR. Lord Foley's involvement in the coming of the railway to Claygate was passive but his brother, the Hon Fitzalan Foley, spotted the development opportunities in Claygate, which the New Line to Guildford stimulated.

When Henry Thomas Foley died childless in 1905, he and his family had established themselves as figureheads in Claygate life more through their benefaction to the villagers than from any titular position such as Lord of the Manor, a role held by the absentee Lord Lovelace. The family, although having no connection with Claygate since 1919 (when the realisation of the family landholdings began) has left its name to the village in various ways, not least in the *Foley Arms* public house where the Foley family motto *Ut Prosim*, 'That I May Serve', is still retained.

Source:
The Claygate Book: Malcolm Peebles, 1983.

Fitzalan Charles John Foley, 6th Baron Foley (1852-1918) developer, landowner

Fitzalan Charles John Foley became the 6th Baron on the death of his elder brother, Henry Thomas Foley in 1905. Until that time he was known as the Hon Fitzalan Foley, and he lived in *Ruxley Lodge* (later renamed *Ruxley Towers*) until his own death in 1918. He was Deputy Lieutenant of Surrey (the Earl of Lovelace was Lieutenant until his death in 1893), a Justice of the Peace and had an Army career as a Captain in the Sherwood Foresters. Like his brother and sister-in-law, he was active in village affairs, becoming president of Claygate Cricket Club. It was the Hon Foley who was quick to spot the opportunity for residential development which the opening of the New Line would bring to Claygate: he purchased many acres of farm land to the east of the railway and, after planning the lay-out of the estate roads, not all of which were built, he parcelled up the land for sale as individual building plots. Some of the development inspired by the Hon Foley is today preserved within the Foley Estate Conservation Area.

In 1918 the unmarried 6th Baron died childless and the Barony passed to his cousin, Gerald Henry Foley (1898-1927) who, as the 7th Baron, disposed of *Ruxley Lodge*, its associated land and the 22 'villa residences' which Fitzalan Foley had developed and still owned in Albany Crescent, Gordon Road and Foley Road, Claygate. With the auctioning of the Foley estate in 1919 the near 50-year involvement of the Foley family with Claygate came to an end. The 8th Baron, Adrian Gerald, inherited the title as a four-year old in 1927.

Source:
The Claygate Book: Malcolm Peebles, 1983.

James Staats Forbes (1823-1904), railway administrator and art connoisseur

James Staats Forbes was a Scot, long-settled in England. Showing skill as an engineering draughtsman, in 1840 he entered the office of the legendary I K Brunel, who was then constructing the GWR, a railway Forbes joined as a booking clerk. He achieved rapid promotion, reaching by successive steps the post of chief goods manager at Paddington.

In 1857 Forbes joined the staff of the British owned Rhenish Railway, then on the verge of bankruptcy, and soon rose to the post of general manager, restoring comparative success. This was the beginning of a long involvement with railway companies in financial difficulties.

The first of these was the LC&DR, which was in the hands of a receiver when in 1861 he was appointed general manager. Menaced by creditors and lacking funds, the company was fighting for its very existence against two powerful competitors on routes into London – the SER and the LB&SCR. Under Forbes' bold and skilful leadership the LC&DR held its own, and in 1871 he joined the board of directors, succeeding in 1873 to the post of Chairman, which he held jointly with that of general manager until 1898. In his management of the company's finances, in his tact and skill in presiding at meetings of shareholders, and the exceptionally good terms that he secured for the LC&DR in a later amalgamation, Forbes proved himself a skilled diplomatist of great ability.

Forbes excelled as an administrator on broad lines and in boldly taking an initiative, perhaps obsessively, but had no taste for details. The measure of Forbes' capacity is demonstrated by the fact that he combined his posts with the LC&DR with the restoration of the fortunes of another near bankrupt concern, the District Railway, whose board he joined as a part-time director in 1870, becoming Chairman from 1872 till 1901. For 25 years (1870-95) the rivalry between Forbes, of the LC&DR and the District Railway, and Sir Edward Watkin, of the SER and the Metropolitan Railway, was a source of anxiety to the shareholders on both sides, while yielding much profit to lawyers. This antagonism caused considerable damage to the railways concerned, through wasteful, confusing, and inefficient competition. Forbes was involved in the District Railway's expansion of the 1870s to the west and south west of London. Services were established partly over LSWR trackage, to Hammersmith, Ealing, Hounslow, Richmond and Fulham, and by connecting these suburbs directly with *Mansion House*, huge increases in traffic volumes were obtained, but not enough to pay a continuous and worthwhile dividend to ordinary stockholders. This was exactly the intention when Lord Onslow promoted the Guildford, Kingston and London Railway Bill, an initiative that Forbes claimed to have come from others, but few doubt that Forbes deliberately played down the role of the District

Railway, in order to avoid the taint of its own precarious financial position contaminating the nascent company whose Bill it was. He was a frequent witness before parliamentary committees.

Forbes was connected with several other railways, most of them needing help to bring them out of difficulties. His financial ability was widely sought, and at the height of his career he was also Chairman of three important electric light companies, a director of the Lion Fire Insurance Company, and president of the National Telephone Company. He exuded charm and was even-tempered but was not averse to showering shareholders with deceitful optimism.

Sources:
The Oxford Dictionary of National Biography.
The Metropolitan District Railway: Charles E Lee, 1956.

Frederick Gould, twice Mayor of Kingston

It is unclear whether Frederick Gould was active in Kingston affairs in the early 1830s, or indeed if he had any but anecdotal knowledge of the attitude of the town towards Giles' plans for the London & Southampton Railway. What is much more certain is that Gould spent much the greater part of his active life in seeking to redress the economic damage done to the town by its earlier failure to embrace the railway. Historical works give scant attention to his activities, but it is plain from contemporary records that he was active in getting the LSWR into the town, albeit by the back door – via Twickenham – and even then after he had led the local fight to have the line bridge the Thames instead of terminating, as was proposed, in Hampton Wick. Later Gould was pressing for the direct link to *Waterloo* to be opened, via *New Malden*, and when it was, trying to get the LSWR to improve its somewhat second rate service to the town.

When Lord Onslow promoted his Guildford, Kingston and London Railway Bill, Gould embraced it enthusiastically, even to the extent of obtaining the Council's approval of equity investment and representation on the board. When the opposing schemes for railways through Surbiton to Guildford were compromised, with the New Line being built but with the District Railway route through Kingston dying a slow death, Kingston had lost the only chance it had had to reverse its folly of 50 years earlier. Although

Gould had worked tirelessly to achieve such an elevation in Kingston's railway status, in the end he failed.

Sources:
Various testimonies to Select Committees considering local railways.
Surrey Comet.

Frederick Lovell Keays, commuter

Frederick Lovell Keays owned property in Surbiton where he had lived before moving out to *Fairmile Court*, Cobham. Travelling to London every day he was one of Cobham's first commuters, at first from *Esher* to *Waterloo*. He was a Promoter of the Guildford, Kingston and London Railway Bill and a keen critic of the LSWR's train service, citing the lateness of trains in the middle of the day, and high prices for parcels and goods. But it was not simply as a means of breaking the LSWR monopoly that caused him to oppose their proposal to offer an alternative to Lord Onslow's scheme.

His enthusiasm for the latter was based on a misapprehension. Keays believed that the Kingston scheme would allow direct access into the underground railways of the time. He claimed, but with dubious veracity, that Forbes of the District Railway had told him that through trains would be run from *Guildford* to *Mansion House*. The attraction of this to Keays, were it to have been so, would have been that he could avoid the troublesome and slow transfer by cab from *Waterloo* to St James's Square, where he conducted his business. Forbes, who ran the District Railway, was adamant that no access would be allowed by trains from the country to the Inner Circle. That Keays believed otherwise led him to be a supporter of Onslow and, somewhat selfishly, to be forthright in his objection to the LSWR proposal to take their alternative railway through Cobham. To argue as he did that Oxshott would be a convenient station for Fairmile, where 'a good many gentlemen are residing' who are 'engaged in business in the City' and that a station in Cobham was not required, was a mental contortion. The alternative of Stoke D'Abernon as a site for a station put Keays in direct conflict with Phillips, and with all those many Cobham residents who wanted a station there. In the end Keays and the enclave of wealthy Fairmile residents exchanged their journey to *Esher* to catch the *Waterloo* train with one to *Oxshott*. It may be going too far to attribute to Keays' influence the decision by the LSWR to by-pass Cobham when they compromised with Lord

Onslow over the route of the New Line, but his advocacy of the Stoke D'Abernon route was in flagrant disregard of what he knew were the express wishes of a public meeting at the *White Lion Hotel.*

Source:
Testimony to Select Committee considering the Guildford, Kingston and London Railway Bill, May 1881.

William King-Noel, First Earl of Lovelace (1805-1893), landowner, arboriculturalist, architect, engineer, Lord Lieutenant of Surrey

William King-Noel, 1st Earl of Lovelace was a descendant of the 1st Baron King of Ockham, who purchased the estate of *Ockham Park* in 1707. After Eton and Trinity College, Cambridge, William entered the diplomatic service but a promising career ended with his recall to England on the death of his father in 1833. In 1835 he married the only legitimate daughter of Lord Byron, the romantic poet, who had the eye and ear of her cousin Lord Melbourne, the Prime Minister. In 1838, Lord King was created First Earl of Lovelace. He continued to be favoured when in 1840 he was created Lord Lieutenant of Surrey, the highest social and political position to which a man could aspire in English county society. In the 1840s and 1850s Lovelace consolidated his land holdings into central Surrey. Having acquired *East Horsley Place* with its 2,200 acres, he made it his seat, *Ockham Park* to which he had 'taken a dislike' being let.

Ockham Park had been a short distance from the *Talbot* in Ripley whence coaches left for London, to which Lovelace travelled often, but after the opening of the railway at Woking in 1838 (and from 1859 at Leatherhead), he had a quicker means of reaching his West End clubs or his town house. Of the Promoters of the Guildford, Kingston and London Railway, Lovelace was perhaps the one whose personal convenience benefited most from the new station at *Horsley*. When the Bill was presented to Parliament in 1880, Lovelace had already profited by selling land to the railway companies in the Midlands.

Lovelace was an authority on farming, estate management and particularly, arboriculture. Large areas of the Horsley estate became extensively wooded, as he had been planting trees ever since he had acquired it. He is particularly remembered for his architectural legacy the most notable but not only example of which is *Horsley Towers*, the renamed *East Horsley Place*, from which Lovelace created the neo-Gothic mansion. To his agricultural and architectural interests can be added brick-making and engineering; he was a fellow of the Royal Society and an associate of the Institution of Civil Engineers. The timbers used in the roof of the banqueting hall at *Horsley Towers* were bent by the application of steam heat – a process acclaimed by the famous I K Brunel.

In 1856, through the death of an obscure aristocrat, Lovelace's son Ralph (1853-1906) inherited a title through Lady Byron and for 30 years was in the unusual position of sitting in the House of Lords with his father.

Lovelace's family life was tumultuous and at times tragic but he threw himself wholeheartedly into Surrey affairs, not just as its greatest landowner: he had transformed the village of East Horsley. In his office as Lord Lieutenant his most absorbing field of activity was his responsibility for the county militia. From 1852 he supervised the reconstitution of three regiments and took command of the 2nd Royal Surrey Regiment, a position he filled 'with both zeal and energy' and which brought him into contact with the Commander-in-Chief of the Army, HRH the Duke of Cambridge, who was also an enthusiast for the Guildford, Kingston and London Railway.

Lovelace led an abstemious life and died aged 88 in 1893. His son, the 2nd Earl lived in *Ockham Park*, and that estate and other lands went into the female line being ultimately broken up for disposal. In 1919 the 3rd Earl Lovelace sold *Horsley Towers* and its land to T O M Sopwith, the famous aeronautical designer from Kingston.

Sources:

William, Earl of Lovelace, 1805-1893: Stephen Turner, *Surrey Archaeological Collections*, vol 70 1975 (for 1974), The Surrey Archaeological Society.
Charles Lennox Tredcroft and the Earl of Lovelace: Stephen Turner, unpublished, held by The Surrey Archaeological Society.
The Oxford Dictionary of National Biography (including Ralph Gordon Noel King, Second Earl of Lovelace 1839-1906).

William Hillier Onslow, 4th Earl of Onslow (1853-1911), landowner, parliamentarian, government minister

William Hillier Onslow was born at the family home in Alresford, Hants in 1853. His father died two years later but it was not until 1870, at the age of 17, that he became the 4th Earl of Onslow when his great-uncle, the estranged member of the dynasty, Arthur George, died at the age of 94 having during his lifetime abandoned *Clandon Park* (built by a previous Lord Onslow in the early 18th century) to a 'grievous and uninhabited decay'. William Hillier inherited an estate of 13,500 acres in Surrey and Essex and, being no idle or ordinary youth, resolved to occupy and restore the great house, which had not been occupied for 43 years. Everything he did was done well and fast: 'he was always jumping into carriages or trains, to be taken here or there with all imaginable speed.' As soon as he became of age in 1874, he was appointed a Deputy Lieutenant for Surrey (Lord Lovelace was the Lieutenant) and took his seat in the House of Lords. The youthful Earl married in 1874 and the couple settled with a vast enthusiasm into the affairs of a country estate; and the restoration of the great house, in the course of which Lord and Lady Lovelace, their neighbours from East Horsley were entertained. *Clandon Park*: 'his work, his delight, his exalting purpose', required vast funds but the agricultural depression from 1878/9 saw a sharp fall in farm incomes. Soon after, William Hillier became the leading figure in the promotion of the Guildford, Kingston and London Railway Bill, as a means of realizing large sums by the sale of land, both for the railway itself and for development of land he owned in Guildford.

In 1880, when the great task of planning the promotion of a railway company took place, Onslow's unfamiliarity with business and of railway affairs were no barrier to his leadership of a group of landowners who first challenged the LSWR monopoly, then caused that great enterprise to build a railway it had tried its best to prevent for want of viability. The New Line would never have been completed but for the 4th Earl who melded together a formidable group, which, with immaculate timing out-manoeuvred the LSWR at a short-lived vulnerable period. It was a project that would bring economic relief to his own farm and those of his tenants, some of whom succumbed to the ravages of the depression and great benefits to his landowner friends, while doing nothing but damage to the shareholders of the LSWR. Even as this project was developing William Hillier became a Lord-in-Waiting to Queen Victoria, who saw the Crown lands at Oxshott increase in value by his initiative. The generational gap – Lovelace was 75 years old when the Bill was presented but Onslow was only 27 – is reflected in the fact that Onslow was a contemporary at Oxford and a lifelong friend of one of Lovelace's stepsons.

Prominence in government, and in Parliament, proclaims the Onslows' genetic attraction to politics, a dynasty which includes three Speakers of the House of Commons and a Chancellor of the Exchequer. The 4th Earl was himself deputy speaker of the House of Lords. In 1888, three years after the New Line had opened, he was appointed Governor of New Zealand. Reviewing his life-achievements in 1905, when he was Chairman of Committees of the House of Lords, a popular contemporary journal observed that he was 'a man of talent and diversified accomplishments'. He had held three Under-Secretaryships of State (one of which was India) before entering the Cabinet as President of the Board of Agriculture and Fisheries, during which time he had 'reduced the inflammatory protests of farmers with a grievance' with his 'tact and common sense' (and knowledge of the industry). He travelled around Britain's agricultural areas taking sympathetic interest, as he was especially qualified to do, in the effect of the railway freight charges upon farmers.

Clandon Park was given to The National Trust by his grandson, the 6th Earl.

Sources:
The Onslow Family 1528-1874: C E Vulliamy, 1953.
Vanity Fair: Men of the day. No 960. 1905.
Clandon Park: The National Trust, undated.
The Oxford Dictionary of National Biography.

The Revd Frederick Parr Phillips (1811-1903), landowner, clergyman

The Revd Frederick Parr Phillips was Lord of the Manor, patron of the living and Rector of St Mary's, Stoke D'Abernon. As 'a young man of great possessions' he had bought the living of St Mary's in 1851 and a year later the whole of the parish of Stoke D'Abernon, with its some 1,000 acres of land, his mother having lived as a tenant in the Manor House since several years previously. The parish included Oxshott at that time, and Phillips devoted effort to re-establishing that end of the parish, particularly by

reopening the Royal Kent School, as well as rectifying the substantial disrepair of St Mary's during the neglectful absence of the existing incumbent. Once his predecessor had died in 1862, Phillips appointed himself rector – a post he held until 1890. He served the church either as curate, rector or churchwarden for over 50 years, having combined these posts with being Rural Dean of Leatherhead (1874) and an honorary Canon of Winchester (1894), from which time he was known locally as 'the Canon'.

The Revd Phillips showed himself to be railway phobic: he had objected to Bell's narrow gauge proposal of 1870 to serve Cobham. That this railway was not built owed more to Queen Victoria's dislike of it than to Phillips' weak rationalisation that there would be no traffic to support it. Eleven years later, his objection to the railway, although more soundly based, was in the end futile. The route proposed by Lord Onslow bisected his estate and, eschewing the economic benefits it would bring to him personally, he hated the very notion of a railway, which one of his detractors said he considered would damage the 'rustic simplicity' of Stoke D'Abernon – with a population at the time of 400 there was some substance in that. Phillips had moved a motion at a public meeting in the *White Lion Hotel* at which there was overwhelming support for the LSWR's alternative route taking the line through Cobham and not Stoke D'Abernon – a motion with which Frederick Keays (of *Fairmile Court*) for private reasons conspicuously disagreed. Phillips' objection to a railway going through Stoke D'Abernon was so passionate that he petitioned Parliament personally against it, and was thus the only landowner of any significance on the route to do so. From the point of view of traffic generation, Cobham was plainly the place for a station. It was Phillips' misfortune that his spirited attempt to keep the line away from Stoke D'Abernon, was not only a solitary one but ultimately doomed to fall under the weight of the compromise hatched by the powerful protagonists of the competing routes. Nevertheless, the LSWR still had to buy some of his land and over £8,000 was paid for it. The £1,516 he had spent fighting the LSWR was reimbursed.

Sources:
A Short History of St Mary's Church Stoke D'Abernon, Surrey: R S Morrish, 1949.
Testimony to the Select Committee considering the Guildford, Kingston and London Railway Bill, May 1881.
Minutes of Court of Directors, and other LSWR records.

The Revd Dr Henry Richards, DD, clergyman, landowner

The Revd Dr Henry Richards was Vicar of Claygate from 1856 to 1884. His involvement as both an objector to and supporter of railway projects was undistinguished. He was an objector in 1870 to Bell's narrow gauge scheme – on account of paucity of demand – and a supporter of Lord Onslow's Guildford, Kingston and London Railway Bill, which would have taken a railway within yards of the vicarage and church of Holy Trinity. His appearance before the Select Committee considering Lord Onslow's scheme was ill-judged: he was forced to alter his opinion about the paucity of traffic in 1870, and justify his support for one in 1881 because the population of Claygate had risen by 212 in the meantime. Moreover, when it emerged that the railway was going to go through his land, his support for it was shown to be mercenary.

Source:
Testimony to the Select Committee considering the Guildford, Kingston and London Railway Bill, May 1881.

Archibald Scott (died 1910), railway manager

Archibald Scott was a railwayman to the tips of his fingers. Starting his career in 1838, he saw railways from their beginnings through their golden age. Before taking office in 1852 as traffic manager for the LSWR, a role which evolved into the general managership, Scott served with three Scottish companies eventually becoming goods manager of the North British Railway. Scott quickly justified the excellent reputation that he brought with him. A life-long bachelor, he was devoted to his work into which he put long hours and much energy. An observer commented: 'I have known him to attend your offices when all other people would expect to be, and would be, at the fireside.' It has been said that Archibald Scott was one of the few whose good effect on the fortunes of the LSWR during its first 50 years was so noticeable. Scott operated all over the system wherever business could be opened up or competition stifled: he was known to every general manager of a railway that had an interface with the LSWR, placing his company in a strong commercial position, especially by arrangements with other companies to secure through traffic.

Scott was at the helm of the LSWR during a period of growth and consolidation for the LSWR during which the great rivalry with the GWR was a dominant but not singular example of the myriad of shifting and at times difficult relationships with other companies. In one affair, dubbed 'an unfortunate episode' by the GWR, Scott by alert action got the better of that company and pulled off a deal much to the benefit of his own shareholders, leaving Paddington to observe of his shrewdness: 'you must rise very early in the morning' to get the better of him. In another famous railway incident – 'the Battle of Havant' – where the LB&SCR obstructed the LSWR from opening up the short route from *Waterloo* to *Portsmouth*, Scott was centre-stage. Expecting trouble when the line was opened, Scott arrived at Havant junction with a goods train, two engines and about 80 men demanding passage along the line. Violence erupted: 'they placed eight or 10 men on our engine, who put the driver and guard forcibly off' and the line was blocked by the LB&SCR thuggery. Sensing a better way than by offering more violence, Scott withdrew under protest, to be rewarded for his judgment a few days later by the opening of the line, which good reason could not hold closed.

A sound, perceptive manager with an excellent sense of judgment, Scott was patient in negotiation and although it was said of him that he was 'not needlessly aggressive', his successful dismissal of all representations to build a railway to Cobham were swept aside without charm. The worst that has been said of his management was that he considered his shareholders much more than his customers. In 1868 *Punch*, an articulate critic of 'The Wags of Waterloo', had sarcastically commented that the LSWR had put a fraction of a per cent into the dividends of 20 thousand shareholders by destroying the comfort and crippling the accommodation of as many million passengers. There was a germ of truth in this, but as General Manager, Scott won unique regard from directors and shareholders alike. In 1862, a high compliment was paid by the Chairman, Captain Mangles, who said that he had been particularly requested by his colleagues to comment on 'the unceasing exertions of Mr Archibald Scott' referring to 'the untiring zeal with which that gentleman had attended' to his onerous and difficult duties.

Scott frequently gave evidence often to Select Committees of Parliament, notably in 1863 when London's urban railway needs were being considered, but did not give evidence on the Guildford, Kingston and London Railway Bill. He was rigidly opposed to any line such as the New Line for want of any benefit to the shareholders in building it. That he was out-manoeuvred on this issue speaks for Lord Onslow's well-timed Bill and of course the intervention of the District Railway. He resigned as General Manager in 1884, after 32 years' service and served as a director of the LSWR until 1903.

Sources:

The London & South Western Railway Vol 2: Growth and Consolidation: R A Williams, 1973.
The History of the Southern Railway: C F Dendy Marshall, revised by R W Kidner, 1963.
The London and South Western Railway: O S Nock, 1965.

Sir John Wolfe Wolfe-Barry (1836-1918), civil engineer

Sir John Wolfe Wolfe-Barry was the youngest son of Sir Charles Barry (1795-1860), the architect of the *Palace of Westminster*. He assumed the additional surname of Wolfe in 1898, the year after he was knighted. A pupil of John (later Sir John) Hawkshaw, he subsequently acted as his assistant resident engineer for the railway bridges and stations at *Charing Cross* and *Cannon Street*. Becoming a leading engineer of his day, his long and distinguished career as a consulting civil engineer began in 1867 spanning the last quarter of the 19th century and the early years of the 20th.

Wolfe Barry and his firm were responsible for numerous engineering projects, including the District Railway extension to Fulham, and for the LSWR, design of the Thames crossing carrying that railway to Putney. He engineered the layout of the Guildford, Kingston and London Railway, having had a significant, albeit undocumented role in bringing together its chief protagonists, Lord Onslow, and James Staats Forbes of the District Railway. During this period he was in partnership with Henri Marc Brunel, the second son of the celebrated engineer, I K Brunel, with whom he designed the Blackfriars railway bridge. Their other works together included the docks at Barry in South Wales. Among the pupils articled to Brunel and Wolfe Barry was Alexander Gibb (later Sir Alexander) who like Wolfe Barry became President of

the Institution of Civil engineers and a notable engineer of his age.

Wolfe Barry's notable main work was in railways, bridges, and docks. In 1884, following his previous 'cut and cover' experience, he completed the final link to form the Circle Line. His other works included the Caledonian Railway's shallow underground lines in Glasgow. He was employed on most of the railway bridges crossing the Thames east of Westminster, as well as the King Edward VII road bridge at Kew. From 1887 he had sole responsibility for Tower Bridge, completed in 1894.

He was also consulted by many railway and harbour undertakings in India, China, and elsewhere. He was a member of many Royal Commissions and was one of the three members of the court of arbitration, which in 1902 determined the price to be paid by the Metropolitan Water Board to purchase the eight London water companies. He was especially interested in the problems of town traffic and served on the Royal Commission on London Traffic (1903-5), having expressed his views on the subject in both the inaugural addresses he gave as Chairman, Royal Society of Arts, in 1898 and 1899.

Wolfe Barry took great interest in the Institution of Civil engineers, of which he was a council member for forty years, and becoming its President in 1896-8. His final paper to the Institution was 'Standardisation ... and its influence on the prosperity of the country' (1918). This chronicled his epoch-making initiative in making mass production possible. Early achievements by Wolfe Barry's committees included reducing the number of patterns of tramway rail from 70 to nine and finding a uniform specification for Portland cement, which combined the best qualities of the many different specifications previously in use.

Wolfe Barry's wide experience, sound judgment, and untiring energy made him a leading figure in the engineering profession.

Source:
The Oxford Dictionary of National Biography.

APPENDIX B

ANNOTATED BIBLIOGRAPHY

English history. It is usually appropriate to set any local history in the context of national and regional histories of the period, but it is especially so where, as is the case with this book, what was happening in London was so central to the story. The following books in *The Oxford History of England* series were consulted: *England 1870–1914*, by Sir Robert Ensor (1936) provides a national perspective on the flood of grain imports from the USA and the subsequent agricultural depression and the political reactions to it. Ensor also describes how the pattern of trade changed in the late 19th century and how London continued to prosper even while the rest of the economy showed a decline in its relative share of world trade. He also discusses the faltering and wrong-headed attempts at Town and Country Planning, which ultimately failed to stop the excesses of the 1930s. *English History 1914-1945*, by A J P Taylor (1965) provides a good insight into the rise of the motor car in the early 20th century (this is also covered by Ensor); the economic crisis from 1929 and the 1930s housing boom, the decline in the numbers of domestic servants and the growth of towns, and population shifts to the suburbs.

London. Stephen Inwood's *A History of London* (1998) gives useful coverage of London's rise as a great city at the centre of world trade and finance also giving a general overview of transport and the suburbs. Alan A Jackson's *Semi-Detached London* is the definitive work on 20th century suburban development in London, with particular reference to the excesses of the 1930s housing boom.

Agriculture. The emergence of the *Guildford via Cobham* project owed much to the agricultural depression of the late 19th century and the decline of agriculture has been a feature of the line's history for 75 years. The development of the USA and its rise as a great grain exporter, made possible by its railways, is covered in Hugh Brogan's *The Longman History of the United States* (1985) but a more focussed account on the growth of the grain prairies will be found in *The Oxford History of the American West* (1994) edited by Clyde A Milner, II and Carol A O'Connor. For the impact of the import of prairie wheat on English agriculture, and changes in agricultural practices as they affected rural life, reference has been made to *The Agrarian History of England and Wales, Vol VII (Part 1) 1850–1914* (2000) edited by Joan Thirsk. The collapse in agricultural prices from 1879 is recorded in *Course of Average Prices of General Commodities in England* by A Sauerbeck (1908). Useful coverage of the impacts of the agricultural depression of the last quarter of the 19th century is to be found in *English Farming Past and Present* (1917) by Rowland E Prothero and in *Agriculture after the War* (1916) by Sir A Daniel Hall. Sources used for the catastrophe of the 1879 harvest were local newspaper reports and for the distress in relation to land values, the *Estates Gazette*.

Planning history. The websites of Surrey County Council and the Government Office for the South East contain useful information on the Metropolitan Green Belt, and planning history. Details of the Barlow report available on The Internet were consulted. The overarching source has been the *Greater London Plan 1944* (1945) by Patrick Abercrombie. The Surrey County Council website is a source of data, on the censuses and the proposed Merrow station.

Railway history. As background reading on Victorian railways two works by Professor Jack Simmons proved valuable: *The Railways of Britain* (2nd Ed 1968) and *The Victorian Railway* (1991). The official *History of the Southern Railway* by C F Dendy Marshall, published in 1936, is not as useful as the revision by R W Kidner, published in 1963. It is a wide-ranging work but the greatest value of the revised edition is its encyclopaedic schedules of officials of the railway and constituent companies, dates lines were opened, electrified and closed, dates stations opened and closed and major changes to station names. More detail is offered by the two-volume work by R A Williams: *The London & South Western Railway vol 1: The Formative Years* (1968) and *vol 2: Growth and Consolidation* (1973). The third volume of the intended trilogy, *The LSWR in the 20th Century* (1988) was written with J N Faulkner; all three works have been consulted extensively. Faulkner also wrote *To Guildford via Cobham* for the *Railway Magazine*, September 1959. Another history of the LSWR to be consulted was the nostalgic *The London & South Western Railway* (1965) by O S Nock and S G Spark's vignette of the New Line: *Via Cobham* (1978)

A totally different style was adopted by Sam Fay in *A Royal Road* (first published in Kingston in 1882). Fay was a railwayman through and through, active when the New Line was in its infancy; his comments about the role of the District railway are valuable because of their contemporary provenance. Charles E Lee's *The Metropolitan District Railway* (1956) was taken as the history of that underground railway as useful background to the story, specially the character of James Forbes and the expansion into the West London suburbs, which Forbes so wanted to follow further south west. H P White's *A Regional History of the Railways of Great Britain, Vol 2 – Southern England* (1982) gives a good account of the context of the New Line and a commentary on the electrification project, but the definitive work on the latter is G T Moody's *Southern Electric 1909-79* (5th edition, 1979). This gives a thorough account of the project including technical details. *Branch Lines Around Effingham Junction* (1990) by Vic Mitchell and Keith Smith, is a picture album particularly valuable for details of mileages and gradients. David Wragg's *The Southern Railway Handbook 1923-1947* (2003) is a concise account of the major events and personalities in the SR's short life.

The Railway in Surrey (1999) by Alan A Jackson gives a comprehensive discussion of the evolution of the various railways that have been developed in the county and of their impact on development, which has been consulted extensively. This was found valuable not least for its scrupulous research and devotion to accuracy.

The South Western Circle is the historical society for the LSWR and its journal, *The South Western Circular*, together with the Circle's archive of researched monographs on particular aspects of LSWR operations is a rich source of detailed historical material sometimes not found in the published literature.

Primary source. Happily for historiography the Guildford, Kingston and London Railway Bill was opposed in Parliament and the *verbatim* record of all the proceedings of the Select Committee involving witnesses is available at the House of Lords Record Office. All the evidence, maps and schedules were consulted. It is a rich seam, with many important personalities of the time called as witnesses. This source is, naturally, highly focussed on the subject, and because of that appears not to have been given any prominence by earlier writers. The references to the House of Lords papers are:

HC/CL/PB/2/28/34 - Opposed Private Bill Committee Evidence, 1860, volume 34. London and South Western Railway (Kingston Railway Extension) bill; and other matters.

HC/CL/PB/2/49/29 - HC/CL/PB/2/49/30: Opposed Private Bill Committee Evidence, 1881, volumes 29 & 30. Guildford, Kingston and London Railway bill; London and South Western Railway bill, and other matters.

HC/CL/PB/2/38/9 - Opposed Private Bill Committee Evidence, 1870, volume 9. Cobham Railway bill; and other matters.

For those events that concern Queen Victoria the *Royal Archives* at Windsor were consulted and material from that source in relation to the Queen's objection to railways close to her house at *Claremont*, Esher, proved useful.

Tourism history. A number of late 19th century books aimed at contemporary tourists provide an otherwise rare commentary about places which come into the New Line story, often describing them before the railway came. Although not aimed at tourists, *The Victoria History of the Counties of England, A History of Surrey* (4 Vols edited by Arthur Doubleday) is a useful reference point for its occasional mention of the 'New Line cluster of villages'. Books of the late 19th century, largely designed to guide those exploring London's countryside contain useful references to the New Line villages: *Tourists' Guide to the County of Surrey* (1887) by G Phillips Bevan; *Greater London: a Narrative of its History, its People, and its Places* (two vols, 1883, 1884), by Edward Walford; *A Handbook for Travellers in Surrey, Hampshire and the Isle of Wight* (1888) by John Murray and by the same author, *The Environs of London* or *A Picturesque Tour of the Thames in its Western Course* (1845); *Handbook to the Environs of London* (two vols 1876) by James Thorne; and Louis J Jennings' *Field Paths & Green Lanes* (four editions, 1877-1884). A later work published in 1923 but written in 1908 with revisions a year later in a second edition, is Eric Parker's *Highways and Byways of Surrey*, which contains many references to the New Line cluster of villages. Local guides and rambling books consulted include: *SURREY'S CAPITAL: A handbook for Guildford and its surroundings* (The Homeland Handbooks series – No 11): Joseph E

Morris, 1910; *Ramblers' Guide to Guildford and Environs* (Geographia Ltd, undated) and *Field-Path Rambles comprising routes round Gomshall …*: Walker Miles, 1910; and *Southern Rambles for Londoners*: S P B Mais (5th edition, undated c1923). The undated LSWR publication *The Pleasure Grounds of the South-West* captures their promotion of holidays in the West Country as a means of generating rail travel.

Social history. The definitive general work on social history is G M Trevelyan's *English Social History* (1st English edition, 1944). In Chapter XVIII the second half of the Victorian era (1865-1901) is covered including the fall of English agriculture, late Victorian society, the penetration of rural life by ideas from the cities and the end of the railway age. For vivid descriptions of the rural scenes in Surrey, its wild life and bucolic rhythm there is Richard Jefferies' *Nature near London* (1887), written while the author was living in London while Flora Thompson's *Lark Rise to Candleford* (1945) is a classic of its genre, steeped in country village life in the period when the New Line was being built and beyond. *Country Girls Preferred* (1998) by John Pink provides an interesting and illuminating account of domestic service in Surbiton, which reflects the decline in agriculture and the drift to the towns. George Bourne's *Change in the Village* (1912) provides a sympathetic, apologetic, account, based on years of observation, of how a small village near Farnham had change wrought upon it by newcomers attracted to establish new commuter homes in a rustic community; a process which led to what Bourne describes as a 'notice to quit' on the former contented peasants living in the area. John Connell's, *The End of Tradition: Country Life in Central Surrey* (1978) is an academic study of 20th century change in the villages of East and West Clandon and East and West Horsley. It is partly in the style of Bourne but based on research rather than observation, and from a later period, when the motor car had arrived: it presents a valuable and objective study of the social change in these villages, which was induced by incomers. Both books are essential reading for a deeper understanding of social change in Surrey.

Local history. To write on the impact of the New Line would not be a practical proposition without the many local histories that have preceded this book. Of the 19th century histories, *Surbiton: Thirty-two years of Local Self-Government 1855-1887* (1888) by Rowley W C Richardson, the some-time Chairman of the Surbiton Improvement Commission; W D Biden's *The History and Antiquities of … Kingston-upon-Thames* (1852); and F S Merryweather's *Half a Century of Kingston History* (1887) are valuable works in themselves but the more so for their coverage of railway history. On Claygate there is Malcolm Peebles' *The Claygate Book* (2nd edition, 1999); on a lesser scale but with a few treasures within it, is *Claygate Surrey* (1953) (the so-called *Golden Book*) edited by J R Salter and published by The Council of the Claygate Village Hall Association, and which can be seen at Surrey History Centre. John King's *The development of a commuter village. A case study of Claygate, Surrey* is an unpublished thesis of 1972, which is available at Esher Library. Charles McLeod, a former official of Claygate Resident Association, analysed the 1881 census for Claygate in *Claygate 100 years ago*, a painstaking piece of work which is also available at the Surrey History Centre.

B S Gidvani's *Oxshott: the Story of a Surrey Village* (1996), is a book which supplemented a series of articles for the Oxshott Parish magazine published in 1943 under the umbrella title: *Old Oxshott 1812–1943*, and authored by 'a resident' only thinly disguised as the vicar. These articles are available at Surrey History Centre.

David Taylor has authored many local histories of Cobham including *The Book of Cobham: 1982*, supplemented by a later edition: *Cobham: A History. A Short History of St Mary's Church, Stoke D'Abernon* (1949) compiled by R S Morrish, is useful in relation to the Revd Phillips. S E D Fortesque has written about the Bookhams in *The story of two villages Great and Little Bookham* (1975) and *People and Places Great and Little Bookham* (1978). These are usefully supplemented by Bill Culley's *Bookham in the Twentieth Century* (2000). Pam Bowley's *East Horsley: The History of A Surrey Village* (1995) was consulted; A M Conisbee's *More Memories of our Village* (1944), available at Surrey History Centre, is a set of homespun East Horsley anecdotes. Stephen Turner's article: *William, Earl of Lovelace 1805-1903*, in Surrey Archaeological Collections, LXX, 1974 is a useful source on Lord Lovelace. The folksy collection of vignettes in *The Clandons: a look into the past*, 1991, is a compendium of memoirs of village life.

E R Chamberlin's *Guildford* (1982) is a discourse on the development of Guildford and a valuable authority on the subject; June Sampson's *All Change: Kingston, Surbiton & New Malden in the 19th Century* (1985) provides a useful source based largely on contemporary newspaper reports. The author's *Hinchley Wood: the origins of a 1930s settlement* (2002) gives a detailed account of that district and its development since 1929.

The Southern Railway's well-illustrated residential guides, published under various titles from 1926, offer much information on contemporary housing projects and prices around each station as well as train services, ticket prices and local amenities. This factual material is supplemented by descriptions of the districts as seen through the sometimes rose-tinted glasses of the SR's publicity team. Surrey was not covered after 1937 but what was written in the decade and a bit after the electrification of the New Line is of great value. For this book extensive use has been made of the 1929 volume, *Country Homes at London's Door*, in the library of the Surrey History Centre. The *Surrey Comet* archive held at the Local History Room of Kingston Museum has been consulted together with the *Surrey Advertiser* at the Newspaper Library at the British Library, Colindale.

Subscribers

Alan A Jackson
Philip Hutchinson
Alan Williams
London's Transport Museum
Surrey History Centre
Local History Room: Kingston Museum and Heritage Service
Surrey Archaeological Society
Institution of Civil Engineers
Royal Institution of Chartered Surveyors
South Western Circle

The following lists in order of receipt those individuals and organisations whose subscriptions to this book were received before 11 May 2006 on which date the list was closed.

1	The Earl of Onslow
2	The Lord MacLaurin of Knebwoth DL
3	Ian Taylor MBE, MP
4	Anne Milton MP
5	Cllr Terrence Patrick
6	Cllr Mrs Jennifer Powell JP
7	Cllr Keith Taylor
8	Cllr Anthony Sheppard
9	Colin Chivers
10	Jeremy Price
11	Bruce Davies
12	Martin Corry
13	Len Chandler
14	Christopher Gill
15	David Barls
16	Tony Goodbody
17	John Mellbourn
18	Nicholas Harmer
19	Bryan Chapple
20	Gordon Stevenson
21	Keith Wheal
22	Henry Ashby
23	John King
24	Sean MacDonald
25	Tony Allen
26	John Russell
27	Jim Spriggs
28	Mike Dawes
29	Jeanne Fry
30	Paul Sutherland-Waite
31	John Wilton
32	Mr and Mrs J A C Smart
33	Malcolm and Gill Aish
34	Charles Hibberd
35	Lally and Chris Farara
36	J C Broderick
37	Peter Swift
38	Miichael Badcock
39	Richard Beardon
40	Sarah Friday
41	Ruth Strong
42	Jim Thornton
43	Paul Langton
44	Geoffrey and Lesley Tregaskes
45	Leslie O'Keefe
46	John LeGrove
47	Andrew Crocker
48	Malcolm McLaughlin
49	John Surrey
50	Cliff O'Donnell
51	Tim Madge
52	George Gunson
53	Nigel Harris
54	Robert B Wood
55	Paul Roffey
56	Martin Box
57	Mr and Mrs Stuart Mellstrom
58	Robert Avis
59	Ian Palmer
60	Stephen Bishop
61	Susan Watson
62	Roy Ekberg
63	Cedric F Jeffery
64	John T Macdonald
65	John Peverel-Cooper
66	Hugh Crawford
67	Adrian D Wimbush
68	Laurie Tribe
69	Virginia Abrahams
70	John S Parker
71	Russell Longley
72	Douglas Fleming
73	Colin Wheatley
74	David Wheatley
75	Michael Hornby
76	Anna Lise and Richard Gordon
77	Ian Gunner
78	Roger Vincent
79	Dr Robert N Hayes
80	Tim Grose
81	Bill Chilcott
82	Tony Doherty
83	Ronald Day
84	Christopher Relleen
85	Jon Davey
86	Mike Guest
87	Douglas & Helen Post
88	The Maxwell Family
89	Stephen Pizzey
90	Chris Taylor
91	Eric T Smith
92	Mark Giles
93	Dick Jarrett
94	Dean Casswell
95	Douglas Edwards
96	Jenny Gretton
97	Anthony Neal
98	Timothy Williams

99	Ian Wallis	155	Joyce Tatlow	210	Nigel Forrest
100	Jack Woodhead	156	Nigel Ferguson	211	Simon Coy
101	Martin James	157	John Harmer	212	Ian Jewell
102	A W Hutchins	158	J R Main	213	Peter Brown
103	Feiona Mitchell	159	Nicky & Bob Wilson	214	Iain Pearson
104	Robert Fulton	160	Gerry Acher	215	Peter Swift
105	George Findlay	161	Rupert Eastell	216	Philip Thompson
106	Gerald B Hall	162	Andy Piekarski	217	Michael Baldock
107	Jon Budd	163	Mr N B Carter	218	Richard Davies
108	Harry Manders	164	Mrs G D Carter	219	Margaret Hawes
109	Chris and Felicity Ingram	165	Henry Theobalds	220	Alan Gregory
110	John Pincham	166	Gareth Clutton	221	Nicholas Gregory
111	Richard Gan	167	The Orozco Family	222	Ken Head
112	Stephen Thompson	168	Moorad Choudhry	223	Pauline Hulse
113	Michael Taylor	169	John & Gil Salter	224	David Cockle
114	Sheila Farrell	170	Derek Street Esq	225	Christopher Harrison
115	Virginia Catmur	171	Patrick Wainwright	226	Hugh Tomkins
116	Celia Wannan	172	Phil Collins	227	Hugh Stephenson
117	Jo Richards	173	Nick Anderton	228	"The Station Master's House",
118	Janet Gaymer CBE	174	Roger Hateley		Claygate
119	Mike Day	175	Mike Dawes	229	John Hemsley
120	Gladys Dedmen	176	Craig Templer	230	Mrs Anne Cane
121	Jonathan Griffiths	177	Antony Jones	231	Alan Leakey
122	Michael Clift	178	Arthur Brocklehurst	232	Colin Crispin
123	Margaret Newman	179	Tim Lintott	233	John M Boult
124	Philip A R Carter	180	Alex and Antonia Wilson	234	Andrew Jones
125	Robert J Avery	181	Ray Bartlett	235	Sutton Local Studies Centre
126	William Mclaughlin	182	Dr. Harold Lewis & Mrs. Andrea	236	Penny & Ashley de Jonge
127	Simon A Archer		Lewis	237	Elizabeth Ball
128	G T Ritchie	183	Roger Whittaker	238	Michael Hutchison
129	Jean & David Hayes	184	Sheila & John Crichton	239	Michael Conlon
130	Brian Hamilton	185	William de Segundo	240	David Curtis
131	Nigel Brockwell	186	Norman Pattenden MVO MBE	241	Mrs Lucia Moser
132	Rosalind Hepple	187	David G Ventry	242	Nita Rodd
133	Eric Penn	188	John Hookham	243	Mrs Brenda Golden
134	Goron Cove	189	Peter Watt	244	Ian Royce
135	Sheila Forbes	190	Ian Harvey	245	N W Hill
136	Cllr David Smedley	191	Ann Taylor	246	Anthony Sandifer Mallard MBE
137	Janice Robe	192	Jeffrey Karoly	247	J N Smith
138	Patrick Berton	193	Martyn Mullard	248	Peter Swift
139	John Bound	194	P Gardner	249	Peter Hopson
140	Bruce Gyngell	195	Stephen Tudsbery-Turner	250	Arthur & Marlene Field
141	Eileen Griffiths	196	Eric Hall	251	Becky & Clive Moorman
142	Alan & Mary Roome	197	John Dunman	252	Peter Banister
143	Tony Page	198	W T O Wallace	253	Chris Banister
144	Sue Bellworthy	199	David E Taylor	254	David Banister
145	George Pickstock	200	John Neve	255	Huw Banister
146	Joyce and Dick Wilkins	201	Duncan Mirylees	256	Rachel Banister
147	Maurice John Chapman	202	John Manners	257	Anthony Allen
148	Tony Mallinson	203	Victoria and Edward Bosch	258	David Bennett
149	P A Ottaway	204	Peter Stevenson	259	Anthony D Page
150	John Maycock	205	Ivan Smith	260	L C Taylor
151	Leslie Cousins	206	Henry Bousher	261	John Hickey
152	John Reekie	207	John Downham	262	Mrs Gaynor Rowland
153	Jean & David Griffiths	208	Terence Page	263	Mrs Janet Amos
154	John Woodland	209	Roger Taylor	264	Christopher Bell

265	Subash Tavares	280	Nigel Hutchinson	295	Robin Cobb
266	Hilary Marshall	281	James McLeod	296	Eric Bartholomew
267	John Kopij	282	Charles McLeod	297	Peter J Smith
268	Bryan Simmons	283	John Franklin	298	Steve Haywood
269	Richard Golding	284	Elizabeth Baker	299	Bryon Smith
270	Barry Searle	285	Michael Major	300	Margaret Emery
271	Robert Wragge-Morley	286	John Telfer	301	Charles Hindle
272	Simon Howell	287	Ralph C Dyson	302	Charles Hewlett
273	Tony Elliott	288	Major James More-Molyneux	303	Anthony Heath
274	B H Cook	289	John Woollhead	304	Ron Hancock
275	Howard Satchell	290	Alison Jane Hague	305	Stephen Spark
276	Antony Hall	291	Graham Cocks	306	Philip Rubery
277	Martin Cooper	292	The Lewis family	307	Alice and Guy Pashley
278	Anthony Bevis	293	Jim Winborn	308	Ken Jenkins
279	Doug Scott	294	Diana Balfour	309	Sir John and Lady Hall

Index

H

I

K

L